The Cost of War

For Judith Allen, David Walker, and the Gumnut Tea House

The Cost of War

War, Return and the Re-Shaping of Australian Culture

Stephen Garton

SYDNEY UNIVERSITY PRESS

This revised edition published by Sydney University Press

© Stephen Garton 2020
© Sydney University Press 2020
First published by Oxford University Press in 1996.

Reproduction and Communication for other purposes

Except as permitted under the Act, no part of this edition may be reproduced, stored in a retrieval system, or communicated in any form or by any means without prior written permission. All requests for reproduction or communication should be made to Sydney University Press at the address below:

Sydney University Press
Fisher Library F03
University of Sydney NSW 2006
AUSTRALIA
sup.info@sydney.edu.au

sydneyuniversitypress.com.au

 A catalogue record for this book is available from the National Library of Australia.

ISBN 9781743326756 paperback
ISBN 9781743326749 epub
ISBN 9781743326763 MOBI
ISBN 9781743326824 PDF

Cover image: bullet casings, iStock.com/ra-photos.
Cover design by Miguel Yamin.

Contents

Abbreviations	vi
Preface to the Revised Edition	vii
Preface to the First Edition	xix
1 Return	1
2 Remembering	31
3 Repatriation	75
4 Soldier Settlement	119
5 Shell-Shock	145
6 Home Fires	179
7 Prisoners of War	213
8 Korea and Vietnam	235
Epilogue	267
Select Bibliography	271
Index	275

Abbreviations

AA	Australian Archives
ABC	Australian Broadcasting Commission (later Corporation)
ACTU	Australian Council of Trade Unions
AGPS	Australian Government Publishing Service
AIF	Australian Imperial Force
ALP	Australian Labor Party
ANU	Australian National University
AWM	Australian War Memorial
CRTS	Commonwealth Rehabilitation Training Scheme
CUP	Cambridge University Press
DVA	Department of Veterans' Affairs
JRAHS	*Journal of Royal Australian Historical Society*
MJA	*Medical Journal of Australia*
ML	Mitchell Library
MUP	Melbourne University Press
NLA	National Library of Australia
OUP	Oxford University Press
RKP	Routledge & Kegan Paul
RSA	Returned Soldiers Association
RSL	Returned Services League
RSSILA	Returned Sailors and Soldiers Imperial League of Australia
SUP	Sydney University Press
TPI	totally and permanently incapacitated
UQP	University of Queensland Press
VVA	Vietnam Veterans Association of Australia

Preface to the Revised Edition

As the old cliché goes, books are of their time and place; that is part of their fascination and significance. *The Cost of War*, first published in 1996, reflected both a personal intellectual journey and more general currents in social and cultural history in the early 1990s. But the world moves on. The history of war in terms of themes such as memory, grief, mourning, memorialisation, identity, language, the myriad complex cultural and social currents transformed by the reality of damaged, ill, injured returned servicemen and women and bereaved families, and the changes return wrought in public and private life in the aftermath of war have become major currents of contemporary scholarship, swelled in recent times by the centenary of the Great War. While *The Cost of War* canvassed some of these themes (a few in considerable detail), with the passage of time, new lines of enquiry emerge, what has gone before becomes the ground for critical conversations, absences in earlier studies are identified, different theories, methods and approaches are deployed, other questions asked; all greatly adding to the history of the impact of war on individuals, societies and cultures. We now know much more about the history of the troubled return of servicemen and women in Australia (and overseas) and the social and cultural impact of our collective efforts to manage these troubles than we did in the late 1980s when I began working in this field. *The Cost of War* was an early intervention into the social and cultural history of the aftermath of war in Australia. Nonetheless, despite its evident limitations some of the key themes of *The Cost of War* are still the subject of debate and critical commentary, and it is for this reason that a revised edition seems appropriate, especially as we enter the centenary of return from the Great War.

The original edition of *The Cost of War* was published in 1996 by Oxford University Press. The acknowledgement of all those, including the publisher, who assisted in the realisation of the first edition is outlined in the 'Preface' to that edition, reproduced here. This revised edition reaffirms the great debt owed to all those who helped along the way for the original publication: some sadly no longer with us. A number of years ago Oxford passed back the rights to enable me to republish with another press. Other duties have long delayed the search for an alternative publisher but as the centenary of Anzac approached, I felt I should make an effort. For this edition I'm very grateful that Susan Murray, Agata Mrva-Montoya and the team from Sydney University Press agreed to take on this task. Their support has been invaluabl,e as has that of the Fisher Library, and the then University Librarian Anne Bell, where the Press is based. Although she was acknowledged in the first edition my ongoing debt to Julia remains incalculable. Since then I owe a similar debt to our daughter Anna.

The personal intellectual journey that led to *The Cost of War* was, like many research endeavours, a curious mixture of serendipity and persistence. In the 1980s I had published a history of insanity in Australia, and one of the pivotal moments in that larger narrative was the impact of theories of shell-shock on the nature of psychiatry and the provision of psychiatric services in Australia.[1] A few years later I wrote a general history of poverty and social policy in Australia, where again one of the key turning points in the larger story of Australian social policy was, from 1916 to the 1940s, the creation of two distinct welfare states in Australia: a niggardly welfare net for civilians, most of it created in that brief period of 'state experiments' after Federation, and a far more generous set of provisions governing invalid and widows pensions, hospital and rehabilitation services, housing, land settlement, training, and employment preference for returned servicemen and their families and the families of those who perished from war-related injuries and diseases. This second welfare state consumed a fifth of all Commonwealth expenditure by the early 1930s.[2] These two threads, coming together, suggested that a project on returned service personnel and Australia's repatriation system might be worth pursuing.

A further stimulus came from my first ever visit to the United States thirty years ago. Unlike many who visit America, mine was not a journey to the west or east coast but to a conference in Indianapolis. Unbeknown to me at the time, although my morning stroll around the town soon opened my eyes, was the fact that Indianapolis was the headquarters of the American Legion (something like the RSL) and the site of an extraordinary number and variety of war memorials covering most of the conflicts America had been involved in from the War of Independence onwards. The physical forms of these memorials seemed very familiar – cenotaphs, grand columns, faux classical and art deco memorial buildings, neo-classical and religious statuary atop grand plinths. What was unfamiliar and disorienting was the rhetorical framing of all this memorialisation. This was not the poignant minimalism of 'Lest We Forget' or 'Their Name Liveth for Evermore' but something more grandiloquent, extensive paeans of praise to those who fought and died for the nation bringing freedom to so many; a land

---

1 *Medicine and Madness: A Social History of Insanity in NSW 1880–1940*, UNSW Press, Kensington, 1988.
2 *Out of Luck: Poor Australians and Social Welfare 1788–1988*, Allen & Unwin, Sydney, 1990.

that was a beacon of democracy and freedom in the world. I came away from my sojourn in Indianapolis persuaded that form does not necessarily dictate content and, more importantly, that Australia was different and had to be seen in its specificity, a theme I have elaborated on more recently with respect to an argument that Australian nationalism after the Great War was shaped by what I call 'Empire nationalism', a peculiar and unique post-war nationalist discourse remarkably different to the emergent nationalism in other Dominions – Canada, New Zealand and South Africa – as well as other parts of the British empire, such as Ireland and India.[3] In a transnational framework, the Australian response to the Great War seemed distinctive, despite the shared experience of loss by so many nations.

The wider currents in social and cultural history are more difficult to pin down. Any list of influences is perforce somewhat idiosyncratic. But in the late 1980s and early 1990s, when I began to think about a returned soldier project, there was little work in the field. There was an abundance of Australian military history, some important studies of the Australian home-front during the Great War and a plethora of works on the Anzac legend.[4] Some of these works, such as Bill Gammage's *The Broken Years* (1974), were inspirational, but my focus was to move beyond the experience of combat to explore the aftermath of conflict. At that time most Australian military history ended, like C.E.W. Bean's official histories, with Armistice and demobilisation. While there were rare exceptions notably, A.G. Butler's three volumes on the medical history of the Great War (1930–43), which contained a wealth of information and insight into the post-war plight of returned servicemen, the cessation of hostilities and the return to Australia, like many of the diaries of ordinary soldiers themselves, seemed to be the natural endpoint of the narrative. *The Cost of War* was an effort to argue that for many Australian servicemen and women and their families the war continued for years afterwards.

Nonetheless, there were a few shafts of light. Ken Inglis had written important essays on the Anzac legend, where he canvassed his early ideas on war

---

[3] 'Demobilization and Empire: Empire Nationalism and Soldier Citizenship in Australia after WWI – in Dominion context', *Journal of Contemporary History*, vol. 50, no. 1, 2015, pp. 121–43. See also my 'The Dominions, Ireland, and India' in Robert Gerwarth and Erez Manela (eds), *Empires at War 1911–1923*, Oxford University Press, Oxford, 2014, pp. 152–78. Simultaneously Mark Hearn also coined the term 'Empire nationalism' but covering a different aspect of Australian political culture – the efforts of the Australian Labor Party to reconcile Empire loyalty with Australian nationalism in the first two decades after Federation. See Mark Hearn, 'Bound with the Empire: Narratives of race, nation and empire in the Australian Labor Party's defence policy 1901–21', *War & Society*, vol. 32, no. 2, 2013, pp. 95–115.

[4] And while in the early 1990s I thought the Anzac legend somewhat exhausted as a topic, many excellent studies have proved me wrong. See for example, Graham Seal, *Inventing Anzac: The Digger and National Mythology*, UQP, St Lucia, 2004 and Carolyn Holbrook, *Anzac: The Unauthorised Biography*, New South Books, Sydney, 2014. More importantly Joan Beaumont's richly rewarding history of Australia during the Great War, *Broken Nation: Australians in the Great War*, Allen & Unwin, Sydney, 2014, demonstrates powerfully that in the right hands, military history, enlivened by social and cultural history, still offers vital insights into the history of Australia.

memorialisation in Australia that later became the basis for his wonderful magnum opus *Sacred Places* (1998). Ray Evans's study of the 1919 'red flag riots' in Brisbane opened up questions about the extent of social unrest in the immediate post-war years.[5] The most direct and powerful influence for me, however, was Marilyn Lake's path-breaking study of soldier settlement, *Limits of Hope* (1987).[6] While there was an existing historiography on soldier settlement (the one aspect of the post-war experience that had generated a reasonable body of work), Marilyn's brilliant evocation of the gender dynamics of life on the land for damaged soldiers and their families, particularly the experience of women and children, generated important new vistas in gender history, cultural history and the history of Australian national identity. This was a direction of travel that held enormous promise and one that influenced much of what I wrote thereafter.

Another stimulus, of course, was the opportunity to engage with an exciting body of overseas scholarship in the cultural history of war and memorialisation. I was keen to read more thoroughly in this field, inspired as I was by the work of historians such as Paul Fussell, George Mosse, Eric Leed, Modris Eksteins, David Cannadine, Sonya Michel, Margaret Higonnet, Samuel Hynes, Tom Laqueur, Klaus Theweleit and Jay Winter. One of the joys of researching the social and cultural history of war was the opportunity to read much more widely in this field, where there were abundant works of great interest, not to mention novels and films from *Her Privates We* and *All Quiet on the Western Front* to *Platoon* and *Apocalypse Now* (although I'm not sure the family always appreciated my continued efforts to shape our viewing habits through classic war films). Jay Winter's *Sites of Memory, Sites of Mourning* (1995), was a revelation. Jay's pivotal argument that the cultural response to war, contrary to earlier scholarship which positioned the Great War as a progenitor of modernism, was often backward looking, conservative, craving classical certitude in a time of collective grief, economic and political upheaval and cultural discord, put the question of how, culturally, polities and individuals strive for meaning in the face of meaninglessness, at the centre of historiographical debate. This became an important line of enquiry in *The Cost of War*.

Thus in 1991, supported by an ARC grant, I was ready to start in earnest. Equally important, while it had been a protracted struggle, I was finally given access to Department of Veterans' Affairs repatriation case files. I've always been someone who considers archival files invaluable 'texts' requiring similar care and diligence to interpret as literary sources, but when read carefully (and often against the grain) they can genuinely illuminate historical experience. Buoyed by funds and access I set off to research the Australian repatriation system: who had it impacted, how had it worked, what were the wider social and cultural tensions around this provision, what had been the patterns of support, what would the files

---

5   Ray Evans, *The Red Flag Riots: A Study of Intolerance*, UQP, St Lucia, 1988.
6   Marilyn Lake, *Limits of Hope: Soldier Settlements in Victoria 1915–38*, Oxford University Press, Melbourne, 1987.

tell us about the stresses and strains of war after return? It was to be a history from the Great War up through to Vietnam. I had a particular personal interest in the Vietnam experience. Although I was too young to have faced conscription, I found the Moratorium Movement of the early 1970s, and later the 1987 'Welcome Home' march for Vietnam veterans, particularly affecting. More personally, I had a university holiday job for a couple of years mixing and then spraying a weed killer – 2,4-D and 2,4,5-T. Just wash your hands after mixing it and before eating your sandwich was the advice of fellow workers. Only later, as a consequence of the agitation of Vietnam veterans, was it revealed that the poison I had been spraying with careless abandon in shorts and a t-shirt was 'Agent Orange'. There were many reasons to explore the fate of Australian veterans in the aftermath of war.

The shape of the work, however, was altered considerably by an unanticipated development. The research was well advanced but serious writing was yet to begin when I heard on the grapevine that an extensive history of repatriation by Clem Lloyd and Jacqui Rees was soon to go to press (it appeared in early 1994).[7] This required a considerable reorientation of approach. A setback became an opportunity. I was freed from the burden of having to craft a reasonably comprehensive account of Australian policy and practice and could attempt something more reflective and thematic; themes such as return, remembering and repatriation could animate the analysis, allowing me to explore larger questions across a range of conflicts. One of those questions was how different (if at all) was the experience of return and re-integration for veterans of WWI, WWII and Vietnam. Underpinning this was the broader current of thinking of the time that the experience of Vietnam veterans had indeed been different, particularly contested and had produced undue stress and strain on these veterans. Australian society had rejected them, and this could be seen in the extent of post-traumatic stress disorders in Vietnam veterans. Had it been collective guilt that prompted the Welcome Home march of 1987, a symbolic effort to embrace belatedly and apologise to these veterans? Reflecting back now I think there is something about the 1987 march that signalled (perhaps even initiated) the extraordinary current revival in public interest in the Anzac experience.

Thus, a theme that runs through *The Cost of War* is the question of the experiences of the veterans of different conflicts. The more I dug into the files the more I was persuaded that the differences were small. Alienation, social discontent, chronic psychological problems, alcoholism, domestic violence, lack of interest in one's family, a general feeling that civilian life was unsympathetic, a craving for the mateship of other veterans, and anger that governments were failing to recognise and reward their sacrifice seemed to be persistent themes in the lives of many Australian veterans. The experience of Vietnam veterans was not that different to those who had served in earlier wars. In an age when we now talk openly

---

7   Clem Lloyd and Jacqui Rees, *The Last Shilling: A History of Repatriation in Australia*, Melbourne University Press, Melbourne, 1994.

about the extent of post-traumatic stress disorder in any conflict (Iraq, Afghanistan, East Timor and more) a sense that this is a persistent syndrome that needs to be managed is commonplace. In the early 1990s this was less well understood, at least in historical scholarship. This theme also underpinned some of the more specialised thematic chapters in *The Cost of War*; was the experience of prisoners of war different to other veterans and in what ways did the Vietnam veteran campaign for recognition of Agent Orange as a war-caused complaint mark them out from other veteran movements for recognition of diseases (less than might be expected was my conclusion).

A pivotal chapter was that on shell-shock. This had, after all, been the starting point for my interest in this topic. A focus of the research was on charting the history of the concept of shell-shock. While much of the scholarly literature had seen the idea of shell-shock as essentially a phenomenon of modern warfare – suggesting that the intensity and fire power of warfare since 1914 created unique conditions for the emergence of a new form of psychological problem. It was a concept that emerged in response to conditions in the Great War, although a few historians suggested that there was some evidence for such conditions in soldiers who fought in the Russo-Japanese War (1904–5) and possibly earlier in the American Civil War (1861–5). Reading early nineteenth century military manuals, however, suggested even earlier instances of behaviours that would later be called war neurosis. Then they were termed forms of malingering, requiring punishment. Malingering remained a theme in theorisations of war neurosis in the Great War but as the incidence of stress-related behaviours increased the first recourse was to a physical theory (the vibrations to the brain caused by exploding shells – the origin of the term shell-shock) till eventually the weight of evidence suggested a psychological explanation (and hence for medical officers the preferred term became war neurosis). It is likely that such conditions were widely under-reported, as Jay Winter has suggested, given the initial resistance to the concept itself.[8]

For subsequent conflicts, however, the lessons still had to be learnt. Some came to blame the inherent mental weaknesses of the soldiers themselves, thus a focus of recruitment in WWII was psychological testing of recruits to weed out the mentally weak. It didn't work. Combat fatigue or battle exhaustion, as it became known, emerged regardless of these tests if combatants remained in conflict zones for a considerable length of time. Eventually this led to the idea of a 'tour of duty'; service personnel only served for 12 months at a time to ensure that combat fatigue didn't arise. Nonetheless, during the Vietnam War, despite (or because of) tours of duty, post-traumatic stress disorder (where the stresses showed after return rather than at the front-line) emerged as a major

---

8   Jay Winter, 'Shell shock, Gallipoli and the Generation of Silence' in Alexandre Dessingué and Jay Winter (eds), *Beyond Memory: Silences and the Aesthetics of Remembrance*, Routledge, Abingdon, 2016, pp. 195–208.

problem. Indeed, for American soldiers (not for Australian) it was exacerbated by the idea that men served as individuals for 12 months, moving in and out of combat units on the basis of a personal year of service. Australian soldiers were seemingly more resilient because they usually entered and exited as a unit, maintaining close comradely bonds, which subsequent research has shown is vital for managing psychological stress in war. Nevertheless, the incidence of post-traumatic stress disorder remained high. While the concepts that have framed the problem and the policies to manage it have changed, psychological stress remains an endemic condition in modern warfare.

Perhaps the least satisfactory chapter in *The Cost of War* was on soldier settlement. After Marilyn Lake's work there seemed little that could be added but given the importance of the scheme in the overall repatriation effort and the tragic consequences of this failed policy initiative, it couldn't be ignored. There is a rich historiography on soldier settlement, much of it focused on local accounts illustrating the wider tragedy. By 1929, the Commonwealth Commission of Inquiry led by Mr Justice Pike found that at least 40 percent of those who had taken up a soldier settlement block had left the land, indebted, impoverished and often broken in spirit. Marilyn had highlighted the cost on marriages and the lives of wives and children, many of whom bore the brunt of failure. Struggling for something original to add, I highlighted the fact that despite the failures, 60 percent of soldier settlers remained on the land in the 1930s. Importantly, I was then able to take the story up through the settlement schemes for veterans of WWII, which demonstrated that the government had learnt the lessons of earlier policy failures. Greater care was taken to select servicemen for settlement, pick suitable land and offer adequate training to ensure they had the skills to work the land. Far fewer were settled but a higher proportion succeeded. Shifting the focus, a little, towards success, while still highlighting the personal and policy tragedy, was a minor contribution, nothing in comparison to the significance of Marilyn's work. But the idea of success has had some subsequent theoretical airing, notably in Bruce Scates and Melanie Oppenheimer's excellent general history of soldier settlement after the Great War, *The Last Battle* (2016).[9]

Pioneering is a much over-used concept. Nonetheless, given the relative paucity of Australian scholarship on the aftermath of war in the 1980s and early 1990s, I think *The Cost of War* did establish some themes and highlight questions that had received little attention to that point in time and the theme of the aftermath of war has since stimulated ongoing scholarly work. Much of this work has moved well beyond the questions and themes first sketched in *The Cost of War* (as it should). Some of it, notably Bruce Scates's innovative and highly original study of 'pilgrimages' to Anzac Cove and the Western Front since the Armistice up to the present day, has explored aspects of the aftermath

---

9   Bruce Scates and Melanie Oppenheimer, *The Last Battle: Soldier Settlement in Australia 1916–39*, Cambridge University Press, Melbourne, 2016.

of war never envisaged in *The Cost of War*.[10] Although *The Cost of War* laid some groundwork for understanding the significance of returned services organisations in shaping twentieth century Australian political culture, Martin Crotty has gone further, publishing important work on returned soldier organisations (especially the RSL) and their impact on post-war Australia.[11] Christina Twomey's work on civilian prisoners of war has been genuinely illuminating.[12] Other work, notably on the history of Aboriginal and Torres Strait Islander servicemen and women, the numbers who enlisted and what faced them on return, has built a vital corpus of knowledge and insight that wasn't available twenty-five years ago.[13] Since *The Cost of War* there has also been a flourishing and illuminating scholarly literature on the role of memorialisation in managing public and private grief and mourning. Ken Inglis's marvellous *Sacred Places* (1998) stands tall in this field, exploring the ways war memorials have given shape to and helped create the 'secular religion' of Anzac in Australian culture. Subsequent Australian work in this field is in many respects a conversation with Ken's work, but some of the most important contributions have moved away from public memorialisation to explore how individual families crafted consoling (and sometimes embittered) memorial tributes to husbands, fathers, sons and brothers killed in war: Pat Jalland's work on 'death denial' and the emergence of 'privatised grieving', Bart Ziino's study of 'In Memoriam' columns in newspapers and Colin Bale's research on family epitaphs on headstones in military cemeteries on the Western Front.[14]

The focus on grief and mourning has been an important historiographical turn. While *The Cost of War* explored some of the impact of angry, disgruntled and violent returned soldiers on families, these effects were read through the

---

10 Bruce Scates, *Return to Gallipoli: Walking the Battlefields of the Great War*, Cambridge University Press, Melbourne, 2006.
11 See, for example, his 'The Returned Sailors' and Soldiers' Imperial League of Australia, 1916–1946' in Martin Crotty and Marina Larsson (eds), *Anzac Legacies: Australians and the Aftermath of War*, Australian Scholarly Publishing, Melbourne, 2010, pp. 166–86.
12 Christina Twomey, *Australia's Forgotten Prisoners: Civilians Interned by the Japanese in World War II*, Cambridge University Press, Melbourne, 2007.
13 See for example, James Bennett, 'Lest We Forget Black Diggers: Aboriginal Anzacs on Television', *Journal of Australian Studies*, vol. 38, no. 4, 2014, pp. 457–75, Ann Curthoys, 'National Narratives, War Commemoration and Racial Exclusion in a Settler Society', in T.G. Ashplant, Graham Dawson and Michael Roper (eds), *The Politics of War Memory and Commemoration*, Routledge, London, 2000, pp. 128–44 and Philippa Scarlett, 'Aboriginal Service in the First World War: Identity, Recognition and the Problem of Mateship', *Aboriginal History*, vol. 39, 2015, 163–81. Aboriginal and Torres Strait Islander experience is now also being seen in a transnational context. See for example, Timothy C. Winegard, *Indigenous Peoples of the British Dominions and the First World War*, Cambridge University Press, New York, 2012.
14 Pat Jalland, *Changing Ways of Death in Twentieth Century Australia: War, Medicine and the Funeral Business*, UNSW Press, Sydney, 2006; Bart Ziino, *A Distant Grief: Australian War Graves and the Great War*, UWA Press, Crawley, 2007; Colin Bale, *A Crowd of Witnesses: Epitaphs on First World War Australian War Graves*, Longueville Books, Haberfield, 2015.

repatriation files with their inevitable bias towards the actions of men. While a strength of *The Cost of War* was its focus on the history of masculinity, particularly male sexual anxieties, and by implication their impact on families, how wives and families actually coped with disgruntled and resentful men didn't receive the attention it deserved. Joy Damousi's path-breaking studies of wartime mourning and bereavement turned *The Cost of War* on its head, exploring the ways women and families coped with the psychological burdens of bereavement and forged new political identities that re-shaped Australian culture and politics. Her work charted innovative methodological and theoretical terrain in the history of emotions and individual psychology.[15] Some of the subsequent work of scholars following her lead, such as that of Marina Larsson, has been genuinely illuminating.[16]

But there are risks in this focus on individual emotional responses. How can one historicise grief, mourning and bereavement, mark them as distinctive to war-time and post-war Australia, rather than as some ahistorical psychological response to any mass trauma (genocide, natural disaster and so on)? There are pitfalls evident in efforts to uncover war-caused trauma by reading the sources uncritically through this lens. Some recent scholarship, for example, has sought to use mental hospital case files as evidence that war grief caused mental breakdowns. And while war undoubtedly caused severe mental strains for some, there are two methodological dilemmas here, not always well navigated by historians. The first is that diagnoses and descriptions in case files are not definitive judgements but rather 'family narratives'; efforts by relatives, friends and doctors to explain away the inexplicable. They are not conclusions that can be used to mount an historical argument about the actual cause of a breakdown. The second is that the incidence of mental breakdown in Australia and overseas, in both world wars, declined rather than increased.[17] The brilliance of Damousi's approach, however, is that having explored the emotional and psychological dimensions of bereavement, she pulls back to assess the social, cultural and political impact of bereavement through the making of new identities – the war widow, the childless father, the sole mother, the fatherless family – which grounded war bereavement in meaningful historical contexts.

Other recent work, however, is taking a welcome and refreshingly different approach to the aftermath of war. There is now an emerging historiography on the 'benefits' rather than the costs of war. Modern war is commonly a crucible for rapid developments in manufacturing, logistics, armaments, engineering, chemistry, medicine, surgery, the control of infectious diseases and many other areas of scientific endeavour. The pressure to secure a decisive military advantage through

---

15   Joy Damousi, *The Labour of Loss: Mourning, Memory and Wartime Bereavement in Australia*, Cambridge University Press, Melbourne, 1999 and *Living with the Aftermath: Trauma, Nostalgia and Grief in Post-War Australia*, Cambridge University Press, Melbourne, 2001.
16   Marina Larsson, *Shattered Anzacs: Living with the Scars of War*, UNSW Press, Sydney, 2009.
17   For an example of these dilemmas see Tanja Luckins, *The Gates of Memory: Australian People's Experiences and Memories of Loss in the Great War*, Curtin University Books, Fremantle, 2004.

science and the need to manage major health issues on a mass scale has, in the twentieth century, been a significant impetus to innovation, which has then often been translated into benefits for civilian populations thereafter. The mobilisation of expertise, utilising university staff and graduates in areas in which they had expertise, rather than in normal combat units, was slow to take off in the Great War, but once it did many areas of knowledge and practice were transformed. The aftermath of war witnessed the return of veterans at the forefront of developments in science, engineering and medicine and many of these men and women deployed their newfound knowledge and skills in post-war society. In Australia, this line of inquiry is being pursued by the 'Expert Nation' group and results of this research are beginning to be published.[18]

Given the explosion of scholarship on the aftermath of war in Australia, *The Cost of War* remains an early and necessarily exploratory intervention into this field. The diversity and depth of the current scholarship awaits a synthesis but in issuing *The Cost of War* again my hope is to both acknowledge its limitations and its contribution in time and place, and to offer points of reference for new generations of scholars to go well beyond its boundaries in undertaking work in a fertile area of scholarship where there is still much to be done. Thus, this revised edition is largely the text as written in the early 1990s. I have corrected a few errors, added an occasional sentence or two when current scholarship has really made some of my original claims redundant, and added a small section on Korea. In the original responses to *The Cost of War* a number of veterans of the Korean War complained that they had been 'overlooked again'. While *The Cost of War* was meant to be a thematic rather than a narrative study, it does seem appropriate to acknowledge that Korean War veterans are part of this larger story. I haven't, however, canvassed the fate of service personnel who have served in numerous other conflicts (such as the Malayan Emergency and Timor Leste, let alone Afghanistan and Iraq) but I have inserted one or two sentences, where appropriate, to acknowledge that many of the challenges and dilemmas outlined here remain pressing and relevant for the veterans and their families of other conflicts – notably Afghanistan and Iraq – and conflicts yet to come. The public and public policy challenge, given what we know about the likely effects, is how to do a better job supporting veterans and their families.

History can help us to consider more carefully not just the political and foreign policy implications of committing our armed services overseas, but also the long-term social and cultural consequences of war given what we now understand about the aftermath of war. That Australians have managed the aftermath of wars

---

18   The chief investigator of this project is Tamson Pietsch (UTS). The other chief investigators are Julia Horne and Stephen Garton (Sydney), Kate Darian-Smith (Tasmania) and James Waghorne (Melbourne), ably supported by Liz Gillroy (UTS and Sydney). The first fruits of this work include Kate Darian-Smith and James Waghorne (eds), *The First World War, Universities and the Professions*, MUP, Melbourne, 2019.

Preface to the Revised Edition

without major political upheaval is remarkable – and part of the story must be how this has been achieved – but the personal costs for returned service personnel and their families and friends have at times been enormous and left major economic, emotional and psychological scars that have been transmitted across generations. We underestimate the cost of war at our peril.

Stephen Garton
Sydney, May 2019

Preface to the First Edition

Why write about war? It is a question I am often asked, but one difficult to answer. I have never been in combat, and although my father fought in New Guinea, he saw more action in supply than on the front line. Moreover, the war of my memory is Vietnam, and though I was too young for the draft (and perhaps too young to grasp fully the political issues), my sympathies lay with the anti-war protesters. I am singularly ill-equipped, then, to write about war or its effects, and I dare say some who read or review this book will despair of my ignorance of things military. Even the reply that this is not a book about war but one concerning the impact of war on Australian culture may not completely satisfy, for if this study deals with anything, it is the effects of combat, the emotional and physical scars born by returned men and women, the impact of return on veterans, their families, and friends, and the efforts of Australians to understand this pain and tend the bodily, psychological, and cultural wounds of war. And, in pursuing these problems, I have been selective, examining only a few twentieth century theatres of war – The First World War, the Second World War, Korea and the Vietnam War – although the dynamics of return sketched here seem to apply and continue to apply more generally.

How did I come to be interested in such problems? There is a conventional route. In the early 1980s I was researching mental illness, particularly the shift from an asylum system of treatment to new forms of psychotherapy. It seemed that a crucial factor in this transformation was the impact of shell-shock on psychiatric thinking (now, having done more work, I am less sure). But certainly shell-shocked soldiers forced a greater awareness of psychological factors in mental illness. Later I began to write a history of social welfare in Australia. Here I found that most of the historians who had preceded me had naturally traced the emergence of 'the welfare state'. But few had acknowledged that the repatriation system represented a second welfare state, running parallel to, and almost as large as, the official one. In fact, this book began as a history to redress this absence, but fortunately, early in its gestation, I became aware of the work of Clem Lloyd and Jacqui Rees. Their book, *The Last Shilling* (1994), is an excellent study, and readers interested in a comprehensive account of repatriation could find no better guide. It is a work that, thankfully, freed me from the daunting obligation of writing a narrative of war-service welfare. Instead I have tried to incorporate repatriation into a study of the problem of 'return'. And the more I worked on return, as both a cultural 'fact' and a social one, the more convinced I became that this experience has shaped the lives of many Australians. Over the last few years I have spoken with many people on the street, on phones, behind counters, casual acquaintances and close friends, about my research, and out tumbled troubled memories of disturbed returned-soldier fathers. What has emerged is not a single thesis but a series of linked essays and reflections on questions arising from the return of servicemen and women from war: What was their experience of return? What problems did they face? How did they and their families cope with return? What systems of assistance were provided for them, and how effective were they? How was the experience understood? And finally, how did these understandings shape the response to, the memory of, and the history of return?

But there were other routes to this book. Underpinning the research was a more curious imperative. I have no experience of war, nor any real knowledge of military history, but few things move me more deeply than remembrance ceremonies, and few pieces of music wrench at the heart more than 'The Last Post'. What is it about the Anzac ethos that can work such effect? Here a consideration of the meaning of 'return' is offered as one way (but certainly not the only way) of exploring this question. Perhaps this will turn out to be a rather old-fashioned quest, for how can the Anzac legend have meaning for generations who have no experience of war, or for Australians whose experience of war has nothing to do with Anzac? Recent events, however, suggest that Anzac might have some continuing, if shifting, meaning. High attendances at Anzac Day marches and 'Welcome Home' marches for Vietnam veterans, public mourning for Weary Dunlop, the creation of the Tomb of the Unknown Soldier, and celebrations of the anniversaries of the Anzac landing or the end of the Second World War all attest to widespread emotional involvement in the legend – an involvement that goes some way towards transcending the barriers of age, gender, and ethnicity. And, while I am convinced that we should embrace our differences, it is instructive to understand what can bind us. But understandings emerge from critical scrutiny, not unquestioning acceptance. This study seeks to uncover problems and contradictions, and while this disposition means that it is far from complete – indeed it is deliberately partial – it is offered as a contribution to debate. It focuses on the darker side of return, partly because this is a side too often ignored in national celebration, and on ambivalences in the construction of meaning, because legends both create particular identities and deny others. But it is also a means of marvelling at the extraordinary cultural performance involved in turning something so painful into a political imagining of enduring significance.

A project as large as this would not have been possible without a generous grant from the Australian Research Council. This much-maligned body (not enough grants and never enough money) deserves sincere thanks and apologies for this meagre return on investment. The Faculty of Arts and the History Department at the University of Sydney also provided much-appreciated financial assistance. Most of these grants were expended employing three excellent research assistants. Maryellen Galbally and Lesley Whalen got the project off to a good start. Lesley contributed even more by revealing her own experiences of the repatriation system. But Tessa Milne, who worked on the project for two years, not only performed all that was required of her with remarkable efficiency and good cheer; she also opened doors and established relationships of immeasurable benefit. When the research began, I was only given access to case files in the Australian Archives, but very quickly Tessa persuaded the Department of Veterans' Affairs to let us have access to all files. Access to this material was a key feature of this project, adding a vital dimension to the research, and it would have been difficult to achieve without her.

For facilitating access to the Department's restricted records, I am particularly grateful to Colin Hassall (who certainly did not live up to his name). Once we had access, Tessa visited each of the State offices of the Department of Veterans' Affairs and the Australian Archives. We would like to thank the staff in all these places for their enormous help and assistance, most particularly Noel Day, Narelle Wallace, Wendy Simmons, Debbie Bryce, Betty Walters, and Mira Setton. I am also grateful to Ann O'Hea of the Australian Archives, who guided me through the mysteries of the department's holdings. Books also need publishers, and I am thankful that Jill Lane and Oxford took an early and enthusiastic interest in this project. Good publishers find good editors, and Lucy Davison was in all respects an excellent choice.

One of the great pleasures of this research has been the opportunity to visit libraries and archives in each state. There are untold cultural treasures in these repositories, and it is disheartening to see that financial problems threaten public access to some of these institutions, particularly those in Victoria. But I greatly appreciate the assistance provided by staff in the Mitchell, La Trobe, John Oxley, Mortlock, Crowther, and Battye Libraries. Equally, staff in the New South Wales, Western Australian, Queensland, Tasmanian, and South Australian State Archives, and in the Public Record Office of Victoria proved to be ever helpful. Some of the most important sources for this study were the papers of the RSL, held at the National Library of Australia. I am grateful to Rollo Brett, Deputy National Secretary of the RSL, for permission to consult these papers, and to Greg Wilson and other staff of the Manuscripts Room, who did so much to assist me in getting through this mountain of records. My greatest pleasure, however, was the opportunity to use the Research Centre of the Australian War Memorial. This is an invaluable archive, and it continues to be staffed with unfailing efficiency and patience.

Early in the project's history I decided it was essential to embark on some comparative history to test the reputation of Australia's repatriation system. I am grateful to the staff of a number of institutions and to friends and colleagues who made my overseas visits more enjoyable. In London, I was able to taste the wonders of the British Library and make use of the Wellcome Institute for the History of Medicine Library, which must rank as one of the most efficient research institutions in the world. While there, I was also attached to the Sir Robert Menzies Centre, and staff and friends there – particularly Kate Darian-Smith, Brian Matthews, and Jane Arms – made my stay more than worthwhile. Pat Thane was a generous friend and introduced me to the Modern History Seminar of the Institute of Historical Research. Others who enlivened my stay include Clive Emsley, Michele Field, Dorothy Doherty, and Mike and Brenda Latham. In Cambridge, Massachusetts, Helen Hardacre provided a roof over our heads, many laughs, and much more besides. And trudging to the Widener Library each day through snow drifts and −14° Celsius represented a new dimension of the research experience. In Washington, Roy Rosenzweig and Deborah Kaplan, and Owen and Dorothy Harries treated us to meals and convivial conversation. At Indiana University, Judith Allen was ever generous and a source of endless good times. While there I was able to use the excellent resources of the Kinsey Institute for Sex Research, and I am grateful to the then Interim Director, Stephanie Sanders, Todd Smith, Curator of Art and Photography, and all the staff for their assistance. Also at Indiana, Jim Diehl and John Ephron listened to my thoughts on repatriation, offered encouragement and assistance, and provided congenial company. In Winnipeg, Jean and Gerry Friesen were wonderful hosts. The memory of our trip up the frozen Red River still remains vivid.

Back in Australia I have benefited from the advice and guidance of many colleagues. Some passed on the fruits of their own research, notably Penny Cuthbert, Grahame Harrison, Beverley Kingston, Greg Patmore, John Reeve, Jill Roe, Michael Roe, Catherine Snowden, and David Walker. Brendan O'Keefe offered some useful advice at an interesting moment. My colleagues at Sydney – particularly Barbara Caine, Iain Cameron, Brian Fletcher, Ian Jack, Ros Pesman, Penny Russell, and Glenda Sluga – did much to lighten the daily grind. Richard Waterhouse did all this and more, revealing something of himself and his own family experience of return from war. And I certainly could not have finished this book without Shane White, who dragged me from the trenches each week to rest in the Elysian Fields of Moore Park. More than this, he proved to be, as ever, a fount of relevant references. Others also helped. Athol Moffitt, prosecutor at the War Crimes trials in Borneo, gave freely of his experiences and put me in contact with the children of former prisoners, whose memories did more than anything else to hit me with the reality of return. Much of my time researching this book was spent in the nation's capital, and I am forever grateful to Chris Cunneen and Kerry Regan for their wonderful hospitality and friendship (not to mention the best food and wine in Canberra). In Western Australia, Pen Hetherington, Charlie Fox, and Tom Stannage provided the first opportunity to put my preliminary ideas before an audience. Others kindly agreed to read early drafts of the manuscript. Barry Smith subjected it to his searching gaze, pointing to many follies and errors, for which I

Preface to the First Edition

am ever grateful. Ken Inglis gave me the benefit of his inestimable knowledge in this field, gently chiding me for my ignorance and subtly urging me to think again. He also encouraged me to continue at a time when I thought it was all too much.

Without such encouragements, the book may never have been finished. Two 'anonymous' publisher's referees, Alistair Thomson and Paula Hamilton, were more than generous in their criticisms. I have benefited immeasurably from these readings and, while I may have failed to live up to their standards or meet all their demands, the book is much better for their efforts, while the many remaining weaknesses are a result of too many meetings, mental fatigue, and my own intellectual and imaginative shortcomings.

Families are also important in these endeavours. There is, of course, the family of friends who I have already thanked, particularly the two to whom this book is dedicated. There is also the family of relations. Perhaps the origin of this book goes back to my early childhood fascination with my father's campaign medals and the mysterious samurai sword under the parental bed. But more importantly, without the support of Lyn, Pat, Gloria, and Lesley over many years, none of this would have been possible. My second family also helped. Donald and Myfanwy provided a mountain retreat to revive tired minds and flagging spirits. But they have done much more in so many ways that I am embarrassed there is only this to thank them. Nick also brightened many dark days with his wit, good humour, and, on special occasions, his singing. Last, but certainly not least, in these thanks is Julia, who insisted, quite rightly, that her writing project was far more important than mine. The gestation may have been slower, but it benefited from this time for reflection. More than this, without Julia I could not have borne the struggle of facing the academy each day and the book at night.

Stephen Garton
Sydney, February 1996

1
Return

Every return was different in its own way, and yet it was also something more general, shared, and universal. The soldiers, sailors, airmen, nurses, and servicewomen who returned to Australia after war had their particular negotiations to make – with themselves, family, friends, and the place they returned to – yet each faced a common problem: returning, when they felt that they themselves had changed and everything around them also seemed to have changed. Plucked from familiar surroundings and associations, they left home for years at a time, undergoing experiences so profound that many were never able to talk about them again. They were experiences that most felt had marked them forever. Although they returned in joyous expectation of seeing loved ones again, they also returned to people and places that seemed at once familiar and yet strangely different. People at home had grown older and gone through their own experiences, tests of character, advances, and setbacks. Places were different: new buildings, people, pets, trees, and clothes. A whole spatial and cultural geography had undergone subtle, and sometimes not so subtle, transformation.

In one sense, returning servicemen and women faced the familiar problems of the traveller who comes home after a long journey; in another sense, their return was very different. In part this was because of the particular nature of their experience, but it was also because their return was of greater significance. These men and women had participated in a global drama, and were seen by Australians as having contributed to the formation of national identity itself. From the first reports of the landing at Gallipoli, newspapers proudly proclaimed that Australians had won 'imperishable fame'. In the months following this momentous event, the Gallipoli landing also came to be seen as a moment of 'awakening'; in the words of one commentator, the Anzacs had 'given infinite confidence in the manhood and destiny of Australia'.[1] And in all subsequent military conflicts Australian servicemen and women were expected to live up to this founding ideal.

---

1   Adelaide *Advertiser*, 8 May 1915; *Age*, 25 November 1918.

Under these circumstances, they could not be left alone to their private and personal efforts to repatriate.

I

Each war seemed to have its own rhythm of return. For the 167,000 Australian men and nearly 1000 women in service overseas at the end of the First World War, it was slow. At the end of the war they were far from home in camps in France, Britain, and the Middle East. Ships were in short supply, many having been destroyed in Atlantic battles and others tied up assisting Britain and Europe's recovery from the economic shocks of war, bringing refugees and prisoners of war home, and returning troops to the USA, Canada, New Zealand, and India. It took a considerable diplomatic and administrative effort on the part of Australian politicians and military authorities to garner the necessary transport to complete demobilisation.

It took 172 journeys by ship to bring them all home. And the last Australian soldiers and nurses to set off for home had to wait almost a year before departing. Decisions had to be made about who had priority in boarding and how those who remained behind were to be occupied. The ill and injured were a priority, although the timing of their return was also dependent on the extent of their injuries and their fitness for a voyage that lasted as long as six weeks. Nurses returned with the sick and injured. The principles governing the return of the majority, however, had to be determined. There was some debate over this: should men be evacuated on the basis of whether they had skills vital to Australia's post-war economy? their marital status? their unit? or how long they had been away from home? The latter course of action, with some modifications based on marital status, became the preferred policy, and one seen by its advocates and its historian as a triumph of Australian 'fairness'.[2]

While awaiting their return, men had to be occupied, and this proved to be an intricate administrative exercise. Libraries, reading courses, lectures, and trade classes were provided in the camps. There men could read from an eclectic, practical, but rather highbrow selection of books, including Arnold Toynbee's *Industrial Revolution*, G.D.H. Cole's *World of Labour*, Francis Galton's *Hereditary Genius*, and Meredith Atkinson's *Trade Unionism in Australia*; receive instruction in such subjects as arithmetic, French, German, book-keeping, shorthand, and economics; and listen to lectures on 'Slavs and their Problems', 'India', 'My Experiences under Bolshevism', and 'Irish Wit and Humour'. Those stationed in Britain could enrol in local colleges and universities, undertaking training in such trades as forestry, carpentry, pig-breeding, commerce, drawing, wool-classing, and telegraphy, and university education in varied courses, such as anthropology, moral philosophy, history, and medicine. Many eagerly embraced these offers to extend

---

2   E. Scott, *Australia During the War*, UQP, St Lucia, 1989 (1936), p. 827.

their knowledge and training at government expense. Corporal E.J. Leary-Smith wrote to thank the AIF Education Service for the chance to pursue his piano studies at the Royale Conservatoire in Brussels. Being in Europe also afforded the opportunity to attend concerts and operas, ensuring that 'my power of appreciation of good music profited immeasurably'. Some used their time to travel. They went on tours and visited the sights of Britain, Ireland, and Europe, fulfilling the desires of some of those who hoped the war would offer a means to see the world.[3]

The flurry of education, travel, and the general round of parties, drinking, and gambling embraced by soldiers who had 'done the job', however, masked a deeper problem during the hiatus before return. Soldiers were temporarily at a loose end. They were neither soldiers nor citizens, but something in between. This gave them a space and a freedom they would rarely achieve again: to behave in ways that would not be normally sanctioned, to revel in pleasures dreamt of at the front, and to reinvent themselves anew in professions and trades they might have aspired to but had never found the opportunity to pursue. Long delays fuelled strange rumours in the camps, a phenomenon parodied in the soldier journal *Aussie*: 'A bloke was tellin me that they are goin to keep all the ... cockies for two years after the war to plough up all the old battlefields in France'.[4] The rootlessness of the soldiers' state, however, worried those in charge of demobilisation. They noted a 'strange unrest' and an 'unsettling of the mind'. The men seemed 'irregular' and suffered from bouts of lethargy punctuated by 'spasmodic effort'. They feared that these were symptoms of a loss of the 'moral tone' and 'character' that had marked the AIF in battle. Attendances at courses and lectures fluctuated wildly – much more than might have been expected, even with the difficulties of providing adequate resources, instructors, and educators. Even some of the nurses seemed to lose interest in their work once the Armistice was declared. The men and women were restive, and for many of them, the lectures and instruction did little to offset their sense of unreality or to substitute for their desire to return home as quickly as possible[5].

This sense of being 'in-between' was only exacerbated by the long return by sea. Angela Thirkell has given us a wry parody of the Australian Anzac 'larrikin' in her account of the voyage. Here 'the digger' engages in all manner of 'typical behaviour': extraordinary bouts of drinking and brawling, ridiculing officers through female impersonation and abusing 'natives' in foreign ports.[6] And while Thirkell exaggerated to good effect, there is little doubt that some of the men took one of their few remaining opportunities to 'live it up' before demobilisation. Skylarking and gambling may have momentarily relieved the tedium, but in the endless hours

---

3   See AIF Education Service, 1914–18, AWM series 20. See also R. White, 'The Soldier as Tourist: The Australian Experience of the Great War', *War and Society*, vol. 5, no. 1, May 1987, pp. 63–77.
4   *Aussie*, no. 10, January 1919.
5   AIF Education Service, AWM 20, items 6403 & 6437. See also J. Bassett, *Guns and Brooches: Australian Army Nursing from the Boer War to the Gulf War*, OUP, Melbourne, 1992, pp. 92–3.
6   A. Thirkell, *Trooper to the Southern Cross*, Sun, Melbourne, 1966 (1934).

of waiting, men and women also had time to reflect on home – on what they would see and do on their return. The anticipation for some was intense, and the sense of relief accompanying their first sight of home – the lights on Rottnest Island, off Fremantle – overwhelming. Oliver Woodward, for one, would 'never forget the thrill occasioned by that light. To us it meant home after all these years of war, and I think the majority of us welcomed the darkness to hide our tears of joy'.[7] Soon after the first sighting of home, the ships docked at Fremantle, and the returning men and women were given tumultuous welcomes by families, friends, and well-wishers keen to acknowledge the glorious achievements of the AIF.

These emotional scenes were repeated at the next landings, in Adelaide and then Melbourne. Flags flew from every mast, streamers and bunting decorated the wharves and streets, and 'prolonged co-ees' from the soldiers were greeted with enthusiastic 'hurrahs' from the crowd. There were shrill screams, waving hats and handkerchiefs, the throwing of cigarettes, sweets, flowers, and confetti, cries of recognition, and passionate embraces as the soldiers marched through Melbourne to the Exhibition Building before formal demobilisation. Some had a few days leave before their departure to other towns and cities. They were granted free suburban railway and tram tickets, half-price theatre tickets, and a 25 per cent reduction on all food and accommodation by members of the Licensed Victuallers Association in appreciation of their sacrifice.

The return of the First AIF was a public event. Notices of returning ships were well advertised in newspapers, and forewarned crowds thronged disembarkation points, jostling for a sight of the men. In each town and city, the men marched to the accompaniment of bands and choirs. Speeches by the Governor-General, governors and numerous local mayors proclaimed the honour of meeting the men who had proved themselves to be 'second to none in military prowess and virtue'. Even the weather could not deter the celebrations. In late November the streets of Melbourne were choked with swirling dust whipped up by hot northerly winds, but the crowds remained enthusiastic. For May Tilton, a returning nurse taking her place in the soldier procession, 'it was a wonderful welcome ... I was weeping the whole way'.[8]

The press, in case anyone remained unaware of the significance of the return, trumpeted its meaning for their readers. For the Melbourne *Age*, 'here were the very men – sound in body and limb – of whose deeds and valour the whole world has sung paeans of praise'. The welcome sent the message that 'to those warriors who had roamed the globe, amidst dreadful scenes and privations, there was no place so sweet as home'. For the press, these returns also afforded an opportunity to stress again their belief that these soldiers had realised the latent racial potential of the bushman and the pioneer:

---

7   Oliver Holmes Woodward Papers, Fryer Library, MSS F2266, vol. 2, p. 169.
8   As quoted in G. Robinson, *The Forgotten Women*, self-published, Mt Gravatt, Qld,1989, p. 140.

> The thoughts of many; of course, must have been beyond the Great Divide, where the bush, the fern, the thrush, the parrot, the lyre bird and the wallaby are part of home; back home among the corn with the 'old man', to whom absence from the loved one had been an absence of self from self – the deadliest form of banishment.

But this was also a moment to reconcile the conflicting pull of city and country, of Australia and Empire; all had contributed to the formation of the new nation. The same paper remarked that, 'to a good proportion, the plane and elm tree, the old cable cars, the tall buildings, the dusty streets and the smoky factories were the dear familiar sights of that great home place in which they had started life's long wonderful, stirring race ... and made the immortal name of Anzac'.[9] Whether from the city or the bush, these men had sprung from the soil of a distinctive land and had made it known to the world that this place produced the finest people in the world.

From Melbourne, returning soldiers caught ships or trains to Sydney, Hobart, and Brisbane, and then travelled on to their home towns and suburbs to receive similar welcomes. On the dock, railway station, or just striding up the street to home, many walked expectantly into the arms of loved ones. Oliver Woodward, having survived the fanfares in Perth and Melbourne, arrived in Brisbane and 'caught sight of [his] mother and sister and then ... knew what joy could really mean'.[10]

The return of the soldiers, sailors, airmen, nurses, and members of the women's services at the end of the Second World War was not nearly as protracted. Although Australian forces had fought in European, Mediterranean, and North African theatres of war, most of these men had returned to Australia in 1942 and 1943 to strengthen the fight against the Japanese. Some 3000 airmen continued to fight in Europe, and about 8000 were in German prisoner-of-war camps, but the majority of the forces at the end of the war were much closer to home than had been the case in 1918. The majority, in fact, were home already, or at least on Australian soil. Of the 595,000 men and women in the services at the end of the war, only about half were actually overseas, and of these most were in New Guinea and on nearby Pacific islands. Another 14,000 were in Japanese prisoner-of-war camps in South-East Asia. Since early 1944 nearly 200,000 had been returned to civilian life before the cessation of hostilities.

Although the last of the forces were finally demobilised in February 1947 (although a small contingent remained in Japan as part of the occupation force until 1950), most had returned to Australia within a few months of the surrender of Japan. There was some waiting then, but these men did not require the extensive education services of the First AIF. Instead they were occupied: ensuring that Japanese forces on numerous small islands in the Pacific were repatriated to Japan, guarding Japanese accused of war crimes, freeing prisoners of war, and assisting in the reconstruction of transport facilities in Asia and the Pacific. Nonetheless,

---

9   *Age*, 25 November 1918.
10 Woodward Papers, vol. 2, p. 170.

there was plenty of idle time in the camps, only alleviated by occasional films and theatrical performances, and lectures on the benefits a grateful nation would provide on their return. This prompted many complaints, even the occasional demonstration, about the slowness of the demobilisation process.[11] The frustration was all the more intense because home was so close and few had any desire to explore the tourist potential of their surroundings. Government and military authorities were also worried that the sight of emaciated prisoners might alarm friends and relatives back home. These men had to wait until they regained a respectable measure of health before they could be returned.

Once the decision was made, however, the return for many was much quicker than for the veterans of the First World War. Some were brought back by plane – Catalina sea planes – landing first in Darwin and then in Rose Bay, Sydney, in just under a day after leaving Malaya. More, however, returned by ship. Their first sight of home was Queensland as they steamed down the coast to dock in Brisbane. From there, some caught trains, which sped them on to their homes in other states. Others remained on the ship to dock in ports further south. The expectations of these servicemen and women were probably no less intense than those of earlier veterans. Although they had less time to mull over their future, the sense of relief for many was palpable. Alan Hoyle felt 'delirious delight at being alive' and surviving without serious injury. Their moments of reunion were no less joyous. J.P. O'Brien walked into his home in Plummer Street, Graceville, in Brisbane, 'to the tears of joy from Mum and Dad and a big lump in my throat after being away for six years'.[12]

The return of servicemen and women from Europe, Asia, and the Pacific was also marked by public celebration. Men were greeted at wharves and airports by 10,000 or more enthusiastic friends, relatives, and well-wishers. Crowds lined the streets cheering each returning contingent, throwing confetti, and shouting 'good on yer' and 'well done' to the men, shaking their hands and shouting them drinks at every opportunity. These were familiar scenes. But there was also something different about these welcomes. Most notably, there were far fewer speeches celebrating the valour and glory of the men, who, while delighted by the warm welcomes, were reported to be keen to avoid such celebrations, preferring to slip more quickly and quietly back into the embrace of their families.[13]

This attitude marks a change in the character of Australia's involvement in war. While the Australian forces in the Second World War were almost twice the size of those in the First World War and played decisive roles in North Africa, New Guinea, and Melanesia, fewer servicemen saw actual front-line combat. Moreover, the ending of the later war had been a more protracted and expected outcome. The

---

11 See *Courier Mail*, 4 January 1946.
12 See A. Hoyle, *Into the Darkness*, self-published, Canberra, 1989, p. 96; J. P. O'Brien Papers, John Oxley Library, OMSS 618, p. 128.
13 See, for example, *Sydney Morning Herald*, 4 August 1945.

First World War had ended suddenly and to the surprise of many. With the Second World War, there had been a sense of steady and inevitable progress towards victory after the invasion of Normandy in June 1944. Successive celebrations of each step towards victory focused attention on the future and sapped vitality for the present. In the last months of the war, many soldiers themselves were aware that they were engaged in a difficult and dangerous mopping up campaign but one that was not on the leading edge of confrontation with Japan. Their thoughts turned all too frequently to home as they ached for the completion of hostilities and prayed that they would survive unscathed.

But there were cultural forces also at work. The Second World War had not been embraced by the nation's opinion-makers and many of its citizens with the eagerness for national glory that had marked the attitudes of their counterparts in 1914. Rather, many had gone to war with a certain measure of dutiful determination, all too aware of the horrors of war that awaited them. Equally, the reputation of the Anzacs had already been cemented. The soldiers of the Second World War, particularly those at Tobruk and Kokoda, had confirmed the continuing vitality of the tradition but were not seen to have added anything new to it. There was also greater fatigue on the home front. The war had been longer and had affected the lives of many civilians materially and physically. The largest crowds and parades were victory parades, and our lasting visual image is of Australians dancing in the streets, not soldiers marching. They were celebrating an end to hardship more than the glory of sacrifice, and the crowds that gathered to see the return of individual units were often comparatively small. Perhaps even more significant was the plight of prisoners of war. They embodied the suffering and privations of war more vividly than ever before. The torture they had been subjected to was reported in sombre tones in the press. The poignancy and ambiguity of these brave men, who both confirmed and contradicted the warrior ideal, unsettled conventional representations of returning men. This troubled authorities and the public was banned from the wharves for the return of the worst affected former prisoners. This was hardly the time or the place for bombastic rhetoric about the glories of war and the return of heroes; it was an occasion only of relief at its ending.[14]

If the return of soldiers from the First World War had been slow, for the 17,000 who served in Korea and the 50,000 servicemen and women who had served in Vietnam, it was fast – too fast for some. These men and women, unlike their predecessors, now had a defined tour of duty designed to alleviate 'combat fatigue'. Their lives, fears, and anxieties were inevitably shaped by the calendar of their tour: would they be injured or killed before it was up? More importantly, finishing a tour was not a tidy point of resolution. Those returning from Vietnam, in particular, were all too aware that this was an undeclared war, increasingly unpopular at home, and one that would continue after their departure. For Vietnam veterans, demobilisation was not a point of completion but something more ambiguous.

---

14   See the *Age*, 6 October 1945; *Sydney Morning Herald*, 4 October 1945; *Courier Mail*, 9 October 1945.

Fighting an enemy that was often unseen and indistinguishable from the civilian population, in a war that seemed to have no ending in sight, meant that servicemen and women not only left the combat behind at the end of their tour, but also friends and comrades. They could not come home as victors, but only as cogs in a military machine that continued to grind.

The process of leaving amplified these ambiguities. Improved transport and communication meant a rapid transition from front line to home front. One day they were in the towns and villages of Vietnam, uncertain who was friend or foe, and by the end of that day they were preparing to land in Australia. Many Vietnam veterans returned by plane, and the abrupt change in their circumstances was unsettling. Some declared that return seemed like a blur, which heightened the unreality of home. They often found it difficult, having returned to civilian life, to eradicate the habits of combat. They were cautious and on edge in public. Some started at backfiring cars, hitting the ground in combat positions to the amusement of friends and relatives. Others found Australian cities claustrophobic. Many more continued to dream of the horrors of combat. But the sense of relief and joy at seeing friends and relatives again was no less intense than it had been for veterans of earlier wars. For one veteran, the 'reunion was quite an emotional event. I remember the tears flowing freely'. For another, 'the flight to Perth was tremendous ... My mother and I hugged and cried together. Even some of my mates and I embraced. We'd never done that before and haven't since'.[15]

The public reception, however, was more ambivalent. In the 1966 federal election, the Labor Opposition, led by Arthur Calwell, had campaigned strongly against Australia's involvement in the Vietnam conflict and had been soundly defeated. But by 1967 the anti-war movement in the USA and Australia was a small but active voice of opposition to the war. In October 1967, crowds of 10,000 people protested the war, and by 1970 there were moratorium marches of 100,000 people in Melbourne and large gatherings in many other cities. Vietnam soldiers were well aware of these developments and deeply resented them. One young infantryman wrote to the *Courier Mail*, angrily condemning Jim Cairns and the moratorium movement as 'doubters, traitors and spreaders of dissension'.[16] Such cries did little to halt the march of opposition. Protesters began to picket returned soldier parades, shouting anti-war slogans with devastating effect. Some soldiers were flown in at night to protect them from protesters. Instead of warm family welcomes, they found themselves in cold customs sheds in the hours before dawn awaiting transport home. Some veterans recall being abused and ridiculed. A few fought back. Michael Prowse, a navy veteran, earned a few broken ribs and bruises in a stoush with protesters, although was satisfied that he had repaid this favour in kind. But the malaise was deeper than this. The continuing struggle and the

---

15   N. Giblett (ed.), *Homecomings: Stories of Australian Vietnam Veterans and their Wives*, AGPS, Canberra, 1990, pp. 29–30.
16   *Courier Mail*, 19 June 1970.

perception that they were losing the fight made some veterans feel as though they were the 'black sheep of the Anzac tradition'. Robert Gay, like many returned Vietnam soldiers, 'felt disgraced' on Anzac Day: 'we didn't bring any glory or honour home ... we didn't return as a victorious army'.[17]

II

Images of the glorious consecration of the founding Anzac achievements in 1918, the delirious celebrations of victory in 1945, and the surreptitious and troubled return of Vietnam veterans are well ingrained in popular memory. But such memories have as much to do with conscious efforts to foster particular ideals, and the struggle between competing groups to claim the Anzac tradition for their own purposes, as they do with the realities of return. Our image of the Anzacs has been forever cemented by C. E. W. Bean's moving account of their exploits, the affecting and humbling testament to Australian sacrifice at the Australian War Memorial, the self-conscious maintenance of the tradition by veterans and their organisations on Anzac Day, and the countless speeches, books, and articles by Australians, both well-known and unknown, that have kept the flame of remembrance alive for over a century.[18] To say, however, that this is a particular type of remembering does not diminish the sacrifices of these men and women. Anzac, and even Vietnam – the 'black sheep' of Anzac – is legend: a complex mix of fact, remembering, forgetting, and longing.

It is impossible to deny the fertility of Anzac (the Cove, the battles, the men, and the legend) in the formation of national identity. In recent years, it has become fashionable to talk of Anzac and other images of national identity as inventions, developed by powerful interest groups and propagated among a pliant population. In the case of Anzac, such formulations, while undoubtedly containing a grain of truth, obscure other cultural processes. Although many of the First AIF saw it as their duty to enlist to defend Great Britain, their 'homeland' (nearly one-quarter of the First AIF had been born there), many also took wallabies, possums, koala bears, and other emblems of Australia to war. Some proudly promoted Aboriginal recruits as troop mascots (even though, legally, Indigenous Australians could not enlist to fight), wrote diaries for the first and last time in their lives, and eagerly gathered souvenirs of battle to bring back to Australia.[19] This suggests a certain self-consciousness on the part of many soldiers of their Australianness and the

---

17 G. Edwards (ed.), *Vietnam: The War Within*, self-published, Salisbury, SA, 1992, pp. 62 & 91.
18 See K. S. Inglis, 'The Anzac Tradition', *Meanjin*, no. 1, March 1965, pp. 25–44.
19 See D. Huggonson, 'Aboriginal Diggers of the 9th Brigade First A.I.F', *JRAHS*, vol. 79, 1993, pts 3–4, pp. 214–23; A. Jackomos & D. Fowell, *Forgotten Heroes: Aborigines at War from the Somme to Vietnam*, Victoria Press, Melbourne, 1993. On the gathering of souvenirs, see M. McKernan, *Here is their Spirit: A History of the Australian War Memorial 1917–1990*, UQP, St Lucia, 1991, pp. 30–61.

historical significance of their endeavour. The speed and enthusiasm with which the landing at Gallipoli was transformed into a symbol of national pride and embraced by a broad cross-section of the population points to the pervasive cultural hunger of a colonial population for recognition of the worth of their society, and for symbols to represent their hard-won maturity. This sense of a distinctive Australianness was refined and sharpened for the soldiers themselves, and for Australians more generally, by the experience and stories of Anzac larrikinism and valour, and of British formality and alleged bungling. The digger image may have had a close association with the earlier bushman image – neither image reflecting the lived experiences of women, Indigenous Australians, or the many men who lived in cities and suburbs – but Anzac transcended these barriers and spoke to the hopes and desires of large sections of the population.

The conjunction of Gallipoli with the very idea of Australia has done much to shape the historical memory of the reception afforded returning soldiers. The images of our embrace of First and Second World War veterans, and of the isolation of those who served in Vietnam, as well as veterans' own memories of these events, attests to the power of the Anzac legend. This is not to suggest that such images and recollections are wrong. On the contrary, the evidence to support them is strong. But there is also evidence for alternative accounts of return. Like all popular historical memories and legends, the conventional narratives are selections, distilled and recalled from a mass of individual moments. Their force comes from their ability to shape and to speak to a public consciousness that evolves and crystallises over time. With regard to the First AIF, it fosters an idea of their return as easy and uncomplicated: as C.E.W. Bean suggested, they 'merged quickly and quietly into the general population'.[20] In contrast, Vietnam veterans, who felt they had failed to achieve the victories of their forebears, recalled an ambivalent public attitude to their war and remained bitter in their sense that they had been betrayed by the society that had sent them away to do their duty. Where the original Anzacs stood for Australianness itself, Vietnam veterans represented (until recently) alienation and anger. But many returned servicemen and women from each war had experiences that cut across these familiar memories and stories, and these are equally significant for any understanding of return.

In 1918 F.V. Culverhouse returned from France. His diary and notes about life in the trenches are graphic, detailing the gruesome fatalism of front-line life, and the horror of choking with gas and lying in blood-soaked casualty stations. For him, the 'merry-making and wild delight' at the 'declaration of peace' was beyond compare. His return, however, was less delightful. He found work scarce and prices high, and encountered lingering bitterness from the anti-conscription campaigns and, worse still, jealousy of soldier repatriation benefits. He and his comrades 'were ashamed and afraid' to wear their badges, given by the Department of Defence to

---

20   C. E. W. Bean, *Anzac to Amiens*, AWM, Canberra, 1983 (1946), p. 529.

every man who had seen active service. This was a common experience. Soldiers and their organisations had pushed for a distinctive emblem to symbolise their sacrifice and special status. The Repatriation Department published its own journal, *Repatriation*, with the header 'Help the Man with the Medal', and retailers advertised discounts for these men. Governments also asked employers to give returned men job preference, but this made them targets for resentment and abuse. Newspapers reported that men were removing their badges to avoid getting 'a rough time' and were being jeered for having been 'fool enough' to fight.[21]

These undercurrents of antagonism persisted for some time. As late as 1938 Norman Campbell reported that very few men were prepared to wear their badge. Throughout the 1920s and 1930s occasional outbursts from minor officials and public figures give us a glimpse of the usually hidden antipathies to returned men. In these years some candidates for election who sought to gain votes by proclaiming their returned-soldier status were heckled. In 1928 a magistrate at Tamworth found himself the object of a series of outraged letters from returned men when, in rejecting a convicted man's plea for leniency, he declared 'the war has been over for ten years now, and it is time, those who went realised that they are now civilians'. A few years later an Alderman for the Windsor Municipal Council, near Sydney, found himself the object of a similar campaign of criticism when, during a heated debate about the planting of a garden around the local war memorial, he shouted that 'it was a pity that all returned soldiers did not stay "on the other side" '.[22]

Some of these attitudes reflected longstanding resentments against anyone who received welfare. Underlying Victorian charity was a belief that many of those who received benefits were 'undeserving' and 'imposters' who hoped to fool gullible philanthropists rather than undertake honest work and self-help. What is remarkable is the longevity and persistence of these ideas. They stretch from the first criticisms of the 'Old Poor Law' in England in the late eighteenth century to media attacks on 'dole bludgers' in the 1990s. What is surprising is that returned soldiers in receipt of benefits for war injuries and illnesses did not escape this undercurrent of antagonism. Repatriation pensioners were often said to be 'on the pig's back'. The correspondence files of the Repatriation Department contain numerous letters from neighbours and workmates 'dobbing in' war pensioners they believed were 'undeserving'. Even Second World War veterans were not immune to such charges, as one typical letter makes clear. Writing in 1957, Harold L stated:

> there is a fellow employee in the Department on a good salary but he is an inveterate gambler and drinker. He loses a great deal and the worry has affected his health ... he was advised to apply for a war pension ... he succeeded ... he is the

---

21 See F. V. Culverhouse, Diary and Notes: Three Black Lights, John Oxley Library, OMSS 64-31/7; *Age*, 4 January 1919.
22 See N. Campbell, 'The Great War is Not Over Yet', *Life*, March 1938, p. 18; *Sydney Morning Herald*, 14 October 1927, 17 February 1928, 13 July 1931.

master of the fake and with a pension he will be better able to carry on his betting at the expense of the overloaded taxpayer ... there is another man in the next office who is drawing a pension for injuries received to his leg ... [which] has long since healed so that he can complete hours of dancing ... have you any means whatsoever to protect people from these vultures.[23]

But contempt for pensioners cannot fully explain the resentment returned soldiers faced after 1918. Their ambivalent reception was shaped by the troubled context of the war and immediate post-war years.

The First World War may have created the symbols by which Australians would recognise themselves, but on the home front it was a deeply divisive war. It imposed severe economic burdens on individual households. Patriotic funds raised over £12 million by subscription during the war, and at the same time, governments were raising war loans, to the tune of £250 million. This was the equivalent of £260 for each household, when the average male wage in 1919 was just over £193 a year. This represented a significant patriotic investment in the war, but for some poorer households even a small contribution meant hardship. These economic strains were increased by rampant inflation, with the price of many basic foodstuffs (such as milk, bread, and butter) and other essentials (such as clothing and footwear) nearly doubling. Wages were also rising but failed to keep pace with prices. This was the source of much anger, particularly when it became obvious that some companies and stores were making significant profits. Workers, unions, and housewives protested vigorously, claiming that profiteers were 'starving the families of our soldiers at the front'. Governments failed to keep a lid on prices, despite promises to do so, perpetuating the populist belief that this was a war in which the workers were sent to die at the front while capital grew even fatter at the expense of ordinary families. In this context of economic strain, housewives marched on Parliament demanding a 'fair price', and unions went on strike for a greater slice of war profits. In 1917 a series of crippling strikes – most notably the General Strike, which spread from the railways to other transport unions – involved 173,000 workers and resulted in nearly five million lost working days.[24]

The most bitter divisions, however, occurred over enlistment and conscription. The First AIF was a voluntary force. Although this was the source of much pride, by 1916 declining enlistments were of great concern to the Prime Minister, William Morris Hughes, who had promised Britain a quota of recruits that he was

---

23 Harold L to Repatriation Department, 26 March 1957, Department of Veterans' Affairs, Correspondence, AA, SP 1375, box 400.
24 Figures from Scott, *Australia during the War*, pp. 499–665. See also H. McQueen, 'Shoot the Bolshevik! Hang the Profiteer! Reconstructing Australian Capitalism 1918–21', in E. L. Wheelwright & K. Buckley (eds), *Essays in the Political Economy of Australian Capitalism*, vol. 2, ANZ Book Company, Sydney, 1978, pp. 185–206; J. Smart, 'Feminists, Food and the Fair Price: The Cost of Living Demonstrations in Melbourne, August–September 1917', *Labour History*, no. 50, May 1986, pp. 113–31.

increasingly unable to fill. Hughes's attempts to institute conscription by popular mandate through two, ultimately unsuccessful, referendums in 1916 and 1917 polarised the nation. There were bitter clashes between pro- and anti-conscriptionists, and the narrow defeat of the referendums only served to heighten these tensions. In the public campaigns, Irish Catholics (angered by Britain's brutal suppression of the Easter 1916 uprising in Ireland), trade unionists, and large groups of Labor Party supporters were conspicuous voices against conscription, while Protestant middle-class employers and professionals were prominent supporters. Recent research suggests other political fissures. Women, primary producers, British migrants, and Western Australians were inclined to support conscription, while Catholics were divided, and the split in the Labor Party over the referendums indicates that the issue was more than a clash of class and sectarian loyalties.[25]

Opposition to conscription, however, was not about participation in the war. Most anti-conscriptionists were in favour of the war but supported voluntarism rather than compulsion. This points us in the direction of another major division in Australia: the division between those who volunteered and those who did not. Most historians of the First World War are fond of stressing that nearly half of all those men aged between eighteen and forty-five years who were eligible to enlist did so – undoubtedly a high proportion (although it was less than the British rate). This only highlights that over half did not enlist, even if half of these again failed on health grounds.[26] Despite all the public campaigns to foster enlistment, the clear expressions of loyalty to Empire, the emergent nationalism that supported it, and the more secret subterfuges of white feathers and ridicule, it seems that from one-fifth to one-quarter of all eligible men fit enough to go refused to enlist. Some had families to support; others had brothers at the front and were required to stay at home to look after ageing parents or the family business. This was the case for one of the most famous refusers: future prime minister, Robert Gordon Menzies. Whatever the reason, a clear distinction, fostered by soldiers themselves, emerged between the returned soldier, 'the man with the medal', and the 'shirkers', the 'men-in-the-street', the 'stay-at-homes', who had remained in Australia. This became a major point of tension in the interwar years.

These conflicts and disputes shaped the reception of returning soldiers. The more these men sought to claim a special status, the more they opened themselves up to jealousy, rancour, or antagonism from those who had remained behind, especially those who had opposed conscription or had suffered at the hands of 'shysters' and 'profiteers'. These divisions were exacerbated by difficult post-war

---

25 G. Withers, 'The 1916–1917 Conscription Referenda: A Cliometric Re-appraisal', *Historical Studies*, vol. 20, no. 78, 1982, pp. 36–47.
26 Lloyd Robson estimates that about 40 per cent of all Australian men aged from eighteen to forty-five years enlisted. See L. L. Robson, *The First AIF – A Study of its Recruitment 1914–1918*, MUP, Melbourne, 1982, pp. 202–3.

economic conditions. The short-lived post-war boom was followed by recession in 1920 and 1921. Oversupply on world markets sent commodity prices down significantly, undermining national income and making it more difficult to repay war loans. Unemployment almost doubled (rising to 11 per cent), and in this context the claim of returned-services organisations to employment preference threatened the livelihood of other Australians. There were complaints on both sides. Soldiers, promised by governments and employers that their jobs would be secure, came home to find employers reluctant to let good workers go, jobs occupied by 'stay-at-homes', and as conditions worsened, positions being cut rather than filled. Workers competing in a tight labour market feared that returned men would receive employment preference, and trade unionists, some of whom were returned soldiers, were concerned that this policy would undermine the hard-won gains of union preference and the closed shop.[27]

Employment preference was not the only issue that diminished the enthusiasm of some Australians for returning Anzacs. Some of these men also brought back diseases, such as influenza, venereal infections, and tuberculosis. None of these were new to Australia, but concentrated as they were in a young population and with the capacity to spread to other Australians, they represented a serious public health problem. Tuberculosis could mask its insidious effects for some years, but venereal and influenza infections were immediate and obvious. The high incidence of venereal diseases and their debilitating effect on manpower had been of particular concern to military authorities during the war. Extensive measures were undertaken to combat them, including the provision of lectures, condoms, clinical care, blue light depots for early treatment, and detention and pay deductions for those who failed to report their infection. Nonetheless, government authorities estimated that about 50,000 Anzacs contracted a venereal disease. But how many actually returned infected is more difficult to estimate. A. G. Butler, the official medical historian, offers a figure of only 1474, all returned to Australia in the first two years of the war as unfit, and a further 2000–3000 requiring further treatment at the end of the war. But this is likely to be an underestimate, ignoring men who contracted infections in the final months of the war or after the cessation of hostilities. Regardless of the actual number of infected returned men, informed citizens were concerned about the potential spread of infection, establishing such organisations as the University of Sydney Society for Combating Venereal Diseases and the Racial Hygiene Association during and after the war to warn of the danger and inform about prevention. All the states legislated so that it was compulsory for doctors to notify the authorities of persons suffering from venereal diseases (although South Australia failed to implement the provisions), and most established public clinics for their treatment. Although information on venereal

---

27 See H. Radi, '1920–29', in F. Crowley (ed.), *A New History of Australia*, Nelson, Melbourne, 1974, pp. 357–414; S. Macintyre, *The Oxford History of Australia*, vol. 4, OUP, Melbourne, 1986, pp. 168–97.

diseases in the interwar years is patchy, what evidence exists suggests that the incidence of these diseases declined, perhaps as a result of the success of these campaigns, but also partly because of a decline in their virulence. But this misses the point. These campaigns arose out of a climate of fear.[28]

Of even more immediate concern was the influenza pandemic. The 'Spanish Flu' first appeared among United States forces in 1918, but by 1919 it had spread to civilian populations around the world, killing an estimated thirty million people. Australians feared that returning soldiers would bring the flu home, and deaths on board troop ships prompted swift action. Australian authorities introduced stringent quarantine measures involving detentions of more than a week if cases of infection were discovered. Such measures were condemned as a 'flu muddle' by soldier organisations, who blamed authorities for allowing the troop ships to dock in infected ports. A few angry Anzacs, desperate to see home, broke out of quarantine in Australia, and although it is difficult to tie the outbreak of the pandemic in Australia to these sources, 12,000 Australians died from influenza in the immediate post-war years. As possible bearers of the 'red plague' or the 'Spanish Flu', returning soldiers after the First World War came home not just as heroes but also as potential 'scourges'.[29] The closer we examine the reality of return for soldiers, the more the sharp distinction between Vietnam veterans and Australian veterans of earlier wars begins to disappear. The odd ones out are not the Vietnam veterans but those from the Second World War, who returned to a vigorous policy of post-war reconstruction, high levels of growth in employment and income, and a population supported by a significant welfare safety net. In contrast, returning servicemen from the First World War sometimes faced social ostracism, ridicule, and disaffection from sections of the population, just as Vietnam veterans were to, although in neither case was ostracism inflicted by the majority of the population.

Even when we look at the public celebrations of return, the distinctions begin to blur. Although the first Anzacs received fulsome acknowledgment of their achievements, the vast public celebrations were most obvious in the last few months of 1918, when the exaltation of victory was fresh. During 1919, as the ships began to dock at regular intervals, the celebrations became more muted. One or two inches of column space announced the return of men, and their welcomes were restricted to relatives and 'Red Cross kitchen teas of ham, eggs, jellies, cakes and scones'. These were no doubt welcome and warm occasions, but they were a far cry from the mass parades of earlier months. Bureaucratic bungling spoiled the return

---

28 See Inter-Departmental Committee, 'Report on Infectious Diseases in Connection with Demobilisation', *British Parliamentary Papers*, vol. 30, 1919, pp. 427–52; A. G. Butler, *History of the Australian Army Medical Services in the 1914–18 War*, vol. 3, Angus & Robertson, Sydney, 1943, pp. 148–89, 786. Figures on the incidence of venereal diseases after the war are contained in the *Commonwealth of Australia Year Books*, 1923–29.
29 See Editorial, 'The Flu Muddle', *The Soldier*, 14 February 1919. See also H. McQueen, 'The "Spanish" Influenza Pandemic in Australia 1918–19', in J. Roe (ed.), *Social Policy in Australia: Some Perspectives 1901–1975*, Cassell, Sydney, 1976, pp. 131–47.

for some. Tasmanian officials complained that they were misinformed about the arrival of ships, with the result that men arrived to no public welcome whatsoever.[30] Vietnam veterans, despite all the myths of rejection, often returned to rousing public receptions, reputedly attended by up to 300,000 people. These figures are probably exaggerated, but crowds were large nonetheless, and protesters were only ever a small and insignificant presence at these returns. More usually, Vietnam veterans were wildly cheered, showered with ticker-tape, and kissed by members of the crowd. Soldiers declared that it was 'great to be back' and 'there was no place like home', and were impressed by their reception. This account is a long way from our image of Vietnam veterans being shunned by the public. More commonly, it seems that the warmth of the welcome depended more on the timing of return, and on whether men and women returned as part of a unit or as individuals, than on which war they returned from.[31]

There were undoubtedly significant differences in the receptions for returned servicemen and women from the two world wars and those for Korean and Vietnam veterans, particularly for those Vietnam veterans who arrived as the anti-war and moratorium movements gained momentum. Clearly the extent of overt public protest against Vietnam veterans was far greater and more visible than anything returned soldiers from the First World War ever faced. Certainly, for a significant section of the population, the Vietnam War was more morally ambiguous than the First World War or Second World War, thus compromising the tenor of public celebration. But veterans of the earlier conflicts did face resentment, and many of those who served in Vietnam did arrive home to rousing welcomes. Some Vietnam veterans, however, returned as individuals rather than units, and this experience framed their memory of welcome. These memories have also been shaped by the historical and popular narratives that have been written about each war. Where the First World War and Second World War were noble victories, Korea had faded from public memory and Vietnam was shrouded in failure. The power of the Anzac myth could undermine as much as it could inflate. And this points us towards a broader problem: the emotional and cultural baggage that returned servicemen and women brought home with them, and their efforts to make sense of war experience long after return.

III

In 1935 'Alan Tiveychoc' (a pseudonym) attempted to give narrative shape and meaning to his war experiences, then almost twenty years past. His is an account inevitably coloured by memory, time, and his own shattered health and morphine addiction arising from extensive war injuries. The description of his moment of

---

30 See *Courier Mail* 27 October 1919; *Age*, 8 January 1919.
31 See *Sydney Morning Herald* and *Courier Mail* 9 June 1966.

return, still on the ship outside Fremantle, concludes with these brief reflections: 'he felt not the glamour of heroics but rather the pathos of this eventide that signified the passing of so much – the venture, the great experience had ended – the sun had set'. Not the least interesting aspect of this passage is that it is written in the third person, signifying a rupturing of past and present selves, and serving to highlight the contrast between the pure world of war and mateship, and the present world of 'eventide'.[32]

This account is far from unique. It resembles many others, some published, many lying in diary and note form in libraries and archives. Equally, it reflects the experience of Australians from different wars. Second World War returned airman Alan Hoyle, to take just one of many examples, found that 'I was home and the greatest adventure of my life was over'. Time and again these accounts position war experience as the defining moment of existence. After it, nothing seemed to match it for intensity or meaning. For some, like Tiveychoc or Hoyle, this was a moment of nostalgic and melancholic recollection of a richer past, but for others, like E.J.H. Joseph, it was an embittered cry for a lost self that could never be recovered: it was if he 'had completed a life's work', a feeling that so paralysed him that he felt incapable of ever summoning up the energy to engage in productive employment again. Some of these meanings achieved a higher literary formulation. Second World War poets, such as Alexander Turner, could write: 'Though we give freedom to the race of men/ Yet who shall give us back Ourselves Again?'. Here war experience takes on a different inflection, as the death of an innocent 'true self'. In these accounts the loss of self frames the years after return as a time when soldiers would wander in the wilderness. In diverse ways, the period after war, in literature and private recollection, is represented as a time of loss and darkness, in which returned soldiers are forever condemned to live in the past tense and the third person.[33]

This sense of loss is an effect of time and memory; who does not look back from the infirmities and responsibilities of age on youth as a time of excitement? Even so, the transformation of war into nostalgia requires an enormous effort of memory and, perhaps, a painful period of decline. But the ubiquity of these feelings of loss is nowhere more apparent than in the efforts of military and repatriation authorities to give voice to them in order to ease readjustment. Perhaps Australians in 1919 were unprepared for the disillusionment that would engulf returned men, but by 1945 governments had clearly learnt by bitter experience that the reassimilation process would be far from easy. One story, 'Man Before A Window', in the returned-services journal, *As You Were*, encapsulates this effort:

---

32 A. Tiveychoc, *There and Back: The Story of an Australian Soldier*, RSSILA, Sydney, 1935, p. 224.
33 See Hoyle, *Into the Darkness*, p. 99; E. J. H. Joseph, *The Long Road Back*, self-published, Hobart, 1985, p. 14; A. Turner, 'The Soldiers', in I. Mudie (ed.), *Poets at War*, Georgian House, Melbourne, 1944, p. 141.

he stared towards the rain and the unseen movement of the trams five floors below. Somewhere in the past there was other rain. Rain across the bellies, knotted with hunger and cramp ... He grinned as he remembered what he never admitted to anyone but himself. That he hugged very closely every minute of his living in the army, that he and the men he'd known, the things they had said and the things they'd done would be with him a lot of his life until he quietly left it.[34]

Other efforts were more humorous and whimsical. In armed services and repatriation journals, such as *Salt*, *Change Over*, and *As You Were*, there were often cartoons and drawings of men in dreary offices dreaming of the sunny and comfortable life on the front-line contrasted with the same man at the front, slogging through the miserable wet and dreaming of a nice comfortable bed at home, or a wife making the bed for her returned husband, a navy man, as a hammock strung from the bedroom ceiling. Through these modes of address, authorities sought to inculcate the idea that problems of readjustment were shared rather than individual. This was a way of easing the path to seeking help from 'experts', who now saw readjustment as a psychological, as much as a material, task. Authorities had long observed that some returned men seemed unable or unwilling to give up their fixation on the war and, whether through counselling, therapy, and vocational training or through melodrama, pathos, and humour, sought to provide a cathexis for the release of these feelings. Years afterwards, many still considered their war years as the most meaningful of their lives, and repatriation officials believed that such obsessions hindered the process of readjustment.[35]

Similar fixations are apparent in the recollections of some Vietnam veterans. One veteran, Ray, returned to his wife and young son but found that he 'couldn't handle it. It was like a void. Nothingness. For the first month all I could think of was how to get back there [Vietnam] ASAP'. The experience was so overwhelming that Ray, like so many others, seemed incapable of talking about it. Years later he believed that the problem had been the sudden shift 'from intense camaraderie to extreme alienation and isolation'. Similarly, Jack, after his return, found himself 'wondering every day what my mates [back in Vietnam] were doing'. Another veteran's reunion was 'overshadowed by the feeling that I should not have been back. The job was unfinished. I belonged back there'. Some enlisted for a further tour of duty. Like their counterparts in earlier wars, Vietnam veterans remembered front-line experience as a defining event of their lives.[36]

In oral testimony, diaries, memoirs, visual representations, and literary accounts, the return of Australians from war is seen as a rupture. It served to

---

34 S. O'Leary, 'Man Before a Window', *As You Were*, 1948, p. 60.
35 See Australian Army Education Service, *Human Problems After the War*, Government Printer, Melbourne, 1946; A. H. Martin, *Welcome Home Serviceman!*, National Defence League Pamphlet, Sydney, c.1946.
36 Giblett, *Homecomings*, pp. 28–45.

demarcate and divide the self into discrete parts: the warrior and the civilian; the real self and the lost self. Sometimes it enabled self-discovery. In the memory work and life narration of returned servicemen and women, the war was frequently positioned as pivotal. It was the turning point, oftentimes a protracted one, that pushed them through trauma either to some point of self-realisation or to some point of unresolved crisis, which served to explain subsequent failure in life. We can see a triumph of genre in this memory work. In conventional narrative forms there is always some event or experience that gives the story shape and meaning, and similar processes structured the life stories of many returned men and women. War looms large in all these accounts, overshadowing much else, particularly the immediate post-war years. What is remarkable about so many of the diaries, autobiographies, and memoirs of returning servicemen and women is how many of them finish with the cessation of hostilities. Even a description of the actual return journey is rare. A few pick up the threads again, seeing the war as the event that pushed their lives in a new direction. These are most often autobiographies, written sometime after the war, in which the comfort of time, distance, and perspective allow for reflection on the meaning of war for life. But even in these accounts the immediate post-war years are curiously absent, occasionally covered in a few pages or sentences, or shrouded in vague allusions to a time of darkness and restlessness. Here the post-war years are a hiatus, an abyss, all the more troubling because no one seems to have a language adequate to describe them.

The difficulty of rendering the return from war is equally apparent in literary accounts. Much Australian war literature is obsessed with perpetuating the myth of Australian heroism in war, ennobling the distinctive characteristics of the digger, and proclaiming the birth of a nation. This is particularly the case in the interwar years, when numerous literary accounts trumpeted the achievements of the Anzacs. The cinematic companion to these writings is Charles Chauvel's *Forty Thousand Horsemen* (1940). Most of these novels and films finish at the front at the moment of victory. In contrast to this triumphalist literature, however, was a dissenting tradition, which problematised war by focusing on post-war trauma. A number of interwar novels are peopled by disturbed and suicidal returned soldiers: Vance Palmer's *Daybreak* (1932), Katharine Susannah Prichard's *Intimate Strangers* (1937), and Martin Boyd's *The Montforts* (1920) are some of the most notable. In these narratives war is a dark, corrosive force that undermines and destroys returned men. Of course, there is not much narrative play to be made of happy returned men, but it is important to see that Australian literary efforts to question war found it easier to use life after war, rather than war itself, to frame these explorations. This may be a testament to the popularity of Anzac, but in a few hands the moment of return served to question war, undercutting the heroic tradition.[37]

---

37 See R. Gerster, *Big-Noting: The Heroic Theme in Australian War Writing*, MUP, Melbourne, 1992; R. Nile, 'The Anti-Hero and the Anzac Tradition: Australian Literary Responses to the

This is especially evident in Martin Boyd's final volume of the Langton Quartet, *When Blackbirds Sing* (1962). Here the central character, Dominic Langton, is a curiously mute character: a physical, almost animalistic, and yet raw and sensitive young man, a product of the most civilised of families and yet somehow a primitive creature, whose very spontaneity of feeling and response acts as an accurate register of the emotional undercurrents of the emerging barbarism of war. Dominic is a rather poorly developed character – a major flaw in the novel – but his very lack of development leaves him free to function as a blackboard for the inscription of more global deformities of the mind and spirit, deformities that afflicted a generation, not just an individual. This allows Dominic to represent a universal darker side – almost a collective subconscious, perhaps even a submerged everyman – which makes the novel a type of social diagnosis of cultural malaise rather than a rounder portrait of a complex character. Here, however, the description of return is truncated, confined to a few brief reflections in the final chapter. But peculiarities in the novel point to a deeper problem. This is the only volume in the quartet in which the central character is represented in the third, rather than the first, person, and when Dominic returns from the war, his response cannot be described but can only be represented in metaphor – with Dominic throwing his medals in the dam. The experience of return seems, in many ways and in many forms, to be literally unspeakable.

It is not surprising that for many Australians the glories of war, rather than the disillusions of return, were the focus of memory and narration. But the structure of narration can tell us something important about the meaning of return, for war and return operated as defining opposites, not just in the dichotomy of glory and disillusion, but more fundamentally in the gendered frames of war-front and home-front. The traditional war narrative of men is one of self-realisation. War represented the attainment of an ideal of manliness – in physical action, bravery, self-control, courage, and, more importantly for many, male comradeship. This ideal was fostered in institutions such as school, in sporting contests and boy scouts, in popular histories of wars, from Troy to Waterloo and on to Mafeking, and in literature, from Homer to *Deeds that Won the Empire*. In Australia after 1915 these narratives were doubly burdened with the coalescence of manhood and nationhood. Anzac confirmed this tradition. This war narrative shaped representations of return. Common to accounts of return were the dichotomous meanings of the front and of home, the front being a place of masculine embrace, while home was a feminised space. It was the place of women, domesticity, constrained masculinity, and the 'shirkers', 'stay-at-homes', and 'bureaucrats' – the 'non-men'. Return meant having to come to terms with this feminine world, of having to adjust to the everyday humdrum routine of meaningless work, domestic responsibility, of being a breadwinner rather than a warrior.[38]

1914–1918 War', in A. Seymour & R. Nile (eds), *Anzac: Meaning, Memory and Myth*, Sir Robert Menzies Centre, London, 1991, pp. 63–78.

This dichotomy of war and home is complicated, however, by the experience of nurses and servicewomen, particularly those who served overseas. Many of them described feelings of restlessness and dissatisfaction on their return to civilian life, just as their male counterparts did. They missed the vibrancy of war and felt like 'walking vacuums' on return. They believed that those at home were uninterested in their war life and did not comprehend the enormity of their experiences. They craved the company of former colleagues and treasured the bonds that tied them to the other men and women who had served. Some, like Elizabeth Burchill, a Second World War nurse, tried to maintain these bonds by joining the local branch of a returned-services organisation. But she soon discovered that, as the only woman in her branch, she was cramping the 'members' style'. The mateship of combat was, after all, a male preserve, despite occasional efforts to incorporate nurses in the legend – notably in the Hall of Memory at the Australian War Memorial. Even if some women had been at the front, they had not fought and so could not comfortably fit into those organisations that served to remember the camaraderie of combat. This did not stifle the craving of servicewomen for association with those few who had shared their experiences. They formed and joined their own ex-servicewomen's organisations.[39]

The readjustment difficulties and memory work of returned servicewomen may have paralleled that of men, but for servicewomen the return from front to home could not be a return from a romanticised male world to an impoverishing feminised existence. Theirs was in some ways a more difficult dilemma. Part of this arose from the diverse implications of their participation in war. Was war work an extension of femininity or its abandonment? The very ambiguity of service suggests that it could be both. Nurses had a quintessential feminine nurturing role. Combat nursing, however, was also dirty, rough, intense, and often dangerous. It both allowed women to be women and afforded them the opportunity to escape from conventional expectations of what a woman should do. More than this, in a century when women gained political citizenship but were often still denied the opportunity to fulfil their potential, combat nursing and front-line service seemed to offer a means for women to perform women's work, but work that, for once, was seen as making a significant contribution to the nation.

Return to normal roles for these women was often as problematic as it was for men. They seemed equally ambivalent about trading the intensity of the front for

---

38   See J. Damousi & M. Lake (eds), *Gender and War: Australians at War in the Twentieth Century*, CUP, Melbourne, 1995; H. M. Cooper et al. (eds), *Arms and the Man: War, Gender and Literary Representation*, University of North Carolina Press, Chapel Hill, 1989; M. Higonnet et al. (eds), *Behind the Lines: Gender and the Two World Wars*, Yale University Press, New Haven, 1987; M. Cooke & A. Woollacott (eds), *Gendering War Talk*, Princeton University Press, Princeton, NJ, 1993.

39   E. Burchill, *The Paths I've Trod*, Spectrum Books, Melbourne, 1981, pp. 184–95. See also Bassett, *Guns and Brooches*, pp. 71–101; S. McHugh, *Minefields and Miniskirts: Australian Women and the Vietnam War*, Doubleday, Sydney, 1993, pp. 86–99.

the routine and predictability of conventional marriage and motherhood. Perhaps this was because they were women who, in the very act of enlisting for war service, were searching for an escape from domesticity. Others may have been transformed by the experience itself. Whatever the cause (and perhaps it was sometimes a combination of both) some of these women did not adjust easily to home. For them also, it seemed to be a world constrained by narrow expectations, which they no longer felt able to embrace or enjoy. Patricia Ferguson found civilian nursing unfulfilling after her return from Vietnam. It seemed trivial after the front, and although recently married, she thought of war nursing often, longing to return to the vividness of that experience. There is also evidence to suggest that some returned nurses, unable to abandon their war, succumbed to the nightmares and sleep disorders that plagued many returned men.

This restlessness is sometimes more evident in the silences of returned women than in their words. Elizabeth Burchill's autobiography is revealing here. In a long account of her inspiring and interesting life as a war nurse, and later as a nurse for Aboriginal women and children in the Northern Territory, the immediate post-war years appear as a minor disruption, confined to a few pages. Here are the familiar tropes of restlessness and readjustment. On her return she went fruit-picking and worked on radio, before eventually realising that she was happiest when facing the challenge of difficult nursing work. Unlike traditional narratives of a female life, her marriage is dealt with in just one sentence: 'After a brief unhappy marriage I went back to nursing'. Here, in its very brevity, we can glimpse a profound ambivalence about returning to a conventional female role. Marriage, so central to the lives of many women and promoted as an important life goal, is here just a speck, a few words drowned by so many other phrases. In combat zones, front-line nurses experienced a heightened sense of worth. On return, some found marriage or work mundane, their contribution marginalised, and the housekeeping, pay, and conditions that marked the domestic and working lives of many women riddled with petty discriminations. Life for them never quite regained the same meaning, value, or intensity. It left them thinking of the past in preference to the present.[40]

A defining trope in all these accounts – oral, visual, and written – is this distinction between front-line and home-front. And underpinning each is a reluctance to negotiate the return from one to the other. For the small number of women returning from war, such ambivalences would appear to indicate a search for a more meaningful female role, for men return seemed to represent a direct conflict between their maleness, newly strengthened at the front, and its opposite – a stifling feminised world. Whether expressing the sudden realisation of alienation, a growing boredom with work and domesticity, or the romantic nostalgia for a lost comradeship, these accounts exhibit profound contradictions

---

40 See Burchill, *The Paths I've Trod*, p. 195. For an account of Patricia Ferguson's experiences, see Edwards, *Vietnam: The War Within*, pp. 28–40. There are a small number of cases of women diagnosed as suffering stress disorders in Department of Veterans' Affairs, Case Files.

both in the experience of returning home, and the accretions of memory and history that sought to explain that return. The reasons for this are elusive. In one sense, these feelings reflect the profusion of negative representations of domestic life for men. There is a rich cultural stream of contempt for men who seemed unable to escape the domestic sphere (signified by such epithets as the 'hen-pecked husband') and a widespread view that routine work, particularly office work, was unmanly (poignantly represented in such works as 'Clancy of the Overflow').

There are alternative streams of representation that support an ideal of men as breadwinners, husbands, and fathers, but these abraded against the fear of the domestic. The return of many soldiers to Australia after 1914, however, coincided with profound economic and cultural changes that made the prospect of urban domesticity more common. The masculine ideal of the lone bush worker fostered in journals such as the *Bulletin* – free to roam the outback and finding solace in mateship – was never typical, but the drift from the country to the city, suburbanisation, the growth of urban manufacturing and commerce, and higher rates of marriage increasingly rendered it even less so as the twentieth century unfolded. War threw men into an older world of male camaraderie, and return meant an abandonment of this supportive embrace for the lonely challenge of breadwinner. Moreover, for a significant minority of those who returned, war injuries and illnesses prevented them from ever achieving the breadwinner ideal. They were marooned in a limbo of unmanly dependence.[41]

Were these gendered distinctions between home and front peculiar to the Anzacs? The perpetuators of the Anzac legend believed that mateship was something unique to the Australian forces and the key to their success. For C. E. W. Bean, war historian and passionate promoter of the Anzac ideal, mateship was a product of two factors: the Australian 'character' and the experience of war. For Bean, the distinctive qualities of the digger lay 'in the mettle of the men themselves', in their 'idea of manhood', and in the refusal to 'give way when his mates were trusting in his firmness'. All of these characteristics were a product of the peculiar race of men and the democratic culture bred in the Australian bush. But these characteristics were also quickened, and given discipline and order 'in the flame of the whitest heat': battle.[42] Stripped of its nationalist and social Darwinist rhetoric, Bean's description is structured around a natural dichotomy of front and home: on the front, men forged intense bonds of camaraderie – bonds that could only be shared by men who had experienced combat and that irrevocably divided them from those at home.

Other research, however, suggests that many of the elements of the digger legend were far from unique. Eric Leed argues that front-line experience in the

---

41 See M. Lake, 'The Politics of Respectability: Identifying the Masculinist Context', *Historical Studies*, vol. 22, no. 86, April 1986, pp. 116–31.
42 C. E. W Bean, *The Story of Anzac: The Official History of Australia in the War of 1914–1918*, vol. 1, UQP, St Lucia, 1988 (1921), pp. 605–7.

First World War profoundly altered the identity of soldiers on all sides of the conflict, forever forging a deep division between those who fought and those who remained behind. The unrelenting and sustained nature of modern war, the extraordinary increase in the power of modern weapons of destruction, the agony of long periods of passivity while being subjected to shelling from enemies miles away, and the grim realisation that modern weapons could in an instant destroy all bodily trace served to make twentieth-century wars qualitatively different from the more measured engagements of traditional European conflicts. High casualty rates were not new, but this was the first war in which the majority of casualties died from wounds rather than disease. Moreover, the majority of combatants were citizens rather than mercenaries, and the numbers killed and injured were on an unprecedented scale. The only comparable precedent was the American Civil War, but even the scale of this tragedy paled in comparison to the Great War. The experience of modern war, argues Leed, lead to a pervasive effacement of self, an estrangement from all that was familiar, a sense of resigned fatalism, and a loss of dignity among the soldiers on all sides. But in the midst of this sustained attack on identity, veterans found something positive and intrinsically rewarding in the experience – comradeship – which 'erased "artificial" social barriers, [and involved] the sharing of a common destiny and the equality of condition that transcended rank and even enmity'. Similar psychologies emerged in front-line soldiers during the Second World War. There the fire-power of modern weapons, extensive casualties, and the ceaseless oscillation between periods of sustained passivity and intense combat undermined normal social bonds and forged new ones based on the 'tiny fraternity of comrades who shared the suffering'. This exacerbated tensions within armies, between those at the front-line and those in supply and support, but in combat units the bonds were very strong. In fact, rather than soldiers being inspired by broader patriotic ideals, many fought increasingly for their comrades, to maintain these bonds and to ensure the survival of the unit. The tragedy of Vietnam was that the tour of duty policy weakened the bonds of comradeship that were so essential to maintaining morale in combat.[43]

Comradeship may not have been the exclusive preserve of Anzacs, but particular features of Australian forces strengthened it. Anzac forces were certainly hierarchical, but they lacked the class divisions between officers and men that characterised British forces or the racial tensions that divided American units. Equally, in Vietnam, Australians were more likely to undertake a tour of duty as a unit than as an individual. In a relative sense, then, Australian forces seem to have been more egalitarian, which served to cement comradely bonds.[44] This was

---

43 See G. Belenky, 'Introduction', in Belenky (ed.), *Contemporary Studies in Combat Psychiatry*, Greenwood Press, Westport, Conn., 1987, pp. 3–5. See E. J. Leed, *No Man's Land: Combat and Identity in World War I*, CUP, Cambridge, 1979; J. Ellis, *The Sharp End of War: The Fighting Man in World War Two*, David and Charles, London, 1980, pp. 310–20.

44 For a useful overview of the structure and nature of the Australian fighting forces, see J. Grey, *A Military History of Australia*, CUP, Melbourne, 1990. For an analysis of the development of

a difference of degree rather than of kind, but its effects were all too apparent in the keenly felt division between those who fought and those who did not. That this divide was rendered in gendered terms – between the manly comradeship of the front and the effeminate and constraining bonds of home – served to highlight its depth. Even the complex dilemma facing servicewomen – the choice between different forms of femininity – served to perpetuate the divide between front and home, now rendered as a contrast between a vibrant, purposeful, and independent feminine role and domestic femininity. Many returning men and women may have embraced the comfort of domesticity after the horrors of war, but even this embrace had to negotiate a period of transition from one state to another. It is this psychology of returning servicemen and women that helps explain the reports of their widespread lethargy and restlessness. Anecdotal evidence and individual testimony suggest that many of these men and women found that they could 'do nothing for six months', would find distractions such as swimming, flying kites, or shooting rabbits to avoid work, would go bush for months at a time, or would turn to drink, neglecting their families and ruining their businesses. For some it was a temporary state; for others, something more permanent.[45]

IV

The case of Hugo Throssell is suitably cautionary. Throssell was from a well-to-do Western Australian family. In 1914 he enlisted, seeing extensive action at Gallipoli and in the Middle East. He served with great distinction and courage, quickly winning promotion to lieutenant and later captain. He was awarded a Victoria Cross for his actions at Hill 60, Gallipoli, and was widely touted as a hero on his return to Western Australia. But his disaffection with post-war Australia was apparent in his growing commitment to radical politics, a shift facilitated by his marriage to novelist and communist Katharine Susannah Prichard. His public sympathy for the communist cause alienated him from the returned-services community. In these years he also engaged in a number of failed business ventures, and the onset of the Great Depression left him severely indebted. He became withdrawn and depressed, and in 1933 committed suicide. Was his death a consequence of war experience and an inability to readjust to the demands of civilian life, his alienation from fellows who had shared his experiences at the front, tensions in his marriage, economic downturn, his failure to adequately provide for his family, or some combination of all of these? Would his economic setbacks have

---

mateship bonds in an Australian unit in WWII, see M. Barter, *Far Above Battle: The Experience and Memory of Australian Soldiers in War 1939–1945*, Allen & Unwin, Sydney, 1994.
45 See, for example, Joseph, *The Long Road Back*, p. 16; Woodward Papers, vol. 3, p. 3; L. Whittaker, 'Recollections of a Life on a Farm in Northwest Victoria 1904–83', Leonard Whittaker Papers, La Trobe Library, MS 12515; Giblett, *Homecomings*, pp. 35–47; S. Rintoul, *Ashes of Vietnam: Australian Voices*, Heinemann, Melbourne, 1987, pp. 179–229.

been sufficient to drive him to suicide, as it did other men who had not been to war, or does war experience somehow predispose a person to suicide?[46]

One of the few direct comparisons between returned soldiers and the broader population was undertaken for the 1933 Commonwealth census, in response to pressure from returned-services organisations, who claimed that these men were suffering severe disadvantages that warranted increased government compensation. The findings were mixed. For instance, fewer returned men were unmarried than their civilian counterparts, which runs counter to arguments that ex-servicemen were alienated from women and family life. But the difference was slight (only 1 per cent), and it was still the case that 15 per cent of returned men remained bachelors. In terms of income, the government statistician concluded that the differences between returned soldiers and the rest of the male population were relatively insignificant. Returned men were represented in the major occupational groups in similar proportions to the rest of the workforce and, as a consequence, seem to have been spread across the income spectrum in much the same way as the general population. Such findings offered little comfort to returned-services groups. More striking were the findings on mortality. Here the government statistician found that the life expectancy of the returned man was two years less than his civilian counterpart. But this calculation was not particularly sophisticated, based as it was on a simple comparison of the proportion of returned men still alive in 1933 with the equivalent figure for adult men aged over thirty years. There are too many possible extraneous variables. Moreover, A.G. Butler, the official war medical historian, cited evidence from actuarial studies that found war service had no effects on mortality.[47]

More recent studies of Second World War and Vietnam veterans support the view that there is little to distinguish between the health, mortality, and morbidity patterns of veterans and those of the comparable civilian population. The notable exceptions are those who returned from Japanese prisoner-of-war camps. Here there is overwhelming evidence for serious health and mortality problems.[48] The evidence on the plight of returned nurses and servicewomen is equally striking. They have received far less attention than servicemen, and their smaller numbers make it more difficult to make adequate comparisons. But nurses in the First World War and servicewomen who saw overseas duties in the Second World War seem to have suffered significant economic hardship in later life. Over one-quarter of the latter group were in 'difficult financial circumstances' by 1985, and an extraordinary

---

46 See R. Throssell, *My Father's Son*, Mandarin, Melbourne, 1990, pp. 3–141.
47 See Commonwealth of Australia, Census, 1933, pp. 397–407; Butler, *The Australian Army Medical Services*, vol. 3, pp. 817–18. For a discussion of this evidence, see R. White, 'War and Australian Society', in M. McKernan & M. Browne (eds), *Australia: Two Centuries of War and Peace*, AWM and Allen & Unwin, Canberra, 1988, pp. 401–3.
48 See, for example, O. Dent et al., 'Post-war Mortality among Australian World War II Prisoners of the Japanese', *MJA*, vol. 150, April 1989, pp. 378–82; *Australian Veterans Health Studies, The Mortality Report*, Department of Veterans' Affairs, Canberra, 1984.

four-fifths of them were receiving a war pension or treatment for war-related injuries and illnesses. Some of these disabilities resulted from normal processes of ageing, but the high incidence of health problems in this group in comparison with the general population was of some concern to repatriation authorities. Poverty in this group also reflected the more endemic disadvantages faced by women. The high incidence of returned service-women who remained single, combined with the traditionally lower wages for women's work, made it difficult for servicewomen to provide for their retirement years.[49] With these exceptions, however, there is little to confirm the widespread view that returned men suffered disproportionately.

Part of the problem with any such conclusion is the difficulty of defining the returned. Implicit in many discussions of returned servicemen is an assumption that, with the exception of prisoners of war, the experiences of the men are comparable. There are many pitfalls in this assumption, not least of which is the idea that enlistment meant combat. This is far from the case. In the First World War, of the over 400,000 enlistments in the AIF, three-quarters served overseas, and the majority of these saw combat. In the Second World War, however, far fewer servicemen experienced front-line duty. Of the over 800,000 enlistments in the services, only half went overseas, and of these only about one-third were directly involved in combat. The majority were engaged in the vital tasks of supply, engineering, and other support services. In fact, there were sharp divisions within the Australian services, and particularly within the army: those who volunteered for active service and who served in combat units overseas set themselves apart from those in supply units; and, in turn, these two groups were antagonistic towards the militia men – the 'chocolate soldiers' or 'chockos' – who remained on home duty. Front-line men resented the easy life of 'chockos', charging that they were not doing enough to assist those actually fighting.[50]

If combat was a crucial factor in forging a soldier identity and psychology that was antipathetic to home, and in creating specific dispositions that made reintegration into civil society difficult, then we can no longer take veterans as a homogeneous group. Some experienced the most horrendous front-line conflict, but many others saw very little, if any, combat. If we are to gain a better glimpse of the problems confronting returned soldiers, we need to look beyond a comparison of veterans and the general population to one that focuses on the differences between combatants and other veterans, and between those who fought and the general population. One way round this issue is to look at war pensioners more closely, to see the prospects of those who were awarded compensation for war injuries. If we take a random sample of war pensioners from the First World War, Second World War and Vietnam, and begin to investigate their readjustment, it is

---

49 Department of Veterans' Affairs, *Study of Returned Servicewomen of the Second World War*, Department of Veterans' Affairs, Canberra, 1985. On the problems confronting nurses from the First World War, see Bassett, *Guns and Brooches*, pp. 96–8.
50 See Ellis, *The Sharp End of War*, pp. 332–3.

clear that they suffered higher rates of employment disruption, suicide, vagrancy, and marital instability than ordinary Australians.[51] One-third of all war pensioners sampled had significant time off work as a result of illness, and one tenth of these were chronically unemployed during periods of economic prosperity after 1945. This is double the rate for the general population. Our group was also from two to three times more likely to be vagrants or 'whereabouts unknown to families or police' than other Australians.

Some of these figures might be the result of casual and seasonal work rather than vagrancy, just as a person classified as unknown may just as easily be a man fleeing maintenance payments as a homeless person. Nevertheless, they do give some indication that there was a small group (as much as 3 per cent of pensioners) who failed to return to a settled way of life. Suicide among pensioners was definitely more frequent than among the general male population: about one-third higher for men from the First World War and Second World War, and double for veterans of the Vietnam War. Such figures give credence to the widespread belief that returned men were in the grip of a 'suicide epidemic'. In 1919 George Taylor, editor of the journal *The Soldier*, gave poignant voice to this concern in his poem 'The Suicide': 'How oft we see that headline grim. / Ah! You who sit and calmly scan that headline think/ – He Was A Man ... / Whose nerves unstrung in noble strife, / went through Hell in earthly life'.[52] But this 'epidemic' continued for veterans of all wars. Finally, the evidence on marital instability, particularly divorce, shows that war pensioners had a consistently higher divorce rate, usually double that of other Australians.

In one sense, these figures merely state the obvious. It is only to be expected that men with chronic injuries, ill health, and, sometimes, mental instability should also suffer social and psychological problems. Moreover, these afflictions placed a disproportionate burden on families, leading in some instances to divorce and separation. Was it war itself, or merely the pensionable consequences of war, that caused these social disabilities? These are the imponderables that frustrate attempts to diagnose the return problem. But our problem also needs to be seen in context. If war pensioners represented about one-fifth of returned men from the First World War and one-tenth of those from later wars, what of the majority? They are largely beyond our statistical reach and, for all intents and purposes, did 'merge quickly

---

51 This sample of 1412 pensioners from WWI, WWII and Vietnam was taken randomly from Department of Veterans' Affairs pension case files for each state. They include both active (that is, continuing) cases and inactive (a euphemism for deceased or, less often, no longer in receipt of a pension) cases. This sample has then been compared with the equivalent census figures for the general population for every census from 1921 to 1971. In some instances, this comparison is not particularly easy. There are differences in the definition of terms and in the forms of calculation between the files, which cover long periods, and censuses, which focus on particular years. I have tried to make allowances for such differences. Our focus in this comparison has to be on servicemen, as the numbers of servicewomen who saw overseas service in this sample is too small to be of statistical significance. Individual cases referred to hereafter are numbered according to this sample.

52 G. Taylor, 'The Suicide', *The Soldier*, 14 November 1919.

and quietly' into the population. Some, even those who witnessed combat, saw their experience in a positive light. For them, war meant a rapid transition to manhood (for some it meant experience of sex and gambling) and a growing confidence in their skills and abilities.[53]

In the end, it may be that oral testimony, memoirs, and diaries are more reliable guides to the contours of the return experience than statistics. Through these sources we can glimpse a cultural current of anxiety and concern about returned men. Some who seemed to have made that readjustment – fitting back into family, work, and social life – inexplicably collapsed later in life. Donald Horne's father fought in the First World War, and returned to establish a family and a career as a respected school master. By the 1930s, however, he seemed increasingly irritable, and alternately withdrawn and abstracted. Moments of fun and humour became rare. He began waking at night and wandering around the house. Finally, there were complaints about his behaviour at work, and he was relieved of his duties, diagnosed to be suffering a 'nervous breakdown', and admitted to the 'repat' ward at Callan Park Mental Hospital. Some months later he was released, having been pronounced cured, but to his family he never seemed to regain his former élan; he seemed 'empty inside'.

Similar problems afflicted Second World War veterans. Earle Waterhouse was a respected school inspector. He never talked of his war experiences and seemed to lead a successful professional and family life. Years later, tortured by his guilt at being the only member of his RAAF crew to survive the war, he collapsed into a fit of depression and refused to speak. He required a short hospitalisation and, after a few months, returned to work. His family never talked of this episode until after his death, but they remain convinced that it had something to do with his war experience. Sometimes there was no breakdown to provide a clue to the behaviour of these men. Germaine Greer recalls her father as aloof and emotionally withdrawn. In her poignant search for an explanation, she came to see the war as the cause of the family drama that ensued. Neither the Greer, Waterhouse, nor Horne families, nor anyone else, will ever be able to really tell whether they are right in their interpretations. The stumbling block is the problem of attribution. Were these problems a result of war, or were other factors at work? Perhaps what is most significant is how often relatives of returned servicemen have similar stories to tell.[54]

These examples can be multiplied a hundredfold, and the frequency of such experiences must stand for something. Perhaps these were problems unique to veterans, but equally they may reflect more general problems arising from

---

53 For a positive recollection of war and manhood, see Interview with Lloyd Hewett, University Oral History Project, University of NSW Archives, OH 92. See also J. McCalman, *Journeyings: The Biography of a Middle-Class Generation 1920–1990*, MUP, Melbourne, 1993.

54 See D. Horne, *The Education of Young Donald*, Angus & Robertson, Sydney, 1967, pp. 152–73; Interview with Richard Waterhouse, 25 May 1991; G. Greer, *Daddy, We Hardly Knew You*, Penguin, Melbourne, 1990.

masculinity, unemployment, domestic tension, ill health, or mental disturbance. Perhaps an explanation of some of the discernible differences between the war-pensioner population and the general male population lies in some combination of war and civilian life. Caution is advisable here. What we can know is that the image of the troubled veteran is a powerful one, but one that increasingly has to jostle in the marketplace of ideas to explain the life histories of returned men and women. Singly they are stories of individual pain and anguish; together they may indicate something unsettling and troubling in the readjustment of many returned men and women. What is certain is that war functioned as a means of explaining personal and social problems. It was an available idea that served returned men and women, their families and friends, and repatriation authorities. It helped people to understand the unfathomable events of ordinary lives made extraordinary by their participation in war.

Returning men and women certainly believed they had been transformed by war, and in this belief many came to fulfil war's promise for good or ill. This is not to dismiss the profound impact of war on the men and women who experienced it, but rather an attempt to broaden the horizon of its effects, which were not merely psychological, physical, or economic, but also cultural, social, and even spiritual. Out of the horror of combat, and war's intense bombardment of their identity, many forged a new identity – that of a returned man who was now part of a fraternity or, less commonly, that of a returned woman. They joined a brotherhood and sisterhood who had survived the horror and were forever bonded by their experience. While some sought to put the past behind them, many others sought to keep the flame alive. Although many returned to lead ordinary lives, happy and unhappy, others seemed to have reserved some small part of themselves, secreted away from family and civilian friends, to recall the war. Some felt that a part of themselves still belonged back at the front with the mates who had died there. In 1993 Australians witnessed the ceremonial return of the ashes of war hero, doctor, and medical officer on the notorious Burma-Thailand Railway, Edward 'Weary' Dunlop, to the site where he had cared for and buried so many men. He wished some part of himself to return to them. Many more probably felt this way. One was Oswald Bates, who had returned from the trenches in France. In 1928 he swallowed poison and turned to another returned man, Henry Stringer, asking him not to get help, but instead to light him a cigarette, stand him up against a fence, and let him fall on his face 'like the good lads on the other side'.[55]

---

55 *Sydney Morning Herald*, 4 April 1928.

2
Remembering

In 1932 Colonel Arthur Graham Butler, a medical officer at Gallipoli and in France, and then official historian of the Australian medical services in the First World War, wrote to a colleague: 'I should love to go the front-line again [and] stay there'.[1] This desire reflected the anguish of a man uncertain of his financial future and prospects, and struggling, under an enormous weight of expectation, to complete his life's work. But it also demonstrates the wonderful power of memory to forget. Here, as in many recollections of war, it was comradeship, rather than horror, that was remembered. The sickening shock of combat and the gruesome realities of death and wounds were the stuff of nightmares, momentary flashbacks, and private grief, not everyday conversation. Instead, understandably, such matters were masked and displaced, but obliquely acknowledged in metaphor and allusion. Soldier organisations, patriots, and politicians provided a framework for this type of remembering through a language of sacrifice, honour, and national self-realisation. Sometimes soldier organisations stretched the boundaries of this language with protestations that returned men were 'racked with wounds' or 'chained by pictures that are burned in the brain ... by things that will grip their soul until death shall release them'.[2] Even here, however, it is cliché that dominates the mode of expression. Who could, or would want to, develop a language for such horror? Novelists, painters, and poets perhaps – but few others.

Servicemen themselves negotiated the reality of war through humour and their own rich language. Front-line 'lingo' was littered with words to register the harsh realities of warfare – words such as *Blighty* (wound enabling one to be evacuated to Britain), *whiz-bang* (exploding shell), *jellies* or *windy* (suffering from shellshock), and *konked-out* (died slowly of wounds) – in an effort to speak, and yet deflect, the horror of war. There were also more formal efforts to represent the feelings of the 'diggers'. In the carefully selected collection of soldier stories, poems, drawings, and

---

1   A.G. Butler to Dr H. Pern, 24 September 1932, A. G. Butler Papers, AWM, series 41, box 68.
2   See *Reveille*, 1 November 1927; *Whiz-Bang*, 1 July 1933.

recollections edited by C.E.W. Bean in 1916, *The Anzac Book*, there are references to the horrors of war, but these are taken as illustrations of heroism and serve to highlight Bean's view of the digger spirit as nonchalant bravery. Bean was careful to reject contributions that compromised what he believed to be the tone of the real Australian soldier response to war. Grim realism or unrestrained sentimentalism are rarely present, while classical allusions to the Trojan War serve to invigorate the stories with a serious and heroic message. The humour was of a debunking kind: mocking, sending up, and sharpening the divide between home and front. In this context, a drawing of a seriously wounded man (bandage round the head and over the eye, and sticking plaster on the cheek); subtitled 'complaints of the season', was not a testament to the effects of war (the man is smoking casually and standing) but a representation of phlegmatic perseverance. In the front-line journal *Aussie*, a cartoon of two frozen soldiers laying wire and being fired on by enemy soldiers (entitled 'The Next War: The Aurora Borealis makes things very difficult for a wiring party on the Esquimaux [sic] Front') was not an image of the dangers of shell-fire but an attempt to satirise the officers who sent men to do ridiculous, life-threatening tasks.

Similar modes of humorous displacement are evident in Second World War soldier books, such as *Khaki and Green* and *Soldiering On*. In the latter a drawing of two soldiers crawling out of their trench during fierce shelling is undercut by the caption 'Air raid be blowed! Wasn't that a Blonde?'. Such stories and drawings were reputedly popular with servicemen, probably because they rendered them heroic without bombast and heightened the ironic contrast between the reality of their situation and the stupidity of army bureaucracy, and between the soldier's knowledge of war and the ignorance of those at home. They appealed to families, relatives, and friends back home because they provided a comforting picture of normality (men chasing after pretty blondes) and an image of unruffled fortitude (and hence a sense of indestructibility) under fire.[3]

In private and public memory, then, there was precious little space and even fewer words to signal the horror of war. Nonetheless the scale of sacrifice demanded some means of resolving its effects. It is worth recalling these facts, well known as they are, in order to acknowledge the difficulty of this task of resolution, both personal and public. In the First World War 60,000 men died, and a further 150,000 returned injured and ill, many permanently affected. These casualties represented nearly one-quarter of all Australian men aged from eighteen to forty-five years. Few families would have remained unaffected by these tragic statistics. In the Second World War casualties were fewer, but even so, nearly 25,000 men died, and a further 40,000 returned wounded or ill. Korea and Vietnam were much smaller engagements. Yet even here 340 and 500 service personnel were killed respectively, with over 3000 other casualties (from both conflicts). All this represented a

---

3   See C. E. W Bean (ed.), *The Anzac Book*, Cassell, London, 1916; *Aussie*, no. 10, January 1919, p. 4; *Soldiering On*, AWM, Canberra, 1942, p. 182.

quantum of mourning difficult to grasp. Returned servicemen and women, friends, and relatives had to find their own private ways to mourn dead mates, sons, daughters, spouses, and lovers, and had to find the fortitude to suffer the torments and difficulties of those who returned injured and ill.

But this was also a wider cultural problem. These men and women had been killed and injured as part of a national commitment, and they required a public display of mourning and commemoration. These were simply stated yet infinitely complex dilemmas. How could the unreasonable be made reasonable? How could such a sacrifice be explained and resolved? In what ways could the extent of sacrifice be justified? Moreover, Australians faced the problem of deciding what to commemorate. What had such a sacrifice meant, not just for those who served but also for the nation as a whole? We have conveniently obscured the cultural complexity of this process through comforting reference to the 'Anzac legend'. But for historians the task has been to explain the making of this legend – its meaning, how it was maintained, and, perhaps more importantly, the significance of this legend for the returned men and women themselves. It was the emerging legend that gave shape to the expression of mourning. In this it served a positive purpose, providing a field of meaning that eased the burden of loss. It also had a coercive function, closing off other ways of understanding the nature of war and the sacrifice of so many lives.

I

One of the first tasks confronting Australians with the onset of the First World War was how and where to bury the dead. Under the intense conditions of the front this was an easy decision. A quick and simple burial (if a body could be found) near the battle field was the obvious and immediate solution. Men buried their comrades in cemeteries at Gallipoli and in France and the Middle East, marking the spot with a simple cross, a name, sometimes a few words, and an occasional memento to acknowledge the life of a friend. Others could not be buried: those killed in no man's land or behind enemy lines, and those lost in the mud in France, never to be found. While the USA and France gave families the option of having the bodies of fallen soldiers returned home, the Australian government, mindful of the cost of returning the dead from distant shores, decided, as did Britain and her other dominions, to leave their war dead in cemeteries near the battlefields. First in 1915, with a special Red Cross unit, later with the National Committee for the Care of Soldiers Graves, and finally in 1917, with the Imperial War Graves Commission, an elaborate bureaucracy was established, charged with the responsibility for burying, often re-burying, and commemorating the war dead.[4]

---

4   On the Imperial War Graves Commission, see F. Ware, *The Immortal Heritage: An Account of the Work and Policy of the Imperial War Graves Commission 1917–37*, CUP, Cambridge, 1937.

These matters were not straightforward. Choices had to be made: should burial and commemoration be individual or collective? Christian or secular? local or national? Out of decision and debate came remarkable invention. The striking aspect of war memorialisation after 1914 (in all combatant nations) was the overwhelming desire to name the individual dead on the one hand, and to represent their collective death on the other: what historian Thomas Laqueur has termed the 'hyper-nominalism' of sacrifice. This was a break with tradition. Except for the occasional officer, the soldiers who died at Waterloo in 1815, in the Crimea, or in the Sudan did not receive individual burial. Rather, in the time-honoured way, they were placed in mass graves with a monument to mark their collective resting place. The graves of soldiers in the Boer War who were not privately buried were marked by small iron crosses but were only 'haphazardly named'. The first real glimmering of a concerted effort to 'name' came during the American Civil War. Those who died at Gettysburg were buried in named graves in a carefully maintained lawn cemetery. But this was the exception; individual burial was common, but not naming. This gives us one clue to the desire to name. The soldiers in many of the conflicts of the nineteenth century were professionals who died in the commission of their work. Other war dead, notably those in Germany in 1813, were martyrs to a revolutionary cause. But the majority of those in the Civil War were ordinary citizens called upon to defend a particular national ideal. The emergence of citizen armies fostered an acknowledgment by the state of the individual's sacrifice for the nation.[5]

A deeper cultural current impelling naming was romanticism and death. Since the sixteenth century, mass graves and charnel houses had slowly disappeared to be replaced by individual burial plots. And from the late eighteenth century a new sensibility shaped this custom. Cemeteries were removed from city centres into natural parklands, and headstones and ostentatious statuary used to mark the individuality of each life. In complex ways, these practices represented the growing importance of the productive citizen (to families, economies, and nations increasingly concerned with piety, domesticity, effort, self-help, and civic virtue). Its obverse was the practice of burying paupers in mass or unmarked graves until the late nineteenth century. And with this acknowledgment of the individual came a desire to symbolise the spiritual transcendence of each death.

From 1915 these diverse imperatives towards individualisation came together in war memorialisation for citizen soldiers. It was difficult to overlook the enormous problem of grieving faced by so many families who, miles from the battlefields (thousands of miles for Australians), had no tangible effects to bury or mourn. Each day, newspapers printed lists of names of the war dead. In fact, names were all that many mothers, fathers, wives, fiancés, and children had. In all combatant nations local communities erected simple war memorials, dominated

---

5 See T. Laqueur, 'Memory and Naming in the Great War', in J. Gillis (ed.), *Commemorations: The Politics of National Identity*, Princeton University Press, Princeton, NJ, 1994, pp. 150–67.

by the names of those residents who had died in the service of their national ideal. As one of the few armed forces comprised entirely of volunteers (Ireland and Newfoundland also rejected conscription), Australians went one step further in acknowledging the sacrifice of its citizens. On many local war memorials, all those who fought, not just those who died, were recorded.[6]

The popular appeal of naming influenced official memorialisation. The Imperial War Graves Commission was charged with the responsibility of providing some recognition of those citizens who had died in service. Each man's name was accorded an individual place, either marked by a simple headstone in a war cemetery for those whose body was found, or named on a monument, such as the Menin Gate, to commemorate those whose grave was unknown but whose sacrifice was to be equally acknowledged. The essential equality of sacrifice was marked by the absence of distinction between officers and soldiers. In addition, there were also representations of collective sacrifice. From 1920 'tombs for the unknown soldier' became common in European cities. Such tombs, often in conjunction with an eternal flame or stone of remembrance, came to represent the sacrifice of all those who had died. Likewise, the proliferation of cenotaphs (empty tombs) represented a collective resting place to acknowledge the sacrifice of all who died in service. They gave a tangible presence for mourners separated from the dead, allowing them to remember their individual loss and link that particular sacrifice to a larger national story. The individuality of death was effaced by the symbolism of the collective, where nation and citizen merged as one.

The coalescence of death and nationhood, however, posed a particular dilemma for those crafting military commemoration. Burial was usually a Christian ceremony, but the meaning of death in war was also seen in secular terms: as sacrifice for the nation. The melding of these two representational traditions created interesting tensions in the symbolism of military cemeteries and memorials. On the one hand, traditional icons, such as the cross, and simple Christian statements, such as 'Known unto God', retained a central place on military headstones and monuments. On the other hand, many of the monuments replicated classical Greek forms, evoking a longer tradition of warrior sacrifice for democracy. More recent systems of meaning also made their mark. Memorials were adorned with distinctly modern statements, such as 'Justice, Liberty, and Patriotism'. At Australia's memorial in France, at Villers-Bretonneux, the architect Edward Lutyens attempted to design a monument 'redolent of the open air, of the young country that sent forth the flower of its manhood'. The monument echoed the shape of a classical Egyptian temple, and on each corner there was a sentinel representing a 'greater dawn', each marked by a specific message – Mercy, Truth, Righteousness, and Peace. The image

---

6   See K. S. Inglis, 'Entombing Unknown Soldiers', *Journal of the Australian War Memorial*, no. 23, October 1993, pp. 4–12; J. Phillips and K. S. Inglis, 'War Memorials in Australia and New Zealand', in J. Rickard and P. Spearritt (eds), *Packaging the Past? Public Histories*, MUP, Melbourne, 1991, pp. 179–91.

of the rising sun was present, as was a six-pointed star signifying the sacrifice of the men of each state in the Commonwealth.[7]

These and other themes are evident in the proliferation of war memorials in Australia during the 1920s. Many of these were local expressions of memorialisation. In the Mitchell Library, there are two large volumes of newspaper cuttings devoted to the many local memorials erected mainly in New South Wales from 1919 to 1922. This is just a small selection of the vast number of such memorials erected in Australia after the war. Even in this limited sample, the number and variety is extraordinary. Most were erected by local municipal and country town councils, commemorating either the dead or all those who served from their locality. But there were also school and university honour rolls, and memorials erected by particular organisations, such as the Order of Oddfellows Memorial and the Monument to Fallen Cricketers in Moore Park, Sydney. In form, they mostly consisted of Egyptian obelisks, Greek stele, columns, arches, or more elaborate variations on these simple forms, sometimes crowned by a figure of a soldier (either standing or in fighting pose), occasionally by an angel of mercy, and on a few, a figure of a crucified Christ. Many bore simple statements and phrases to acknowledge the sacrifice, commonly Rudyard Kipling's selection from the 'Apocrypha' for Imperial War Graves Commission memorials: 'Their name liveth for evermore', or variations on this theme, such as 'And their glory shall not be blotted out', 'Honour the brave' and 'Our noble dead'. Another popular form of memorial was the avenue of trees, notable examples of which are in Perth and Ballarat. Each individual tree was named for a particular serviceman, but with the avenue signifying collective transcendence and life after death – mixing Christian with natural symbolism.[8] All this memorialisation required enormous public effort, donations, subscriptions, and fund-raising events run by councils, ex-service organisations, and women's groups. In these memorials is ample evidence for the emotive power of Anzac sacrifice and the emergence of a cult of the war dead.

The attempt to provide some significant public memorialisation proved more difficult. Although large memorials were planned, particularly in Melbourne and Sydney, and design competitions held in the early 1920s, many considered the cost of such grand schemes exorbitant in the context of Australia's interwar economic difficulties. In the immediate aftermath of the war, soldier organisations were critical of these proposals. They urged 'practical memorials' in the form of hospitals, employment preference, and increased benefits for those who had returned injured and ill rather than useless blocks of stone.[9] By the mid-1920s, however, soldier

---

7   J. C. Waters, *Crosses of Sacrifice: The Story of the Empire's Million War Dead and Australia's 60,000*, Angus & Robertson, Sydney, 1932, pp. 89–90. See also J. Winter, *Sites of Memory, Sites of Mourning: The Great War in European Cultural History*, CUP, Cambridge, 1995, pp.78–116.
8   Mitchell Library, Newspaper Cuttings, vols 241–2.
9   See *The Soldier*, 28 November 1919 and 16 January 1920.

organisations (the fire having gone out of their campaign for increased benefits) had come round to the idea of public memorials, and they, particularly the Melbourne Legacy Club, were notable contributors to the effort to raise funds by subscription. Despite grumblings about cost from a few quarters, particularly with the onset of the Great Depression, impressive memorials were built in both Melbourne and Sydney. The 1934 opening ceremonies were attended by large crowds, – 300,000 in the case of Melbourne – testifying to the continued desire for commemoration.

In their form, both these memorials continued the tradition of mixing Christian and classical imagery. In Melbourne, the memorial was called a shrine, it contains a sanctuary, and the path up to it is emblazoned with the statement 'let all men know this is holy ground'. But the inspiration for the actual shrine was Greek, evoking the spirit of warrior sacrifice for democracy, while the corners are buttressed by statues representing Peace, Patriotism, Sacrifice, and Justice. In Sydney the memorial, designed by Bruce Dellit, has a sanctuary and hall of memory, the centrepiece of which is a statuary group of women, one with a child, supporting a shield, on which lies a dead warrior. The sculptor, Raynor Hoff, sought here to represent the essence of victorious sacrifice, a nation's triumph but a legacy or grief and mourning for those at home, particularly the thousands of women who lost sons, husbands, fathers, friends, and lovers. Sydney's Anzac Memorial is also one of the few without individual names of the dead, but the dome is adorned with stars, one for each the 120,000 men and women from New South Wales who served. Outside are reliefs depicting battle scenes, and statues representing each of the armed services.[10]

The attempt to erect a national memorial was equally protracted. C.E.W. Bean was the driving force behind this scheme. He envisaged something that would be both a museum, to instruct Australians in the story of the Anzac contribution to the nation, and a memorial, for the commemoration of their sacrifice. The temporary exhibitions of war relics, models, and educational material – first in Melbourne and later in Sydney – that were to become the heart of the Memorial collection, were enormously popular. The viability and importance of the educative function of a war museum was clear. Despite this, moves to erect a permanent home for the collection in Canberra were slow. One factor was cost. The Commonwealth was already committed to some considerable expense in moving its operations from Melbourne to Canberra. Nevertheless, in 1927 the Federal government accepted the worth of the memorial proposal but imposed a budget of only £250,000 on the project – a sum equivalent to the cost of the Shrine of Remembrance in Melbourne.

---

10 National War Memorial of Victoria, *The Shrine of Remembrance*, National War Memorial of Victoria, Melbourne, 1941; A. Pratt & J. Barnes, *An Interpretative Appreciation of the Shrine of Remembrance and the 1939–45 War Memorial*, Shrine of Remembrance Committee, Melbourne, 1957; R. Hoff, 'Anzac Memorial Figures', Home, May 1932; Anzac Memorial Committee, *The Anzac Memorial, Hyde Park, Sydney*, Anzac Memorial Committee, Sydney, 1936.

It was a tall order, and one that placed considerable limitations on architects and planners. Although the War Memorial was opened in 1941, important elements of the building, particularly in the Hall of Memory, remained unfinished until after the Second World War. But fulfilling the ideal of a combined museum and memorial was not just a financial problem; it was also an artistic one. How were two diverse functions to be incorporated and given equal value in one building? What were the appropriate forms and icons for such a building? In answering these questions, it was the memorial function that proved to be the most burdensome. Bean favoured a classical form, evoking Greek and democratic traditions. It was difficult, however, to escape religious imagery, and in his references to the memorial as a shrine and sanctuary the confusion and pull of diverse traditions was apparent. In its final form, the building looks less like a Greek temple or mausoleum than an art deco rendering of a medieval basilica, an impression reinforced by the use of a dome, atrium, cloisters, and stained-glass windows.

Familiar motifs and techniques were utilised in the plans for the memorial. There was to be a roll of honour (although how to organise the names – alphabetically, by locality, or by unit – was the source of continuing controversy), a stone of remembrance, a cloistered garden and pool to evoke an atmosphere of respectful contemplation, and crowning all this, a hall of memory, the spiritual centre of the building. The domed hall itself is impressive, although less impressive than Bean had hoped after the proposal for increasing its height was rejected. The aesthetics and iconography of its decoration, however, were the source of greater debate. Napier Waller and Leslie Bowles were commissioned to furnish the hall with stained glass, mosaic, and statuary. Some of this had strong religious connotations. The mosaic, for instance, was reminiscent of Byzantine church decoration. The iconography, however, was secular, with representations of soldiers, sailors, airmen, and nurses, and images of peace and liberty. The statuary proved to be the most controversial. Bowles's first model of a half-draped woman in classical style, symbolising a youthful nation, was abandoned as trite. In 1941, his new design for a sword-like cross, composed of four emblematic figures – representing freedom of speech, freedom of worship, freedom from want, and freedom from fear – was criticised by politicians and returned soldiers as modernist and inappropriate to the 'Australian ideal of sacrifice'. In 1954 the decision was made to install a large statue of an Australian soldier, erect and triumphant. This was an aesthetic travesty, heightening the effect of the mosaic images of the fighting forces, and together making the hall more of an exhibition space than a place for contemplation and commemoration. This tension in the hall was not resolved until 1993, when the entombment of an unknown soldier restored to the hall a spiritual function. Bean, one feels, would have been pleased by this development.[11]

---

11 See K. S. Inglis, 'A Sacred Place: The Making of the Australian War Memorial', *War and Society*, vol. 3, no. 2, September 1985, pp. 99–126; McKernan, *Here is their Spirit*, pp. 209–16.

In many memorials there was a rich profusion of secular and Christian imagery, and classical and modern forms. Certainly, while trying not to deny the Christian implications of death, memorialists were anxious to prevent sectarian sentiments from disrupting their aspirations for an essentially modern, democratic, and egalitarian form of commemoration. This left a void. And it is not surprising that classical symbolism served an important function in representing the nobility of sacrifice. This search for an ennobling tradition is all the more significant because, by 1918, there were disturbing signs in Britain and Europe of a loss of faith in the meaning of war. Important writers, poets, and artists had come to question the nature of war and its significance for Western culture. They saw the war as a violent rupture with the past, as a questioning of Victorian culture, and a demand for modern forms of expression. They sought a means of representing the alienated and senseless world ushered in by war. Writers such as Robert Graves, Siegfried Sassoon, and Wilfred Owen in Britain, Remarque in Germany, and Barbusse in France, as well as painters such as Paul Nash, all combatants, stressed the waste and futility of war. Others, overwhelmed by the experience, turned not to modernism but to older spiritual and apocalyptic traditions in the search for meaning in mass bereavement. But more than a few, such as Muirhead Bone, John Galsworthy, and Rudyard Kipling, clung to older themes of sacrifice, patriotism, and social permanence. For Samuel Hynes, the war and immediate post-war years were a time of contest over how the war was to be 'imagined'. In this cultural flux, it is not surprising that official memorialisation should fall back to an older tradition of classical symbolism in an effort to represent continuity, transcendence, and the essential nobility of the war. The alternatives were bleak despair, catastrophic allegory, or ironic cynicism.[12]

II

Australia shared some of these cultural dilemmas, but from the very first, public opinion was shaped by a less ambiguous embrace of the classical and nationalist traditions. From the announcement of the Gallipoli landing, there were effusive proclamations of the achievements of the Anzacs, from politicians, from nationalists, and, as Bill Gammage makes clear, from soldiers themselves. But although many came to see this as the 'birth of a nation', the obviousness of this moment was less clear at the time. The first public reports of Australian fighting at Gallipoli filtered back to Australia five days after the landing. In reply to congratulations from the British government, the Governor-General expressed his gratitude that the Australians had acquitted themselves well. Even when British war correspondent Ellis Ashmead-Bartlett's 'paeans of praise' for Anzac bravery

---

12 See S. Hynes, *A War Imagined: The First World War and English Culture*, Collier Books, New York, 1990; Winter, *Sites of Memory*, pp. 145–203.

were trumpeted in the Australian press, nationhood was not the first thought. More commonly it was seen as a triumph of race and manhood rather than nation, and instead of Anzacs being seen as unequivocally the greatest fighters in the Empire (as later commentators claimed), they were at this point merely 'amply worthy to fight side by side with the heroes of Mons ... Ypres and Neuve Chappelle'. This was high praise, but within two days the Gallipoli campaign had been relegated to a small column by reports of the sinking of the *Lusitania*. Even at the end of the campaign it could still be seen as something 'glorious' in the 'annals of our race', meaning the British race, not the Australian people.[13]

Australians were rightly proud of these efforts. And within a month of the landing, Empire Day celebrations were suffused with talk of Gallipoli. Empire loyalists such as Rev. W.H. Fitchett (author of the best seller *Deeds that Won the Empire*) proclaimed the distinctive 'touch' of the Australian soldier, which made Gallipoli the equal of Waterloo. But for Fitchett, like many others, Australia and Empire were inextricably linked. The Australian 'touch' was something that strengthened the Empire. In complex ways, the themes of Empire, race, manhood, bravery, valour, and nation were present from the first announcements of Gallipoli, but the balance of imagining began to shift from Empire to nation. Gradually the diverse strands of meaning were woven to say something new about the nation. Returned-soldier groups and commentators, such as Bean, played important roles in constructing these meanings. The first anniversary of the landing became a moment when this message could gain final confirmation. In reporting the 1916 Anzac Day celebrations, the *Sydney Morning Herald* could proudly proclaim: 'the great awakening came ... they made a new Australia ... when Australia suddenly emerged to adult nationhood'; Similarly, a Returned Soldiers' Association publication, *In Memoriam*, pronounced Gallipoli as: 'the first great fruitage of Australian nationhood ... on that day of testing Australia became fully one with the Empire ... as a true man goes to his bride, they dared the embraces of Death. We are a nation of freemen cemented heart to heart by the blood our brothers shed for us'. The metaphor of the bridegroom dominated this and other contributions. It suggested that Australia had finally achieved nationhood through a marriage to Britain – in this instance a marriage in which Australia was the groom and Britain the bride – a hint perhaps that Australia could now stand alongside Britain on an equal, if not superior, footing. Other accounts used a similar metaphor to that of the *Sydney Morning Herald*, depicting Australia as the son or the daughter who had finally grown up. Whether as bridegroom or grown child, numerous statements proclaimed Australia's achievement of national maturity.[14]

---

13 See *Sydney Morning Herald*, 30 April 1915; *Age*, 7 May 1915; Adelaide *Advertiser*, 8 May 1915; *West Australian*, 8 May 1915. For a later report, see *Sydney Morning Herald*, 22 December 1915. See also B. Gammage, *The Broken Years: Australian Soldiers in the Great War*, Penguin, Melbourne, 1975, pp. 84–113.

14 See *Sydney Morning Herald*, 25 April 1916; Returned Soldiers' Association, *In Memoriam*, RSA, Sydney, 1916;. 'Advance Australia', in Returned Soldiers' Association, *Anzac Memorial* RSA,

This idea of national self-realisation was built on a long heritage of nationalist aspiration, stretching back to the mid-nineteenth century republican campaigns of John Dunmore Lang and continuing with the *Bulletin* writers and artists, such as Lawson, Paterson, and Livingston Hopkins. They attempted to represent Australia in new and definably Australian ways. The emergence of the bushman as emblematic of a distinctive Australian type, different from his British or Irish forebears, owed much to pervasive social-Darwinist ideas of the evolving colonial. The unique frontier environment of Australia shaped a special type: tall, straight-backed, laconic, resourceful, and independent. This image stood in marked contrast to the depiction of the typical Englishman as an urban industrial type: decadent, weak, and nervous. Here we have an emergent iconography for Australian national identity – a sense and an image of Australian difference from the parent society. But the story is more complicated than this. The Australian type also sat alongside a sympathy and respect for things British, a faith that Britain was the homeland of Australians, and a belief that Australia's continued security as a European, colonising society was dependent on the maintenance of British naval and military power in the region. In this context, Australia could still be represented not as a man but as the 'little boy from Manly'.[15]

As Henry Lawson sensed in his metaphor of blood staining the wattle, without some epochal event, true nationhood would be elusive. This may not necessarily be so, but within the terrain of Victorian and Edwardian culture, death for one's country was a potent signifier of nationhood. Australians could look at the historical narratives of other nations' births to see this – the War of Independence in the USA, the French Revolution, Germany in the Wars of Liberation, and even further back, Scotland at Bannockburn, and England at Hastings, Agincourt, and numerous other battles (none were truly national, but each, by the early nineteenth century, could be read as founding moments). Drawing on a classical heritage, and looking even further back to battles such as Thermopylae, it seemed to many that democracy, citizenship, and now nation had to be established on the basis of offering one's body in defence of these ideals. Marilyn Lake has highlighted the complex gendered imagery of Australia's national birth at Gallipoli.[16] For it was through the idea of blood, and its association through metaphors of fruit, harvest, and watering the soil, that men could lay claim to something paralleling the blood and birth experience of women. Furthermore, in the warrior ideal of Western culture, the sacrifice of life was the only means by which men could give birth to

---

Sydney, 1916. See also K. S. Inglis, 'The Australians at Gallipoli, I-II', *Historical Studies*, vol. 14, nos 54–5, 1970, pp. 219–30 & 361–75; R. Ely, 'The First Anzac Day: Invented or Discovered?', *Journal of Australian Studies*, no. 17, November 1985, pp. 41–58.

15 For a summary of these developments, see R. White, *Inventing Australia: Images and Identity 1688–1980*, Allen & Unwin, Sydney, 1981, pp. 63–109.

16 M. Lake, 'Mission Impossible: How Men Gave Birth to the Australian Nation – Nationalism, Gender and Other Seminal Acts', *Gender and History*, vol. 4, no. 3, 1992, pp. 305–22.

something – a nation – thus rendering the life-giving capacities of women puny by comparison.

This was a powerful cultural field, which shaped much of the understanding of war in Australia after 1914. Prominent poets and writers worked within the confines of this tradition. Vance Palmer, Hugh McCrae, Dowell O'Reilly, and Christopher Brennan all trumpeted the nobility of Australia's youthful sacrifice and the nation's new-found place in the world. Palmer lauded the 'dauntless heart of youth ... [whose] name shall keep the house we build secure against the world'. Others, like Mary Gilmore and H. L. Galway in his poem 'The Australiad', strained for classical references to Troy to represent the nobility of Gallipoli. These poems, published in official commemorative volumes, are not entirely representative. But there is a sense in which the profusion of nationalist sentiment occasioned by Gallipoli was also culturally constraining. This was partly direct, as censorship provisions of the *War Precautions Act 1914* prevented the publication of seditious work. But constraint was also indirect. The heavy weight of nationalist sympathy made alternative views difficult to articulate. Even feminists such as Rose Scott (a prominent pre-war pacifist) and Louisa Lawson were persuaded to contribute to these volumes. And although they avoided the worst excesses of nationalist bombast, their contributions were caught within the rhetoric of bravery and sacrifice.[17]

This emphasis on the nobility of war and the glory of Anzac achievement is not surprising; especially given the nationalist longings of many Australians, the glowing reports of Anzac bravery by British commentators such as Ashmead Bartlett and John Masefield, the staggering loss of life, censorship, and the widespread popular and media condemnation of German aggression. It paralleled similar national outpourings in Britain. Of more interest is the continuation of this tradition after the war. Australian war writing during and after the Great War was peculiarly obsessed with perpetuating the ideal of noble Anzac sacrifice and bravery. From C. J. Dennis, who in *The Moods of Ginger Mick* (1916), saw war as the catalyst for turning the urban larrikin into a noble (and martyred) soldier, to the post-war novels of Frank Dalby Davison, Ion Idriess, and many lesser writers, an enormous amount of creative energy was devoted to elaborating a particular ideal of the Australian soldier. This literature is peculiar precisely because so much post-war literature in Britain, France, the USA, and Germany focused on the futility and senselessness of war. The now classic works of Remarque, Graves, Sassoon, and Hemingway (to name but a few) were characterised by an ironic sensibility, a spare realism, and an abandonment of traditional narrative techniques in favour of episodic development. But this contrast between heroic traditionalism in Australia and ironic modernism in Europe is too stark. There was much bombastic, nationalist, 'big-noting' literature in Britain and Europe. Moreover, some of the

---

17 All these contributions are collected in RSA, *Anzac Memorial*.

ironic classics, notably Frederic Manning's *Her Privates We* (1929), are caught in an uneasy tension between irony and a romantic sense that in the horror of the trenches men found their true selves. Manning's central character, Bourne, is freed from doubt, self-consciousness, and a nervous temperament (ailments of the modern age) in the camaraderie of combat. Far from representing futility, some of these ironic works grappled with the confused meanings embedded in war – waste and official incompetence, but equally nobility and comradeship. And out of this arose a cultural struggle to imagine (to use Hynes' useful phrase) the war. Nonetheless, there is something peculiarly Australian in the absence of an ironic tradition. The imaginative struggle was too one-sided; the emphasis on the ennobling sacrifice of Australian soldiers held stronger sway against alternative representations and sensibilities.[18]

A similar trend is evident in war painting. The most popular post-war depiction of the war in Australia, for politicians, returned soldiers, and the general public alike, was Will Longstaff's *The Menin Gate at Midnight*, first publicly displayed in Australia in 1929. This is a remarkable painting despite its conventional form and romantic imagery. Here a dark and sublime sky overhangs the Menin Gate Memorial, near Ypres, which is painted in striking gold colours, giving it an inviting warmth in contrast to the sky. The memorial, however, is in the background; in the foreground are open fields, and upon those fields are what at first glance might be flowers but on closer inspection are the ghostly shapes of soldiers. This confusion between soldiers and flowers gives the scene a pastoral quality, but contrasted to a sublime sky and a golden memorial, it works beautifully to evoke a feeling of sombre awe, counterpointed by a feeling of spiritual wonder at the sense of continuing existence (the spirits/flowers) and the transcendence of death. Here the subtle mix of the pastoral and the sublime creates a conventional but arresting image.

It was not just the emotive power of the Anzac legend that inspired writers and artists. In a direct pecuniary way, returned-services organisations, State governments, and increasingly the Commonwealth directly sponsored writers and artists through the official histories and the war artists program for the proposed Australian War Memorial. Even without this direct sponsorship, the public response to the paintings of Longstaff, Dyson, and other war artists ensured that there was a receptive and appreciative audience for such work. On the other side, however, there was also a climate antagonistic towards alternative views. There were active campaigns to suppress modernist sensibilities born of war. Remarque's *All Quiet on the Western Front* was banned from sale in Australia during the interwar years. Similarly, soldier organisations, patriotic art critics, and traditionalists

---

18 See Gerster, *Big-Noting*, Frederic Manning, *Her Privates We* (first published as *The Middle Parts of Fortune*), Hogarth Press, London, 1986. For arguments about the 'ironic' tradition, which I suggest exaggerate the force and impact of irony, see P. Fussell, *The Great War and Modern Memory*, OUP, Oxford, 1975.

dismissed modernist war paintings, such as those by Paul Nash (who had been a British soldier), as 'silly trash' and decadent rubbish, in no way representative of the experience of war – seen by these institutions and individuals as a noble reality. For them, the meaning of Menin was more truthfully evoked by Longstaff than the fractured, geometrical, and desolate landscape of Nash.[19]

Interwar literary and artistic culture in Australia has been seen by many as conservative and anti-modernist. In painting, classical themes and forms, and in literature, optimistic narratives, often with a bush or Anzac focus, commanded critical praise and patronage. But this masks deeper cultural problems and conflicts. Pre-war novelists and dramatists of the nationalist school, such as Frank Wilmot, Louis Esson, and Vance and Nettie Palmer, who might have embraced the triumph of the bush legend at Anzac, instead lapsed into interwar despair and, for some, like Esson, creative paralysis. They lamented what they saw as the capture of the bush ethos by conservative forces. Where such writers ventured critical perspectives, they did so not to question the bravery of Anzac but to chart the decline of the Anzac on his return. Many of these writers and artists, aware of new cultural movements overseas, seemed overwhelmed by the conflict between the desire to represent a national ethos, on the one hand, and the broader modernist aesthetic that sought to break with traditional forms, on the other. The solution seemed to be either a backward-looking and nostalgic recovery of the roots of Australian identity in the bush, or silence.

There were some active, assertive, and confident artistic movements in the 1920s that sought to transcend the melancholy of war. One of these revolved around Norman and Jack Lindsay, and the journal *Vision*. Here the Lindsays propagated a vitalist ethos, proclaiming the power and youthful sexual energy of the Australian spirit, free from the decadence of Europe. But aesthetically and intellectually this manifesto was a dead end. It could find no new forms for this ethos, instead relying on old classical themes and symbols, which rendered its sexual vitalism stale and two dimensional. This bohemian tradition thrived upon a dated belief that Australia was a haven of manly vigour (proven at Anzac Cove), in contrast to enfeebled Europe. It was this article of faith, a cliché, evident among bohemians and conservatives alike, that justified formal and informal barriers against the incursion of European artistic movements. These groups sought to isolate Australia from decadent culture, much as the 'White Australia' policy sought to protect the 'racial purity' of the population.[20]

This clash between modernism and a backward-looking traditionalism rooted in classicism and realism was hardly unique to Australia. The conservatism of

---

19   See 'Silly Trash', *The Soldier*, 22 November 1918. See also D. Walker, *Dream and Disillusion: A Search for Australian Cultural Identity*, ANU Press, Canberra, 1976, p. 157.

20   For discussions of these cultural developments, see G. Serle, *From the Deserts the Prophets Come: The Creative Spirit in Australia 1788–1972*, Heinemann, Melbourne, 1973, pp. 89–118; Walker, *Dream and Disillusion*, pp. 119–67; J. F. Williams, *The Quarantined Culture: Australian Reactions to Modernism 1913–1939*, CUP, Melbourne, 1995.

Australian interwar culture was a matter not of absolutes but degrees. Many Australians were aware of modernist movements – the novels were read (even the banned ones), the plays occasionally performed, and the paintings reviewed in art journals, and seen in art shows and collections. But the audience sympathetic to such approaches was small. Some of its early practitioners, such as Roland Wakelin or Roy de Maistre, fled to the more congenial artistic climate of London. Some of its most notable proponents and practitioners were women, such as Margaret Preston, Grace Crowley and Grace Cossington-Smith in the visual arts, and M. Barnard Eldershaw, Katharine Susannah Prichard, and Eleanor Dark in literature. Women, in one sense, had greater freedom from the artistic tyranny of the Anzac myth because of the very masculinity of the tradition. They were free to turn their attention to the realities of women's lives: personal and family relations, marriage, sexuality, the conflict between the private and the public spheres, work, and children. And in their search for forms of expression, they felt more able to adapt modernist ideas to cultural practice. Nonetheless, the overwhelming ambivalence towards modernism in interwar Australia, evident in outright rejection, selective adaptation, and belated embrace, is one sign of the broader cultural impact of the First World War. The Anzac ideal was a powerful cultural force, which demanded that many writers and artists respond in some way to its effects and significance. In the end, it probably acted to stifle rather than stimulate cultural production. It narrowed the artistic world, forced it into the unhelpful strait-jacket of contrasts between pure Australia and decaying Europe, thus isolating Australia from broader cultural movements, and alienating and undermining those who felt uncomfortable in these narrow confines. More significantly it fostered a culture that proclaimed an ideal of noble sacrifice that appealed to Australians.[21]

III

How did this particular Anzac tradition come to have such force during the war and interwar years? There is no simple answer. But one cannot overlook the seminal contribution of writers like C.E.W. Bean in the formulation and propagation of the legend. It was more than Bean of course, as the enthusiastic embrace of the reports of the landing at Gallipoli (well before Bean's own account arrived) testify. But Bean, through the official war histories and the Australian War Memorial, gave it the ring of historical truth and much of its specific character. Bean, from an Imperial family with connections to India and the English public school system, was born in Bathurst, educated in England, and seemed, in his early manhood, to be torn between his love for, and loyalty to, two countries: Britain and Australia.

---

21 For discussions of modernism between the wars and the central role of women in the arts in this period, see the works of Serle and Williams already cited, and J. Hoorn (ed.), *Strange Women: Essays in Art and Gender*, MUP, Melbourne, 1994.

He was in some ways the quintessential Anglo-Australian. In other ways, however, he differed. His love for Australia grew stronger on greater acquaintance with the land of his birth. This, in part, arose from his immersion in a social-Darwinist world. As a young reporter travelling around the bush and writing stories on the Australian wool industry, he became fascinated with the race of men bred there. In two interesting accounts of his travels, *On the Wool Track* (1909) and *Dreadnought of the Darling* (1911), he marvelled at the vigour of the men raised in a harsh pioneering environment. Unlike Britain, where urbanisation and industrialisation had supposedly brought the evolution of the race to a standstill, he saw in Australia a place where the true potential of the Anglo-Saxon race could flower. Adversity brought out the best characteristics of the race: resourcefulness, independence, comradeship, and a fierce democratic spirit. He was not alone in such views; they resembled those of other commentators on the Empire and colonial nationalism, such as Richard Jebb and Rudyard Kipling, and they strike a chord with the influential frontier thesis, proposed only a few years before, by the American historian Frederick Jackson Turner. It is stating the obvious to say that Bean was a man of his time, and it is to this that he owed much of his influence.[22]

Bean, first as war correspondent and later as official historian, brought these ideas to his understanding of the war. He was a conspicuous presence near the front lines and kept a keen watch on all the major engagements of the Australians in the war, documenting the nature of combat in minute detail. His concern, however, and the source of his literary originality and cultural influence was not with the niceties of strategy and tactics, or the perception of generals who commanded, it was his focus on the men themselves: the ordinary soldier – their every step, effort, advance, and retreat. For Bean, the actions of the Australians in war confirmed his view that here was an exceptional race of men, who, by dint of their innate individualism, resourcefulness, egalitarianism, comradeship, and now courage, had been able to triumph even in defeat. For Bean:

> Australians came ... from a stock more adventurous, and for the most part physically more strong, than the general run of men. By reason of the open air life in the new climate, and of the greater abundance of food, the people developed more fully ... Bred of such stock, and left to develop in their own way, Australians came to exhibit a peculiar independence of character.[23]

This was written in 1921 and betrays Bean's social-Darwinist stamp. Although he remained committed to these views, they nonetheless underwent subtle change. Some years later he further elaborated on this theme:

---

22 See K. S. Inglis, *C.E.W. Bean: Australian Historian*, UQP, St Lucia, 1970; M. Roe, 'C.E.W. Bean: Progressive and Nationalist', *Veritas*, vol. 3, no. 1, 1980, pp. 1–9; M. Roe, 'Comment on the Digger Tradition', *Meanjin*, no. 3, 1965, pp. 357–8.
23 Bean, *The Story of Anzac*, vol. 1, pp. 4–5.

Social equality in civil life had produced men with the habit of thinking for themselves and acting on that decision ... The Digger's unspoken, unbreakable creed was the miner's and the bushman's, 'Stand by your mate.' ... Whatever the merits or faults of democratic government in war, the freedom that it alone, apparently, ensures to its citizens seems to build the best soldier because it develops the whole man.[24]

By 1942, when this was written, Bean had shed the sharp racialist edge of his interpretation. Such an attitude was uncongenial in the context of a war against fascism. But by then he was also well aware that many Australian soldiers had come from the city rather than the country and that no simple correlation could be drawn between outdoor life and fighting spirit. Here it was less the frontier race than the democratic culture, bred in the bush, that had come to form the national spirit, a spirit that found its full flowering in Gallipoli and France.

Bean's histories are a remarkable achievement. In their focus on the minutia of combat for ordinary soldiers, they broke new ground in the writing of military history. A very different but comparable work was that of Tolstoy, in those extraordinary chapters devoted to the description of battle in *War and Peace*. But where Tolstoy sought to render the randomness of battle, Bean sought to ennoble it. Bean demonstrates a rare talent for dramatic narrative structure, melodramatic caricatures of the 'Hun' and German culture, and an easy resort to classical allusions to enliven his account. It is more than the individual battle scenes, brilliant as they are; it is the history of the triumph of a people and a spirit. They flow with a rare lyrical power, which makes them much more than mere description. Bean's histories, however, have been the source of some controversy.[25] That Bean censored some of his work, emphasised some aspects to the detriment of others, and coloured his account in various ways is of little concern here. What is significant is that they presented a very powerful case for Anzac as a culmination of national evolution. Far from the war being a cataclysmic break with an ordered and civilised Edwardian world, as so many writers, poets, artists, critics, and academics in Britain implied, Bean bequeathed to Australia a vision of continuity. He imagined the war as a fulfilment of the nation's potential. In this he reiterated the views of many commentators in Australia. Bean, however, gave them the legitimacy of history.

---

24 C. E. W. Bean, *The A.I.F. in France: The Official History of Australia in the War of 1914–1918*, vol. 6, UQP, St Lucia, 1983 (1942), p. 1084.
25 See D. A. Kent, 'The Anzac Book and the Anzac Legend: C. E. W. Bean as Editor and Image-Maker', *Historical Studies*, vol. 21, no. 84, April 1985, pp. 376–90; A. Thomson, 'Steadfast until Death? C.E.W. Bean and the Representation of Australian Military Manhood', *Australian Historical Studies*, vol. 23, no. 93, October 1989, pp. 462–78. For an alternative view, see J. Barrett, 'No Straw Man: C.E.W. Bean and Some Critics', *Australian Historical Studies*, vol. 23, no. 90, April 1988, pp. 102–14.

There was much more to the legend than Bean and 'national character'. The linking of Australia's history to a longer tradition of the warrior also made Anzac an assertion of the strength and nobility of Australian manhood. Australian manliness had long been regarded as the hallmark of colonial culture, but now it was able to demonstrate its place on the world stage. Manhood featured almost as prominently as nationhood in the proclamations of Gallipoli's significance. It may seem more than coincidence that this stress on manhood should be so prominent in the only combatant nations (Australia and New Zealand) that had granted female suffrage, but in all the allied and central powers, the symbolism of the manly warrior was a rich cultural resource. What distinguished Australia was that warrior manhood was not taken to confirm a tradition but to initiate one, and to proclaim the emergence of a new and vigorous people. Here was an opportunity to prove that the nation had not been enfeebled by female suffrage and to reaffirm the importance of men to nation-building. Although there were occasional attempts to incorporate nurses into the Anzac legend, as 'Anzacettes', the masculinity of Anzac, in its focus on bravery and feats of arms, is overwhelming.

Anzac, however, was a complex and contradictory signifying field. If it had not been so, it is doubtful that bellicose pronouncements of masculinity and nationhood would have stood the test of time. In some forms, it also represented friendship and a spirit of collectivism that echoed more traditional understandings of Australianness. In other ways, the forms of masculinity and national sentiment it embodied represented tragedy, pathos, and melancholy – tropes that appealed to many women who mourned the dead. Even the representation of masculinity itself was curiously open-ended. One of the enduring symbols of Gallipoli was not 'the fighter' but the man and his donkey. Simpson was a stretcher-bearer – a symbol of nurturing, almost feminine, sacrifice, made all the more potent by his martyrdom at Anzac Cove. Similar images emerged in the Second World War. The Damien Parer photograph of the wounded soldier being supported by a mate on his return from Kokoda is one of the most poignant of the war. Here Anzac could represent vulnerability as well as fortitude, life as well as death, and it was the diversity of these meanings that gave the legend much of its emotional power. What it required, however, was a means of linking these representations to the nation. This was the function and the genius of commentators like Bean.[26]

Bean was not alone in seeing Anzac as a fulfilment of national destiny. Nor was he alone in investing the legend with a historical lineage. A.G. Butler traced the digger idea back to the crusades, to Cromwell and Winstanley, to Wat Tyler and Irish rebels, and finally up to the pioneer and the selector.[27] Others, before

---

26 On the idea of the 'Anzacette', see *The Soldier*, 20 April 1917. See also M. Lake, 'The Power of Anzac', in McKernan and Browne (eds), *Australia: Two Centuries of War and Peace*, pp. 194–222; P. Cochrane, *Simpson and the Donkey: The Making of a Legend*, MUP, Melbourne, 1992.
27 A. G. Butler, *The Digger: A Study in Democracy*, Angus & Robertson, Sydney, 1945.

and after Bean and Butler, took the war and the digger as evidence that there was something unique in Australian culture, and that conventional accounts of its history were misplaced. Anzac had the potential to recast the history of Australian colonisation. In 1916 writer, traveller, and essayist, Randolf Bedford, argued that Australians were actually better than the British because they had come from the pick of the British. Here typical social-Darwinist ideas could be turned to the rewriting of Australian history. According to Bedford, during the gold-rushes only the most enterprising, healthy, and entrepreneurial had elected to undertake the difficult journey to Australia in order to escape from industrial decay and find their fortune. Once here, the 'best climate and the most lavish country' made them a vigorous and healthy race. Thus, the Australian is a better man than any of the recently imported, because he came of the 'pick of a bold and adventurous stock and his peerless country improved him in two generations out of all comparison with his grandsire'. The British, in contrast, were the 'queer little weaklings' left behind by this migration, 'whose grandchildren swank around to this day and criticise Australia with the bitterness of their own inferiority'. Few would have shared Bedford's extreme colonial nationalism, but the essential truth of his history seemed to some to have been proved at Gallipoli.[28]

The convicts, however, represented a difficulty for Bedford. They disrupted his sense of racial superiority and were brushed aside with the cavalier comment that Australians were more ashamed of the gaolers than the gaoled. More importantly, the penal system was swept away as quickly as possible and its biological inheritance swamped by the gold-rush immigrants. But another writer, with more respectable historical credentials, took the convicts more seriously. In 1921 George Arnold Wood, Challis Professor of History at the University of Sydney, delivered a controversial paper on the convicts to the Royal Australian Historical Society. Wood argued that the convicts were 'children of misfortune', not crime. For Wood, British aristocratic society robbed honest toilers of their small plots of land and forced them to petty crime to avoid starvation. In his view, the real criminals (the aristocrats) were left behind, and the innocent victims were punished by transportation. The convicts were 'village Hampdens' (rebels against unjust authority), not genuine criminals. They were usually convicted of minor offences – many of them, by the 1920s, summary in character, warranting no more than a small fine. Wood's interpretation was undoubtedly influenced by recent scholarship on the social impact of enclosures. But it was also sharpened by his reflections on the significance of Anzac. Echoing Bedford, Wood argued that in the colonies, free from aristocratic corruption and the need to steal, each generation 'rose to greater worth, until the day came at Gallipoli' when 'the Australian-born proved themselves to be among the greatest and noblest souls who have ever grown among the British race'.[29]

---

28   R. Bedford, 'The Australian in Australia', *The Soldier*, 15 December 1916.
29   G. A. Wood, 'Convicts', *JRAHS*, vol. 8, pt 4, 1922, pp. 177–208.

Wood, like Bedford and Bean, spoke to the reality of Anzac and its significance for an emerging national consciousness. Gallipoli was widely seen as a culmination of a particular history, a realisation of the potential of Australia and its people. The speed with which such a view was embraced points to long-simmering colonial nationalist sympathies in Australian culture. It was a view that seemed logical and, moreover, historical. But the war was not just the completion of a linear development; it was also the occasion for particular understandings of Australian nationalism, patriotism, and politics, some of them new and some of them not so new. There was a curious double edge to these understandings. While traditional loyalties were affirmed, traditional institutions were condemned. Leading the critique of existing political institutions were returned servicemen and those who sought to advance the interests of this particular group. A new force stepped onto the political stage – the returned serviceman – and the pursuit of a new returned-soldier politics did much to cement the Anzac legend within Australian culture and shape the memories of Australians.

IV

The one quality of the Anzacs that all commentators noted, be they returned servicemen themselves, contemporaries, or later historians, was mateship. In the trenches of Gallipoli and France, in the deserts of Palestine, later in the frozen wastes of Korea or the jungles of New Guinea and Borneo, and Vietnam, soldiers formed intense bonds with their fellows. These were the bonds forged from living at close quarters, and in many ways, as Bean and others argued, they replicated the mateship ethos of civilian society. Men needed mates to calm their nerves, to drink and yarn with, to share leave with, and to look after each other. This bonding found its cohesion in opposition to others: either the British, one's own officers, or those from other units; sometimes the lines of division were drawn within one's own unit. Small groups formed, including some and excluding others. Each group shared a code and an ethos, a way of presenting themselves to the world, and a way of speaking, eating, laughing, and acting; there were a thousand small ways of drawing boundaries. But more importantly, these bonds of male friendship were quickened by the chasm of immanent annihilation that confronted each man at the dawn call. Without the comfort of being in the company of friends, of having those beside you who shared your thoughts and fears, and without the feeling that there would be someone there to protect you if you stumbled, or mourn you if you fell, it is difficult to imagine how men could summon the courage to charge forth time and time again.[30]

---

30 The evidence for this is apparent in any number of accounts of Anzacs and the war. One of the best, now a classic, is Bill Gammage's *The Broken Years*. But this was not solely an Australian

The intensity of these bonds is hard to gauge. Such things defy measurement, almost as much as they do definition. Looking at photographs of soldiers in the First World War, particularly those of men resting in the trenches or enjoying themselves behind the lines, I am always struck by their easy familiarity. There is often a warm, unselfconscious bond between them – a hand on the shoulder, a closeness of the bodies – which points to an intimacy in these relations. In our more psychological age, it is tempting to suggest that this is evidence of a strong homoeroticism in the trenches. From the 1920s the popularisation of Freudian notions of repression may have problematised such easy familiarity. Photographs of diggers in the Second World War still demonstrate a relaxed, informal, and friendly attitude between men, but the bonds seem less intimate somehow. Perhaps this is merely the effect of a selective reading of an unrepresentative sample. This is not to deny that there was homoeroticism in the trenches – there was, much of it probably latent – but as more recent studies suggest, there are usually secretive (necessarily so, given the attitude of military authorities to such practices) homosexual subcultures in military forces. There is no reason to think that such a culture did not exist among the Anzacs. But the obvious and unselfconscious display of mateship in the photographs suggests that for many Anzacs this behaviour was homosocial in character – intense and psychologically intimate – where the bonds between the men were of friendship.[31]

Not surprisingly, after the war, many soldiers sought to maintain these comradely bonds. War had acted to dramatically transform the identity of the individual soldier – from civilian to Anzac – and the difficulty and uncertainty of returning to civilian status fostered a desire for a continuation of the digger identity. In the difficult years after the war, many hungered for 'trench mateship'. Anzac Day was one means of satisfying this desire. Here they could openly mourn their comrades without impugning their manhood, proclaim their importance to the nation, and return to the intimacy of the front line. For Alan Tiveychoc, Anzac Day was when they could 'silently [grip] the hands of their old cobbers ... the men with whom they went to war, and whom they learnt to love'. Herbert Moran, returned soldier, medical officer, and prominent Sydney doctor, believed that this bond was fanned by the lack of sympathy for their plight: 'fighters felt the chilling atmosphere around them ... for warmth they gathered together'.[32] But this begs the question. Returned men felt the 'chilling atmosphere' precisely because they sought

---

phenomenon: it defined all forces in all the major twentieth century wars. See Ellis, *The Sharp End of War*, pp. 310–20.

31 See C. J. Williams & M. S. Weinberg, *Homosexuals and the Military: A Study of Less than Honourable Discharge*, Harper & Row, New York, 1971; A. Berube, 'Coming Out Under Fire', *Mother Jones*, February–March 1983, pp. 23–45.

32 See A. Tiveychoc, *There and Back: The Story of an Australian Soldier*, RSSILA, Sydney, 1935, p. 283; H. Moran, *Viewless Winds: Being the Recollections and Digression of an Australian Surgeon*, Peter Davies, London, 1939, p. 160.

to differentiate themselves from civilians and claim particular privileges unavailable to other citizens.

Numerous organisations, founded by returned servicemen and women, emerged after 1914 to advance the interests of returned men and women, and to perpetuate the 'Anzac spirit', which had served Australia so well in 'preserving the nation from foreign aggression'. Their strength is evident in the peculiar Australian celebration of Anzac Day. While Australia shared Armistice Day with Britain, France, and other allied nations to celebrate the ending of the war and commemorate the war dead with 'the silence' and 'the poppy', it also had its own day, shared only with New Zealand, equally commemorative of the dead, but more directly a celebration of achievement. This day institutionalised national respect for sacrifice, but returned-services groups sought to move beyond commemoration to more concrete political programs. The most influential of these groups was the Returned Soldiers' Association, founded in June 1916. It later underwent a number of name changes (such as Returned Sailors and Soldiers' Imperial League of Australia, and Returned Servicemen's League) before evolving into its present incarnation as the Returned and Services League, popularly known as the RSL (and for ease of reference, I will use this for all its manifestations). Its original aims were to maintain the bonds between returned men, to fight to ensure adequate compensation for their sacrifice, and to defend and preserve Australian society against all those who would undermine its greatness. Membership was restricted to those who had seen active overseas service.[33]

The RSL was only one of numerous organisations that perpetuated a soldier ethos or sought to assist soldiers and their dependants after the war. Others, some of them in direct competition with the RSL, included the Returned Soldiers' Labour League, the Returned Sailors, Soldiers and Citizens' Loyalty League, and the Returned Soldiers and Patriots' National League. In addition, there were organisations for servicewomen, such as the Returned Soldiers and Nurses' Association, and the Returned Army Nurses Association; organisations for specific groups of returned men, such as the Limbless Soldiers' Association, the Tubercular Sailors, Soldiers and Airmen's Association, and the Totally and Permanently Incapacitated Association; support groups of relatives, such as the Sailors and Soldiers Fathers' Association; welfare groups, such as the Soldiers' Home League and, most importantly, Legacy, which cared for the widows and children of deceased servicemen. The list expands with new groups established after the Second World War and later conflicts, such as the Australian Legion of Ex-Servicemen and Women, the Services' Welfare Fund, the Malayan and Far Eastern Association, and the Vietnam Veterans' Association. Some of these

---

33 See A. Gregory, *The Silence of Memory: Armistice Day 1919–1946*, Berg, Oxford, 1994. For general histories of the RSL, see G. L. Kristianson, *The Politics of Patriotism: The Pressure Group Activities of the Returned Servicemen's League*, ANU Press, Canberra, 1966; P. Sekuless and J. Rees, *Lest We Forget: The History of the Returned Services League 1916-86*, Rigby, Sydney, 1986.

emerged in response to the strict membership rules of the RSL, which until the early 1970s excluded all those who had not served overseas; others targeted specific interest groups in the belief that the RSL did not cater for their particular needs; and still others, notably the Vietnam Veterans' Association, arose from a deep sense of dissatisfaction with the RSL. The number and variety of these organisations is astounding – surely a testament to the power of the Anzac ideal. Some were rather short-lived, but others continue to be large and important welfare organisations.[34]

Australia was not unique in this development. Most combatant nations in the major twentieth-century wars witnessed the creation of societies for returned servicemen and women, notably the British Legion, Canadian Legion, American Legion, and after the Second World War, the American Veterans' Association. Nor was this development confined to allied nations. In Weimar Germany disabled veterans were represented by the *Kriegsopferverbände*. Equally, this was not just a phenomenon of twentieth-century wars. After the American War of Independence, an officers group, the Order of the Cincinnati, was established to maintain links between the men who fought. Similarly, after the American Civil War, the Grand Army of the Republic was established to lobby politicians for pensions for Yankee veterans. It proved to be remarkably successful in mobilising the soldier vote and won significant pension concessions. The distinguishing feature of all these organisations is that they arose among men from citizen armies. These men did not have the continuing bond of being professional soldiers. Their involvement was often voluntary, and certainly only lasted for the duration of the war. But out of these groups rose a peculiar ethos, which George Mosse has called the 'myth of war experience'. The citizen soldiers in all the forces that contested the great nationalist wars of the nineteenth century, and the Great War in the twentieth, returned with a desire to make their war experience a meaningful and sacred event. Through organisations such as the RSL, Australian returned men sought to sanctify their fallen comrades and render their own contribution sacred. Memorialisation was only the most obvious way of making war experience into a secular religion. But these organisations were not only concerned with perpetuating a sacred memory. They also engaged in a particular politics, claiming a special right, as citizens who had actually fought for their country, to determine the direction of post-war society. The emergence of a returned soldier politics is a crucial part of the veteran experience and the construction of war memory.[35]

Was there a distinctive soldier politics in Australia after the First World War? The answer (like too many answers) is both yes and no. We can answer in the negative because returned servicemen had divided loyalties. Although many sought

---

34 The histories of very few of these organisations have been written. The notable exception is M. Lyons, *Legacy: The First Fifty Years*, Lothian, Melbourne, 1978.
35 G. L. Mosse, *Fallen Soldiers: Reshaping the Memory of the World Wars*, OUP, New York, 1990. On earlier soldier organisations, see Dixon Wecter, *When Johnny Comes Marching Home*, Houghton Mifflin, Cambridge, Mass.,1944, pp. 51–251.

to mobilise them as a single force, no one group commanded the whole. Some men preferred to forget their wartime experiences and shunned all association with returned-servicemen's organisations. This is evident in the membership numbers. After the first flush of enthusiasm in 1919 and 1920, membership declined sharply. Even by the most generous estimates, by 1923 less than two-fifths of all those who returned were affiliated with one of the major returned-services organisations. Soon after, many of these organisations lapsed or went into terminal decline. There were other hurdles to soldier politics. Many returned men and women had loyalties that proved stronger than their soldier identity: class loyalties. We can see this in the proliferation of class-based returned-soldier organisations, some affiliated with labour and others with conservative parties, and all condemned by the RSL as a betrayal of the true non-partisan stance of the genuine returned man. These organisations attempted to appeal to a returned-soldier identity but shift the balance of the returned serviceman's vote towards either end of the political spectrum. They failed, which says something important about this soldier identity. But this does not mean that class loyalty was negligible. On the contrary, many returned men came home to resume careers as trade unionists and Labor politicians, and others as advocates of loyalist and conservative politics. Some labour men came home and joined the RSL, only to be repulsed by what they saw as the conservatism of the organisation. Other groups broke away from the RSL in the 1930s – notably some Queensland sub-branches, which formed their own 'Diggers Association' – charging that the League's conservative alliance was blunting its capacity to obtain better repatriation benefits for members. Accusations of conservative bias were a continuing problem. After his return from the Second World War, J.P. O'Brien joined the Sherwood Branch (Queensland) of the League but left a few years later because of the League's sympathy for cold-war politics. After this he became more involved in the trade union movement. This was a common story. What it suggests is that returned servicemen and women had diverse allegiances. They had to negotiate the pull between their loyalty to their service comrades and their civilian affiliations. For many, the latter were more important. Others juggled the two, participating in reunions, Anzac Day marches, and RSL functions, but also participating in other organisations, institutions, clubs, and societies, and voting as they saw fit.[36]

Nonetheless, despite many ups and downs in membership, the RSL survived and, at times, thrived. Overall the League seems to have been able to claim a membership of roughly one-third of all those who fought overseas. Membership alone does not make a politics. Through effective organisation and leadership, and a clear charter of principles, the League was able to achieve a political influence greater than its membership would warrant, and far greater than some other

---

36 See O'Brien Papers. The 'Diggers Association' is reported on in *Whiz-Bang*, 1 July 1935. For broader RSL accusations of betrayal of the non-partisan cause, see *The National Leader*, 15 September 1916.

comparable groups, such as the British Legion. The leaders of the League were an effective lobby group, with an extraordinary access to the political decision-making process. One of the strengths of the RSL was its rigid adherence to a non-partisan and non-sectarian stance. Although many doubted the non-party political stance of the League (believing it to be conservative rather than Labor in sympathy), its professed principle gave it a mandate to criticise and exert pressure on all governments. Another factor was that many politicians were returned servicemen, often members of the League, and certainly with some sympathy for the League's aims. More significant than this, however, was the League's command of a particular political rhetoric – a rhetoric of patriotism, sacrifice, and national well-being – that was coherent, impassioned, and difficult to argue against without appearing disloyal.[37]

Another source of the League's appeal was that it conferred a superior status. It proclaimed returned men and women as a special breed. It signified this through badges, oaths, memorials, marches, and moments of silence. And at every turn it cemented bonds between members. It sought to unite them into a brotherhood (and, through the ladies' auxiliaries, a sisterhood) that replicated the supposed mateship bonds of the front. It was remarkably successful. As Ken Inglis has argued, Australia was the one country in the interwar years where the term *returned soldier* was always spelt with a capital R and a capital S.[38] This sacred status was regarded by the RSL as transcending all others – be they those of class, religion, gender, or even more remarkably, race. But of these, race proved to be the most difficult to reconcile. The RSL was a strong advocate of the White Australia policy. There was, however, an evident ambivalence about Aboriginal Anzacs, which created complex tensions inside the organisation. Despite a history of government discrimination against Aboriginal soldiers; the original sanctions against Indigenous enlistment, and lower pay scales and repatriation benefits, the RSL came to the defence of some Aboriginal returned soldiers. In 1921, the League protested the refusal of the Lithgow Small Arms Factory to employ an Aboriginal returned soldier. Even more remarkably, the returned serviceman in question, Doug Grant, later came to be President of the local RSL sub-branch. Similarly, in 1951, the Alice Springs Sub-branch of the League sought to remove the restrictions on Aboriginal drinking to allow Aboriginal returned soldiers to fully participate in League functions. And in 1953 the South Australian Branch of the RSL sought full entitlement to old age and invalid pensions for Aboriginal ex-servicemen and women, and the National Secretariat petitioned the Federal government for full citizenship rights for Aboriginal returned servicemen and women, even those on reserves. This is striking evidence that the identity of 'returned soldier' was for some RSL members more important than social status. On the other hand, many branches of the RSL

---

37 These figures are taken from Sekuless & Rees, *Lest We Forget*, pp. 55–7 & 167–75.
38 K. S. Inglis, 'Returned Soldiers in Australia 1918–39', in Institute of Commonwealth Studies, *The Dominions Between the Wars*, Seminar Papers, London, 1971, pp. 57–65.

directly or indirectly discouraged Aboriginal membership and many Aboriginal Anzacs were refused entry to the RSL club bar. There were limits to Anzac solidarity, even for those who served, and that limit was race.[39]

Another attraction of the RSL was its organisational structure. Although there were tensions between the national, State and local levels of the League, it was an extraordinarily open organisation (except for Aboriginal Anzacs). Its strength lay in the numerous local sub-branches. These varied in size from just a few men to over a thousand, but each had control over their own membership (within guidelines set by the League), organised their own functions, had their own commemorative occasions, raised their own money, and spent it as they wished on local causes (after giving some to the state and national branches). This sometimes lead to debilitating demarcation disputes between different sub-branches, but it also gave League members prestige and power in local communities. It was one of the most significant voluntary welfare organisations in the country, with an annual welfare budget of over $6 million by the early 1980s. The genius of the structure, however, lay more in the decision-making process. Reading the archives of the League, one is struck by the extraordinary number of motions put to State and national conferences each year. Any sub-branch could move a motion, usually related to some complaint about the inadequacies of government funding or the harshness of repatriation tribunal decisions. The vast majority of these were passed and then conveyed by the League's state or national secretariat to the relevant repatriation or parliamentary authority. The vast majority of these claims and arguments were rejected by governments. The almost ritualistic nature of this process might raise doubts about the supposed influence of the League, but this would be to miss the point of the exercise. When it came to the hard bargaining over legislation and budget allocations, League officials were often very effective in getting a better deal for returned servicemen and women. The same officials were probably aware that the vast majority of motions passed at League conferences had no chance of success, but these motions gave the members a say, an avenue for complaint, and a means to voice their dissatisfaction with repatriation policy and administration. And, just sometimes, these local ideas were taken up by the national executive more formally. The League was a complex institution, shaped as much from below as from above. Through these diverse forums, the League developed a distinctive political voice, although it took some time to evolve the tone familiar to us today.[40]

The first journal of the League (or the Returned Soldiers' Association as it was then) was *The Soldier*, which started publication in 1916 with the subtitle 'A Journal of Australian Nationalism'. This chimed in with its numerous articles proclaiming

---

39 *Lithgow Mercury*, 14 September 1921. See also RSL Archives, NL, MS 6609, 2248C. For a broader discussion of discrimination against Aboriginal servicemen, see R. A. Hall, *Black Diggers: Aborigines and Torres Strait Islanders in the Second World War*, Allen & Unwin, Sydney, 1989.
40 This structure is apparent throughout the extensive archival records of the League.

Gallipoli as the birth of Australian nationhood. More directly perhaps, it reflected the progressivism of the journal's founder and editor, George Augustine Taylor, a man of restless energy and firm faith in the nation's future. But, as the journal of the League, it also represented the voice of the returned soldier, and there were tensions and contradictions in this voice. The title 'Australian Nationalism' is one. We are accustomed to think that organisations such as the League saw nationalism as inextricably linked to Empire. There was nothing new in this: Australian patriots had long trumpeted the virtues of Empire, and few saw any contradiction between loyalty to Empire and national patriotism. Early issues of *The Soldier*, however, disrupt this comfortable perception. There was much on the virtues of the Empire, the greatness of Britain, and the obligation of Australians to defend the 'old country'. But the pages of this journal could also include Randolf Bedford's stinging attack on the sanctimonious 'weaklings' in Britain and the virtues of Australia's difference from the homeland, as well as arguments such as the following:

> Although some kings are better than others; it remains an unhappy fact that the Kaiser type predominates ... The products of royalty are pretty well all tarred with the one defiling brush. The British King and the British system of limited monarchy are exceptions. But neither justifies the continued domination of Europe by a crowd of congenital idiots, following the track of moral assassins when dynastic purposes are served. France awakened long ago to that fact.[41]

The initials of the author (O'C) and the timing of the article (before the second conscription referendum) point to Irish Catholic, anti-conscription motives. His contribution may not be representative, but, even so, 'O'C.' was a regular columnist, and the journal felt able to publish this contribution. There are other oddities. Articles appear on the importance of women's contributions to the war effort and one suspects that Taylor's wife Florence, a prominent Sydney architect, had a strong influence here. And while there were some sentiments affirming the natural differences in the roles of men and women, there was also a regular column, 'Mothers, Wives and Sweethearts', that had a poem, 'The Awakening of Women', as its epigraph: 'They are waking, they are waking/ ... As she throws off old traditions and is free,/ And the world shall quickly render to woman what is hers'. In another significant regular feature, the 'Australia First' column, it was argued that 'the War has worked many changes, but none more than the awakening of Australia', and later that 'Anzac has transmitted a soul to the people. "Made in Australia" is assuming a new meaning – its real meaning. Australia is coming first in the hearts of its people.'[42]

The existence of nationalist, republican, and even feminist sentiments alongside Empire loyalty is unsettling. It certainly suggests that returned-soldier politics was

---

41 *The Soldier*, 29 June 1917.
42 *The Soldier*, 24 August 1916.

a more plural and diffuse phenomenon than previously thought. From late 1917, however, the tenor of *The Soldier* begins to change; its politics begins to harden into a more familiar mould. Some of the changes are very obvious. The 'Mothers, Wives and Sweethearts' column dropped 'The Awakening of Women' as its epigraph and replaced it with more conventional sentiments: 'A mother's heart is always for her children, a wife is the key of the house. A Sweetheart's counsel is certainly unselfish'. Similarly, the 'Australia First' column now became 'Empire and Australia First'. Some changes are less obvious. These are to be seen in the increasing frequency of stories on labour unrest, 'shirkers', strikes, attempts to undermine the war effort, and the vacillation of politicians in the face of these crises. At the end of the war the impact of these changes is signified in a change of subtitle – from 'Journal of Australian Nationalism' to 'Journal of Australian Patriotism', and still later, 'Journal of Comrades of the Great War'.

What is in a change of name? Nationalism or Patriotism: is there any significant difference? In popular usage, the two are often closely related, even synonymous. But there is a subtle difference, and one that Taylor and the League may have felt was significant – sufficient, at any rate, to justify a change of name. Nationalism was obviously a more recent concept: a commitment to an ideal of nation, the ideal of a people unified in belief, culture, and sometimes race, within a defined geographic boundary. The concept of patriotism – a love of one's country, specifically (in etymological terms) one's fatherland – had a longer lineage. It is precisely because of the ambiguity of Australia's colonial heritage that such a difference is significant. In one sense, Britain was the true 'fatherland' of Australian colonists (except for those of Irish descent and Indigenous Australians) – culturally, politically, and for some, emotionally and actually. Patriotism, then, embraced a commitment to Empire as much as it did the nation, and this is evident in the other changes of tone and emphasis in the journal. *The Soldier* gradually abandoned the confident assertion of a new spirit of national birth and retreated to a comforting embrace of the familiar dependence on the Empire, where nationalism and Empire loyalty became synonymous. Those tendencies were always present in the journal, but the alternative, optimistic vision faded from its pages; it ceased to be a journal of diverse voices and came to enunciate a singular vision, the one that we have come to know as returned-soldier politics.

The reasons for this shift are obscure. Michael Roe suggests that growing tensions between Taylor and the League, and within the League itself, played a part. Around 1917, the RSA was subsumed by a broader national organisation, the RSSILA, and this may have occasioned some shift in emphasis. Equally, Taylor's numerous involvements may have meant a withdrawal of his interest in the journal, leaving it more firmly in the hands of the League.[43] But the shifts in tone also reflect the broader war context. The nationalist euphoria of Gallipoli could not be

---

43 See M. Roe, *Nine Australian Progressives: Vitalism in Bourgeois Social Thought 1890–1960*, UQP, St Lucia, 1984, pp. 185–209.

sustained once it became apparent that the war was going to grind on, at great cost, for some considerable time. The mounting death toll was enough to stifle optimism. Equally, the crises of the conscription referenda, the problem of war profiteering, strike activity, and the prospect of working-class revolution (evident in Russia) make the end of 1917 a crucial turning point in the understanding of Australia's participation in the war. The effect was to shift soldier politics, and conservative politics more generally, into a defensive position. Instead of an optimistic embrace of the potential of the nation to take its place on the world stage, the political upheavals of 1917 suggested that Australia's commitment to the war effort was being white-anted by forces from within the nation. What the war came to mean now was not just the defeat of German aggression, but also the defence of an Australian way of life against the corrosive forces that threatened its newly won nationhood from within.

In the pages of *The Soldier* we can see an ever-more-elaborate demonology at work, and one that helped shape post-war soldier politics. In October 1916, a provocative image featured for the first time, and it appeared repeatedly in the following years. Called 'Swat the Fly', with the inscription 'Kill that fly or he'll kill you', and drawn by Harold Cavill, a returned soldier, it depicted a large fly with the head of a man. The man had the distinctive long, upturned *'junker'* moustache favoured in caricatures of the 'Hun', and on each of the four legs of the fly were the words 'shirker', 'slacker', 'strike', and 'treason'. On the body of the fly were the initials PLL (Political Labor League) and IWW (Industrial Workers of the World), and the slogan 'go slow'. Here we have a less than subtle linkage of those who refused to enlist, obstructionist trade unionism, with its strategy of strike and 'go slow', the Labor Party, a revolutionary socialist group, and treason (although, after the war, 'PLL' and 'IWW' were usually dropped from the image). It was a powerful linkage, and one that would appear in various guises and variations: in the campaigns in support of conscription, in the more hysterical pronouncements of the Prime Minister, William Morris Hughes, and for some time after the war, in the journals of returned-soldier organisations.[44]

There was another crucial element to this returned-soldier demonology. This was the vacillating, ineffectual, and sometimes corrupt politician, evident in the strident criticisms in the journals of the RSL. One obvious target was the repatriation system. Returned soldiers were highly critical of repatriation policies, both for their lack of generosity and for the slowness in enacting them. Senator Millen, the minister in charge of repatriation policy, was nick-named 'millennium' (because it was clear that his promises would not be filled until then). Some of the depictions were more sinister. In one drawing, a man named 'the public' is bound

---

44 *The Soldier*, 6 October 1916. The broader history of domestic conflict has been examined in numerous histories, from Scott, *Australia During the War*, pp. 320–430 & 658–98, to more recent accounts, such as M. McKernan, *The Australian People and the Great War*, Nelson, Melbourne, 1980, pp. 14–42.

and gagged to a chair, by bonds called 'political party ties'; opening the safe and taking 'public funds' is another man wearing a hat emblazoned with 'politician'.[45] The more usual representations of the political process, however, involved variations on themes such as the public being squeezed by the competing vested interests of employers and unions, or Australia being undermined by party politics. Underpinning these representations was a profound distaste for pluralism and democracy. What ailed Australia was party politics, which divided the nation, made it the victim of vested interests, and undermined its capacity to confront urgent problems. What the war had demonstrated was that politicians were incapable of acting decisively. They had allowed strife, division, and conflict to undermine support for the men at the front, and now soldiers seemed to be saying that politicians were failing in their duty to returned men for the same reason. This disillusionment and the fear that the interests of returned men would be sacrificed to vested interests lay at the heart of returned soldier populism, with the assertion that action was needed. And who better to act than those who had already demonstrated their capacity for decisive action: returned soldiers.

The leading voices of returned-soldier opinion laid claim to the special right of these men to speak, and to their right to determine the course of Australian politics. As an editorial in *The Soldier*, just after the Armistice, declared:

> Already in this alleged 'Democratic Australia' it is apparent that true democracy does not exist ... already it is proved that the community is divided ... already the returned man has to fight and compete for his right to live and exist ... Is there a remedy[?] ... the remedy is in the hands of those who ... appreciated their country's needs ... the spirit of comradeship must be maintained.[46]

If this spirit was maintained, it was argued, then returned men could act as a political force to quench the fires of anarchy (depicted literally on the cover of one issue) and to 'build our beloved Australia in the way she should be built'.[47] League statements were replete with images of the new broom, sweeping aside old divisions, and of beginning all over again with returned men at the helm. There were also more sinister undercurrents to returned-soldier politics.

One of these was the preparedness of returned soldiers to take matters into their own hands. In the immediate post-war years, there were numerous riots and street fights between returned soldiers and labour radicals throughout urban and rural Australia. The flashpoint for such conflicts was usually a demonstration of support for socialist ideals. In Townsville, a few days after the Armistice, fifteen men marched up the main street, reputedly singing 'The Red Flag'. They were attacked and beaten by men shouting 'diggers to the rescue'. This was just one

---

45 *The Soldier,* 10 January 1919.
46 *The Soldier,* 29 November 1918.
47 *The Soldier* 15 November 1918.

of hundreds of minor affrays. Occasionally, however, they erupted into serious conflicts. In early 1919, speakers at worker meetings in Brisbane were pushed off their soap-boxes and beaten. In response, workers marched through the streets carrying red flags, and banners sporting Bolshevik and Sinn Fein slogans. A few days later several thousand returned soldiers and Empire loyalists stormed across the Victoria Bridge to attack members of South Brisbane's small Russian community, believed to be a haven for Bolsheviks. Shops and houses were smashed and looted, the Russian Hall destroyed, and men on both sides injured, some seriously. Sporadic fighting continued for the next three days, and soldiers marched through the streets with their own banners proclaiming their loyalty to the Union Jack. These incidents were symptoms of an emerging soldier politics?[48]

Were these sudden outbursts born of returned-soldier frustration, or were they more systematic efforts to subvert the democratic process? They were both. The number and spread of these clashes throughout the country points to the unplanned, momentary effusion of anger among soldiers. The heat of the moment, and the mad, compulsive throb of the crowd could overcome peaceful debate. In some cases, houses were stoned on the basis of rumours that the inhabitants were German, Russian, or Irish republican sympathisers (or any one of the other targets of hate), only for it to be discovered that the inhabitants were innocent – and, in one case, even returned soldiers themselves.[49] After many years away, nourished by stories of their own heroism and of disloyalty and apathy at home, and resentful of delays in demobilisation and inadequate repatriation policies, some returned men were bitter and frustrated. There was a widespread unsettledness was evident among returned men. They found it difficult to readjust to civilian ways, and in their liminal state, hovering somewhere between soldier and civilian, but not quite either, it was as easy to slip back to soldier ways as it was to make the step into the civilian world. In the immediate post-war period, reluctance to make this shift was amplified by returned-soldier unemployment, anger at government ineptitude, and union opposition to soldier preference. In this context, it was understandable that some would focus on groups perceived to be opposed to what soldiers had fought for. This reading of soldier protest is reinforced by the rapid dissipation of conflict. By the early 1920s the frequency and violence of these loyalist returned-soldier riots had diminished. A crucial factor in this was that most returned men had made some adjustment to civilian life – jobs, family life, and reasonable repatriation benefits meant they were no longer on the margins of civil society, hovering as a threat, but citizens with responsibilities.

But evidence of police, RSL, and Commonwealth security force involvement in the conduct of some of these loyalist demonstrations also suggests that there

---

48 On the Townsville incident, see *Courier Mail*, 16 November 1918. On the Brisbane riots, see R. Evans, *The Red Flag Riots: A Study of Intolerance*, UQP, St Lucia, 1988; R. Evans *Loyalty and Disloyalty: Social Conflict on the Queensland Homefront 1914–18*, Allen & Unwin, Sydney, 1987.
49 *Courier Mail*, 12 November 1918.

were forces orchestrating opposition to radical elements in Australia. One of the best sources for understanding these forces, strangely perhaps, is D. H. Lawrence's novel, based on his 1922 visit to Australia, *Kangaroo* (1923). The central characters, Harriet and Richard Lovat Somers, fresh from England, strike up a friendship with their neighbours, Jack and Victoria Callcott. Jack is a returned soldier, deeply involved in an organisation of 'Digger Clubs' run by prominent Sydney Jewish lawyer Benjamin Cooley, nicknamed 'Kangaroo'. These clubs contain an inner cell of men committed to maintaining the 'digger spirit' and ready to mobilise in defence of digger interests; more particularly, to act as agents for cleansing the society of decadent and corrupt elements. At the climax of the novel, a trade-union meeting addressed by labour leader Willie Struthers is broken up by the diggers, led by Jack and Kangaroo. In the ensuing fight, Kangaroo is wounded and dies some weeks later. Harriet and Richard Somers leave for the USA.

Kangaroo conveys more than this bare outline of the plot indicates. There are evocative passages on the nature of the Australian bush and the Australian people, – some typically Lawrentian ruminations on gender relations, and a strongly vitalist account of the decadence of Europe and the youthful exuberance of the New World. But historians have understandably taken a particular interest in the accuracy of its account of soldier politics, particularly the material concerning a secret organisation of soldiers.[50] What is striking, is not the literal accuracy of the story but the tone of Lawrence's account of the returned-soldier ideal. Jack, Kangaroo, and the other returned men see themselves as crusaders for an ethos of solidarity, born in Gallipoli. They stand in opposition to the vested interests of capital and labour, and yet draw from each: the stress on individual initiative and enterprise from capital, and the principle of collective responsibility from labour. This populist ideology seems to mirror, with remarkable accuracy, the tenor of returned soldier politics. In its account of the desire to act, to bypass the choking corridors of traditional power for the 'greater good', it divines the mood of the loyalist returned-soldier organisations. Jack, Kangaroo, and the men take matters into their own hands. This resonates with the pronouncements of returned-soldier leaders, notably W.A. Fisher in Queensland, who during the Red Flag Riots declared that 'we feel it is our bounden duty to warn the authorities that grave breaches of the peace will ensue' and, further, that 'we have a large number of Returned Soldiers here who are fully determined to use every means necessary to effect our purpose'. There is also evidence that actual secret organisations, such as the Old Guard, the 'white army', and later the New Guard, largely composed of returned soldiers, continued to exist throughout the 1920s and 1930s. Many were closely allied to new conservative groups, such as the King and Empire Alliance, the Sane Democracy League, the All for Australia League, and the Constitutional Clubs. These groups

---

50   It is generally agreed that Lawrence modelled some aspects of his central characters on actual people, and that secret organisations existed. See R. Darroch, *D. H. Lawrence in Australia*, Macmillan, Sydney, 1981.

promoted the ideals of Empire, patriotism, individualism, and the virtues of family and work, but more importantly they targeted labour organisations, trade unions, and radical worker groups, characterising them as enemies of the Australian way of life.[51]

These organisations were extreme echoes of more mainstream messages of returned-soldier journals and pamphlets: politics was paralysed by party loyalties and inept politicians; what was needed was a new force in politics, one committed to decisive action for the national good. Returned-soldier organisations believed that they were this third force, and that, at Gallipoli, they had inherited a privileged role as citizens. Some even proposed that election to Parliament should be confined to returned servicemen; a parliament of servicemen alone. In the end, however, Australians rejected this appeal, preferring to maintain their traditional party allegiances. Despite efforts to form a 'soldiers' party', influential organisations such as the RSL were relegated to a lobbying role. In the final analysis, the exclusive populism of returned-soldier groups alienated trade unionists, Irish Catholics with no love of Empire, and men who had not served – hardening commitments to traditional political loyalties. Moreover, the overweening masculinism of returned groups – the idealisation of an essentially male ideal of citizenship – may have repulsed many women, who had contributed significantly to the war effort, who bore the burden of mourning, and who were newly exercising their political rights. But we cannot underestimate the force of returned-soldier rhetoric. In its insistence on targeting disloyalty, in its focus on maintaining the flame of remembrance, and in its faith that the freedoms won at Gallipoli were constantly under threat, this politics did much to strangle alternative visions for Australian society. In doing so, returned soldier groups helped perpetuate a national ideal that framed public and private memories of Anzac.

V

After the effluxion of the immediate post-war years, official soldier politics settled into familiar patterns. Returned soldier concerns focused on injustices and inefficiencies in the repatriation system. The RSL, however, always saw itself as having a wider mandate to speak on issues of national importance. In the branch journals and newsletters, such as *Reveille* (NSW), *Duckboard* (Victoria), and *Whiz-Bang* (Queensland), and at the State and federal annual conferences, there

---

51 The Fisher quote is from Evans, *Red Flag Riots*, p. 140. For broader discussions of radical conservative groups, see T. Matthews, 'The All for Australia League', *Labour History*, no. 17, November 1970, pp. 136–47; K. Richmond, 'Reaction to Radicalism: Non-Labour Movements, 1920–9', *Journal of Australian Studies*, no. 5, November 1979, pp. 50–63. On secret armies, see A. Moore, *The Secret Army and the Premier: Conservative Paramilitary Organisation in New South Wales 1930–32*, UNSW Press, Sydney, 1989; M. Cathcart, *Defending the National Tuckshop: Australia's Secret Army Intrigue of 1931*, McPhee Gribble, Melbourne, 1988.

were always assertions of the right of returned men and women to safeguard Australian society. As Colonel H.B. Collett, President of the RSL in Western Australia, asserted in 1926, 'We know no politics, but I do think there are questions of a national character in which a League of this nature and importance should interest itself'. He went on to enunciate a wide-ranging brief, encompassing immigration, national insurance, public health, housing, land settlement, railway and road problems, and 'last but not least, the elimination or reduction of foreign film and its pernicious influence'.[52]

Such calls became even more insistent during the Great Depression. As representatives of the Newcastle Branch asked in 1931, 'is this sad condition [the economy] not a call to the Anzac spirit?'. It may have been, but the proposed remedies were rather shallow. There was, of course, much spirited rhetoric about 'keeping bright within Australia the ideals of loyalty and patriotism' (as if the depression was a consequence of disloyalty).[53] When it came to actual policies, however, the League retreated into a narrow sectionalism, defending the rights of returned men and women, and campaigning vigorously to exclude war pensions from the Federal government's proposed budget cuts. The League adopted a 'defend the members first' policy rather than a national strategy, succeeding to a limited extent when the government maintained war pension rates but reduced some allowances for dependants. Underpinning the League campaign, however, was a belief that returned men had special citizenship status, which exempted them from demands for further sacrifice in the national good; it was the turn of other (implicitly lesser) citizens to bear the brunt of hardship.

This was a politics of protectionism taken to new heights. It was a politics justifiably calculated to serve the interest of its members, but also one that embraced populist ideas from both labour and anti-labour groups: protect the territory with Empire loyalism, the nation's economy with tariffs, the race with immigration restriction, the culture with censorship, the standard of living with high wages, pensions and national insurance, and the Anzac spirit with patriotism. In these ideals we can see the legacy of the war and home-front conflict. The assertive, confident nationalism of the first years of the war was replaced by suspicion, sectionalism, and bellicose loyalism. Soldier politics, and Australian politics more generally, took up a defensive and protective posture, one based on the belief that Australia had to remain dependent on the Empire and, at the same time, repress dissension at home. In the interwar years, part of the reputation of the League rested with its ability to both defend the interests of members and articulate a social vision in accord with the mainstream of Australian political culture.

---

52 Col. H. B. Collett, Tenth Presidential Address, RSL, WA Branch Conference, Perth, 29 September 1926, p. 2.
53 Newcastle Branch of the Returned Sailors and Soldiers Imperial League of Australia, *A Service Record of the A.I.F.: Work, Methods, Humour*, RSSILA, Newcastle, 1931, p. 3.

The League bequeathed this politics to a later generation of soldiers. During the Second World War representatives of the League again asserted the right of the soldier to determine the shape of post-war society. The by now familiar refrain about the danger of party politics and the need for a single voice in national politics (the soldier's voice) gained further significance in the next war. As *Reveille* reported; 'those serving as a result of the spiritual ecstasy of comradeship are granted a clearer perception of a necessary social condition than any others'. One soldier representative even revived the old idea of a 'serviceman's parliament' to overcome the problems of party divisions.[54] Even before the war's end, the League saw itself playing a significant role in the formulation of the government's policy of post-war reconstruction. Added to the demand for a say, however, was a new addendum: it was imperative to avoid the mistakes of the last war. Governments, it was asserted, needed to act decisively this time to ensure adequate reward for the sacrifice of servicemen and women. This was a basis for a renewal of the traditional League campaigns for greater benefits for returned men and women, including employment preference, adequate training for employment, pensions, sufficient housing, land settlement, and increased hospital and medical benefits.

They were rarely happy with the results. In 1947, the New South Wales Branch of the League were asserting that:

> There's quite a few things wrong with Australia. There are industrial disputes, a shortage of workers and commodities, a scarcity of smokes, and bottled beer is hard to get... but tragedy is stalking our midst ... the authorities are complacent ... [get] the bureaucrat to take his head out of the sand ... [we need] houses for people ... the Minister of Immigration is running round the world urging all and sundry to Come Down Under ... where is he going to put them?[55]

This was a familiar litany of woes. But the fact was, despite the very real problem of the post-war housing shortage, the home front to which servicemen and women of the Second World War returned was far less troubled than the one that confronted the first generation of Anzacs. There had been no major conflicts and divisions on the Australian home front from 1939 to 1945. There had been strikes, but these were minor, and limited conscription had not become a major point of conflict. Moreover, Labor's policy of post-war reconstruction bore fruit in a significant rate of economic growth, fuelled by high tariffs, population growth through a higher birth-rate and increased immigration, and an expansion in manufacturing. The economy was capable of absorbing returned men and women, with little unemployment. Equally, greater government investment in training and education

---

54 Editorial, 'New World Order', and E. J. Brady, 'The Serviceman Awakes', *Reveille*, 1 November 1942.
55 Editorial, 'A Golden Age', *Reveille*, 1 October 1947.

programs for former service personnel equipped many to enter the workforce at a level they may not have envisaged before enlistment.

This did not prevent the RSL from seeking to maintain its role as a watchdog of national health and prosperity. Here the politics of cultural protectionism continued to reign. Throughout the post-war years, even until the 1990s, prominent League spokesmen (sometimes even women) stressed the need to safeguard Australia from the perils of communism, non-British immigration, pacifism, and more recently republicanism. For many years the greatest concern was communism. In 1948 the League passed a resolution banning communists from membership of the League, even if they were returned men. A few years later the League was a prominent advocate of the politics of cold-war vigilance, views that commanded popular support. In the late 1960s this led them to condemn pacifists, student protest groups, and the moratorium and anti-Vietnam War movements as communist front organisations.[56] Given the obvious presence of communists in these movements, such a view probably did not seem unreasonable, but it was an overly simple view, which blurred the distinctions and diverse motives of different groups within these movements. Increasingly, however, League views were out of touch with new elements of Australian political culture. In the minds of many younger Australians, it became a generational organisation – a group of ageing men alienated from youth culture. This was the force behind new, critical representations of the League. In the 1960s, in documentary programs such as *Four Corners*, in books and plays, such as Alan Seymour's *One Day in the Year*, and in radical journals such as *Oz*, the League came to be seen as a haven for old, conservative men, irrelevant to a changing world. In the 1980s and 1990s the League's support for restrictions on Asian immigration and its opposition to a republic alienated it from Labor governments, republicans, and supporters of multiculturalism. Increasingly the League was being seen as a sectional interest group. It has always been so, but the key difference is that between the wars and in the 1940s and 1950s the League seemed to be in the mainstream of Australian politics, whereas by the end of the century, although still popular with many Australians, it was seen by many others, including some Vietnam Veterans who preferred their own organisation, as an anachronism.[57]

To concentrate on the public politics of the RSL, however, is to miss important dimensions of the organisation. It remains a relevant and influential organisation, which has demonstrated an extraordinary capacity to renew itself. In part, this is a consequence of a relaxation of its rigid membership rules. With a declining membership in the 1970s, the League had to admit, first, ex-servicemen and women who had not served overseas and, finally in 1983, anyone (provided they were acceptable to the membership), whether they had served or not. By opening up the clubs to all Australians, especially younger Australians, the League was

---

56 Sir William Yeo, 'State President Puts Views', *Reveille*, 1 July 1969.
57 See Sekuless & Rees, *Lest We Forget*, pp. 116–67.

trying to counter its generational image. Moreover, it has retained a loyal membership and continues to serve as an umbrella organisation for a number of diverse groups – limbless and tubercular soldier societies, ladies' auxiliaries, returned nurses' organisations, and permanently incapacitated servicemen's associations – that do much to ensure the welfare of former servicemen and women, and their dependants. But perhaps its continuing influence stems from its central role in Australia's most prominent public ritual: Anzac Day.

Although alternative celebrations, such as Armistice Day, have faded in significance, and newer claimants, such as Australia Day, have struggled for support, Anzac Day still commands national attention. Although the ranks of returned men and women are thinning, the dawn services and marches are still televised, enjoyed by many servicemen and women, and attended by large and supportive crowds. It would seem then that 'the myth of war experience' – the need to sanctify the sacrifice of citizen soldiers – remains a defining aspect of Australian national identity. The case of Australia certainly stands in contrast to other countries, such as Germany, Britain, Japan, and Italy, where the 'myth of war experience' was strong in the interwar years but collapsed during the Second World War, or Russia, where victory over the Nazis is a major celebration but one attributed to all Russians, not just its soldiers. Other nations, such as the USA and India, celebrate Independence more than any particular war, and even for our closest counterparts, Canada and New Zealand, the focus is more on remembering the war dead than on celebrating the founding of a nation.

This is not to suggest that Anzac Day emerged spontaneously in the hearts of Australians. Although Anzac exploits were celebrated by many Australians, the dominant meanings of Anzac had to be made, and such making did not go uncontested. Although celebrations were held from 1916, enthusiasm waned after the Armistice, with many thinking it better to assert the importance of life as citizen rather than as soldier. Only through the intense lobbying of returned-soldier groups did governments come to see the worth of celebrating Anzac as a national day. This was the resolution of the 1923 Premiers Conference, but it took some time before every State government had legislated for it to be a public holiday. Such caution arose from difficulties in defining the ideals of Anzac. Although soldier organisations enthusiastically promoted the first anniversary of Gallipoli with marches and commemorative volumes, the shift in soldier politics that we have noted from 1917 made the nationalism of the event problematic for conservatives. Some thought that Empire Day should continue as Australia's most important national day. During the war and immediate interwar years, a cultural struggle took place to define Anzac as either a radical nationalist or an empire loyalist event. In the end the RSL was able to incorporate elements of both (notably the racism, xenophobia, and protectionism of Australia's pre-war radical nationalism with traditional loyalism) in its presentation of Anzac, thus broadening its appeal, but robbing it of its radical potential. Only by 1927 did Anzac Day gain a secure place in the national calendar – a place that became more significant with the affirmation of the myth of war experience in subsequent wars.⁵⁸ But we are left with the question of why Anzac has retained popular support.

One clear factor is the impact of the Second World War on civilian populations in Europe and Asia. This was a war of mass destruction, which in many respects eroded the distinction between soldier and civilian. More civilians died in this war than soldiers, particularly in Germany, Poland, and Russia, where there were almost fourteen million civilian deaths. Even Britain, which was never occupied by Axis forces, lost 60,000 civilians in air raids and rocket attacks, which is more than twice the number of Australian soldiers killed in the war. In these countries it was impossible to sustain the argument that soldiers were a singular group that had made a special sacrifice in war; instead the entire community bore the brunt of conflict.⁵⁹ Australian civilians, on the other hand, were largely insulated from war, and certainly there were no significant civilian casualties. War, although it came very close to Australian shores (in New Guinea and in naval engagements off the coast) and, in Darwin and Sydney Harbour, even breached our defences, never seriously threatened Australian soil or the civilian population. In this context, the special status of the Australian serviceman and woman as the defenders of our way of life was maintained.

Australia, of course, was not the only allied nation whose population was insulated from the horrors of combat. The USA, Canada, South Africa, and India are other notable examples. But although soldier cults were strong in these nations, most particularly the USA, they never came to represent the nation as a whole. There is a real puzzle regarding the role of Anzac as the emblem of Australian national identity. How could something that happened to the few stand for the whole? Here we have to see Australia's colonial heritage in context. Nations such as the USA, South Africa, Canada, and India had other events and legends on which to draw for national ideals – the War of Independence for the USA, ancient traditions and the modern national liberation struggle for India, the Great Trek for Boers in South Africa, and for Canada, a fragile and fractured identity shaped by the conflict between two different populations (English and French). Australia had little other than Anzac. There had been no struggle against the colonial power of Britain, and racism prevented (until recent times) any resort to Indigenous culture as the source of national symbols. Australian national identity, caught in a schizophrenic pull between Empire and nation, struggled for sustenance in arid soil. Informed by the Western cultural fixation on battle, blood, and nation, Gallipoli became the defining event in the absence of any other. Despite recent efforts to define Kokoda, a battle fought in defence of Australian soil, as a more

---

58 See G. Fitzpatrick, *Anzac Day: Past and Present*, AWM, Canberra, 1992, pp. 3–10; Bob Bessant, 'Empire Day, Anzac Day, The Flag Ceremony and All That', *Historian*, 25 October 1973, pp. 36–43. On the emergence of the legend as a conservative symbol, see G. Serie, 'The Digger Tradition and Australian Nationalism', *Meanjin*, vol. 24, no. 2, 1965, pp. 149–58.
59 See Mosse, *Fallen Soldiers*, pp. 201–25. For casualty figures, see J. Ellis, *The World War II Data Book*, Aurum Books, London, 1993.

appropriate symbol for national identity, Gallipoli retains its pre-eminent status.[60] It does so, in part, because Australia's participation in the Second World War was not understood as a rupture with the past, as in some other nations, but as an essential continuity.

For many, there seemed an unbroken line in the Anzac tradition from Gallipoli to Kokoda. This was a view embraced by the RSL, which wanted 'to see the comradeship, the unselfish spirit of the Digger, born on Gallipoli, nurtured in France and Palestine, and matured from Libya to Borneo, burn with a quenchless fire'.[61] Of course, the League at this time was still in the hands of veterans of the First World War, and they had no interest in developing a battle myth to rival that of Gallipoli. But the sense of continuity has never been seriously questioned in Australia. This is reflected in memorialisation. Although there were some separate statues and memorials to the AIF, the air force, and the navy, as well as monuments to individual battles in the later war, more usually the names of the war dead from 1939–45 were added to the vast number of existing local memorials and honour rolls throughout Australia. Their names appear in the cloisters of the Australian War Memorial in Canberra, alongside their brothers and sisters of the earlier war. Additions were made to other memorials to recognise those from the Second World War. At the Shrine of Remembrance in Melbourne, stones in the shape of a cross, inscribed with 'We Shall Remember Them', were laid in the forecourt of the shrine. In the area surrounding the shrine, separate statues and memorials commemorating the individual services in the Second World War and particular areas of combat were added. In 1954 these additions, bearing the inscription 'Greater love hath no man than this, that a man lay down his life for his friends', were dedicated by Queen Elizabeth II.[62]

This sense of continuity was even maintained for veterans of the Vietnam War. Despite the troubled reception these servicemen and women received on their return, the RSL proclaimed that 'our boys return home ... so lets bring them into the RSL'. More than this, it asserted an essential link between Vietnam and Gallipoli: 'Anzac Day ... is a general symbol of brave men and heroic action as exemplified in the battle arenas of World War I ... World War II and even in the campaigns of Korea, Malaysia and Vietnam'.[63] The linking phrase 'and even in' suggests some underlying ambivalence about the connections between Korea, Malaya, Vietnam, and the Anzac legend – an ambivalence of which some veterans, particularly those from Vietnam, were aware. It led some to form their own organisations, separate from the RSL. But many Vietnam veterans marched on Anzac Day, the names of the Vietnam war dead were added to those already inscribed on the walls of

---

60 For an early statement of this argument, see H. McQueen, *Gallipoli to Petrov: Arguing with Australian History*, Allen & Unwin, Sydney, 1984, p. 4.
61 Editorial, 'What Do We Want from the Post-War World', *Reveille*, 1 October 1945.
62 Pratt & Barnes, *An Interpretative Appreciation of the Shrine of Remembrance*, pp. 2–20.
63 Editorial, 'Our Boys Return Home', *Reveille*, 1 January 1972; 'Anzac Day: The Changing Vision', *Reveille*, 1 April 1967.

the Australian War Memorial, and eventually there were specific marches and a Vietnam Memorial in Canberra to recognise these veterans.

These were seen as reconciliation gestures. It was a reconciliation not only with the nation, but also with the Anzac legend. As the official booklet for the dedication of the Vietnam Veterans Memorial states, this was a gesture to place their names 'alongside those who made the supreme sacrifice at Gallipoli, Pozieres, Kokoda and Alamein'.[64] This was a crucial process in linking Korea, Malaya, and Vietnam veterans into an unbroken historical tradition. And, in this continuity, the Anzac legend has managed to maintain its place at the centre of national symbolism. This is the public memory uniting the men and women who served Australia in war. It is a memory of extraordinary power and significance for many Australians, and one that has shaped our understanding of our own history – although, like all memories, it is selective, blocking out alternative historical narratives and remembering.

VI

In April 1920 Charles Elmore sat in his lounge room in Murrumbeena, Melbourne, surrounded by friends and sympathetic onlookers. Slowly he began to drift into a trance-like state; on the table before him was a notebook and pen. He picked up the pen and began to write in a quick flowing script, without pause; it was a 'Message to the Bereaved' from those 'slain in war'. The 'slain' sought to reassure their readers:

> We wish to bring thoughts of love and peace to the thoughts of the bereaved mothers especially ... in regard to the fate of their boys ... their loved ones are kindly taught and cared for and brought to understand their new conditions of existence. And there is a spirit of comradeship amongst these young men ... they are gradually beginning to see the tragedy of this great upheaval. Those whom they fought against ... and in hatred slew, they now ... meet on grounds of brotherly love.

Elmore was a spiritualist medium, and the reports of his contact with slain soldiers of the Great War were published for a wider audience eager to find solace in the thought that death was not an ending but a beginning. Moreover, as Elmore's ghostly informants revealed, the mateship of the trenches was transcended by the mateship of the afterlife. Later that same year, Sir Arthur Conan Doyle, British writer and spiritualist, toured Australia to bring a message of 'consolation to bruised hearts and bewildered minds' overwhelmed by the enormity of their loss in war. His message was 'the practical abolition of death', and although condemned by sections of the press as 'evil witchcraft', the idea of continuing existence found a

---

64 Australian War Memorial, *Vietnam: Their Place in History*, AWM, Canberra, 1992.

receptive audience in Australia. His numerous lectures in town halls were 'filled to overflowing'.[65]

Spiritualism was not new; it had a lively presence throughout the late nineteenth century. But war gave it a new following: families grieving over the loss of sons, brothers, and fiancés, ever hopeful that their loss had been neither permanent nor in vain. It provided a means for easing the pain of memory. Not all, however, could find comfort in the idea of transcendence. Jack Ramsay, a well-known bird photographer, conducted a profitable trade after both the First World War and the Second World War 'touching-up' the photographs of men killed in war. Families who lost sons and brothers often had no photographs of them in uniform. Ramsay took old photographs, removed from them any clues to their civilian context, and drew and painted the deceased in military uniform, complete with medals. These 'heroic' portraits could then find pride of place on the family mantelpiece. At the height of this trade, Ramsay employed forty-three assistants, testifying to the widespread desire to remember not just sons and brothers but Anzacs. Photography and spiritualism were just two of the many ways Australians sought to assuage their grief. Many found relief in the idea of nobility of sacrifice; there was no comfort in the futility of war. In private and public memory, and in the meeting of both in memorials, remembrance ceremonies, and marches, Australians sought to invest the Anzac sacrifice with a larger meaning. Only thus could grief find a means of rest.[66]

Each returned man and woman also had his or her own ways of remembering the significance of participation in war. Alistair Thomson's innovative account of the different ways returned soldiers recalled their war experience has illuminated this process of coming to terms with the horror of war. Some repressed their memories of the experience, others displaced them through humour or conventional stories of Anzac larrikinism that were almost as if they were taken directly from Bean's history or the *Anzac Book* (1916). Only slowly was Thomson able to puncture some of these barricades of memory (and then not in every case) to allow these men to dredge up some of the more difficult memories of their war experience. It was clear, however, that each had come to some accommodation of the Anzac legend, either by largely rejecting it as 'not how it really was' or through some placement of the self within the larger public narrative. The latter reaction was more common. Many embraced the Anzac legend in important ways, read Bean's histories, remembered the familiar stories (even if they had not always experienced them), joined the RSL, and marched on Anzac Day. Over time the lines blurred

---

65 See F. Elmore (ed.), *A Message to Humanity: Definite, Vital and Urgent Communications from Beyond the Veil* E. W. Cole, Melbourne, 1921; Sir Arthur Conan Doyle, *The Wanderings of a Spiritualist*, Hodder & Stoughton, London, 1921. For a brilliant elucidation of the spiritualist fervour in relation to war, see Winter, *Sites of Memory*, pp. 54–77.

66 See C. Snowden, 'Private Monuments: Photography and the Construction of Truth', *Public History Review*, vol. 2, 1993, pp. 19–34.

between their actual experience of war and the public narrative of Anzac.[67] For some, they became one and the same thing.

Commemorations, such as Anzac Day, also had private meanings and rituals that reinforced the public message of sacrifice. These were times for reunion with comrades. In the popular understanding of Anzac Day, these occasions involved much drinking, gambling, and reminiscing. In the toleration of excessive drinking and normally illegal pastimes such as two-up, Anzac Day contains elements of the classic 'carnival', during which normal social relations are reversed. In this 'world turned upside down', and with the sanction of alcohol, men could embrace, laugh and cry, reaffirm comradeship, re-experience intimate male bonds, expiate guilt at having survived, or collectively engage in the melancholy of remembering dead mates. They could momentarily escape the strictures of masculine self-control to participate in collective and acceptable displays of mourning and grief. In other respects, however, this was not a 'world turned upside down' but one that was 'right side up'. As Alan Tiveychoc wrote in 1935, 'this party ... was attended ... not because he wanted to drink, but because, unknowingly, he wanted to recapture some of the old care-free atmosphere and light-heartedness that prevailed on the other side'.[68] In the temporary return to an old 'larrikin' spirit, these men could slip back to an imagined world of 'pure mateship', free from the burdens of the home front. It was a ritual, then, that helped to perpetuate the disjuncture between front and home, affirming the freemasonry of returned men and women.

For many of those who returned, and for those who stayed behind and mourned, ideals of sacrifice – whether privately or publicly affirmed – offered a means of taming grief, but they also imposed obligations. Many were deeply committed to repaying the debt to those who sacrificed their health and well-being for the good of the nation. The extraordinary range and variety of returned-services organisations, fund-raising ventures, and welfare services was evidence of the vitality of this voluntary commitment. Much of this fund-raising was organised through local branches of the RSL, Legacy, Legion, and the myriad other societies catering to the welfare of returnees. These branches also provided a social venue for returned men and women – places to meet with comrades who shared their experience. The great number of meetings, socials, dances, poppy day sales, picnics, smokos, fetes, and outings organised by local branches provided continuing social interaction for comrades and financed ongoing welfare services. Through the money raised, these organisations provided employment for out-of-work veterans, homes for the aged and infirm, bursaries for children at school, clinics for the vocational guidance of children, and emergency funds for impoverished veterans. Sometimes the minutes of the meetings of these branches make for depressing reading, documenting constant struggles to raise and distribute funds in the face of an ageing and shrinking membership. While some branches were strong and

---

67   A. Thomson, *Anzac Memories: Living with the Legend*, OUP, Melbourne, 1994.
68   Tiveychoc, *There and Back*, p. 234.

vigorous, others were located in areas of declining economic significance, usually in small country centres. Here members had to overcome the problems of a diminishing veteran population, a local economy in decline, and a population moving to cities and towns. Some went under, absorbed into larger regional branches. Nonetheless, it's hard not to admire the commitment of these groups. For some, it represented an extraordinary investment of time and energy. This perseverance and fortitude are some of our most important clues to the intensity of the Anzac spirit of comradeship.

The records of individual branches provide a glimpse of this commitment. The Bridgetown sub-branch of the RSL in Western Australia, a small county branch, has records for the period from 1919 to 1950. Its first significant function, in September 1919, was a welcome home for returned men at the local Mechanics Institute. For the remainder of the year, the branch committee busied itself with assessing applications for soldier land settlement and establishing a Soldiers Appeal Committee to raise funds. Thereafter it engaged in the politics of being a local branch, following the lead of the national League in writing to local councils, and State and Federal governments in support of soldier settlement, employment preference, and increased repatriation benefits. But it also tackled exclusively local issues, protesting the lack of adequate roads for local soldier settlers, the need for orphanages in the area, the removal of a local soldier settler to a mental hospital, and more.

Throughout the 1920s and 1930s it ran picture nights at the local hall, organised poppy day, ran a repertory club and old-time dances, had 'smoko' nights, and held fetes. During the early 1940s, declining membership forced it to develop relationships with the Country Women's Association and the Girl Guides in order to provide entertainment for members of the Second AIF on leave. After 1945 it ran 'Popular Girl Competitions' (beauty pageants) in an effort to appeal to a new generation of soldiers and their families. They also established a Soldiers' Welfare Fund, a War Veterans' Home Appeal, an orphanage fund, and an Aged Soldiers' and Sailors' Fund. With these, they assisted aged and infirm veterans, sent food parcels and gifts to veterans in hospitals, funded honour rolls in the local school, laid wreaths on Anzac Day, paid for headstones on the graves of veterans whose families could not afford them, and provided sustenance allowances for struggling soldier settlers. Members of the Ladies Auxiliary of the Bridgetown Branch played a central role in many of these activities, in addition to providing the tea and sandwiches for men's committee meetings. Each week they visited convalescent homes, repatriation hospitals, and wards in mental hospitals to provide gifts, entertainment (songs, choirs, musical recitals, plays, and dances), picnics and trips, and general good cheer for inmates. Local branches also provided holidays and outings for widows and children, sporting events, fetes, and picnics for the children of deceased veterans. It was a busy and exhausting round of activities.[69] In this,

---

69 Bridgetown RSL Branch Minutes, 1919–1950, Western Australia Archives, MN32–825A.

Bridgetown replicated the voluntary activities of many other RSL branches throughout Australia. It was an allotment of effort that contributed significantly to the well-being of many returned servicemen and women, and their families. But the need was on a scale that could not be met by such assistance. The burden of care for returnees and their dependants fell on the public purse. Australians turned to governments to provide adequate compensation for returned men and women.

3
Repatriation

Repatriation is a peculiar word to describe the schemes developed to assist returned servicemen and women. It was certainly not used by any other nation after the First World War. In Britain the preferred terms were *reconstruction* or *rehabilitation*, in Canada *re-establishment* or *reinstatement*, and in the USA they were *rehabilitation* and *reclamation*. As Australian critics at the time never tired of pointing out, its literal meaning was 'to return to one's native land', hardly adequate to describe the pension, housing, training, education, medical, and hospital policies for the re-establishment of returned men and women. These policies, after all, were not focused on the process of return but on the serviceman and woman after return. Such critics proposed alternative terms, such as *recognition, assistance, acknowledgment,* and *gratitude,* to better characterise this field of public endeavour. Government ministers and military authorities often used words such as *reestablishment* (for the able-bodied) and *rehabilitation* (for the incapacitated) when talking about particular policies, and almost all used *demobilisation*, either singly or in tandem with *repatriation*, to describe the actions involved in bringing servicemen and women home. In 1919, the Hughes government declared that *demobilisation* was the preferred term for the process of returning servicemen and women. Pedants cautioned that *repatriation* should denote the return of the soldiers, and *demobilisation* their discharge from service. And when John Monash was overseeing the return of the forces to Australia after the First World War, he was made Director-General of Repatriation and Demobilisation. But by then there were 'repatriation funds', the Commonwealth *Australian Soldiers Repatriation Act 1917* and a Repatriation Commission in Australia, all aimed at assisting the process of reinstatement – another popular term at the time. The fine lexical distinctions were soon lost, and *repatriation* was generally adopted as the term to describe all the policies involved in returning, discharging, pensioning, assisting, and training returned men and women, and continuing to assist them throughout their lives. In popular usage, this vast medical and welfare bureaucracy became 'the repat'.[1]

It is tempting to speculate about this peculiar linguistic practice. Perhaps it was simply a consequence of the Australian penchant for a rough and cryptic title, rather than a long-winded official one. But the agitated discussion of the appropriateness of the term suggests that there might have been further reasons. Defenders of the usage pointed to precedents. In Britain repatriation had been used to describe efforts to assist the return of 'detained' Boer farmers to their land after the Boer War. This, of course, was hardly an appropriate parallel – as critics pointed out. On the defensive, advocates of the government's 1916 Australian Soldiers Repatriation Fund Bill declared that the term was already in popular usage, and moreover, since this was legislation to control a patriotic fund already established by private subscription, it was impossible to change the title. This argument just begged the question. Why did prominent philanthropists, such as W L. Baillieu, Edward Grayndler, Samuel Hordern and John Langdon Bonython, choose the term *repatriation* to describe their patriotic fund? Unfortunately, there is no evidence to provide a definitive answer to this question. We do know, however, that the proposal for such a fund arose out of a 1916 conference of Commonwealth and State government representatives to discuss soldier land settlement. Here the idea of a 'repatriation fund' – established by public subscription and subsidised by governments to assist soldier settlers in the purchase of stock, feed, and equipment – was first mooted. Even though it was recognised that more than this would be required to meet the needs of returned men, repatriation was first seen as an effort to settle them on the land.[2]

There was nothing unique in this. Supporters of soldier settlement could point to an ancient custom, Roman in origin, of settling returned soldiers on the land. But the conjunction of this scheme and the term *repatriation* does seem to be more than coincidence. Here *repatriation* meant a literal and a symbolic return to the land. And this return has to be seen in the context of arguments for Australia's newly won nationhood at Gallipoli. As many proclaimed, the Anzacs, in spilling their blood, had created Australian nationhood and had laid a proper claim at last to the legitimacy of colonial occupation. This connection is even more evident when we see that Indigenous servicemen and women were the only ones denied a right

---

1   See Australia, House of Representatives, *Debates*, vol. 80, 1914–17, pp. 7810–77. See also C. Lloyd and J. Rees, *The Last Shilling: A History of Repatriation in Australia*, MUP, Melbourne, 1994, pp. 1–4. On overseas schemes, see Ministry of Reconstruction, *Reconstruction Problems: Pamphlets 1–19*, His Majesty's Stationery Office, London, 1918–19; Wecter, *When Johnny Comes Marching Home*, pp. 263–367; W. Waller, *The Veteran Comes Back*, Dryden Press, New York, 1944, pp. 210–85; D. Morton & G. Wright, *Winning the Second Battle: Canadian Veterans and the Return to Civil Life 1915–30*, University of Toronto Press, Toronto, 1987.
2   See 'Report of the Conference of Representatives of the Commonwealth and State Governments and the Federal Parliamentary War Committee in Respect of the Settlement of Returned Soldiers on the Land', *Commonwealth Parliamentary Papers*, vol. 5, 1914–17, pp. 1457–1517.

to repatriation. Aboriginal and Torres Strait Islander service personnel were given benefits as an Act of Grace by the government (formalised in the Commonwealth *Native Members of the Forces Benefits Act 1957*), not as a right of entitlement on the basis of active service. The use of the term *repatriation*, then, can be seen as a proclamation of nationhood and as a final act of dispossession of indigenous peoples. Through Anzac, non-Aboriginal Australians announced that they had finally and fully won the land with their blood, and returned soldiers were to be given special assistance to ensure that they claimed their 'birthright'.

Whatever the symbolic significance of repatriation, few were under any illusions that the return of servicemen and women would be anything other than complex. In 1917 Senator Edward Millen, soon to be Minister for Repatriation, pointed to the difficulty of drafting legislation for the re-establishment of servicemen and women when there were no similar schemes in existence. Opposition members, such as Frank Tudor, agreed: 'the matter of getting our soldiers back into private life again on their return will prove to be one of the most difficult questions that any Government ... will have to handle'.[3] It was not just a financial or an administrative issue; it was also a cultural one. For those charged with the return of servicemen and women, the transition from soldier to citizen was fraught with problems. 'Civilisation' became a trope for these problems. For politicians and commentators, war had been a failure of civilisation, and now the task was to restore a civilised state. As Lieutenant H.J. Moore, Assistant Director of Education in France, argued in 1919, authorities had to 'help the stricken digger to re-establish himself as a unit of civilisation ... [for] during four years of barbaric warfare and savagery ... much had been forgotten of the refinement of social intercourse'.

Crucial to the success of this scheme was a comprehensive system to re-establish these men and women in civil society.[4] What emerged was a large and complex welfare system. The historians of this system have argued that 'without the Repat, the quantum of human wretchedness, physical pain, mental anguish and poverty in the Australian Community over three quarters of a century would have been incomparably greater'.[5] There could be no quarrel with that conclusion. But 'the repat' was also a field of meaning, of competing claims and beliefs, that tell us much about the problems confronting returned servicemen and women and how Australians struggled to deal with this return.

---

3   Australia, House of Representatives, *Debates*, vol. 82, 1917–19, pp. 183–96, 837–45.
4   H.J. Moore, Report to the Teacher's Conference in London, AIF Education Service Papers, AWM 20, 6423/2/21.
5   Lloyd & Rees, *The Last Shilling*, p. 419.

I

Australia's 'blood sacrifice' during the First World War was the ultimate sanction for a generous system of repatriation. With 60,000 dead and 150,000 injured or ill as a result of combat (almost two-thirds of those sent overseas), proponents of repatriation, particularly returned-soldier groups, established a moral calculus for recompense. They never tired of pointing out that a greater proportion of Australian troops had been killed or wounded than the members of any other armed force. But in terms of the proportion of military-aged men in the population, Britain, France, and Germany actually shouldered a heavier burden of casualties. These are the distinctions of modern social historians. The fact remains that the scale of loss on all sides was overwhelming. The stark obviousness of the casualty figures was a powerful weapon in the campaign for returned-soldier benefits. Moreover, the size of the conflict, the extraordinary increase in the destructive power of weapons, occasioning serious injury to soldiers on a scale never seen or envisaged before, and the parallel developments in military medicine that meant that many survived such injuries, ensured large numbers of injured and ill requiring care after the war. Perhaps the most important medical development was the control of infectious and epidemic diseases. In the First World War many injured and ill soldiers, who in previous wars would have perished from disease, were surviving. The long-term costs in medical care and welfare benefits was a burden on a scale never before encountered in the West. Every combatant nation felt obligated to develop medical and welfare benefits for returning soldiers and the dependants of those who had died. Australia was far from unique in this, and the schemes introduced closely paralleled those in other nations. In one sense, the rhetoric of extreme Australian sacrifice was unnecessary, for in this context, relativities hardly mattered. In another sense, however, the cry of Anzac 'blood sacrifice' was a powerful rhetorical device to press for ever-greater benefits.[6]

In hindsight, what is striking about the early discussions of assistance for returned soldiers is their naivety. How innocent, and yet clinical, were the first debates on the need for a pension scheme. In late 1914, the Fisher Labor government instructed the Commonwealth Statistician, George Knibbs, to calculate the potential cost to the taxpayer of a war pensions scheme. Drawing on other studies, which suggested that the annual mortality rate in combatant forces over the previous hundred years was 5 per cent (although Knibbs noted that the American Civil War rate was 7 per cent), he estimated that Australia might have to provide death benefits for just over 1000 men and pensions for a further 1630, at a cost of £230,000 per annum. Of course, he noted that costs would rise in proportion

---

6 For a discussion of some of the social welfare and medical aspects of war, see T. Skocpol, *Protecting Soldiers and Mothers: The Political Origins of Social Policy in the United States*, Harvard University Press, Cambridge, Mass.,1988, pp. 7–189; R. Wall & J. Winter (eds), *The Upheaval of War: Family, Work and Welfare in Europe 1914–18*, CUP, Cambridge, 1988.

to the number of troops sent and the duration of the war. Opposition members pointed to this flaw in the argument and cited the example of the USA, where they maintained the pension disbursements for all wars since the Revolution amounted to an astronomical four and a half billion dollars.[7] Despite the Opposition bombast, it was clear that no one in the Parliament seriously believed that the nation would suffer a huge pension burden and the Bill passed with little trouble in 1914. These comforting projections were soon made ridiculous. But such condescension misses the point. It is important to recognise the unpreparedness of Australians for the enormity of the repatriation task that would confront them. Policies and programs, and the principles that informed them, were developed on the run, revised, and revised again in the light of changed circumstances and perceptions. In 1914 and 1915 there were three pension Acts, in 1916 an act to regulate repatriation funds, and from 1917 to 1921, four more repatriation Acts, each amending the former. More followed in the 1920s and 1930s, and again during the Second World War, to accommodate a new generation of returned men and women. Suffice to say, the early history of repatriation policy is one of hesitant experimentation.

This is evident in the overlap of public and private provisions for returned servicemen and women. On the one hand, governments recognised their obligation to provide pensions for soldiers and their dependants. Britain had a long history of grants for disabled soldiers, unable to complete their contract of service (which would entitle them to a normal military pension). From 1593, these grants became a statutory right rather than a Royal Bounty. And in legislation passed by Cromwell in 1643, widows and children were entitled to benefits. Public provision extended to institutional care for ill, disabled, aged, and infirm soldiers and sailors, with the opening of the Chelsea Hospital in 1682 and the Greenwich Hospital for Sailors in 1705. Nonetheless, there was still debate about whether disablement pensions should be a right or a bounty from the Crown. With the establishment of the Chelsea Hospital, the responsibility for pensioning was devolved to the commissioners of the hospital, but the pension itself was once again made a Royal Bounty. In 1806, it was made a statutory right again, but within twenty years it had reverted to a bounty administered by the Chelsea Commissioners. And while sailor pensions were a statutory right, army disablement pensions remained a Royal Bounty until the Second World War. On the other side of the Atlantic, the United States Continental Congress undertook to provide for disabled soldiers in 1776. The first general pension law was passed in 1818, and the subsequent provision of pensions was broadly based – so broad that many outside the USA recoiled in horror at the expense involved in pensioning the veterans of the Civil War.[8]

---

7   Australia, House of Representatives, *Debates*, vol. 76, 1914–17, pp. 1896–1902.
8   See E. A. Parry & A. E. Codrington, *War Pensions: Past and Present*, Nisbet and Co., London, 1918; J.M. Hogge & T. H. Garside, *War Pensions and Allowances*, Hodder & Stoughton, London, 1918.

A public obligation to provide pensions for returned men and the dependants of those who perished was an established tradition in Anglophone democracies. Even though the British tradition was technically to provide pensions as a gift, in practice it was a right accorded to all those killed or injured in service. Australian politicians, regardless of party division, were united in their support for a 'fair and reasonable' system of pensions, making 'due provision for our soldiers, their wives, children and dependants'. There were quibbles over the details, the government claiming theirs was the most liberal scheme in the Empire, and the Opposition disputing this liberality. But the principle of public provision and the hope that such provision would inspire patriotism and foster enlistment was shared across the parliamentary spectrum. On the other hand, governments were eager to encourage private contributions to the war effort and, as the war ground on, the increasingly burdensome task of repatriation. As the casualty lists grew longer, beyond all expectations, it was clear that pensions could not be the sole means of assistance.

Governments and patriotic citizens began to realise that there was a need for hospital and medical services, rehabilitation schemes for the incapacitated, and a need to get the returning men back to work. Each week the field of endeavour seemed to expand as new social problems arose. Financing and organising these enterprises, however, was a major concern. Throughout the war, governments raised numerous war loans by public subscription. But private citizens were also active in raising patriotic and comforts funds to aid soldiers overseas. Some of these funds were also used to care for returned soldiers and their dependants. Private organisations established convalescent hospitals, provided food and clothing for impoverished soldier families, contributed to the medical expenses of widows and children, funded the education of children orphaned by the deaths of their fathers at war, and established workshops for the training and employment of incapacitated soldiers. Prominent societies such as Red Cross, St John's Ambulance, YMCA, and War Chest and Comforts funds all played an important role in these activities. Much of this was an extension of traditional philanthropic ventures, and many of the prominent citizens involved in patriotic funds and organisations were the scions of Australia's old philanthropic elite. As with Victorian charity, women were often in the forefront of these endeavours. Lady Helen Munro-Ferguson, the wife of the Governor-General, was a patron of many of these societies. In most states, there was a Lady Mayoress's Fund, a League of Loyal Women, and many other groups led by prominent women, such as Mrs Ann Chisholm in Sydney, and Mrs P. N. Robertson and Mrs T. W. White (daughter of Alfred Deakin) in Melbourne. Men, however, had the financial muscle, and prominent citizens such as Adrian Knox, Norman Brookes, and W. L. Baillieu donated large sums, and enormous time and energy to these activities. It was from this philanthropic impulse that the Australian Soldiers Repatriation Fund was established in 1916. Such efforts were applauded by the government, partly because they were anxious to spread the financial burden, but also because, as the Minister for Defence, Senator George Pearce, declared, 'there is value in what is called the civic virtue of community. There is a value in cultivating in the minds of our people a spirit of generosity and a recognition of our responsibility'.[9]

It is difficult to believe that politicians hoped to rely on private charity to fund repatriation but in 1916 the full dimensions of the problem were yet to dawn on Australians. But they dawned quickly, brought on by more casualties and criticism of the administration of the Repatriation Fund. In the same year, William Holman, Premier of New South Wales, argued that 'it is essential that these matters should be lifted out of the domain of voluntary and spontaneous action and organised by the State itself'.[10] The problem with voluntary effort, for critics like Holman, was that it was burdened with all the drawbacks of Victorian charity: it focused on some groups and ignored others, wasted resources by duplicating effort, and undermined the 'moral fibre' of the recipients by making them reliant rather than self-sufficient. These concerns had been the basis of Australia's first experiments in social welfare at the turn of the century, and while many still valued voluntary activity, there were other voices which proclaimed that the state was the only entity capable of coordinating, funding, and administering repatriation. These voices grew louder. In 1917 the Hughes government introduced a new Bill to create a comprehensive repatriation scheme to be funded from the public purse. Private efforts were still important, and remained so throughout the interwar years, but an 'organised effort on behalf of the community', as Littleton Groom, Honorary Minister introducing the Bill proclaimed, was needed 'to adequately care for those returned soldiers'.[11] Hereafter, the major task of organising soldier repatriation fell to public, rather than private, authorities.

The field of repatriation was charted in the first Repatriation Act of 1917. Although it underwent numerous amendments thereafter, the essential features of repatriation policy were there at the beginning. Senator Edward Millen, soon to be the first Minister for Repatriation, set out the scope of the legislation in presenting the Bill. Pensions for soldiers and their dependants were well established and were now to be part of the repatriation system. In addition, the government sought to assist the re-employment of returning servicemen and women by establishing labour bureaus for the able-bodied, providing gifts and loans for tools and equipment, vocational training to assist those whose apprenticeships and education were disrupted by enlistment, and rehabilitation training for the incapacitated. For the injured and sick, the government undertook to provide free medical and hospital care, hostels and homes for the totally incapacitated and the tubercular soldier, and artificial limbs for the limbless. Schemes were established to settle returned men on the land, and assist in the building and purchase of homes. In 1920 the government also instituted a war gratuity for all returned men, a one-off

---

9 Australia, Senate, *Debates*, vol. 80, 1914–17, p. 7811. On patriotic funds, see Scott, *Australia During the War*, pp. 697–738.
10 W. A. Holman, *The State's Duty to the Soldier*, Government Printer, Sydney, 1916, p. 1.
11 Australia, House of Representatives, *Debates*, vol. 82, 1917–19, p. 838.

payment of one shilling and sixpence for every day of service (although deferred as a redeemable bond for five years). There was also a fund for the education of the children of deceased soldiers, and efforts to ensure employment preference for returned men in the Commonwealth public service.

In the 1930s, new pensions were added for the aged and the permanently unemployable returned serviceman. During the Second World War these benefits were granted to a new generation of returned men and women, although there was much greater emphasis on employment and education training for veterans of this war, with the establishment of the Commonwealth Rehabilitation Training Scheme (CRTS). Where the emphasis after the First World War had been on returning men and women to their pre-war occupations, the CRTS aimed to equip returned men and women with new skills and qualifications that would be appropriate to the developing industrial economy envisaged by post-war reconstruction planners. All these benefits were later made available to veterans of wars and conflicts in Korea, Malaya, Vietnam, and the Middle East. Despite these changes in emphasis and the addition of some new schemes and benefits, then, the central platforms of the public commitment to repatriation were present in 1917.

The principles underpinning these policies were also clear from the beginning. Edward Millen put the case. Repatriation was the means for reinstating 'the fit in their former or similar occupations and to restore as far as ... possible the disabled so that they may regain full participation in the activities of life'. Australia, then, owed an obligation to those 'who fought in defence of the Empire', and the nation was resolved 'to redeem the debt as far as redemption was possible'. He warned, however, that repatriation was not charity, a war bonus, a payment for service, a reward for sacrifice, or a gift of gratitude, but an effort to re-establish the 'returned man' in civil life. 'It cannot make you successful', he stressed, 'but it can provide you with the means of making yourselves successful'. Here were the essential elements of subsequent repatriation discourse: duty, obligation, debt, reinstatement, re-establishment, and independence. These stood in contrast to their opposites: charity and idleness. For Millen, 'every idle man was a loss to the nation'.[12] Similar ideas shaped repatriation rhetoric in the 1940s. Prime Minister, Ben Chifley, talked of the obligation owed to servicemen and the need to repay the debt through efforts to re-establish them in 'useful jobs'. Post-war reconstruction journals talked of the need for initiative on the part of returned men if they were to gain their rightful place in society. Planners of Australia's post-war world, such as H.C. Coombs, had less faith in these traditional entreaties. For Coombs, there was an urgent need for 'a more genuinely humanitarian and less sentimentally charitable point of view' in the treatment of returned servicemen and women. It had to be recognised, he argued, that these people 'can themselves be altered,

---

12 E. D. Millen, *What Australia is Doing for Her Returned Soldiers*, Government Printer, Melbourne, n.d., pp. 1–10; 'Repatriation: Australia's First Great Post-War Problem', *Australia Today*, 21 November 1917, pp. 55–71.

themselves be assisted in a way which will make it possible for them to fit themselves into the post-war world' and allow them to 'contribute genuinely to the work of the community'.[13] Ever present in all these statements was the spectre of idleness and charity. The vision, then, was partly Victorian, in its fear of dependency, and partly modern, in its assertion of a right to entitlement. Despite the emergence of a welfare state and a comprehensive repatriation system, the key principles underpinning these efforts remained the dignity of work and the horror of dependency.

The ideas impelling repatriation may have been clear, but agreement on the best means for administering the range of schemes involved in this re-establishment effort were opaque. Initially war pensions were overseen by a War Pensions Board, composed of prominent citizens. Within a year, the difficulty of administering a national scheme through a single board in Melbourne forced the government to transfer control to the existing Old Age and Invalid Pension Commission, under the umbrella of Treasury. Its structure of local and state Pension Boards facilitated the decentralisation of pensions administration, a reform that was considered essential to the efficient handling of applications. The 1917 Repatriation Act replaced the Pension Commission with a Repatriation Commission comprised of seven honorary commissioners. The following year a Repatriation Department was formed to administer other benefits, although the actual administration of benefits and training programs was devolved to State Repatriation Boards and local repatriation committees. This idea of local assistance was further extended in 1919, with the establishment of the local medical officer system: usually general practitioners registered with the commission to provide free medical care for war-caused problems suffered by returned men and women. Local committees and medical officers would ensure that returned men and women had close contact with government authorities, and that these authorities could respond quickly to the needs of servicemen and women in their area.

Elements of this system, however, were the subject of intense criticism from soldier representatives. They disliked the idea of honorary commissioners because, as the President of the Returned Soldiers' Association complained, it placed 'soldiers in the undignified position of accepting doles from any patriotic committee'. In 1919 the RSL pointed to the essential confusion in the division of responsibility between the Department of Defence, which controlled health and hospital services, Treasury, which controlled pensions, and the Department of Repatriation, which controlled all other benefits. Moreover, State War Councils administered the privately subscribed Repatriation Fund but State Repatriation Boards controlled the public finances and benefits. Soldier groups advocated a

---

13 See J. B. Chifley, 'The Challenge of Peace', in A. W. Stargardt (ed.), *Things Worth Fighting For: Speeches by Joseph Benedict Chifley*, MUP, Melbourne, 1952, pp. 15–16; Editorial, 'Initiative and Mateship', *Change Over*, vol. 1, no. 2, October 1946, p. 2; H. C. Coombs, *The Special Problems of Planning*, MUP, Melbourne, 1944, pp. 3–7.

central commission of three paid businessmen, free of political and ministerial control, with a guarantee that a returned soldier be one of the commissioners, and with all aspects of repatriation to be placed within one department. Most importantly, it was crucial that repatriation not be charity. Unfortunately, they argued, the connection between the administration of war pensions and old-age pensions fostered this impression. Hughes was exasperated by these criticisms, replying 'I can't work miracles'. Senator Millen, the butt of constant jibes in returned-soldier journals about his inefficiency and prevarication, was driven to a grudging apology, conceding that some repatriation policies had been 'less successful', but pointing out that, after all, repatriation 'was a story of experimentation'.[14]

The Hughes government was hardly likely to cede control of repatriation to businessmen and returned-soldier representatives, but in 1920 it did move to resolve some of the endemic administrative difficulties in the scheme. The Repatriation Fund was dissolved, as were the State War Councils, and the administration of pensions transferred from Treasury to the Repatriation Commission. The commission itself was restructured as a board of three paid members. The State Boards and Local Repatriation Committees were retained, although, now with pensions, their responsibilities were considerably greater. Returned-soldier groups were less than pleased with the provision that a representative of one of their organisations 'may' be appointed as a commissioner, but in practice there was always a returned-soldier representative. There were still ambiguities. The commission itself was a statutory authority, but was under the control of a Minister of Repatriation. As such, the officers charged with administering the commission's work were public servants in the Department of Repatriation. Even among those with some acquaintance with the system, there was often confusion in the use of the terms department and commission, something that would remain until the department was renamed the Department of Veterans' Affairs in 1976. A major concern of returned soldiers was that appeals against the decisions of the commission had to heard by the commission. They charged that this was just a system of 'Caesar appealing to Caesar'. In 1929, in response to such criticisms, an Entitlement Appeals Tribunal and an Assessment Appeals Tribunal were established, and although this did not silence the criticism that the commission was still in control, it created important avenues of appeal for returned men and women dissatisfied with either the rejection of their application or the level of their assessment.[15]

---

14 See Australia, House of Representatives, *Debates*, vol. 82, 1917–19, pp. 275–6; Returned Sailors and Soldiers Imperial League of Australia, *Report of Conference of League Delegates with the Prime Minister W.M Hughes, 11 September 1919*, RSSILA, Melbourne, 1919, pp. 3–9; E. D. Millen, 'Foreword', *Repatriation*, vol. 1, no. 1, March 1919, p. 1.
15 See Lloyd & Rees, *The Last Shilling*, pp. 209–40; L. J. Pryor, The Origins of Australia's Repatriation Policy, MA thesis, University of Melbourne, 1932, pp. 12–176. For the 'Caesar'

This, then, was the basic framework for the administration of repatriation. The scale of its operations was enormous and continued to grow. By 1938, 257,000 Australians were being assisted by war pensions – only a few thousand less than those in receipt of old-age and invalid pensions – and a further 3600 were receiving service pensions. In addition, there were 1600 men still in hostels and homes for the permanently incapacitated, and around 23,000 outpatients in repatriation hospitals each year. Similarly, by the late 1930s, 20,000 children had received education assistance, 21,000 homes had been built, over 4000 artificial limbs had been supplied, 133,000 jobs had been found through the department's Labour Bureaus, 28,000 had undergone training courses (many of whom had received sustenance allowances during their training), others had received gifts of tools and furniture, and 40,000 had been placed on the land. All returning men had received a war gratuity. This assistance entailed considerable expense. In 1938 the annual cost of repatriation benefits, including medical services, was nearly £18 million, just under one-fifth of all Commonwealth expenditure.

The advent of new wars and the ageing of the veteran population further burdened the public purse. By 1958 there were over 600,000 war pension beneficiaries and a further 42,000 assisted by service pensions, at a total cost of £55 million. Funds spent on medical and hospital services were the other great expenditure. In 1958 there were 4498 in-patients and 397,000 out-patients in repatriation hospitals, and in all, local medial officers conducted nearly a million repatriation consultations. All this added £11 million to the annual bill. In addition, 70,000 homes had been built and 20,000 Second World War veterans had undergone vocational training and education. Altogether, repatriation was now costing about £86 million a year, or 6 per cent of all Commonwealth expenditure, a lower proportion than in 1938 but this reflected more the shift in Commonwealth and State responsibilities after WWII. Before the Second World War most welfare expenditure and administration had been the preserve of the states, but during the war, the Commonwealth assumed control from the states of income tax revenues and established itself as a major provider of welfare benefits. The cost of repatriation was expanding to meet the needs of a significantly larger repatriation population. Slowly, however, this population began to decline. Mortality and the significantly smaller engagements in Korea, Malaya, and Vietnam reduced the burden. But by the mid-1980s there were still 375,000 war-pension and a further 400,000 service-pension beneficiaries (an indicator of the ageing of the veterans), 59,000 were being treated in repatriation hospitals, and by then, over 100,000 war service homes had been built. Altogether, repatriation services cost over $3 billion a year in the 1980s.[16]

---

comments, see Federal President, Royal Australian Armoured Corps Association to Prime Minister, 18 August 1949, RSL Papers, 3374C.

16 Figures compiled from Repatriation Department, *Annual Reports*, 1921–58; Department of Veterans' Affairs, *Annual Reports*, 1980–90; *Commonwealth Year Books, 1921–86*.

By any standard, the repatriation system was a large and extensive program of social welfare, amounting in many respects to a second welfare state, and one still largely unrecognised by welfare historians. But comparisons between war and civilian welfare systems should not be drawn only in terms of the scale of benefits, the amount of expenditure, or the numbers assisted. It is arguable that the emergence of a large and expensive system of benefits for returned servicemen and women had a significant effect on the growth of the civilian welfare state in Australia. At the turn of the century Australia was famed for its social experiments. In providing old-age and invalid pensions, workers' compensation, a 'living wage', protective factory and shop legislation, and maternity allowances, all before 1914; Australia was at the forefront of social provision. After the First World War, Australia's social welfare system languished, surpassed by most other nations, which introduced similar and usually more extensive benefits. By contrast, there were virtually no new welfare reforms in Australia between the wars. One possible reason was the peculiar nature of the Australian system of social security. It was funded out of general revenue, whereas most other nations developed insurance-based schemes. Defenders of the Australian model claimed that it was more socially just, requiring the 'better-off', who paid taxes, to support the needy. But the other side of this coin was that governments, in order to limit the call on public funds, introduced means, income, and assets tests to ensure that only the 'very needy' qualified for assistance. Critics declared that this system encouraged dependency; instead, they favoured insurance, which required individuals to contribute towards their welfare during their working lives.

The flaw in the Australian model was that general revenue was a well from which many drew, and governments were always reluctant to raise taxes to fund new schemes or increase the benefits of existing ones. Repatriation was a significant drain on public revenue, and was only partly offset by war loans, and by patriotic and repatriation funds. In the squeeze on resources that resulted, it was the civilian welfare system that suffered. In the interwar years, a welfare apartheid emerged in Australia, dividing the civilian population (which had to rely on limited benefits that were restricted to those who met narrow eligibility criteria) from the men and women (and their families) who had served their country in war, and who were entitled to relatively generous pension, unemployment, education, training, and medical benefits. This gap was not narrowed until extensive welfare reforms were instituted by the Curtin and Chifley Labor governments of the 1940s. This increased provision was only possible, however, through the expansion of the tax base, requiring many of the less well-off to contribute directly to general revenue for the first time. Even so, the welfare benefits available to civilians still fell well short of those available to veterans and their dependants.[17]

---

17 See S. Garton, *Out of Luck: Poor Australians and Social Welfare 1788–1988*, Allen & Unwin, Sydney, 1990, pp. 84–150.

This gap between the welfare available to veterans and civilians had particular consequences for Australian women. At the very moment when women had achieved political citizenship through the vote, war intervened to establish new criteria for social citizenship, which effectively excluded them from acceptance as full citizens. Although Australian nurses who served overseas during the First World War were entitled to repatriation benefits, they were few in number. Even with the greater involvement of women in the services during the Second World War, eligibility criteria focused primarily on injuries and illnesses arising out of active service, and different scales of benefits dependent on the theatre of service favoured those who served overseas over those who served in Australia. Women mainly served at home, and this left the majority of them in the lower class of repatriation beneficiaries. Australian governments had made this painfully obvious by referring to 'Soldier Repatriation' in the title of the relevant legislation; it was a scheme designed for men, mainly soldiers, rather than women. The widows and mothers of deceased soldiers qualified for war pensions, but their eligibility was based on their economic dependence on these men and the number of children they had to support. Australian women were doubly disadvantaged. In the civilian welfare system, benefits were restricted to all but the most needy on the assumption that most women would be dependent on male breadwinners, and that they would be supported through the living wage for men (women only received about half the male wage). In the repatriation welfare system, they had few opportunities for extensive benefits, except as dependants of returned or deceased soldiers. Despite enfranchisement, war helped cement the dependence of women on either a male breadwinner or the state.[18]

II

Australian politicians (except when in Opposition) proudly proclaimed the 'liberality' of repatriation. They pointed, with some justification, to the enormous public investment, the extensive range of policies for the reinstatement of men and women in civil life, and the humane care of those whose incapacity rendered them incapable of normal occupation. They pointed also to schemes providing for the widows, children, and even, in some instances, the parents of deceased servicemen and women. But what did the servicemen and women themselves think of the repatriation system? By its very nature, the repatriation archive is more likely to be a repository of complaint than compliment. This takes us to the heart of the psychology of benefit. It was not in the interests of recipients to accept that what they received was generous. Despite the rhetoric of rights and entitlement, both recipients and providers commonly saw their relationship as adversarial. This arose

---

18 J. Roe, 'Chivalry and Social Policy in the Antipodes', *Historical Studies*, vol. 22, no. 88, April 1987, pp. 395–410.

out of the nature of the system, particularly in relation to pensions. Returned men and women, and their dependants, had to prove that any disability or illness arose out of war service. The Repatriation Department had to test the validity of every claim. By its very nature, the provision of benefits pitted returned men and women against the department. It is not surprising, then, that complaint was the more likely response.

Impelling this psychology of complaint, however, was the cultural context in which returned men and women accepted their benefits. As a privileged class of welfare recipients, with more generous benefits than those provided for civilians, they were sometimes the target of envy and resentment. Occasional complaints about soldiers being on 'the pig's back', public campaigns by trade unions against soldier employment preference schemes, and the older tradition of attaching moral opprobrium to welfare dependency made it preferable to assert that benefits were not very generous, and their administration harsh and miserly, rather than admit that they received a fair deal. The threat of public condemnation was ever present, even if it rarely surfaced. When it did, veterans were left in little doubt about their status. In 1919, the *Sydney Morning Herald* ran a series of articles on 'defects' in the repatriation system, declaring that the department 'has been choked with the claims lodged by unworthy applicants' and, worse, that 'a great waste of time, money and effort occurs before the repatriation machine rejects the undesirable'. Fifty years later the *Financial Review* published an article on 'The Repatriation Industry', charging that repatriation was a 'public scandal', pensions were 'a licence to lurk', and pensioners in 'repat' hospitals were mainly 'malingerers, alcoholics and no-hopers'. In between, articles of similar tone appeared every few years. These may not have been representative views, but they did tap into subterranean currents of public antagonism.[19]

The individual response to this atmosphere varied enormously. A few men, believing that they no longer required pensions, relinquished them. One of these was Richard C, a farm labourer in Queensland, who suffered multiple gunshot wounds in the shoulder and back while serving in France. In 1920, however, he requested that his pension be cancelled because he was now 'in good health and permanent employment'. Some others, such as William V of Edenhope Victoria, also suffering from gunshot wounds, were aware of the resentment towards 'repat' pensioners. William wrote to cancel his pension, explaining; 'I feel I cannot face examination in such a public manner ... [this] is a small place and among those in the district are many anti-sympathisers. Being a public man I cannot parade myself for a pension'. Almost 2 per cent of our sample of First World War pensioners voluntarily surrendered their pensions. But others, from all wars, did not even apply for assistance, believing that such action was a shameful admission of

---

19 See *Sydney Morning Herald*, 17–19 February 1919; *Financial Review*, 17–19 January 1973.

weakness. They, like Donald Horne's father, despised those ex-soldiers who tried to cash in on their war service.[20]

These are the cases that leave few records, except in oral testimony and memoirs. But if the considerable number of people applying for benefits is any guide, most returned servicemen and women sought assistance as an earned entitlement of service. In some instances, there was even appreciation of the benefits provided. The Repatriation Department received numerous letters of gratitude, but these were usually from relatives of seriously ill or recently deceased returned servicemen, thanking the nursing and medical staff of repatriation hospitals for the 'wonderful' care provided for the men.[21] More commonly, however, the system was the object of criticism. Men frequently complained that they were treated as 'criminals' and 'malingerers', and sometimes openly abused as 'drongos' and 'hypochondriacs' by officers of the department. Such assertions may be the product of the disgruntled minority, denied what they saw as their legitimate entitlement, but such impressions were fostered by the very nature of provision. Applicants, particularly for pensions, had to answer numerous questions on forms and were later interviewed by commission tribunals to test the validity of their claims. In such a context, it is understandable that some felt as if they were 'on trial' or 'prisoners in the dock'. This underlying suspicion of recipients is still evident. In 1989 Lesley Whalen, a law student, accompanied her father to a 'hearing' before the Veterans Review Board. She was horrified at the formality of the proceedings, the lack of information provided about the nature of the hearing, the type of documentation required, and the presumption by tribunal members that her father was trying to claim a benefit to which he was not entitled. She wrote afterwards complaining of the 'prosecutorial style' of the tribunal.[22] Applicants had to struggle against an entrenched culture of suspicion in the commission. In a 1954 review of pension administration, the committee concluded that many of the men were more concerned with their disability, in the hope of increasing their pension rate, than vocational training. This was 'just a habit of a man trying every avenue to get anything he can'. Even prominent federal politicians, such as Sir Fred Chaney, minister in the Menzies government, were convinced that the system was full of 'discontented soldiers and people wanting more and more from the government' and that most were trying to get 'sicker' to 'get more money'.[23]

---

20 Cases from Department of Veterans' Affairs, Case Files, M, CRS J35 and CRS B73. Calculations from our sample of case files. See also Horne, *The Education of Young Donald*, p. 84.
21 Department of Veterans' Affairs, Correspondence, M, SP 1375, box 401.
22 For details of the 'drongo' accusations, see State Secretary, Victorian Branch to National Secretary, 28 June 1973, RSL Papers, 1988 series, box 33. For comments on the 'trial' atmosphere, see A. P. Derham to Beau, 6 October 1 960, A. P. Derham Papers, Melbourne University Archives, 7/1/2. On the Whalen case, see Lesley Whalen to Veterans Review Board, 30 January 1989 (held by S. Garton).
23 Review of Scheme Report, 11 October 1 954, Department of Veterans' Affairs, Correspondence, M, SPI375, box 447; Interview with Sir Fred Chaney 1983–4, Transcript, Battye Library, OH 636, pp. 275–7.

The criticisms of disgruntled applicants have an obvious basis in experience. But there were other more organised voices of complaint. These were framed and propagated by those who claimed to represent the interests of returned men and women: returned-services groups, chiefly the RSL, and other self-styled champions, notably the sensationalist and populist (not to mention characteristically racist and misogynist) weekly newspaper *Smith's Weekly*, financed by Sydney hotelier, racecourse-owner, and flamboyant entrepreneur, Sir James Joynton Smith. There were some tensions between these champions. *Smith's* frequently condemned the RSL as 'soft'. But such rivalry masks a deeper unity of approach. They were appealing to a particular constituency (readers and members), and success lay in tapping into the well-springs of resentment towards the repatriation system. It was only through criticism that they could hope to increase the pressure on governments to improve benefits. Such organs of opinion were locked in a public campaign of opposition and criticism in the interests of returned men and women. But the increasing influence of the RSL as a lobby group embroiled the organisation in the bureaucracy, making it vulnerable to the charge that they had sold the men out. In the 1930s, and again in the 1960s, disgruntled members resigned from the League, charging that it was not pushing returned-soldier interests hard enough. 'We are not satisfied', they declared, and 'we have not lost the will to fight'.[24]

There was an obvious danger in being seen to be too influential in the formulation of government policy, and the League had to negotiate a difficult path between fully representing the complaints of its constituency and maintaining effective relations with the department; a wrong step either way threatened charges of 'softness' or dismissal as 'cranks'. But the appeal of the RSL and *Smith's Weekly* lay in their voicing of a stream of complaint as a means of pressing for new benefits. In so doing, they challenged the view that repatriation was an overly generous system for the 'loafer'. Of the myriad criticisms, two dominated public discourse: employment preference and unfair pension decisions. The focus on jobs is not surprising. In the context of widespread concern about repatriation being a form of charity, it was vital for soldier representatives to assert that returned men preferred jobs to handouts. As William Fitzpatrick, representative of the Victorian State War Council, declared in 1917, the aim of repatriation was 'to find work for the men'.[25] A key platform in achieving this was employment preference. This was a commitment of the Hughes government, enshrined in the *Public Service Act 1915*, and the principle itself dated back to the *Defence Act 1903*. These Acts sought to ensure that no employer penalised an employee for enlisting in the armed services. But from an early stage, soldier groups declared that employers were not living up to their promises, and in fact, preference was being given to civilians. In 1916, *The Soldier*

---

[24] Veterans to General Secretary RSL, 1 January 1962, RSL Papers, 4795C.
[25] W. Fitzpatrick, *The Repatriation of the Soldier*, Victorian State War Council, Melbourne, 1917, pp. 7–9.

charged that 'those who strike for the Empire abroad are less favoured than those who strike for the enemy at home'.[26]

This was a theme repeated throughout the war and interwar years. In 1919, the League and other returned-services groups organised a march in Melbourne, demanding that the government live up to its preference promise. Spokesmen insisted that all those in the Commonwealth public service who had been eligible but had failed to enlist be dismissed to make jobs available to returned men. *Smith's Weekly* talked of the 'dud preference' scheme, and there were numerous protests about the plight of unemployed diggers and their anger at seeing 'shirkers' and 'stay-at-homes' in jobs that should have been reserved for returned men. Returned soldier groups charged that many had gone to war with the assurances of 'patriotic' employers about job security ringing in their ears. On their return, they discovered that the boss had employed someone else and refused to dismiss him to make way for the legitimate right of the soldier. Worse, in some instances women had replaced men, and even if the returned man came back to his old job, these women had managed to gain promotion: 'imagine a man', *The Soldier* asked, 'returning to a firm who promised to keep his billet and having to take orders from a girl'. These charges persisted throughout the Second World War and the immediate post-war years. Despite the reaffirmation of the preference principle in the *Re-establishment and Employment Act 1945*, returned-soldier groups still proclaimed that, in practice, the policy was 'preference to deserters'. Newspapers carried the complaints of these groups about the post-war jobs scramble and the unscrupulous actions of employers who refused to fulfil their preference promises.[27]

The problem with employment preference lay in vague legislation and unrealistic expectations. These provisions stated that employers should not penalise an employee and, after 1945, that they should actually give preference to returned servicemen. The problem here, as soldier groups continually argued, was the ambiguity of 'should'. In fact, there was nothing to compel employers to reemploy returned men, or to force them to employ them in preference to civilians when new jobs became available. Employers seemed to have a variety of excuses to get around the 'should' provision: the job was no longer available; they could not sack someone who was doing the job well; the job was now different; the returned man no longer had the skills required for the position; the employer had no money to put on extra staff, and so on. Moreover, it was clear that governments faced considerable opposition from business to these stipulations. In 1919, the Premier of New South Wales, William Holman, echoed these business arguments when he explained that

---

26 Editorial, 'Turned Down', *The Soldier*, 14 July 1916.
27 See *Sydney Morning Herald*, 8 January 1919; Editorial, 'Women or Soldiers?', *The Soldier*, 31 January 1919; 'Diggers' Rights', *Smith's Weekly*, 6 March 1920; 'Preference to Deserters', *Smith's Weekly*, 2 February 1946; 'Protests at Jobs Scramble', *Sydney Morning Herald*, 5 January 1946; 'Digger Job Lag' and 'Dedman Scorns Diggers' Threat', *Courier Mail*, 28 February 1946.

preference legislation had to balance the interests of the returned man against those of the decent and patriotic employer. To compel employment preference was to make the patriotic employer vulnerable to competition from the 'unscrupulous' employer, who found a way around these requirements. Implicit in this argument was the view that many of the returned men, scarred by their experiences and weakened by injuries and illness, were not always the best employees. In the end, companies and firms had to be efficient, and this meant interfering as little as possible in the employment practices of business. Governments legislated 'should' rather than 'must'.[28]

There were other pressures that weakened legislative resolve on preference. Like business, trade unions were firm opponents of soldier preference provisions. The unions, arguing that it contravened long-standing labour principles of union preference, maintained a firm opposition to the policy from the very beginning. Labor was rarely in power at the federal level in the interwar years, and so governments did not have to appeal to this constituency for votes, but the threat of strikes and work to rule was a weapon that dissuaded conservative governments from pursuing compulsory preference. Union opposition continued throughout the Second World War. In 1944, the ACTU passed a resolution opposing soldier preference, arguing that it was unnecessary in view of the government's stated aim of full employment. Just in case this argument failed, it went on to assert that 'workers have borne as much hardship and suffering in this war as the men who fought'. Such assertions were dismissed as 'humbug' by soldier groups and the conservative press.[29] But unions were at one with business in opposing rigid preference provisions, much to the anger and resentment of returned-soldier organisations.

The only sphere in which governments could legitimately compel preference was in the public service. Through a series of Acts, the Commonwealth and many of the states legislated for preference. Even here, however, there were hurdles to the full realisation of the hopes of returned-services groups. Public service principles of seniority and permanency militated against careers for returned men. They were often employed at lower levels and had to work their way up the ladder in competition with younger men and women. Moreover, many resented the fact that they were initially employed in temporary roles, rendering them ineligible for promotion to higher positions. In reply to a complaint from a returned soldier being passed over for appointment to a higher grade, the Secretary of the Public Service Commission explained, in best 'Sir Humphrey' style, that 'appointments of persons not on the permanent staff ... are made only in cases where there are no permanent officers ... available with the necessary qualifications to fill the vacancies'. In practice, the only department with a consistent soldier preference policy was the Repatriation Department. This policy was followed partly in response to the

---

28 *Sydney Morning Herald*, 12 March 1919.
29 Editorial, 'Employment Preference', *Courier Mail*, 8 March 1944.

insistence of the RSL that only returned men had the necessary sympathy to be able to deal with the problems of their comrades. The majority of staff in the department, until the 1970s, were returned men and women – a situation that led other sections of the public service to view Repatriation as a 'backwater' to be avoided at all costs.[30]

Although returned-servicemen's groups were insistent that the right to work was their major priority, they were equally adamant that all those who qualified for a war pension should receive their full entitlement. This apparent contradiction is not really so inconsistent when we realise that these organisations had many constituencies to cater for: the able-bodied and partially incapacitated who were capable of holding down jobs, the incapacitated, aged, alcoholic, and mentally and physically scarred returned serviceman, the dependants of these men, and the widows, children, and other dependants of those who died as a consequence of their service. It was the latter groups that deserved pensions, and it was the task of soldier representatives to push for the most generous pensions possible for these deserving cases. Part of the debt owed to these men and women was compensation for irreparable loss of physical and mental health. Returned-soldier groups preferred to see pensions as compensation rather than welfare. They drew the parallel with workers' compensation (and indeed much of the framework of war pension administration was modelled on workers' compensation provisions) as a means of escaping the 'stigma of charity'.

Nonetheless, the voices of returned-soldier opinion were acutely aware that the pension system was inherently adversarial. And while they may have accepted, in principle, the legitimacy of a system under which governments only assisted those whose claims were genuine, they strenuously opposed its consequences. One means of ensuring the best deal for returned men and women was to assist them in their negotiations with the Repatriation Department. Most local RSL sub-branches and each State branch had pension officers to inform members of their entitlements, assist them in filling out the forms, and advise them on any necessary appeals. These officers often also attended commission and tribunal hearings to support the applicant and, in many instances, argue their case. In their view, there was always hope, and occasionally pleasant surprise at the applications and appeals that succeeded. In 1973, the State Secretary of the Queensland Branch urged the RSL to oppose departmental plans to cease sending appeal forms automatically to all rejected applicants. In his view, any attempt to curtail appeals was prejudicial to veterans because he had seen many 'frivolous' cases succeed.[31]

---

30 See Acting Secretary, Public Service Commission to General Secretary RSL, 21 January 1921, RSL Papers, 823A. For the negative view of 'Repat', I am relying on the opinion of a member of the Commonwealth Senior Executive Service; Interview with John Pomeroy, 25 May 1993.
31 State Secretary, Queensland Branch to National Secretary, 12 April 1973, RSL Papers, 1988 series, box 33.

In addition to acting for applicants, returned-services organisations conducted a continuous campaign to safeguard and improve pension provisions. One obvious concern was the actual rate of payment. In the initial pension debates, legislators asserted that pensions were designed to enable those with full incapacity to receive the equivalent of the living wage – the wage sufficient to keep a man, his wife, and three children in 'frugal comfort'. In the end, the top rate was considerably less than the living wage, but considerably more than the old-age and invalid pension – a vital distinction for returned servicemen. In 1920, the living wage was 82 shillings, the 100 per cent war pension 42 shillings, and the old-age pension fifteen shillings per week. War pensioners, however, received allowances for dependent children: ten shillings a week for the first child, seven shillings and sixpence for the second, and five shillings for each thereafter. This brought the base pension closer to the living wage for some pensioners, but even then, only 14 per cent of war pensioners were on the top rate. Of course, things were a little more generous if one had been at a higher rank. The highest paid officers at 100 per cent received 60 shillings a week plus allowances for any children. The gap between the 100 per cent pension and the living wage arose partly because the top pension was not actually the highest rate. As a result of a curious decision, 100 per cent incapacity did not mean total and permanent incapacity; instead, there was a 'special' (or TPI) pension for these men: £4 a week, plus 18 shillings for a dependent wife and allowances for children. A special pensioner, with a wife and three children (the notional living wage family) received 118 shillings and sixpence a week, nearly £2 a week more than the living wage. This was generous, but there were only 535 special pensioners in 1921.

Unlike the living wage, however, war pensions were not indexed to the cost of living. They were increased by a vote of Parliament, cementing the lobbying role of the RSL. Sometimes the League was relatively successful, notably in its campaign to insulate war pensions from budget cuts during the Great Depression. But after the Second World War, its fortunes were more mixed. In 1948, the RSL argued that the living wage had risen by 46 per cent, but war pensions had increased by only 19 per cent. Increases in 1953 and 1962 generally fell well short of the League's claims, and throughout the 1950s and 1960s it had to maintain a vigorous campaign to increase pension payments.[32]

Pension rates were not the only concern. Soldier groups also opposed provisions that threatened a right to a pension. They were particularly critical of the initial provision that no pension application could be made more than six months after discharge, or by dependants six months after the death of the pensioner, except at the discretion of the commission. They complained that war-related problems

---

32 Information on pension rates from *Australian Soldiers' Repatriation Act 1920* (Cwlth), Schedules; Repatriation Commission, Annual Reports, 1921–39. See also Butler, *The Australian Army Medical Services*, vol. 3, pp. 958–63. On the 1931–32 RSL campaign, see 'Report on Auditor-General's Criticism of Pensions', RSL Papers, 5491B. On the post-war campaigns, see, for example, Federal President to Minister of Repatriation, 27 August 1 948, RSL Papers, 2613C and 1955 Federal Executive Agenda, 4382C.

could occur many years after service and that these men should not be denied their entitlement. Equally, dependants, paralysed by grief, were often unable to submit their applications in time. The League was generally successful in these campaigns. These provisions were rarely enforced and were removed from the Act in the 1930s. Another problem confronted widows. Under the 1920 Repatriation Act, widows lost their pension two years after remarriage. *Smith's Weekly* claimed that this encouraged many men to live with war widows so that they too could live off the pension. But widows in these circumstances had their pensions cancelled on the assumption that a de facto marriage was equivalent to an actual marriage for pension entitlement purposes. The RSL took up this 'immorality' clause, arguing that it encouraged neighbours and relatives with a grudge against an innocent widow to 'dob' them in. The commission proved intractable on this issue and the provision remained.[33]

Another concern of returned-servicemen groups was the problem faced by those whose incapacity was deemed to be partial. The pension for these men was reduced in accordance with the extent to which their earning capacity was impaired. This was the principle, but in practice it was arbitrary. In many instances the relationship between disability and employment depended on the job. Some disabilities, such as the loss of a hand, might severely affect a blue-collar occupation but have no effect on a white-collar one. The logic of this was that each case had to be considered on its merits. Such a position was potentially costly and time-consuming, so instead the Repatriation Commission adopted the set scale of disability rates used in workers' compensation tribunals. For instance, a man with two limbs amputated was calculated at 100 per cent incapacity, as was one who lost both eyes. The loss of one limb was calculated at 75 per cent, one eye 50 per cent, and an amputated finger or toe only 10–35 per cent, depending on how much was missing. These were easily calculable rates. The rates for particular diseases, such as malaria, asthma, or gastroenteritis, were far more difficult to determine. Were such diseases a permanent impairment, and if so, to what extent? More difficult to quantify still were psychiatric problems, colloquially known as 'shell-shock'. Although the Repatriation Department used rough and ready tables to draw distinctions between the severity of particular diseases, many of these cases had to be assessed individually.

It was here that returned-services groups were locked in combat with the department. They fought many individual cases for returned men and women whose claim for a pension was rejected or whose rate of incapacity was deemed by the commission to be less than the League considered his or her due. The archives of the RSL and the Department of Veterans' Affairs are stuffed full of such appeals. For the RSL, it was not just a matter of pursuing individual cases. They also sought acceptance of a greater number of illnesses as 'war-caused' and hence

---

33   See 'Widows Pension' and 'Immorality and the Female Pension', RSL Papers, 520A and 6454B.

pensionable. They continually pressed the commission for judgments that diseases such as asthma, and stomach and lung cancer should qualify for a pension. The commission usually replied that there was no evidence linking such diseases to war experience. Some of this is apparent in the commission's rejection of venereal disease as pensionable. The RSL's criticism of this decision stretched the bounds of medical credibility. They claimed that, in many instances, venereal diseases 'were not contracted due to the fault of the serviceman' because many resulted from 'kissing, drinking out of an unclean vessel, and accidental contact of discharge to the eyes, cuts on vulnerable parts'. How these accidents occurred was never canvassed, but for sceptical commissioners, the RSL claim that the 'great majority of cases would not have happened had it not been that these men ... were in countries where VD was rampant' seemed to beg the question. Venereal diseases were generally caught on leave, and while this was technically service, it prevented the soldier from engaging in 'active service'. This was not a condition that the commission thought should be rewarded with a pension.[34]

One of the most significant controversies was over the phenomenon of the 'burnt-out' soldier. By the early 1930s, RSL welfare officers were becoming concerned about the number of cases of ageing and unemployed men seeking assistance. This problem reflected the ageing of the returned-soldier population and the increasing difficulty many faced as the effects of the Great Depression spread. But there were other reasons. Welfare officers were aware that many of these men were probably unemployable regardless of economic conditions. Some were vagabonds and alcoholics; others were surviving on charitable handouts. The problem was that many of these men had no pensionable disability and, not yet being sixty-five years of age, did not qualify for an old-age pension. Australia was not alone in experiencing this problem. In 1930 Canada had introduced a special pension for the 'burnt-out' veteran, and New Zealand followed suit in 1935. The RSL closely monitored these developments and adopted much of their rhetoric. They campaigned for a pension for men who were 'prematurely aged' and 'permanently unemployable' by virtue of their war experience. But the relationship between war and premature ageing was not really amenable to proof. This did not deter the League, who argued that the problem was a serious one and had already been recognised overseas. In 1936, the Lyons government passed legislation to introduce a 'Service Pension' for returned men aged over sixty and women over fifty-five years in impoverished circumstances (determined by a means test), those deemed permanently unemployable, and those suffering tuberculosis (whether war-caused or not). Within two years nearly 2000 service pensions were in place. By the 1950s there were 42,000 people supported by such pensions. But the significance of this pension was not just in the numbers who took advantage of it, but also in the precedent of government support for those who had no clear

---

34 State Secretary South Australia Branch to General Secretary, 14 April 1938, RSL Papers, 7590B.

disability but who struggled to accommodate themselves to the demands of civilian life.[35]

The key to the success of these campaigns for increased returned-soldier benefits was a sympathetic public. Returned-services organisations were very skilled at behind the scenes lobbying, but even this was dependent on the climate of public opinion. These organisations had to become adept at public relations. Duty, obligation, sacrifice, and debt were crucial elements in this repatriation discourse. Another dimension was the assertion that returned soldiers were continuing to suffer from the effects of their service and that the Repatriation Department was failing in its duty. The 'burnt-out' soldier was just one strategy in this broader campaign. Through the press, pamphlets, speeches, and spokesmen in Parliament, returned-soldier groups attempted to focus public attention on the plight of individual returned men, their continuing suffering, and the cruelty of the Repatriation Department in failing to meet their legitimate claim for assistance.

The pages of returned-services journals, such as *Reveille*, *Bayonet*, and *Duckboard*, were frequently the place for detailing the sorry plight of returned men and women. But these journals were merely appealing to an already sympathetic audience of veterans. More important were journals that could reach a wider audience. *Smith's Weekly* established itself as the defender of the interests of the returned man against all those in the repatriation system (League and department alike) who threatened his entitlements. It was committed to the cause but leavened this dour diet with a broader range of news, features, humour, and sporting results, maintaining a viable readership for nearly forty years – at its peaks in the 1920s and 1940s, it had over 200,000 readers. Equally important was the general newspaper press, which saw fit to run the occasional story of returned-soldier suffering, usually accompanied by evidence of departmental neglect, harshness, bungling, or inefficiency. Headlines such as 'Repatriation Grievances', 'Defects of the System', 'Forgotten Inmates of the Military Hospital', 'Thirteen Years Ordeal', 'Digger's Pitiable Appeal to Lyons', and 'Some Distressing Cases' give some sense of the tenor of these stories – from the sober 'Defects' of the *Sydney Morning Herald* to the more sensational and tabloid 'Forgotten Inmates' of *Smith's Weekly*. Through these means, a consistent public discourse depicting repatriation as a problem, and the returned serviceman and woman as grievously wronged and deserving sympathy, was perpetuated. Moreover, it maintained an impression of the Repatriation Commission as unsympathetic, even vengeful. In 1919, in an inspired moment of editorial invention, *Smith's Weekly* dubbed the Repatriation Commission the 'cyanide gang': the group that killed off all legitimate claims for assistance. It sounded good, and the paper returned again and again to this catchy metaphor to criticise the department. The 'cyanide gang' saved 'farthings and wasted millions' and effectively 'hocused the heroes'. It was an epithet that stuck for many years.[36]

---

35 See 'Service Pensions' File, RSL Papers, 7497B.
36 For a few examples, see *Smith's Weekly*, 26 February 1919 and 14 May 1921.

The idea of the wronged returned man, done over by an unsympathetic bureaucracy, had enormous appeal to the press. Their intention was undoubtedly to cultivate sympathy for the plight of returned soldiers, but in moments of extreme sensationalism, a few stories did something more: they presented the returned man as a 'medical freak'. One of the most macabre was 'the man in the bath'. I first heard of this case from a colleague, who had been told the story by his father in the 1930s, a decade after the man had died. He thought the case was probably a myth. But in 1923 *Smith's* had devoted a number of articles to the case of Trooper Rolph, 'flayed alive by barbarous huns' and 'poisoned by gas', and now suffering an 'appalling problem' (psoriasis) in which, literally, his 'skin peeled-off and refused to grow again'. As a consequence, Rolph spent five years in a tepid oil and water bath. A herbalist had tried to cure him by putting potato peelings and cabbage leaves in the bath, but all remedies failed. He was a 'medical curiosity', a 'hopeless case', and worse, 'a nightmare'. He died a year later. The 'man in the bath' is vivid testimony to the persistence in popular memory of the strange and tragic fates that befell returned men.[37]

There is also some sense of the strange, bizarre, and exotic character of returned soldiers in George Johnston's famous *My Brother Jack* (1964). The protagonist, David Meredith, growing up in Melbourne in the 1920s, is surrounded by crippled and injured returned soldiers. His mother works at the local 'repat hospital' and brings many of them home to rest and recuperate for a time. Almost all of them are shadowy figures in the eyes of David, diffused into a composite image. A few are individualised, but generally they remain strange, almost alien, figures in his landscape – sometimes 'nightmarish'. They are fascinating and yet disturbing, different from normal people, and those like his sister, who marries one, are likewise rendered strange rather than sympathetic. This undercurrent of the macabre in the representation of returned soldiers served to widen the already precipitous divisions between the returned men and civilians. Anzacs could be heroes or nightmares, and each stereotype perpetuated a gulf that framed interwar Australian culture. It was a gulf that complicated and perhaps even compromised sympathy for returned men, making it even more the responsibility of returned servicemen and women to look after each other.[38]

III

The official representation of repatriation – in parliamentary debates, reports, commissions, and official war histories – is of a comprehensive system more generous than that of any other country; a view supported by historians of

---

37 See *Smith's Weekly*, 7 July 1923 and 15 September 1923.
38 G. Johnston, *My Brother Jack*, Collins, London, 1964.

Australian repatriation.[39] Any such measure, however, is relative. Overall, the reinstatement systems for soldiers in all Anglophone countries after the First World War and Second World War bear a striking resemblance to each other. All provided hospital, medical, and convalescent care for the ill, injured, and incapacitated; pensions for the war-damaged and for widows, children and the dependent parents of those who died as a result of war service; some assistance for the education of the children of deceased servicemen; artificial limbs for the maimed; assistance with housing; vocational training; and education. And nearly all (the exception being Britain) provided extensive assistance for the settlement of returned men on the land. Both Canada and Australia placed significant resources into these settlement schemes after the First World War, with less than happy results. The significant departure of Second World War reinstatement schemes from their predecessors was the greater emphasis on education and training. Perhaps the most comprehensive program of rehabilitation after the Second World War was that pursued by the USA, through its GI Bill of Rights, which devoted considerable resources to training. In all, nearly eight million American veterans underwent training – half of all those eligible. Moreover, a 1955 World Veterans Federation Report concluded that American veterans received more liberal education and training allowances than any comparable nation. The Australian Commonwealth Rehabilitation Training Scheme (CRTS), which enabled many veterans to pursue university education, or technical and apprenticeship training, with the aid of generous scholarships, sustenance, and training allowances, was undoubtedly smaller in scale and less generous than the American scheme. But in providing assistance for up to two years (more in special cases), it suffered little by comparison. It was certainly far more generous than the British scheme, which funded education, but only for six months.[40]

More importantly, the Second World War scheme marked a significant philosophical departure from similar education schemes. Here the Australian model closely followed the ideas and principles of American planners. In 1918, Australian authorities had looked backwards, seeing their role as one of placing men in their former positions. The Second World War policy, however, was to equip men and women with new skills essential to making a contribution to the modern industrial economy envisaged by post-war reconstruction authorities. In Australia, this meant much greater emphasis on university education. By 1947 university enrolments were more than double those of a decade earlier, and one-quarter of all these enrolments were CRTS students. To this end, post-war planners in Australia placed great faith in vocational guidance and skills-testing to ensure that returned men and women were streamed into appropriate training schemes.

---

39 See Lloyd & Rees, *The Last Shilling*, p. 419; Pryor, '*Origins of Australia's Repatriation Policy*', pp. 30–1.

40 See World Veterans Federation, *Comparative Report on Legislation Affecting Disabled Veteran and Other War Victims*, World Veterans Federation, Paris, 1955.

Similarly, there was a greater focus on ensuring that the disabled were trained for suitable employment. This had always been an aim of repatriation authorities, but those in the Second World War now called upon the skills of the new 'professional experts' – social workers, occupational therapists, physiotherapists, education officers – and their language of 'diversional occupational therapy' and 'pre-vocational assessment' to better manage the problems of the incapacitated. Even servicewomen were not to be denied. Although authorities believed that most servicewomen would marry and become housewives, they were also determined that those who wished to stay in the workforce would be trained to do so. Indeed, there were complaints about a female labour shortage and entreaties to servicewomen, particularly nurses, to stay on in the workforce. Nearly 10,000 servicewomen underwent CRTS courses.[41]

The major area of difference in re-establishment schemes was in pension provisions. All combatant countries provided pensions for those incapacitated by war-related injuries and illness, and for the dependants of those who died as a consequence of service. Nonetheless, the means of doing this and the extent of assistance varied enormously. All combatant countries adopted the criteria that pensions were to be paid to those who, through their war service, suffered incapacitating injuries and illnesses, or aggravated prior conditions, which prevented them from earning a full income. Compensation was calculated on the extent to which one's earning capacity was impaired. Most countries had remarkably similar tables, measuring the notional extent of incapacity for particular injuries and illnesses. These were usually grouped in decile bands from 100 per cent downwards (90, 80, 70 per cent and so on). At some point, the rate of incapacity was considered so slight as to not warrant any compensation. In Australia, because it had half-decile rates, five percent disability was the entry point for a war pension (Canada and New Zealand were 10 percent), all considerably more liberal than the 20 per cent cut off in Britain and the USA. The effect of this decision was to significantly broaden the entitlement to a pension than elsewhere.

Australia also had a category of pension above 100 per cent, the 'special' or TPI pension, for the totally and permanently incapacitated veteran. This pension was double that of the 100 per cent category. It had the advantage of giving the seriously incapacitated a right to an established pension, whereas in Britain such veterans had to apply for specific allowances, albeit generous ones, to supplement their basic pension. Finally, Australia had liberal 'onus of proof' provisions, which allowed returned men to still receive a pension where there was a doubt about the role of war service in causing their disability. This is a complex issue, but its effects are evident in the greater proportion of Australian veterans receiving

---

41 See Ministry of Post-War Reconstruction, *Re-Establishment Pamphlets*, nos 1–9, 1946; Change Over, vols 1–2, 1946–8; Coombs, *Special Problems of Planning*, pp. 3–10; Australian Institute of Political Science, *Repatriation and Rehabilitation*, Australasian Publishing Company, Sydney, 1945.

pensions. Australia supported almost 70,000 more people through war pensions by the late 1930s than did Canada, although Canada had more returned men. Stricter assessments and a refusal to recognise 'shell-shock' as pensionable meant Canada fell short of the generosity accorded Australian servicemen.

Australia's pension scales were also less differentiated on the basis of rank. While an Australian private on 100 per cent pension in 1920 received only two thirds of the 100 per cent pension for the highest-ranking officer, such differentials were far less than those in Britain. In addition, Britain had a special pension scheme, the 'alternative pension', for those whose pension income was significantly lower than their pre-war income. This scheme aimed to address the grievances of many officers, usually men of the professional classes, who could no longer earn an income and had little independent means, and who, in accepting a pension, were going to be in comparatively reduced circumstances. In electing for the 'alternative pension', they were guaranteed a pension of two-thirds their pre-war income, adjusted for wartime inflation. This was an exceedingly generous system, but one that was so expensive that the British government was forced to abandon it after 1922. Similarly, in the USA, soldiers (but, given pay scales, most commonly officers) could contribute to a voluntary insurance scheme that guaranteed more generous pensions. The advocates of the Australian approach believed that reducing the difference between officers and soldiers, and placing all on the same publicly funded footing was more in keeping with the Anzac spirit, but it was a scheme that clearly disadvantaged incapacitated officers in comparison with their fellows in Britain and the USA.[42]

All combatant countries assisted the dependants of servicemen and women. War pension rates were supplemented with specific allowances for each dependant – usually a wife and each child up to the age of sixteen years. Specific pensions were also provided for those who had been dependent on servicemen or women who died as a result of war-related injuries or illness. These were usually widows and children, but they could also include de facto wives, wives separated from husbands but still supporting children, and parents, if it was proved that they had been dependent on the income of the serviceman or woman. There were limits on these benefits. Widows without dependent children received just over half the pension provided for a serviceman, as it was assumed that they suffered no incapacity and were able to earn an income. If they remarried, they lost the pension after two years, because it was believed that the new husband should bear the burden of providing for his wife. The two-year extension of the pension was included because legislators feared that, if the pension was cut immediately, it might discourage many from marriage. Until the civilian widows pension was introduced in 1944, this was the only social security available for widows (except in New South Wales, which

---

42 See Select Committee on Pensions, *British Parliamentary Papers*, vol. 6, 1919, pp. 13–19; Ministry of Pensions and National Insurance, *War Pensions: Some Questions and Answers*, Her Majesty's Stationery Office, London, 1958, pp. 20–1.

had a civilian widows pension from 1927). But like most social-security systems for women, payments for both civilian and war widows fell short of those for men, perpetuating an ideal of men as breadwinners and women as dependants, regardless of circumstances.[43]

But, just as the Anzac legend failed to find an equal place for women who served overseas, so the repatriation system, in the structure of its provisions and its qualifying conditions, presented more hurdles for servicewomen than for men. In Australia, the bias was evident in the title of the relevant legislation – *The Australian Soldiers Repatriation Act* (a title that also aggrieved sailors) – indicating a linguistic priority that was not entirely removed until the enactment of the *Veterans' Entitlements Act 1986*. The central criterion in the pensioning of injuries was 'active service', and this presented particular difficulties for servicewomen. Nurses and those in the women's services who served overseas qualified for pensions, and if they were injured in the course of these duties, they could be adjudged on the same basis as servicemen. The bias against those who served in Australia in the eligibility criteria for pensions, however, was particularly relevant for women. They mainly served on the home front, and this precluded them from the same benefits as many servicemen. Servicewomen faced difficult obstacles in pressing for pension compensation, precisely because it was believed that their home service was less dangerous and stressful than that of men. One such obstacle was the perception of shell-shock as an affliction caused only by combat. Many men were pensioned for this condition even though they were nowhere near the front when they reported their condition. Women, however, because they were in a supporting rather than a combat role, found such a condition far more difficult to prove.

The case of Patricia C, who served in the Women's Auxiliary Australian Air Force (WAAAF), is illustrative. In 1949, she applied for a pension on the ground that she had a pre-existing hysterical condition that had been worsened by the stress of war service. Despite supporting statements from a psychiatrist, attesting to the severity of her condition, which by now was diagnosed as a depressive illness with paranoid trends, her application was rejected. One of the key problems here was the obvious scepticism of the commission concerning the stress involved in women's service at home. A man who served at home in similar circumstances would have faced scepticism, but in the structure of the services, women were far more commonly in the supporting role on the home front, and this made it all the more likely that any illness or injury that arose in these circumstances would not be pensionable. Occasionally, however, there was a loophole that worked to women's benefit. Vera B also served in the WAAAF and, after the war, developed tuberculosis. A pension for this condition was only granted to those who had undertaken active service, which was deemed to be 'service outside a three-mile

---

43 See World Veterans Federation, *Comparative Report*, pp. 36–7. Britain, however, made war widows' pensions taxable, further reducing benefits.

coastal limit'. Vera, while on leave, had travelled to Tasmania, more than three miles from the coast, and as leave was considered service, she won a pension on appeal.[44]

A final criterion for assessing the comparative generosity of the Australian repatriation system is the actual value of a pension. Legislators claimed that pensions were higher in Australia than elsewhere. At first glance, this seems plausible. The standard 100 per cent pension for a private was 42 shillings a week in Australia, whereas in Britain and New Zealand it was only 40 shillings. Comparisons with Canada and the USA are obviously more difficult, but when Australian legislators claimed an advantage, few disputed it. But amounts have to be calculated against the cost of living, and a comparison of this was usually absent from the speeches of politicians defending the Australian system. In the late 1930s the official medical historian, A. G. Butler, did attempt such a calculation, and given his obsessive perfectionism, there is little reason to doubt his figures. He found that, in relation to the cost of living, the purchasing power of the standard pension in Australia was lower than that of the equivalent pension in Britain, France, Canada, New Zealand, and the USA. Moreover, the Australian pension was also the lowest as a percentage of average weekly earnings.[45] It would seem, then, that Australia had a reinstatement system on a par with those overseas. But it was more egalitarian than most, if one defines egalitarian as catering for the greatest number of people and minimising the differences between those receiving benefits. The cost of this 'fairness', however, was that comparatively, while more Australians veterans were eligible for support, they received a lower level of financial assistance than their counterparts overseas.

IV

Repatriation was not just the giving of benefits and the fulfilment of obligations. It was also a vehicle for the transmission of social and cultural values. This was largely due to it being a system of welfare. From the very beginning, soldier organisations were insistent that repatriation should not be seen as charity, a view echoed by the Minister, E.D. Millen. This issue was the focus of continued anxiety. Accusations that war pensioners were 'bludgers', and the long tradition of such popular resentments, go some way to explaining the returned-soldier obsession with ensuring that 'repat' was seen as a right, based on sacrifice, rather a gift. In numerous forums, soldier representatives asserted that the men did not want to 'be kept by the state' but to be given the means to make their own way in life.[46] In 1932 the State Secretary of the Victorian Branch of the RSL, vexed by the continuing link

---

44 On Patricia C, see RSL Papers, 233X, and for Vera B, 245X.
45 Butler, *The Australian Army Medical Services*, vol. 3, p. 960.
46 For example, Secretary of Limbless Sub-Section RSSILA to General Secretary, 23 November 1920, RSL Papers, 701A.

between repatriation and welfare inherent in the word *pensions*, sought to have the term *war pension* replaced by *war disability compensation*. In his view:

> the frequency of attacks upon pensions is affecting the health, confidence and outlook of maimed and sick comrades ... Public criticism of war ... compensation has ceased but there will always be criticism of 'social' pensions ... and the wider the gap between the two classes of payment the better it will be for the ex-soldier and the bereaved.[47]

Clearly there was something disturbing in having repatriation associated with other types of social welfare. Some feared that repatriation might become tainted with the stigma of charity, and the loudness of the denials of this connection – from legislators, returned-services organisations and soldiers themselves – only serves to confirm the pertinence of the connection.

The fear of charity goes to the heart of the cultural context of repatriation. Even in their avid insistence on the need to give men work rather than handouts, and on the necessity of employment preference, training, and education in rehabilitation, legislators and returned soldiers were merely showing the other side of the charity coin. Embedded in nineteenth-century charity discourse was a stark distinction between the dignity of work, self-help, and independence on the one hand, and the shame of dependence on the other. These connections persisted, despite attempts to claim that social-security payments, such as the old-age pension, were a right, not a handout. In 1900 William Morris Hughes, later a staunch advocate of repatriation, argued 'that all men, by reason of their citizenship, should be entitled to an [old-age] pension'. But critics of the new pensions claimed that they led to abuse, undermining the moral backbone of the recipient and encouraging 'idle vagabondage'.[48] Although an idea of welfare as a system of legitimate entitlement was making headway, it had to do so against a strong current of opinion that condemned any type of dependence as moral weakness. Underpinning this belief was the Protestant work ethic and the faith that work of any sort was character-building, ennobling, and preferable in all respects to dependence. Despite all the denials, repatriation benefits, particularly pensions, resembled other types of social welfare payment at a time when welfare was still integrally related, symbolically, to charity.

These connections were doubly troubling because of the gendered meanings attached to ideas of independence and dependence. Central to codes of nineteenth- and twentieth-century masculinity was the idea of stoic and manly independence, exemplified either by the 'lone hand' of the old bush ethos or by the more modern

---

47 State Secretary, Victorian Branch, RSL to General Secretary, 5 December 1932, RSL Papers, 6409B.
48 Hughes, quoted in T. H. Kewley, *Social Security in Australia 1901–72*, SUP, Sydney, 1973, p. 61. For critical comments, see Charity Organisation Society, *Reminiscences of the Charity Organisation Society of Melbourne 1887–1908*, COS, Melbourne, 1908, pp. 3–10.

breadwinner, who had a right to an income sufficient to support a family in 'frugal comfort'. Receiving benefits made a man dependent, and dependency, whatever its other connotations, was a feminised condition. By receiving benefits from patriotic societies, repatriation funds, returned-services organisations, or even the state, men always carried the risk of being seen as emasculated, feminised, and diminished. If these corrosive potentialities were to be successfully overcome, a new rhetoric had to be developed that would wipe away the pension stigma. Those involved in repatriation had somehow to negotiate, deny, or subvert the feminine meanings inherent in welfare.

These concerns are apparent in the efforts of repatriation agencies to encourage active participation in rehabilitation schemes. As the *AIF Education Service Journal* declared in 1919, 'we want our men to return with the right sort of spirit and outlook in order that they may take their share in the formation of another great period in the history of the Commonwealth'.[49] Some conservative groups saw the 'right spirit' as a commitment to national unity in opposition to socialism and trade unions, but usually repatriation authorities avoided such partisan language, preferring to make rehabilitation an individual task, one implicitly encouraging the masculinity of the men. One way of doing this was by deploying the language of combat for the civilian experience. Men now faced a 'new battle' in life, and it demanded all the courage, resourcefulness, and independence that actual combat had required. What characterised the AIF were their deeds of courage, and now, according to Major-General C.B.B. White, the civilian battle required new deeds to let us help ourselves. Brigadier-General Pompey Elliot echoed this view. It was the duty of every returned soldier to 'make his way for himself in life'. Duty, action, deeds, self-reliance – these were the terms of the appeal to returned men, terms that related to their war experience, terms that would deny the difference between war and peace, maintain their pride, and foster the spirit with which they were now imbued. Just as they had not let down the nation in war, they would not let it down in peace.[50]

After the First World War, this appeal was direct and uncomplicated. It was underpinned by pervasive fears about the capacity of men to be independent after the war, but it lacked sophistication or any understanding of the complexities of individual repatriation experience. This is not surprising, but it was a lesson that repatriation authorities learnt slowly during the 1920s and 1930s. The appeal following the Second World War was more cautious. Moreover, it was more inclined to confront the men with the difficulty of the task that faced them. Instead of a direct challenge to be independent, Second World War repatriation rhetoric was full

---

49 'The Australian Service Man as Citizen', *AIF Education Service Journal*, vol. 1, no. 2, February 1919, p. 17.
50 For one example of the conservative response, see National Democratic Council of Queensland, *A National Policy based on Reason, Justice to All, Loyalty to the Empire, Production, Economy, Repatriation and Industrial Peace*, Brisbane n.d.. See also C. B. B. White, 'Men of the AIF', *Repatriation*, vol. 1, no. 11, January 1920, p. 7; 'Message from Brigadier-General H. E. Elliot to Soldiers', *Repatriation*, vol. 1, no. 9, November 1919, p. 4.

of warnings that there would 'be problems in civvy street'. It signalled the dangers of depression, loneliness, disillusion, and apathy; acknowledged that soldiers would inevitably be different and alienated from civilians; advised of the potential for marital discord and the difficulties of relating to women who now had different expectations of life after their own war effort; and forewarned of the psychological difficulties of re-entering the workforce, the family, the club, and old friendships.[51]

Repatriation authorities were hoping to alert men to the task ahead. They sought to make them aware of the signs of distress and to encourage them to seek expert assistance as soon as possible. Repatriation now paraded the virtues of psychological counselling services. There was an emphasis on the teamwork approach: doctors, nurses, occupational therapists, psychiatrists, psychologists, and social workers could now coordinate their efforts to ensure successful rehabilitation.[52] Men were not just left to their own devices but were assisted by modern medicine and psychological science. In the First World War repatriation literature, there was an emphasis on facilitating the merging of the men into civilian life; it was an effort to make the problem disappear. By 1939 it was obvious that this was an impossible aim. Repatriation authorities had come to believe that they had to acknowledge and accommodate the distinctiveness of ex-service personnel. Successful rehabilitation, then, should work with this psychological sense of separation, not disavow its operation.

Despite the greater sophistication of the message and services of the Second World War repatriation effort, its aims were remarkably similar to those of repatriation policies in the First World War. Work was still the key. All effort had to be tailored to the successful placement of the soldier in suitable employment. Self-help remained the prime virtue, as an army rehabilitation pamphlet stated in 1945: 'you have in your hands to shape for yourself in civilian life a career no less worthy than that which you leave now'.[53] The emphasis on independence remained, but it stood in an uncomfortable relationship with the new therapeutic imperative of repatriation policy. The latter implied that the men were not entirely independent, needed assistance and nurturing, and more especially, were not fully in possession of themselves. Creating a discourse of repression and depression explicitly undermined the pride of the men, a problem recognised in the repatriation literature but never adequately resolved. Excessive pride, in fact, became just another warning sign of psychological maladjustment. There was an uncomfortable tension in this literature between the feminising function of therapy and the demand to achieve manly independence.

---

51   See, for example, 'There'll Be Problems in Civvy Street', *Salt*, vol. 10, no. 11, 1945, pp. 1–5; 'How's the Home Front Shaping', *Salt*, vol. 12, no. 4, 1946, pp. 23–7; 'A Bloke's Better off in the Army', *Salt*, vol. 10, no. 11, 1945, p. 26; 'Initiative and Mateship', *Change Over*, vol. 1, no. 2, 1946, pp. 2–3.

52   Australian Army Education Service, *Human Problems After the War*, AAES, Melbourne, 1946; Martin, *Welcome Home Servicemen!*; 'Specialist Team: A New Approach', *Change Over*, vol. 1, no. 8, 1947, p. 4.

53   Australian Military Forces, *Army Rehabilitation*, Department of Defence, Melbourne, 1945, p. 3.

In this context, the rhetoric of independence was central to codes of masculinity, and served as a means of encouraging the men to be self-reliant rather than a drain on the state. This theme was largely implicit, but, in some instances, it was made very explicit, particularly with respect to incapacitated servicemen. In both world wars, Australian soldiers had proved themselves to be men. This was the view of many authorities, but disabled, ill, and injured soldiers faced an uphill task in maintaining their masculine dignity. It was essential, however, that others continued to recognise their spirit and to treat them as men. This theme pervaded much of the literature. But who was being addressed here? Was it the wider society of civilians, the soldiers themselves, or their families and friends. The literature is explicitly addressed to civilians, but it is doubtful that such journals and pamphlets reached a wide audience. A more obvious conclusion is that it targeted the friends and relatives of disabled veterans. But perhaps it also addressed the veterans themselves (they, after all, were the people who received this literature), as a means of inculcating masculine pride in the face of civilian adversity. But regardless of the audience, the proper codes of conduct towards the disabled veteran (and the codes of conduct of the veteran towards civilians) were clear. As Stanley Melbourne Bruce, future prime minister, argued in 1919: 'you other folks – don't treat these boys like babies! Treat them like what they have proved themselves to be – men'. He went on to demand that they should not be spoon fed or coddled because they 'would rather get their own faces down into the blueberry pie and eat it themselves' – a rather strange image, but one that Bruce thought would convey his message.[54]

This theme was pursued in other articles. 'The Menace of Pity' (1919) positioned pity as the greatest threat to the disabled veteran and to the success of repatriation. It undermined their 'courage, ambition and application to adjustment'. It was crucial, then, to embark upon a 'crusade against the habit of harmful sympathy', because pity unconsciously undermined 'the elements of manhood in the disabled soldier'. Here civilians were constructed as the object of discourse, but there were ways in which this address implicated the veteran himself. The article went on to argue that being a 'cripple' was, in fact, a state of mind, a 'wish' or a choice, that had to be overcome by the men. The contrast was clear. The disabled veteran could 'sit and whine' – behaviour that was declared to be un-Australian – or adopt the characteristic Australian 'buoyancy of spirit' and choose to be a man.[55]

This message of 'being a man' was reinforced by contrasting the manly response to that of the 'sissy'. The poem 'The Wounded Man Speaks' establishes the nature of this contrast:

---

54 S. M. Bruce, 'Repatriation: An Individual Duty', *Repatriation*, vol. 1, no. 5, July 1919, pp. 2–9.
55 'The Menace of Pity: A New Outlook for the Cripple', *Repatriation*, vol. 1, no. 2, April 1919, pp. 2–3.

> I left an ear in a dug-out
> When a shell hit made us dance
> And at Belleau Wood where mixing was good I gave up a mitt for France ...
> They certainly spoiled my beauty. And my leg is a twisted curse
> They busted me up like a mangled pup
> But – THEY DID NOT BUST MY NERVE
> And no pussy-footing sissy
> Shall grab my one good hand ...
> Just to make himself feel grand
> For I'm damned if I'll be a hero
> And I ain't a helpless slob
> After what I've stood, what is left is good
> And all I want is – A JOB.[56]

Here humour was used to negotiate an uncomfortable message. It was a strategy used in other poems about the effects of wounds and injuries. A number of poems made great play with the loss of arms, legs, and eye-sight, but usually went on to reassure the reader that, despite these problems, the injured returnee is 'twice the man who went'.[57]

Most of this repatriation literature made work, self-reliance, and independence the hallmarks of masculinity and hence the keys to successful rehabilitation. But there are obviously other dimensions to rehabilitation that vexed disabled veterans and presented problems for repatriation authorities. Sexual performance was a concern, although one difficult to address directly in public forums, given codes of respectability. The lack of discussion of such issues is also evident in the private writings of soldiers – this is not surprising, since much of this was written for family and friends back home. Nonetheless, the fear of sexual impairment is evident in repatriation literature, although humour was a prime means of navigating these troubled waters. This humour was mostly directed at representing repatriation in a positive light. A 1919 cartoon, 'What may in future be seen off "Easy Street" ', in the Army Hospital journal *Remnants from Randwick* depicts a rather healthy soldier in a hospital bed having his pulse checked by an attractive nurse, whose uniform is unbuttoned at the top and who is pulling up her skirt to check the pulse against the watch that is strapped to her thigh. The prospect of future satisfaction is more explicit in a Second World War cartoon in *Salt*. Entitled 'Repatriation can be Successful', it has a vigorous soldier bounding out of his hospital bed in amorous pursuit of a nurse, much to the surprise of the attending doctor. The crude and simplistic meanings are obvious. They may have been a comfort or, more likely, the butt of blacker humour.[58]

---

56   H. Open, 'The Wounded Man Speaks', *Repatriation*, vol. l, no. 1, March 1919, p. 17.
57   Rev. N. J. Cocks, 'Lines on Repatriation', *Repatriation*, vol. 1, no. 6, August 1919, p. 20.
58   See *Remnants From Randwick*, no. 2, 1919, in A. G. Butler Papers, box 8; Salt, vol. 10, no. 11, 1945.

3 Repatriation

The recovery of manhood was not just a task for men. Integral to many representations of the problem of returned soldiers was the requirement of sympathetic responses and sexual readjustments from women. Sonya Michel has shown that the problem of the disabled veteran and female sexual accommodation to disability were central themes in Hollywood films. In many of these films, notably *Big Parade* (1927) and *The Men* (1950), women had to adjust to a role of mother/nurse and negotiate new forms of sexual desire (his and hers) to bring about the 're-masculinisation' of the central male character, the disabled veteran.[59] Such films were an important part of the Australian cultural diet. Taking diverse forms, repatriation was cultural work aimed at ensuring the recovery of manhood in all its connotations, although the evidence of individual cases suggests that it fell short of this aim in many instances. Our sample of cases suggests that 7–11 per cent of pensioner veterans from the First and Second world wars experienced marriage problems, and some of these were related to sexual performance. William F, a Second World War veteran and, after the war, a taxi driver, expressed a common frustration when he said that he had lost all interest in sex after the war. He feared that he was alienating the affection of his wife and blamed all this on his 'nerves'. Such complaints posed a challenge to the psychological counselling services of the Repatriation Department, which responded by warning that restoring adequate sexual relations with wives after long periods of separation was going to be difficult. To alleviate such anxieties, the soldiers were reassured that 'we have proved our manliness and built our self-confidence'.[60]

Repatriation was bounded by narrow and conventional codes of masculinity. Its purpose was evident in the rhetoric of rehabilitation, recovery, re-establishment, and reintegration, each concept signifying, in its way, a return, literally and metaphorically, to what had been: to conventions, practices, and habits that had been before. There is nothing surprising in that. What is surprising is the pervasive nature of the appeal to masculine codes as an acknowledged and central element of government policy. Mostly these policies attended to the material necessities – hospitals, employment policies, rehabilitation services, income support – but embedded within these prosaic concerns were problems of culture, self, sexuality and identity. Soldiers were returning to societies that had changed and carried with them a pervasive sense that they had also changed. Repatriation therefore had to negotiate the problems of change and difference, but its response, particularly after the First World War, largely looked backwards to comfortable certainties of masculinity: the importance of manly independence, self-help, and self-reliance. In the Second World War, it was recognised that such an

---

59 S. Michel, 'Danger on the Home Front: Motherhood, Sexuality and Disabled Veterans in American Post-war Films', in Cooke & Woollacott (eds), *Gendering War Talk*, pp. 260–79.
60 Australian Army Education Service, *Human Problems After the War*, p. 6. For the individual case, see Department of Veterans' Affairs, NSW, Case Files, sample no. 245.

approach, desirable as it might be, was insufficient. Repatriation could not happen overnight and required the efforts of a new scientific approach to re-establishment. But, in making repatriation a problem of individual psychology, the new scientific approach disavowed repatriation as a cultural problem – one that required a negotiation of the habits and expectations of those returning and of those to whom they returned. The new approach to repatriation was conservative and romantic, utilising comforting and idealised norms of an active male libidinal subject and a passive female subject – a breadwinner and a dependant – norms increasingly difficult to sustain, especially for injured and ill returned soldiers.

V

Some of those closely involved in repatriation found that it had failed in its aim of re-establishing the manhood of returned servicemen. Far from transmitting values of manly independence, it fostered the pursuit of dependency. Critics of the system believed that some men devoted their lives to increasing their pensions rather than genuinely seeking rehabilitation and training to equip themselves with the health and the skills sufficient for an independent life. We might dismiss such criticisms as further evidence of the undercurrent of resentment towards those in receipt of welfare benefits. But many of these claims arose among those sympathetic to the needs of returned men. The Repatriation Department was concerned that many pensioners set their sights more firmly on their disability, with the aim of achieving a TPI pension, than on training and employment. There was an increasing tension between those departmental doctors concerned to implement a 'proper system' and returned-services groups, who sought the best deal for the men. As Dr Hastings Willis, Senior Medical Officer in the Repatriation Department in the 1940s saw the situation:

> A Departmental Medical Officer cannot be a 'nice kind doctor' by giving away public monies, he has to be like all Public Servants 'a careful custodian of the public exchequer' ... Moreover the majority of the Department's clients were not heroes but plain men and many of them not as much wounded as they wished to be ... your plea for a 'sympathetic' medical service sounds a bit like the criticism of the Soldiers' League. The Medical Service's reply to that attack is that the term 'sympathetic attitude towards the soldier' was a euphemism ... for a demand that Departmental MOs should make dishonest recommendations for the benefit of soldier applicants.

While many may not have shared his view, its very existence suggests the possibility of endemic conflicts in the provision of assistance to returned servicemen and women. Repatriation was not only a vehicle for social and cultural values, but also an arena of conflict over these values.[61]

The central criterion for entitlement to a war disability pension was an incapacity arising out of, or aggravated by, active service in war. In principle, this meant that any serviceman or woman who became ill or was injured, or whose existing illnesses and injuries worsened, as a result of war service was entitled to a pension calculated on the extent to which they were incapacitated. But the terms *arising* and *aggravated* are vague. Did they mean incapacities that were a direct consequence of war service (most obviously, gunshot or shrapnel wounds), those that worsened as a consequence of service (such as lung conditions exacerbated by exposure to gas), or merely those that arose during service? The last interpretation might include all sorts of conditions that may have manifested themselves whether the serviceman or woman had gone to war or not – for example, cancer or tuberculosis. Legislators intended that pensions should be for those conditions that were a direct consequence of service, but the ambiguity in the terms used to frame the legislation points to the difficulty involved in any such determination. Any system of pensioning, then, inevitably revolved around issues of proof. Given the indeterminate nature of the terms *arising* and *aggravated by* (as well as the state of medical knowledge on many illnesses), repatriation authorities, returned-services organisations, and individual returned men and women were locked into complex debates over the 'onus of proof' and the 'benefit of the doubt' in determining pension entitlements.

The first step in resolving these debates was obviously producing a good set of medical records, from enlistment to discharge, to enable pension tribunals to determine the role of war service in causing or aggravating an illness or injury. At least this was how the Repatriation Commission stated the problem. Returned services groups saw it differently. They constantly argued that any man or woman passed as fit for service at enlistment was exactly that – 100 per cent fit – and that any illnesses or injuries subsequent to enlistment were therefore pensionable. This might be the case with some illnesses, but in the case of conditions such as epilepsy, the commission's usual reply was that any reasonable understanding of the disease could only lead to the conclusion that it could not have been related to war service. Here the commission was relying on the principle of 'reasonable doubt'. But a more difficult issue involved determining what fitness at enlistment really meant. Servicemen and women understandably took the statement of their fitness as a sound medical judgement. But for those with any acquaintance with enlistment, particularly during the First World War, this was far from the case. In the hysteria of wartime recruiting, especially in the later stages of the war, with pressure on the

---

61 Hastings Willis to A. G. Butler, 9 October 1942, in Butler Papers, box 61. For other comments on pensions and the desire of applicants to maximise their benefits, see 'Review of Repatriation Scheme', 11 October 1954, Department of Veterans' Affairs, Correspondence, AA, SP1375, box 448.

Prime Minister, Billy Hughes, to fill quotas without the benefit of conscription, the temptation for enlistment officers to overlook obvious medical problems was great. In 1917 and 1918 Sir Neville Howse, Head of the AIF Medical Services in Britain, frequently complained that many new recruits arriving from Australia had to be sent back because they suffered such obvious defects as deformed hands, missing fingers, flat feet, limps, epilepsy, imbecility, and senility. In all, 16,000 recruits were sent back as unfit, even though they had been passed in Australia. Even so, many probably managed to get through the net. Enlistment medical officers not only turned a blind eye to obvious incapacities, but men also lied about their age and their medical history in order to enlist. And it could work the other way too. Some men did not admit to their illnesses and injuries on discharge for fear of delaying their demobilisation. Weary Dunlop claimed this was especially prevalent in prisoners of war. All these deceptions created enormous difficulties for repatriation authorities after the war.[62]

Even more troubling for pension authorities after the First World War was the absence of adequate medical records. At the end of the war the clinical records of the AIF were housed in the British Museum. These records represented the most comprehensive information on the medical history of servicemen, detailing the diagnosis and treatment of every condition reported by each soldier and, for those soldiers with serious injuries and illnesses who were evacuated to hospitals in Britain, the outcomes of their treatment. In 1919, without warning, the British government, concerned about lack of storage space, destroyed the records. This effectively meant that the archive of material essential for accurate and scientific pension decisions did not exist. There were other medical records held by the Australian Army (enlistment medical reports, casualty clearing station admission and discharge books, and Field Hospital records), but these, as astute observers such as A.G. Butler confessed, were hardly sufficient. Many were written in the heat of battle, and diagnosis was often perfunctory, on the assumption that more considered opinions and treatment would be given behind the lines. In 1933, the RSL challenged the Repatriation Commission and the Department of Defence about this lack of evidence, claiming that it adversely affected pension claims. The Department of Defence countered with the argument that the 'existing system provides all the necessary requirements'. Butler was not so certain. He feared that the lack of concrete evidence made the war-pension system vulnerable to the winds of expediency and 'political bargaining for the wider and wider extension of the scope of compensation'.[63]

---

62 See Sir N. Howse, Report from England, no. 38, 28 March 1918, in Sir Neville Howse Papers, AWM 2DRL 1351, item 45; Butler, *The Australian Army Medical Services*, vol. 3, pp. 739–45. For Dunlop's views, see S. Ebury, *Weary: The Life of Sir Edward Dunlop*, Viking, Melbourne, 1994, p. 535.
63 See Secretary, Department of Defence to General Secretary, RSL, 12 January 1933, RSL Papers, 6435B. For Butler's views of this 'tragedy', see A. G. Butler to Major Stuart Cowen, 11 October 1940; A. G. Butler to C. E. W. Bean, 28 January 1943, in Butler Papers, box 61.

Butler was right about the political nature of pensioning, but he was wrong to see the destruction of the records as a central factor in this state of affairs. It undoubtedly played an important role, but the retention of comprehensive medical records for servicemen and women in the Second World War, Korea and Vietnam did not stem the flow of agitation for greater benefits and more liberal application of the rules governing entitlement. Throughout the 1950s and 1960s the RSL maintained a steady stream of correspondence demanding that the commission reconsider its rejection of particular problems as unrelated to war service. The nub of the dilemma for returned-services groups was the interpretation of 'onus of proof' and 'benefit of the doubt'. This had been the key problem for the commission since its inception. It gained more formal recognition in 1929 when the *Australian Soldiers' Repatriation Amendment Act* established appeal tribunals, and made 'onus' and 'doubt' criteria the basis for determining appeals. This section of the legislation, however, was still open to interpretation. Returned men and their advocates argued that, if medical knowledge was unable to determine the precise cause of an incapacity, if there was any shadow of doubt as to its cause, then soldiers should be granted a pension. In other words, the onus of proof should be on the Repatriation Commission to prove conclusively that the incapacity was definitely not war-caused and, where it could not, the soldier had to be pensioned. The Repatriation Commission and the government approached this problem with a different emphasis. They claimed that they gave ex-servicemen the benefit of 'any reasonable doubt', but their emphasis was on 'reasonable' as much as it was on 'doubt'.[64]

This battle was fought over many years and over many different conditions. In 1928, the RSL argued that since the cause of Hodgkin's disease was unknown then sufferers should be given the 'benefit of the doubt' and their condition recognised as war-caused. The commission, however, argued that since the disease was common in civil life and there was no definite evidence linking it to war service then it was not 'reasonable' to recognise this condition as pensionable. Five years later the RSL tried an even broader attack. It passed a resolution urging the government to declare that a 'prima facie case shall exist whenever a disability exists which might possibly be due to war service'. The Minister for Repatriation certainly did not think such an interpretation was 'reasonable', countering that the resolution was 'so vague and so infinitely broad that it would permit claims being decided without regard to logical discrimination. Absurd decisions would thus be given and adverse criticism of the Department would be inevitable'. But the persistence of League claims ate away at government confidence. In 1943 the Labor Attorney General, H.V. Evatt, attempted to clarify proceedings by arguing that the 'onus of proof' lay with the commission (something the League had been saying for years). The commission, then, had to prove that the condition was not war caused. But, to the frustration of the League, 'beyond reasonable doubt' still operated. This just fuelled

---

64 See, for example, Acting Minister of Repatriation to General Secretary RSSILA, 7 May 1927, RSL Papers, 2898B.

further efforts to expand the range of pensionable diseases. After the Second World War the League argued that, since the causes of cancer were unknown, serviceman should be given the 'benefit of the doubt'. The government invariably replied that, since there was no evidence suggesting 'any general connection between service conditions and cancer', every case had 'to be considered on its own facts'.[65]

Nonetheless, returned-services groups did win important concessions from the commission. In practice, medical opinion was compromised to resolve ambiguities in the onus of proof. This was most apparent in the decision to accept any condition as war-caused if it arose during service. In other words, if diseases such as cancer or tuberculosis appeared at any time between enlistment and demobilisation, they were deemed to be a consequence of service and hence pensionable, even if war was unlikely to be a cause. In the case of tuberculosis, the government went even further. In 1935, concerned about controlling this infectious disease, it legislated for all veterans suffering tuberculosis, whether war-caused or not, to be eligible for a service pension. The trouble with pensions, according to commissioner Sir Richard Stawell in 1931, was that they could be granted 'without effective reference to medical opinion'. He found the idea that the first symptom of a disease appearing during service should be 'taken as equivalent to proof of the disease ... having been caused by service' questionable. Nonetheless, this was the case, and he believed that this was a 'weak spot in the medical armour', allowing 'throngs of applicants to take advantage of it'. Returned-services groups may have resented commission decisions, but on the other side of the fence, many in the commission thought that veterans got more than a reasonable deal.[66]

Despite these concessions, there were still ambiguities that gave returned services groups continuing avenues of legitimate contest. Although it had generally been accepted that the onus of proof was a burden on the commission rather than the veteran, in practice applicants and returned-services groups were puzzled and, more often, angered by what they saw as inconsistencies in the application of these rules. On the one hand, some soldiers with limited front-line experience gained pensions after developing neurotic symptoms after the war, while in 1953 the application of a widow for a pension arising from her husband's death from lung cancer due to mustard gas inhalation was rejected on the grounds that over seventeen different gases were in use in that part of the front and, therefore, the role of mustard gas in the condition could not be determined. To the RSL, this seemed to contravene the onus of proof provisions.[67] It was cases such as these that constantly kept the government on the defensive. In 1962, they sought clarification

---

65 See, for example, Minister for Repatriation to General Secretary, RSL, 6 March 1928, RSL Papers, 3563B; Minister of Repatriation to General Secretary, RSL, 16 March 1933, 6445B; Minister of Repatriation to General Secretary, RSL, 19 February 1947, 2492C; Minister for Repatriation to National Secretary, RSL, 8 August 1962, 4329C.
66 Interview with Sir Richard Stawell, 2 October 1931, in Butler Papers, 1/5.22. On tuberculosis, see Minister of Repatriation to General Secretary, RSL, 21 March 1943, RSL Papers, 1653C.
67 Case of W, Gas Attack, RSL Papers, 4643C.

of the evidence provisions from the Attorney-General, Sir Garfield Barwick. He concluded that the onus of proof for the applicant should only be that the medical opinion accepted 'should be more probably than not the right opinion', but for the commission to rule against an applicant it must be convinced 'that the opinion which they accept is correct beyond any reasonable doubt'.[68]

Barwick's opinion sought to clarify the burden of proof conventions, but it did nothing to allay the concerns of individual servicemen and women or returned-services groups about their application in practice. In 1976, these provisions became a central focus of the extensive review of the repatriation system undertaken by Mr Justice Toose. Toose criticised the adversarial and inquisitorial nature of commission proceedings and concluded that the benefit of doubt provisions were 'unsatisfactory'. If there was any doubt about the role of war service in the subsequent health problems of veterans, he concluded, the benefit of doubt should be in favour of the applicant. Toose drafted new definitions of the proof provisions, which in effect restated the principle that a pension should be granted unless the commission was satisfied beyond reasonable doubt that there were insufficient grounds. This was the first clear legislative statement on the principle of 'reasonable doubt', but it merely reiterated what had been the practice of the commission since the 1920s. The RSL believed that it changed nothing. They were wrong. When the new provisions were tested in the High Court, in such landmark cases as Nancy Law (1981) and O'Brien (1985), the court concluded that applicants only had to provide evidence of a mere possibility of a connection between war service and illness to be granted a pension. This ruling favoured applicants more than the old 'reasonable doubt' rulings of the commission before 1977.[69]

The administration of repatriation benefits, however, was complicated by more than ambiguities in the onus of proof provisions. Pension decisions were enacted in a wider social and cultural context that militated against scientific decision making. This was a contested arena, but the protagonists were not merely the commission, the applicant, and returned-services groups. Governments were also important actors in this drama. They were concerned about alienating RSL support but had to balance this interest against the possibility of public outcry over benefits that were too generous or too expensive. Other protagonists, however, included many of those involved in the actual administration of benefits: local medical officers, departmental medical officers, staff in repatriation hospitals, and administrative staff in the department. Many of these were returned servicemen and women themselves, sympathetic to the plight of their comrades and mates – a situation that had the potential to compromise the system. In order to make fair and just provision for those deserving assistance, the commission was reliant on the quality of the medical advice they received. For some in the system quality advice was

---

68   Minister of Repatriation to National Secretary, RSL, 8 August 1962, RSL Papers, 4329C.
69   See Lloyd & Rees, *The Last Shilling*, pp. 385–6. See also Mr Justice P. B. Toose, *Independent Inquiry into the Repatriation System*, vol. 1, Government Printer, Canberra, 1975, pp. 19–119.

not evident. Dr C. A. Courtney, a returned serviceman himself, and Principal Medical Officer in the Victorian Repatriation Commission throughout the 1920s and 1930s, believed that pension decisions were being made by medical officers and the commission 'on a basis that is untrue to medical knowledge and untrue to facts ... medical science is being prostituted to enable politicians to achieve popularity by being generous with other folks' money'.[70]

Courtney and other critics of the system believed that medical officers were turning a blind eye to the evidence, and at every opportunity determining any medical condition to be war-caused and hence pensionable. This was clearly not the case. Many applicants were rejected, some suffering from severe problems. In fact, from the 1930s to the 1970s, 40–70 per cent of all applications were rejected. There were clearly many diligent officers who analysed cases on their merit. In the case papers of those rejected for pensions, we can see evidence of rigorous investigations. Of course, some were easy to reject. Men who applied for pensions for haemorrhoids and the like were quickly turned down. Others were more difficult. John M from Adelaide fought in France in the First World War. After the Armistice, he was involved in a fight on a train and, in the ensuing melee, was thrown out of the train, hitting his head. A few months later he was admitted to a hospital in France, diagnosed with mania and paranoid delusions. On his return to South Australia he worked for short periods in the bush and on the railways, but by 1933 was admitted to Parkside Mental Hospital. His seemed to be a case of either head injury or post-war unsettledness and mental stress. But the consultant psychiatrist concluded that the real cause of his problem was alcoholism, probably 'congenital', and that this had led to his frequent fights in France and hence his head injury. On this basis, the application was rejected.[71] The issue here is not whether the decision was correct or even just. We cannot really determine this because our framework for understanding the case is shaped by the processes of medical knowledge that selected certain facts as relevant. The significant point is that, within the limits of medical knowledge at the time, thorough investigations were undertaken and rigorous assessments made.

Nonetheless, there is also evidence to support Courtney's conclusions. There are many dubious statements from local medical officers in support of pension applicants to be found in a variety of sources. Some were easily dismissed. In 1926 David F from Western Australia, wounded at Gallipoli and gassed in France, appealed against the rejection of his application for a pension on the grounds of war-induced myocarditis (heart disease). Two local medical officers testified that he had advanced dental sepsis, which had caused emphysema and later myocarditis, and that this was possibly 'contributed by war service'. In 1963 one Melbourne doctor claimed that a former soldier who had developed cancer of the leg deserved a pension as his tumour was war-caused. He argued that the man had been

---

70   C. A. Courtney to A. G. Butler, 19 August 1945, in A. S. Walker Papers, AWM 75, Item 201.
71   Department of Veterans' Affairs, SA, Case Files, sample no. 62.

wounded in France and had subsequently walked with a slight limp. This 'interference in normal locomotion', in his view, 'played some part in the causation of the tumour'.[72] Both these cases were rejected, but they give a sense of the extent to which many medical officers were prepared to stretch the bounds of credibility in order to gain a pension for returned men and women.

There were pressures on these doctors. Returned men and women came to them for assistance, many in a pitiable state. It was natural to try to get the best for them to compensate them for their sacrifice. Some veterans, of course, knew how to exploit both this sympathy and any loopholes in the system. They went to numerous doctors in one day to collect enough scripts to feed their drug habit. Sometimes doctors were implicated in these subterfuges. A few doctors signed blank prescription forms so that veterans could get any drug they liked. Other veterans, however, went to the doctor for genuine reasons, even though there was nothing actually wrong with them: some pleaded for treatment for a range of imagined conditions and problems; others perhaps just sought a sympathetic ear. We can get a brief glimpse of these dynamics in the frequent resort of local medical officers to prescribing harmless treatments. In the 1950s and 1960s the Repatriation Department had to write to local medical officers on a number of occasions to inform them that Ovaltine was a food, not a drug, and should not be prescribed on official forms entitling patients to free medication. It is inconceivable that local medical officers were unaware of this fact, but it was obviously easier to provide a small comfort than turn them away altogether.[73]

Many of these efforts to assist veterans failed, but Courtney and others who were intimately acquainted with the system believed that some also succeeded. Mostly their criticisms were confined to the safe avenues of the bureaucratic memo or were shared with friends. In the 1960s, however, some of these criticisms became public. In 1963, a group of Repatriation Department medical officers published a number of critical letters in the *Medical Journal of Australia*. They argued that many were receiving pensions to which they were not entitled and medical care for conditions that were not war-related. Similar claims were made in 1969 when one former medical officer saw fit to air his frustrations in public. In a thinly veiled account of his time at Concord Repatriation Hospital, John Whiting published a novel, *Be in it Mate!* For Whiting, the repatriation system was out of control, treating far too many for complaints that had nothing to do with war service at enormous cost to the taxpayer. Officers of the department tolerated these 'abuses', preferring to maintain these men regardless of the triviality of their condition or the cause of their disease. Worse, he claimed that employees of the department were colluding in gaining TPI pensions for each other. Whiting was himself a war veteran, and this gave added strength to his claims, which were widely aired in

---

72 See Department of Veterans' Affairs, WA, Case Files, sample no. 13; 'Notes on Cancer', RSL Papers, 4329C.
73 See Department of Veterans' Affairs, Correspondence, SPI375, boxes, 404, 410 & 368.

the press. These were damaging accusations and led to a series of inquiries into the repatriation system in the early 1970s, which concluded that some of Whiting's claims were exaggerated but a few did have foundation in truth. Some of the abuses uncovered by Whiting arose because of the confusions we have seen in the 'burden of proof' provisions. Procedures were tightened and definitions refined, but it was some time before the department escaped the glare of public criticism.

The repatriation system, despite its problems, has delivered enormous benefits to those who deserved recompense for their sacrifice. But a closer look at its operation can lead us beyond such obvious conclusions. Repatriation is interesting not just because it is an institution delivering welfare services, but also because it gives us a glimpse into the dilemmas confronting social welfare. In Australia, the repatriation system has maintained its strength and position because it has been effectively differentiated from other systems of welfare. This division has worked to the advantage of veterans and to the detriment of civilians. The central place of Anzac in the national ethos has, in effect, retarded the legitimate claims of other Australians to an equivalent place in the national polity. This has not been an unalloyed boon for repatriation beneficiaries. It has made them the object of resentment and criticism from those excluded from the system. But more than this, repatriation has been a site for the articulation of particular social values, and also one of conflict over these values. Anzac was, in one sense, a problematic burden for its bearers. It gave them a special place in the heart of the nation, but it also meant that the ideals of manly independence that it embodied were threatened by the reliance of veterans on welfare assistance.

Even sympathisers feared the effects of this assistance. A.G. Butler was a passionate advocate of the Anzac legend, and perhaps this passion explains his disappointment, but even he believed that: 'returned soldiers have been led astray ... after the strange God – strange indeed to the spirit of the AIF – of dependence and gratuity, rather the idea of enforcing their right to achieve independence and self-expression'.[74] In Butler's view, both the men and the organisations that supported them had sacrificed their spirit and their manhood to become just another class of welfare dependant, ever seeking more handouts. The fear of charity stalked the repatriation system, and for some of its critics, the fear had been realised. The more the veterans sought their legitimate right to assistance, the more they were vulnerable to the charge that they had betrayed the spirit of those who had fallen on foreign soil.

---

74 A. G. Butler to C. E.W. Bean, 28 January 1943, in A. G. Butler Papers, box 61.

4
Soldier Settlement

The settlement of returned soldiers on the land was envisaged as the cornerstone of Australia's efforts to compensate the nation's founders. Repatriation itself, as Australia's preferred policy framework, was integrally related to ideas of returning to the land. In 1918 the New South Wales Secretary for Lands, William Ashford, announced that it was 'the duty of the government, to enable soldiers to settle down and more importantly, 'there was no better outlet for personal effort and ambition than ... settlement on the land'. He added something that many others since have come to see as ironic: 'the government is confident of the capability of the land to make adequate return for the work expended on it'.[1] These were common sentiments. In 1916, when Commonwealth and state government representatives met to discuss measures to ease the return of soldiers, land settlement was a central issue. While pensions, training, and the fitting of artificial limbs were necessary for the incapacitated, land settlement, as John Watson, former prime minister and member of the Parliamentary War Committee explained, was the cure for the 'unsettled condition' of the able-bodied returned man. Many returned men, delegates believed, would desire land, and they set about putting this policy into practice. In all, nearly 40,000 First World War men obtained properties under these settlement schemes. But it was the second half of Ashford's statement that proved to be more significant. The land itself did not give an adequate return. In 1929 Mr Justice Pike was charged with investigating the 'causes of failure' of so many soldier settlers. By then many had been forced to leave their farms; others remained, but were seriously indebted, and governments had accumulated losses of £23 million. These conclusions framed later soldier settlement efforts. Access to land was more difficult for veterans of the Second World War and Korea, and measures to ensure the suitability of the land and the capacity of settlers to manage it were more rigorous. No one wanted to repeat the failures of the first soldier

---

1   New South Wales Ministry of Lands, *Land for Soldiers*, Government Printer, Sydney, 1918, pp. 3–4.

settlers. What had begun as rightful compensation was seen to have ended in tragedy.[2]

Stories of hardship and failure among soldier settlers are plenty. They clog the files of State Lands departments, taking on an uneasy familiarity. In 1924, Charles Millen, a Queensland soldier settler, was unable to meet his rent obligations, he explained that 'I am not in a position to pay at present'. There followed an extensive list of problems: he was struggling to get a crop in, last year's crop had been destroyed by drought, and he had used all his war gratuity to pay for new seeds, food, and clothing. Ashby Sikes, was in a similar situation, and left little doubt that he expected some consideration for his difficulties, marking his address Pozieres via Cottonvale. He could not pay, hail had destroyed his crops, his expenses were more than receipts, he owed local storekeepers £57, and he had a wife and child to maintain. No consideration was forthcoming. His application for rent postponement was refused. The land was proving to be a hard taskmaster. Others saw the problem as human, not natural. Patrick Fogarty, a Victorian settler, laid the blame at the door of a 'do nothing government' who had appointed 'inefficient and incompetent' inspectors and supervisors.[3] But whether it was natural or human, failure has structured the dominant narrative of soldier settlement in Australia. With few exceptions, historians have contrasted the optimism of governments and the enthusiasm of returning men for soldier settlement with a melancholy picture of official incompetence, lack of planning and supervision, inadequate and barren land, drought and flood, poorly trained and inexperienced settlers, serious debt, rising costs, and falling prices for produce. According to one historian, it was a 'complete failure' and an 'episode of which the nation was more than a little ashamed, for hardship and deprivation was not the way in which a grateful nation had intended to repay the diggers for their deeds of valour'. Even accounts that depict Second World War soldier settlement as successful, even 'hard to go bung', rely on the contrast with the 'misery and failure' of the earlier scheme.[4]

These pages are being written in the early 1990s (and again in 2019) – unusual, but then again not so unusual, contexts for these claims. In the midst of serious drought, widespread hardship in the rural sector, and accusations of a 'do-nothing' government, it may seem that soldier settlers were not victims of a particular hardship but participants in a longer saga of rural crisis. Was soldier settlement really a policy failure when seen in this broader context of periodic rural crisis, or

---

2   See 'Report of the Conference of Representatives of the Commonwealth and State Governments in Respect of the Settlement of Returned Soldiers on the Land', 1914–17, pp. 1469–73; 'Report of Mr Justice Pike on Losses Due to Soldier Settlement', *Commonwealth Parliamentary Papers*, vol. 2, 1929, pp. 6–24.

3   See Charles Millen to Public Lands Department, 6 September 1924, and Ashby Sikes to Public Lands Department, 18 August 1924, Public Lands Department, Queensland State Archives, LAN/AK 119; Patrick James Fogarty Papers, La Trobe Library, MS 12671.

4   K. Fry, 'Soldier Settlement and the Agrarian Myth after the First World War', *Labour History*, no. 48, May 1985, p. 43. See R. Smallwood, *Hard to Go Bung: World War II Soldier Settlement in Victoria 1945–1962*, Hyland House, Melbourne, 1992.

perhaps a persistent Australian strain of hope often triumphing over reality. It is inconceivable that planners and soldiers did not have some idea of the obstacles ahead. Soldier settlement was the third great government effort since 1860 to establish a self-sufficient yeoman class of agriculturalists in Australia. The first two, selection and closer settlement, had been marred by widespread hardship among the settlers and mixed results in terms of the land under cultivation. These schemes were likewise termed failures. At the 1916 Soldier Settlement Conference, the Queensland Treasurer, E.G. Theodore, warned of the prospect of 'probable failures'.[5] Theodore was alive to the 'lessons of history', but few heeded his warnings. Why was soldier settlement embraced with such fervour, despite the less than satisfactory results of previous settlement experiments? In part it has to be that soldier settlement is as much a cultural artefact as an economic, social and political plan. It was produced by beliefs, ideals, and bodies of knowledge, all of which went some considerable way towards making soldier settlement desirable and rendering its subsequent problems indicators of failure. These beliefs make for a dramaturgy of tragedy, but it is a script that warrants further consideration.

I

The image of outback Australia as Elysian Fields fired the imagination of promoters of soldier settlement. It was an image of considerable duration. When colonists in the 1840s demanded access to land outside the settled districts, their struggle to 'unlock the lands' drew its fire from the belief that agricultural pursuits offered the opportunity for dignity and prosperity, and, further, that the land, in the right hands (non-Aboriginal ones), could be made bountiful. The promoters of this dream, 'the rural boosters', spent many years trumpeting the virtues of agricultural life and the capacity of the land to produce plenty. Civilisation went hand in hand with turning waste land into fruitful fields. And as some began to fear the degenerate effects of the city, so the campaign to move people to the healthier climate of the land gathered pace. For one of the most fulsome boosters, Edwin J. Brady, writing in 1918, Australia was the 'land of milk and honey'. The excesses of his prose are almost farcical, but the popularity of this work suggests the attractiveness of his vision. Brady found in Australia:

Wonder, Beauty and Unequalled Resource. Under the arid seeming of the plains I saw the possibilities of marvellous tilth ... Nor is the message of Australia uttered in tones of predominant melancholy as many alien souls have affected to believe ...

---

5 Report of Conference on Settlement, p. 1467. For discussions of assessments of the failure of earlier schemes, see M. Lake, *Limits of Hope: Soldier Settlement in Victoria 1915–38*, OUP, Melbourne, 1987, pp. 3–24; S. Roberts, *History of Land Settlement in Australia*, Macmillan, Melbourne, 1968, pp. 300–6.

to the sane, healthy native born it is a mother of everlasting youth and beauty, and the freest, richest, happiest land on earth.

He believed that, with irrigation, agriculture could extend over much of the interior, rendering it 'green with growth and yellow with golden harvests'. From there it was only a short step to the assertion that 'Australia can support two hundred millions in the same standard of comfort and security as readily as she is carrying five millions'. Those, like geographer Griffith Taylor, who doubted such visions were subjected to savage rebuttal and ridicule.[6]

The need to develop the land and thereby increase the wealth of Australia after the war was omnipresent. It was there in the views of politicians, such as the Premier of South Australia, Crawford Vaughan, who saw soldier settlement as a means of opening up the country, and in the minds of participants in the Second Australian Town Planning Conference in Brisbane in 1918. There one delegate, a returned soldier himself, declared that 'Australia's greatest need is primary production and the more men who are established on the land the more prosperous and stable will the community be'. It was also there among trade unionists, such as E.J. Holloway, who believed that 'primary industries have been in the past, and must be in the future, the foundation of Australia's prosperity'. Professor Elton Mayo, philosopher and later eminent industrial psychologist, shared this view. He argued that 'the cultivation of secondary industries in Australia is, of course, as far as it goes, excellent ... but we have to remember that many of our secondary industries are really luxuries. In other words, they add little to national income. They merely provide avenues for expenditure'. This being the case, Mayo concluded, the essential task of repatriation was to settle men on the land.

Particular regions also sought to press their own claims for recognition. The Queensland Government Intelligence and Tourist Bureau sought to advertise the virtues of the northern regions of the state, particularly the Atherton Tablelands, describing them as gently undulating tropical jungles with an abundant water supply. Queensland, it concluded, was capable of accommodating 50 million settlers, and no soldier with a 'limited amount of capital, together with a superabundance of thrift, energy, determination and perseverance . . . need have the slightest misgivings about making a success of things'. It was 'an agriculturalist's Eldorado'. Of course, particular regions, keen to develop, had to advertise the virtues of their district to attract soldier settlers, and a bit of hyperbole was always in order in such circumstances. Such views, however, were not confined to Australia. In Britain advocates of Empire settlement accused political economy of

---

6   See E. J. Brady, *Australia Unlimited*, vol. 1, George Robertson, Melbourne, 1918, pp. 13, 56 & 287; G. Taylor, *Australia: In its Physiographic and Economic Aspects*, Clarendon Press, Oxford, 1911, p. 244. On the controversy surrounding Griffith Taylor, see J.M. Powell, 'Taylor, Stefansson and the Arid Centre: An Historic Encounter of "Environmentalism" and "Possibilism"', *Journal of the Royal Australian Historical Society*, vol. 66, pt. 3, December 1980, pp. 163–83.

being 'too urban in outlook'. For them, it was not just wealth that was at stake, but also the future defence and strength of the Empire. Christopher Turnor, an Empire advocate, argued that the 'unpeopled and undeveloped land in our Oversea Dominions is a source of great weakness from the point of view of Defence ... [and] a great economic loss'. A 'new outlook' was required to 'ensure safety of country and stability of Empire', and this required the settlement of British returned soldiers in the Dominions.[7]

There was little to distinguish these views from half a century of rural 'boosterism'. But, for some commentators, the war provided a new and different context. It created specific conditions that made settlement all the more urgent. There was an optimistic view of the relationship between war and land. Former prime minister J.C. Watson believed that the 'outdoor life' of the soldier bred a desire to continue that life – on the land. Our inveterate 'booster' E.J. Brady was even more insistent. He argued that 'no other land can offer the awakened souls of men a continuation of that open life for which the adventure of war has given them a taste'. In other words, war had equipped the soldier with a new willingness and love for the farming life.[8] But there was also a darker side to this faith. Numerous State and Commonwealth government representatives at the 1916 Soldier Settlement Conference spoke of the chaos arising from returning men and the potential unrest of having 'cities congested with idle men'. Unsettled and idle men were vulnerable to the easy charms of dissipation or, even worse, political radicalism, and in either case such an extent of idleness represented a quantum of economic loss the nation was incapable of sustaining. Historians since have sometimes seen the Bolshevik Revolution as precipitating widespread fears about the potential unrest of returned men. It became an important reason, but the fear was present earlier than that. It was part of a longer tradition of concern about the city as a cesspool of decadence for weaker souls. Some Soldier Settlement Conference representatives were convinced that the pull of the city, with 'its lights and music', would prove far stronger than that of the country unless governments ensured the success of settlement. Such views, however, took on a new dimension in war. Underpinning them was an anxiety that the war had transformed men, not into productive outdoor types but into weakened, dissipated, and nervous specimens. The country was a means of reinvigorating these damaged men. In this context, soldier settlement was not just an economic measure to create national wealth, but also a social measure, for continuing peace and stability after the war,

---

7   See Report of Conference on Settlement, p. 1465; Second Australian Town Planning Conference, *Proceedings*, Brisbane, 1918, p. 84; Report of Unemployment Conference and Soldier Settlement, March 1919, RSL Papers, 439; *Sydney Morning Herald*, 1 March 1918; Queensland Government Intelligence and Tourist Bureau, *Tablelands of North Queensland, Atherton and Evelyn Tablelands and Oswald's Track Returned Soldiers Settlement*, Government Printer, Brisbane, 1918, pp. 3–10; C. Turnor, *The Land and the Empire*, John Murray, London, 1917, pp. 1–76.
8   Report of Conference on Settlement, p. 1464; Brady, *Australia Unlimited*, vol. 1, p. 120.

and a cultural measure, to foster an appropriate Australian way of life and restore national vigour.[9]

The obviousness of soldier settlement as a remedy for a variety of ills, however, did not go uncontested. The effect of war on men could be seen in a variety of ways, both positive and negative. The openness of this field of discourse allowed for arguments opposed to soldier settlement, and some of these came from returned soldiers and their representatives. One article in *The Soldier* criticised the 1916 Soldier Settlement Conference for failing to see that there was a 'psychological dimension' to settlement. The returning men were 'temperamentally unfitted' to go on the land because their minds were 'agog with war motion'. The following year similar arguments were advanced: 'after the excitement of battle and the companionship of active campaigning few will suffer the solitude of land settlement'. And another article put the case even more strongly: 'The Australian is a temperamental type – he has got out into a great world, full of interest, agog with motion, excitement and risk. Will he be prepared to return to the placidity of the outback ... land settlement cannot be considered the be all and end all of the repatriation problem'. Such sentiments were balanced by articles from the ubiquitous Brady praising the virtues of settlement, but common to each of these opinions was the view that war had changed the men. The critics of land settlement believed that war had made men unfit for the land, but others believed that the men had become accustomed to outdoor pursuits and that perhaps, after the horrors of war, the land might prove attractive.[10] The latter were buoyed in their optimism after the government surveyed enlisted men. In 1916 it sent out many survey cards to soldiers and found that one-quarter, perhaps as many as 40,000, were interested in being placed on the land. The actual figure was smaller than this: only 18 per cent definitely desired land, but the government factored in the 'doubtful' cases. In their eagerness to push settlement policies, it was convenient to inflate the evidence for the affirmative case. In the end, however, the estimate of 40,000 did not prove to be too far from the mark. If legislators thought that land settlement was a sound policy, so did a fair number of returning men.[11]

It was in this context that Commonwealth and State government representatives met to draft plans for soldier settlement. They carried a historical burden. None wished to repeat the failures of earlier government selection and closer settlement schemes. And few would have been unaware that politicians had borne much of the blame for these nineteenth century failures. The 1883 Morris and Rankin Inquiry into the land laws in New South Wales had left few doubts about the results of these first experiments in government land settlement. In their

---

9   Report of the Conference on Settlement, pp. 1463-76. On the fear of Bolshevism, see R. Gollan, *Revolutionaries and Reformists: Communism and the Australian Labour Movement 1920-50*, Allen & Unwin, Sydney, 1975, pp. 1-32.
10 Editorial, 'Land Settlement', *The Soldier,* 28 July 1916; Editorial, 'Repatriation and Recruiting', *The Soldier,* 25 January 1917; Editorial, 'Repatriation', *The Soldier,* 27 July 1917.
11 Report of the Conference on Settlement, pp. 1464 & 1507.

formulation and administration, the laws were a 'field of abuse and waste ... in defiance of the public interest ... and a waste of the public estate'.[12] Inquiries into the land laws in other colonies echoed these charges. Given this history, accounts of soldier settlement are often tinged with a sense of faint surprise and amazement that a further doomed effort should be made. There may be some justification in this, but to be fair, the prospects for agriculture in the immediate years before the war looked bright.

The amount of land under cultivation since the turn of the century, particularly in Western Australia, had increased considerably, and in most states more effective land administration, and more careful and controlled selection, seemed to be reaping a reward. This does not necessarily mean that a self-sufficient 'yeomanry' had been established. Much of the added area under cultivation was farmed by large agriculturalists. They were able to use mechanisation more effectively and, with improved transport and communication, were capable of producing more efficiently for an overseas market. Given the absence of clear records on the nature of agricultural settlement, however, it is difficult to generalise. Most states were interested in recording the success of their policies in terms of the area under cultivation, rather than the number of settlers, their longevity on the land, or the extent of their prosperity. But if we have difficulty in determining the meaning of these facts, so did legislators. And in the early war years it would have been reasonable to assume that the administrative machinery for the regulation of settlement was by then more efficient, the desire of returned men to take to the land intense, and the prospects for agriculture favourable.[13]

The first task of legislators and planners was to decide who was to take responsibility for the administration of soldier settlement. Repatriation policy was seen to be a Commonwealth activity. As every Australian soldier in the First World War had been a volunteer, there was no doubt that it was a national responsibility to provide pensions and other assistance for returning soldiers. At the 1916 conference and subsequent conferences on land settlement, however, State government representatives made it clear that land settlement should be their responsibility. They had the land, and land policy had always been a major sphere of State activity. There was some sense in this. Each of the states had an elaborate and experienced land bureaucracy. Nonetheless, they made it abundantly clear that they did not have the financial resources to make advances to soldier settlers, bear the costs of redeeming freehold land for settlement, or establish the infrastructure of irrigation, and road and rail transport required for successful settlement. The financial responsibility was the Commonwealth's, and the Commonwealth was urged to provide or guarantee loans for the states to fulfil their responsibilities.

---

12 Report of the Inquiry into the State of the Public Lands and the Operation of the Land Laws, *New South Wales Legislative Assembly Votes and Proceedings*, vol. 2, 1883, p. 106.
13 See Roberts, *History of Australian Land Settlement*, pp. 309–37.

This was agreed to, although Commonwealth representatives were anxious to ensure some uniformity in administration. Participants were reconciled to the division of powers between the states and the Commonwealth, but this created an uncomfortable tension. On the one hand, repatriation was a federal matter, leading to a consistent policy for all returning servicemen and women. In terms of the general principles of settlement, at least, there was a common currency. But in practice, states had widely different means of granting land and overseeing the placement of men. These differences were significant grounds for returned-soldier resentment, as struggling soldiers in one area believed soldiers in another to be faring better. Some returned soldier representatives and their sympathisers feared that state governments were incapable of developing an appropriate sense of 'responsibility' in this sphere and urged the Commonwealth to take a more central role in soldier settlement. These cries fell on deaf ears. The states were determined to keep control of their own land policy. The variety of schemes and policies fuelled the assertions of returned soldier groups and their defenders that repatriation was being strangled in 'red tapeism'.[14]

Underpinning the call for uniformity was not just the desire for equity between soldier settlers; it was also a statement of belief about how best to ensure that soldier settlers did not fail as earlier settlers had done. One of the key concerns was that settlers should have sufficient capital. This had been one of the lessons of selection. Settlers with little capital had expended meagre savings on establishing the land and, at the first bad season, had been left with insufficient reserves to tide them over. Governments were determined that soldier settlers should have a good start. To this end, Commonwealth and State governments agreed that each soldier settler would be given an advance of up to £500 for equipment, materials, stock, and feed, to ensure that they were well established. It was a means of funding essential improvements in order to make the property self-sufficient. When first proposed, there was some debate about whether these advances would be in the form of loans from a bank, direct advances, or subsidies from the 'Repatriation Fund'. Some feared that grants from the fund would appear to be charity, others that if the advance was a direct payment rather than a loan, then settlers might take the money and make few improvements. This was a familiar dilemma for repatriation planners: repatriation was a right, but charities also sought to participate, and both rights and charity, if granted on too liberal a basis, had the capacity (or so it was believed) to render the men dependent. And in the eyes of repatriation authorities, dependency meant lack of initiative, indolence, and waste – all the qualities governments and soldier representatives hoped to avoid. It became a loan to be repaid, albeit on generous terms.[15]

---

14 See Report of Unemployment Conference and Soldier Settlement, March 1919. On 'red tape', see, for example, 'McFarlane's Farm', *Smith's Weekly*, 17 July 1920; W. B. Dalley, *The Case for the Diggers to Mr Hughes KC.*, William Brookes and Co., Sydney, 1919, p. 10.

15 Report of Conference on Settlement, pp. 1477-84.

Despite these tensions, a clear set of principles and policies evolved. There were some differences in emphasis and approach as each state introduced its own soldier settlement legislation, tailoring policies to local peculiarities of availability and use. For instance, New South Wales and Queensland preferred to offer leasehold land, Victoria and South Australia freehold, and Western Australia and Tasmania leasehold and freehold. New South Wales also favoured 'group settlement', to allow cooperative ventures to be undertaken in the belief that these would overcome the perils of isolation. The government would support the latter through assistance for transport, sale of produce, and the establishment of local industries, such as canneries. Some states, notably Victoria, aimed to resume existing land for settlement, while others, such as Western Australia, focused on expanding settlement into new areas. All allowed for settlement on Crown land. But whether freehold, leasehold, or group, settlers in all states were given low interest loans or small rental repayments and, in return, had to agree to stay on the land for a probation period (between three and five years) before they could transfer the lease or sell. All states declared settlers eligible for advances, and most authorised postponement of repayments for up to three years to ensure successful settlement. Perhaps the most innovative proposals, and the ones most indicative of the determination to ensure success, were encouragements for settlers to undertake courses of farming instruction and the establishment of 'classification committees' to assess the suitability of returned men for a life on the land. Both these policies sought to address the most glaring failings of earlier schemes: the unsuitability of prospective settlers, and their lack of knowledge and experience. Added to this, most states established inspectorates to scrutinise the progress of settlers and to offer advice and assistance to those in need. Generous repayments, advances, training, selection procedures, and inspections were the elements of sound settlement policy.[16]

II

Despite these good intentions and careful plans, the troubled history of soldier settlers is now so well known it needs little retelling. Within a few years reports of settler difficulties were rife. In the major newspapers there was a growing tide of criticism and complaint from soldier settlers and their defenders. The official reports of Soldier Settlement Boards also document an increasing incidence of indebtedness and failure. By 1925 nearly one-fifth of Victorian settlers had left their land, and similar figures bedevilled soldier settlement in other states. A series of government inquiries, culminating in the 1929 Commonwealth Inquiry, headed by

---

16 For a general summary of the different State schemes, see Commonwealth Government, *Provisions by Australian Governments for Settlement on the Land of Returned Soldiers and Sailors*, Ede & Townsend, London, 1918.

Mr Justice Pike, painted a dismal picture of 'failure'. Later investigations, notably the 1944 Rural Reconstruction Commission Report, reiterated these findings. By then, accumulated losses from the scheme amounted to £45 million. These inquiries also established a diagnosis of this tragic state of affairs. For Pike, the causes were the want of capital, the want of an adequate home maintenance area, the unsuitability of the settlers, and falling primary produce prices.[17] What went wrong?

The official explanation has much merit. Too many returned soldiers applied, and governments, in that unsettling hiatus of the first few months of return, were anxious to settle as many men as possible. Returned-soldier groups placed sustained pressure on governments to ensure that returned men were given secure occupation. In this climate, hasty decisions were made. Men were classified after cursory examination as suitable for settlement, even pensioner returned soldiers. Others had little farming experience. Official surveys of intending settlers suggest that nearly two-fifths had no farm experience. But there were significant local variations. In Tasmania, 40 per cent had no experience of rural work, being butchers, clerks, hotel keepers, solicitors, and the like before the war. Even more alarming, a similar proportion had suffered some war injury, although not all of these were pensionable. In Victoria, however, only one-fifth of settlers in Geelong and one third in Melbourne had no farming experience. While certainly lower than the official survey, these figures are sufficiently large to indicate the burden of inexperience some settlers carried. This was not wise or prudent administration. And the placement of sick and disabled men on the land was also cause for alarm. The Prime Minister's Office wrote to State premiers in 1921 advising that soldiers who had already received repatriation assistance should not be considered for settlement as too many grants had been given to 'sick men'. By then this warning was too late: many had already settled.[18]

Added to these problems was the fact that training courses in farm techniques were poorly planned, perfunctory, and, worse, not compulsory. In South Australia men were not required to attend, and those that did enrol only had instruction one day a month for twelve months or for one concentrated period of a week. Although the government paid fares and provided free board and lodging, these training schools were often some distance from farms. Moreover, they maintained strict codes of discipline – certainly no alcohol was allowed. None of this would have been an incentive to attend. Worse, there was little pretence that this was thorough training. The prospectus for the Mt Remarkable Training Farm promised lectures

---

17 See Royal Commission on Soldier Settlement, *Victorian Parliamentary Papers*, vol. 2, 1925, pp. 6–23; 'Report of Mr Justice Pike on Losses Due to Soldier Settlement', pp. 6–24; Rural Reconstruction Commission, *Settlement and Employment of Returned Men on the Land*, Government Printer, Canberra, 1944, pp. 3–35.

18 For official figures, see Scott, *Australia During the War*, p. 843. See also Applications for Soldier Selection, Closer Settlement Board, Tasmanian Archives, AB/13; Prime Minister's Office to Premier of Victoria, 18 August 1921, Closer Settlement Board Correspondence, Victorian Public Records Office, VPRS 10645.

from experts, but 'no attempt is made to impart professional or theoretic training'. Presumably this was meant to allay the fears of settlers about impractical education, but it meant that trainees were familiarised with general farming techniques but had little broader understanding to enable them to adapt to difficult and changing circumstances. They were poorly trained, if trained at all, inexperienced, and sometimes suffering pensionable disabilities – this is what Pike meant by the 'unsuitability' of the settlers.[19]

Haste had other consequences. It led governments to open up unsuitable areas for settlement: densely forested terrain in Queensland's Atherton Tablelands, swamps in the Murray river basin of South Australia, dry land in the Western districts of New South Wales, and the like presented enormous obstacles to successful settlement. Some Lands Department officers demonstrated remarkable optimism in their assessments. One investigation near Toombul in Queensland found the land to be low-lying forest, and the soil loose, light, and sandy, which 'could not be considered fertile'. Nonetheless, it was recommended for purchase because 'with fertiliser it might be good for poultry farms'. This proved not to be a sound recommendation. Moreover, haste, the considerable demand for soldier settlement blocks, and the market forces of supply and demand created an upward price spiral in land values and the cost of farm implements, stock, and seed. Settlers' advances bought less and less. To make up the shortfall, they had to spend any savings they had, leaving them vulnerable to economic downturn. This was a situation ripe for profiteering and corruption. Speculators, aware that governments were in the market, sought to exploit these circumstances to their own advantage. Responsible public servants were needed to uncover these scams. In Mudgeeraba, Queensland, an astute local district lands officer advised against the purchase of supposedly suitable land near Tallebudgera Creek, offered for sale to the government by the owner at 'exorbitant' prices. On inspection, the land was found to be of 'very poor quality', covered in tea tree swamps. But not every government officer was so scrupulous. In 1921 the New South Wales Under Secretary of the Lands Department was found by the Royal Commissioner into the Soldier Settlement Administration to have engaged in corrupt practices. He had failed to take proper steps to assess the suitability of soldier settlement land, had earned bonuses for contracting out building work to a particular firm, and had withdrawn applications for soldier settlement land to enable a private contractor to use it for timber cutting.[20]

Even without overt corruption, soldier settlers found themselves having to pay high prices and rents on land purchased by governments at inflated prices. From

---

19 See South Australian Department of Agriculture, *Mt Remarkable Training Farm*, Government Printer, Adelaide, 1918, pp. 1–6; South Australian Minister for Repatriation and Agriculture, *Land Settlement for Soldiers*, Government Printer, Adelaide, 1917.
20 See District Lands Officer to Department of Public Lands, 24 June 1918; District Lands Officer Report, 30 June 1917, Soldier Settlement, Queensland State Archives, LAN/AK 112, Batch 569. For a report on the corruption allegations, see *Sydney Morning Herald*, 12 March 1921.

the moment they settled, some found their debt considerable (often to the full value of the property), with the added burden of advances to repay. Some found their advances eaten up in costly improvements. Some had insufficient capital left to build homes. Families survived in tents, corrugated iron sheds, and caravans for years at a time. Neil Mackenzie spent three years in France and, on his return, wandered from job to job. Out of work and tired of the city, he and a mate 'went bush' with the aim of obtaining a soldier settlement block. In 1922 he took up an orchard block at Barmera, South Australia. He lived in a corrugated iron 'cubicle' for nearly two years before he was able to build a modest house for his new wife. He was one of the fortunate ones: his temporary hardship was the prelude to surviving over thirty years on the land. Others found the going tough. E.J.H. Joseph in Tasmania, for instance, was a war pensioner trying to support a wife and six children on a farm that had only a cow and a few fowls. The family lived in a tent for a few years and survived on rabbit, but unable to afford to build accommodation, Joseph and his family moved into rented rooms in the local town while he undertook casual labouring to pay off debts. They failed and the land was resumed by the government. This is what Pike meant by want of capital and want of a home maintenance area.[21]

Perhaps, in a more favourable economic climate, such obstacles could have been overcome in time. But those most indebted and struggling hardest to establish their farms had little hope of surviving as prices for their produce fell. In 1920 and 1921 oversupply on the world market led to a dramatic drop in prices for agricultural produce. The value of all agricultural goods fell by one-fifth in a year, but falls in some industries – notably dairy produce, fruit, and vegetables – were more dramatic. The price of butter fat fell 75 per cent, and some fruit and vegetables by 50 per cent. High costs, significant debts, and falling income were a disastrous combination for many soldier settlers, as they were for any small farmer. But there were other factors involved. The vision of a yeomanry that had inspired many advocates of soldier settlement also crippled sensible policy. In many areas the ideal of the self-sufficient family farm of 320 acres was inappropriate to the land or the type of crop best suited to it. In drier areas, or in districts best suited to crops that required a large harvest to return an adequate income, such as wheat, small farms were just that: too small. Some were forced to eat up their capital in fertiliser; others were never likely to be able to compete with the larger farmer, who could exploit the efficiency of new farm machinery. Promised irrigation schemes took time, and by then it was too late for settlers on land that was insufficient in size and fertility to sustain a family. It was these settlers who were most vulnerable to falling prices and to the more common crises of farming: drought, frost, hail, and occasional floods. These events were often localised, with the result that farmers in one district faced an uphill battle, while those in another were more insulated

---

21 See N. Mackenzie, Mortlock Library Oral History Transcripts, OH 1/14, pp. 26–32; Joseph, *The Long Road Back*, pp. 16–22.

(for a time) from economic downturn. The problem was that the falling prices of 1920 and 1921 coincided with the first or second harvests of soldier settlers. They hit them at a particularly difficult time, when their savings had been expended and governments were expecting their first postponed payments. In 1922 the Prime Minister authorised soldiers to use their war gratuities to pay off rent to Soldier Settlement Boards, thereby taking their remaining capital. This is what Pike meant by falling prices.[22]

Pike's gloomy but perceptive official pronouncements, however, obscure the underlying tensions and conflicts in the implementation of soldier settlement. The objective conditions of capital, homes, experience, and prices produced clashes between settlers and governments, government inspectors and other land owners. It also produced and fanned conflicts within settler families. In the numerous requests from soldier settlers for relief, are glimpses of their pain and anger as they struggled to survive. They asked for new evaluations of their land to reduce rents, further advances to make essential improvements, and postponements of payments because illness, drought, frost, or pests had prevented them from putting in a crop. All around the country, impoverished settlers were forming Soldier Settler Leagues and Digger's Unemployment Committees to protest their plight. Rural sub-branches of the RSL conveyed the feelings of soldier settlers to government ministers. And angry soldier settlers added their voice to that of other farmers in the formation of the Country Party in 1923. These organisations coordinated the efforts of settlers to obtain a fair deal. They helped cement a strong rural vote in favour of tariff protection and Empire-preference schemes to provide guaranteed markets for produce. And while conservative coalition governments certainly pursued these policies and were rewarded with continuing support (at least at the federal level), the efforts of these soldier settler groups to excuse settlers from any of the blame attached to the failure of the scheme did not go uncontested.

Frustrated politicians and officials were beginning to lose their patience with settlers. Mounting public debt from arrears in rent and unpaid advances fuelled this concern. And out of this arose the disquieting belief that the men were draining the public purse rather than seeking independence. In 1921 the Minister for Lands and Works in Tasmania, Alexander Hean, argued that 'leniency has been extended to soldier settlers ... the Department has dealt liberally, and in many cases the undeserving has received more than his deserts'. Similar ideas underpinned the reply of the Queensland Minister of Public Lands to a deputation of soldier settlers from Beerburrum. They were pineapple growers, struggling to repay debts because of falling prices and anxious for the government to establish a cannery in their district to ensure the viability of their industry. The Minister gave them little comfort, declaring that they 'must recognise that the subsidising of the industry cannot go on forever ... the sooner [the government] knew that the settlers could

---

22 Circular from Prime Minister, 3 May 1922, Closer Settlement Board Correspondence, Tasmanian Archives, AB/13.

not produce pineapples to make a living ... the better for all concerned'. He left little doubt that they should leave the land if they could not make a profit and should not continue to rely on public dispensation for their debts. Here was the familiar injunction to be manly and independent, not undeserving and dependent. The language of Victorian charity was always near at hand to explain away repatriation problems.[23]

Sympathy for returned soldiers could not last. Established landowners often resented the resumption of their land for returned men and the easy loan and lease terms soldiers received. Again, the charge of undeserving was a frequent recourse. In Tasmania one landowner felt obliged to complain about a local soldier settler for whom he had previously written a character reference. According to this man, the returned soldier had been 'earnest, sober and industrious', but since his return 'things have compelled me ... to reverse my good opinion of him'. There was a lesson here, he believed. He was certainly not opposed to returned men – just the reverse. 'I wish you to understand', he assured the Settlement Board, 'I am in sympathy with every soldier but particularly ... those who show that the miseries of the trenches are a thing of the past and are trying to make the Burden placed upon us all lie as lightly as possible'.[24] Having placed men on the land, some clearly felt that the debt they owed returned soldiers had been repaid. The prospect of continuing support, especially for able-bodied men, threatened the manly and resourceful reputation of the Anzacs.

These views also received public confirmation. The 1925 Victorian Royal Commission on Soldier Settlement talked of soldier 'misfits', whose debts would never be recovered. It is tempting to dismiss such charges as the ill-informed prejudices of those who sought to shift the blame from hasty policies and lax administration onto the victims. And while this may be the case, reading the archives of the various State soldier settlement administrations, it is possible to see how such views, blinkered as they were, emerged from the experience of dealing with some settlers. Local inspectors reported regularly on the progress of soldier settlers. Some seemed to be doing well, making improvements on their land, putting in crops, maintaining their stock, and despite occasional setbacks, 'making very good progress'. Others seemed to be doing very little. They appeared uninterested in the land, built no fences, dams, sheds, or stock yards, failed to erect water tanks or even houses, and made 'very poor progress'. When all the settlers in a particular district failed, it was obvious that poor land and administration was at fault, but when some succeeded and some in the same district failed, it appeared to inspectors, locals, and administrators that the fault lay with the 'misfits'. This

---

23 Ministerial Memo re Question in the House, 8 September 1921, Closer Settlement Board Correspondence, Tasmanian Archives, AB/16; Minister of Public Lands to Beerburrum Soldier Settlers Deputation, 26 July 1923, Soldier Settlement, Queensland State Archives, LAN/AK 132.
24 C. B. to Closer Settlement Board, 21 July 1919, Closer Settlement Board Correspondence, Tasmanian Archives, AB/3.

may have been a harsh judgement. It was certainly not one that took account of the fact that some settlers had more experience, more capital, and more resources than others. But it is also clear that some returned soldiers, although attracted to the dream of independence and of 'being one's own boss' after the horror of the trenches, found themselves entirely unsuited to the land. Some were too injured or ill to cope with the rigours of farming life; others found themselves temperamentally unsuited. E.J.H. Joseph failed, but as he later admitted, this arose from his own inadequacies. After the trenches he believed he had completed his life's work and should never have to work again. When it came time to farm he just could not bring himself to do the work. He was dispirited, distracted, and weakened by nervous strain.[25]

The Victorian Royal Commission also laid part of the blame on 'the failure of wives to adapt to country life'. This intriguing claim cannot just be dismissed as misogyny born of official frustration (although it was that as well). Some soldiers talked without rancour of wives who were prepared to work in the house and the garden but refused to engage in farm labour. Household labour, and the rearing of children, were arduous enough tasks, but the official concern about the refusal of some women to assist in farming labour as well tells us much about the flaws in the yeoman ideal. This was really a model of pre-industrial life based on family cooperation and sturdy independence. It was bolstered by the rich pioneer literature of the 1880s, which valorised the labours of settlers, placing them in the canon of noble nation-builders. Here pioneering work was seen as harsh but enriching for the nation and later generations. This legend may have inspired many to go on the land. Nonetheless, some may not have been prepared for the full consequences of their decision. The settlers who went on the land after the war were products of a Victorian world, which had nurtured the separation of the male and female spheres. Over a century of medical science, biology, and etiquette had dictated that woman's natural place was in the home, where they were the experts in the domestic arts and sciences. Moreover, in the context of the declining birth rate that marked all Western nations from the late nineteenth century, there had been a renewed emphasis on the important role of mothering. Numerous magazines, doctors, baby health clinic nurses, and child-guidance experts advised women to breast-feed, supervise the health of infants, and psychologically nurture the growing child. The women who left with husbands to take up soldier settlements, especially those who had no experience of the land, were raised in this world. They were told, on the one hand, that their proper role was as home-maker and child nurturer but, on the other hand, had to face the harsh reality that husbands needed extra help on the farm. Women were never passive consumers of this literature, and the literature itself was never simple in its message. But women were presented with competing ideals – the pioneer woman, the independent, modern woman, and the

---

25 See Victorian Royal Commission on Soldier Settlement, p. 21; Joseph, *The Long Road Back*, p. 14.

nurturing mother – and had to negotiate their own lives within, and against, these expectations. For some, the answer lay in leaving the land, and sometimes their husband, no matter how difficult that decision must have been.[26]

Men also bore the burden of gender expectations. They likewise may have been inspired by the 'pioneer legend' and the prospect of being one's own boss. But they also confronted the ideal of the man as breadwinner, according to which the hallmark of manliness was to be sole provider for one's family. This made some men reluctant to compromise their position by asking wives to help with the planting and harvesting. One study in Western Australia found that some soldier settlers 'refused to enlist their families ... for full time farm work and were thus unable to produce enough'. This, however, was not just a matter of gender. The soldier settlers were seen to be in competition with 'southern European families', who felt comfortable with a peasant mode of production, in which everyone worked on the farm. The adoption of that model threatened the ethnic identity, as well as the manliness, of returned soldiers. There may also be a more pervasive cultural tension in men's relation to the land. Kay Schaffer has explored the myriad ways in which notions of the bush and the land were gendered within Australian culture. The land was predominantly rendered as 'woman', to be conquered and 'tamed' by pioneering men. This cultural imperative – to have culture (masculine) triumph over nature (feminine) – has a long heritage. But, in the context of the harsh conditions in many parts of rural Australia, the fact that nature triumphed over culture, inverting the laws of civilisation, must have been a disturbing and disabling occurrence for the maintenance of masculine esteem. In many ways, then – from the simple material realities of hard work and impoverishment to the deeper cultural currents of gender, ethnicity, and civilisation – settling on the land posed dilemmas and problems for those who sought to establish themselves there. While some triumphed or accommodated themselves to these material and cultural problems, others found this task more difficult.[27]

The reality of the farm forced many couples to quickly shed idealised notions of their roles. The daily struggle to survive extinguished divisions between public and private life, and some may have welcomed this freedom. But, as Marilyn Lake has argued, these competing images represented a fertile context for domestic conflict and family breakdown. Pulled by conflicting demands, some women collapsed under the strain; others took action and left the farm. Sometimes husbands followed; sometimes they did not, preferring to eke out an existence on the land. A few committed suicide. The attempt to impose a yeoman ideal on the soldier settlers

---

26 See Victorian Royal Commission on Soldier Settlement, p. 17; N. Mackenzie, Mortlock Library Oral History Transcript, p. 35. On the pioneer ideal, see J. Hirst, 'The Pioneer Legend', *Historical Studies*, vol. 18, no. 71, October 1978, pp. 316–37.
27 K. Schaffer, *Women and the Bush: Forces of Desire in the Australian Cultural Tradition*, CUP, Melbourne, 1988.

seems to have been a triumph of romantic fantasy over sober reality. It was settlers and their families who shared, but also suffered from, this flawed vision.[28]

For many men and women on the land, however, it was not a flawed vision or their unsuitability for rural life that was to blame for their situation but an incompetent administration and an unsympathetic inspectorate. There is certainly evidence to support this charge. Families settled in areas deemed suitable for cultivation only to be told a few years later by Lands Department officials that the land was unsuitable and they would have to move on. Some settled in areas on the strength of a promise that road or irrigation work would be completed, making the land viable. Public works lagged and settlers found that the proposed improvements never materialised. Some were promised local industries, such as canneries and sugar refineries, only to discover that these industries were eventually developed elsewhere. These events united the settlers into organisations to protest their treatment.

More usually the battle between settlers and administration, however, was an individual one. Inspectors were charged with the responsibility of assessing the worth and viability of settlers, and it was at this harsh coalface that settlers felt the frustration and scorn of officialdom. The inspectors, of course, were only at the end of the official line, but it was on their word that action was taken. We can see this in numerous letters, memos, and reports. In 1919 the Commonwealth Department of Repatriation instructed all State Lands Departments to only pay sustenance allowances to new settlers who 'were in necessitous circumstances and who may reasonably be expected to succeed'. It was the last criteria that placed a burden on inspectors. District officers were instructed to report all cases in which a soldier settler 'has abandoned his block or his block has been forfeited or he has not made a bona fide attempt to work the land properly'.[29]

Soldier settlers in difficult circumstances probably came to dread the visit of the inspector. It could certainly ruin their chance of extra assistance. In one typical case, A.E. Spencer, a Tasmanian soldier settler, wrote to the Minister of Lands requesting a postponement of the rent owing on his block. He promised to pay the balance after the harvest, explaining that he had been in hospital undergoing an operation and 'this put him back a lot'. Worse, he claimed that he had never been informed that his repayments were urgent until the bailiffs had arrived. He pleaded 'to let things stand a while until the stock improves ... as it will crush me altogether if you sell my things now'. The attached note of the local inspector suggests a more complex story. He asserted that Spencer had not carried out promises to make further improvements on the land, and that he seemed unprepared to work the

---

28 See T. P. Field, *Post-war Land Settlement in Western Australia*, University of Kentucky Press, Kentucky, 1963, p. 24. See also Lake, *Limits of Hope*, pp. 143–94. See K. Reiger, *The Disenchantment of the Home: Modernising the Australian Family, 1880-1940*, OUP, Melbourne, 1984.
29 See Repatriation Department to Victorian Lands Department, 24 July 1919; Memo to District Officers, 31. May 1920, Closer Settlement Board Correspondence, VPRS 10645.

land. On this basis, he was 'not inclined to advise giving up our hold over his stock. I should advise him to call a clearing sale and instruct the auctioneers to pay our debt'. The Closer Settlement Board took the inspector's advice and refused to pay Spencer for any improvements made until the debt had been paid.[30] It was a harsh decision, but one that reflected widespread scepticism among inspectors about the seriousness of many settlers.

In evidence before the 1922 New South Wales Select Committee on Soldier Settlements, concerning poultry farmers near Bankstown, the State Poultry Expert declared that 'if a man cannot make a living out of 600 to 800 hens then he cannot make a living at all ... the men are not working sufficiently ... instead they are looking for concessions'. Another inspector claimed that the men 'were inexperienced and had no right to go on the land'. These opinions framed the evidence that all forty-four settlers in this group settlement were in trouble. Settlers, on the other hand, maintained that they had been badly advised by inspectors. They had been informed that 600 birds would guarantee a sufficient income to meet repayments, but the actual return from this number of birds 'was nowhere near it'. As a consequence, 'there was constant friction between the Department and the settlers'. Worse, the men found that the department had put a lien on their egg production, forcing them to sell to the government, with the proceeds being used to pay off arrears. This left them little money to pay off debts to local storekeepers. To get around this problem, settlers were secretly selling eggs on the black market to obtain cash for daily necessities. It was a situation that only exacerbated the tension between officials and settlers.[31]

Many settlers in difficult circumstances engaged in a type of guerrilla warfare with government inspectors and administrators. Once all avenues of appeal for further assistance were exhausted, men and their families left the land, often with considerable amounts owing. Others sought to recoup some of their losses. They sold their stock or any crops, furniture, and farm equipment before inspectors and bailiffs arrived to impound the goods. In Tasmania, for example, the Closer Settlement Board frequently complained of men who left their property without notice, fleeing interstate, out of the reach of police. When inspectors arrived, they found that stock could 'not be traced' and ploughs, carts, saddles, even stoves, all paid for with advances, could not be found. In the first few years, deserting settlers were pursued; sometimes police were called in to trace debtors and the missing stock and equipment. Few were found.[32] But by 1922 the extent of desertion was sufficient, and the obloquy attached to arresting soldier settlers so great, that governments opted to write off debts. Returned-soldier groups and soldier settler

---

30 A. E. Spencer Correspondence, 1 April 1918, Closer Settlement Board Correspondence, Tasmanian Archives, AB/1.
31 Select Committee on Soldier Settlements, New South Wales Parliamentary Papers, vol. 1, 1922, pp. 5–25.
32 On troubles in Tasmania, see Closer Settlement Board Correspondence, Tasmanian Archives, AB/3.

organisations increasingly publicised the 'hard struggle', the 'struggling against hope', and the 'deplorable condition' of settlers. They charged that the 'administration was a failure'. In this context, governments preferred not to be seen as persecuting the men who had sacrificed so much for the nation. In 1929, when Mr Justice Pike came to draw a conclusion on the losses sustained by the states, he faced a situation in which most states had written off their losses and had begun the process of revaluing existing land, stock, and equipment to ensure that the remaining settlers had a fighting chance of survival. He praised the boards in different states for 'dealing with the difficult question of revising the indebtedness of the soldier settlers'.[33]

III

Despite the traumas and well-publicised plight of soldier settlers, enthusiasm for land settlement schemes did not diminish. What is perhaps remarkable is that soldier settlement was still actively promoted as a sound repatriation policy for veterans of later wars. Even the RSL, which had done so much to highlight the plight of soldier settlers after the First World War, continued to promote the virtues of the land. Before the end of the Second World War the RSL even began to rewrite the historical record on soldier settlement, claiming that 'most will admit that there has been a measure of success, and that many of the ... soldier settlers of the last war are now playing a big part in providing the essential foods so necessary to Australia'. Although prudently they warned of the dangers of hasty policy and insufficient safeguards for the next generation of soldier settlers. To this end they argued for generous sustenance allowances, proper irrigation schemes, adequate advances, reasonable land valuations, and high tariff protection for soldier farmers. The League now favoured Commonwealth, rather than state, control of the scheme. But underpinning these proposals was a faith that 'successful settlement plans will be the turning point in our rural life ... leading to a contented and numerous rural population'.[34]

Such assertions were more circumspect than the aggressive 'boosterism' of the early decades of the twentieth century, but vestiges of the old faith in rural plenty and prosperity were still evident. They appear anachronistic in the face of the relentless urbanisation of the population. By the end of the Second World War, half of Australia's population lived in its six state capital cities, a doubling of the proportion since 1880. This only added to the urgency of the League's campaign for

---

33 For publicity on the plight of the settlers, see *Sydney Morning Herald*, 19 April 1922, 22 May 1922, and 6 July 1922. Finally, see 'Report of Mr Justice Pike on Losses Due to Soldier Settlement', p. 25.
34 See K.H. Todd, 'Land Settlement for Ex-Service Men', *Reveille*, 1 August 1943; D.J. Langlands, 'Land Settlement for Servicemen', *Reveille*, 1 June 1944.

a proper soldier settlement scheme. And it was a vision that continued to inspire the League. The RSL supported soldier settlement for Korea and Vietnam veterans. In 1970, in a speech that would have done Brady proud, the future president of the League, Colin Hines, argued:

> Basically I consider we are a 'land-loving' people, so therefore a sound Land Settlement Scheme must have a great appeal to a large percentage of our young Ex-Servicemen. In a country with more undeveloped arable land than anywhere else in the world, this should be ... an obvious course for any progressive government to follow ... to settle and develop that coastal country from Rockhampton ... to the Kimberleys ... is essential. It is quite possible that if we don't develop this area in the very near future someone else will be doing just that for their own benefit.[35]

Australian governments did not pursue a settlement policy for Vietnam veterans, preferring industrial training for a new generation of veterans, but the arguments of Hines point to the tenacity of the rural vision, and it is this that we need to keep in mind in understanding soldier settlement after 1945. Despite the losses incurred from the soldier settlement schemes of the 1920s, Australian governments after 1939 were still prepared to consider land settlement as viable repatriation – the last flowering of rural 'boosterism'.

In 1943 the Commonwealth government established a Rural Reconstruction Commission to advise on policies for the rural sector. The commission believed that soldier settlement would be a natural part of rural reconstruction, as every nation after war had sought to solve the 'age-old problem' of returning soldiers by encouraging them 'to turn their hands from weapons to the use of agricultural implements'. If this was the case, then it was essential that governments act cautiously and in full knowledge of the errors of the past, as the 'stage was set for a repetition of disasters unless precautions were taken'. Much of the commission's report was taken up with an assessment of the reasons for the failure of the earlier scheme, acting as an important propagator of the image of soldier settlement as a disaster. It shared many of Pike's conclusions. Soldier settlement had been destroyed by want of capital, inexperienced settlers, rising costs, lack of markets, and falling prices. Their solution was to 'resist the short-term clamour for land' and ensure that 'qualifications not desires ... determine placement on the land'. This meant more rigorous scrutiny of applicants to ensure that they had sufficient capital and, if not, at least 'high qualifications' for farming life. In addition, settlers needed appropriate guidance and supervision, and expert evaluations of land to ensure that it was suitable. Much of this echoes the plans for the first soldier settlement scheme. The commission, however, was prepared to go further, recommending strict price

---

35   C. Hines, 'National Servicemen on the Land', *Reveille*, 1 May 1970.

controls on capital equipment, and land valuations based on 1939 prices rather than on the expected inflationary prices of the immediate post-war years.[36]

The general framework for post-war soldier settlement was adopted by a joint conference of Commonwealth and State ministers in August 1945, and ratified later that year in Commonwealth and State legislation. Settlement had to be undertaken only in areas where there was a reasonable expectation of successful production; applicants had to be selected on the basis of their savings, their willingness to invest their own resources, and their experience of farm work; holdings had to be of sufficient size to enable settlers to operate efficiently; and adequate guidance and technical advice had to be provided. Although this system, administered by each state, did not meet the RSL's demand for a single government authority, no land could be selected for settlement without the approval of the Commonwealth. Moreover, the Commonwealth, in addition to allocating loans of up to £1000 for improvements, provided all settlers with a living allowance for the first year and required no repayments in that period. Each settler also had to undertake an eight-week residential course in the 'principles of farm management'. Although land valuations were fixed at 1942 prices – rather than 1939, as recommended – in large measure these provisions addressed the main concerns of the Rural Reconstruction Commission.

The commission's warning to resist the clamour for land was astute. For some members of the community, the Commonwealth and state governments had become too cautious. The RSL condemned delays in the survey and inspection of land, and confronted by large numbers of applications, newspapers trumpeted the plaintive cry of 'no land yet for diggers' and 'returning RAAF want to go on the land'. Even in the early 1950s there were long waiting lists for soldier settlement blocks, condemning many men to 'dead-end' jobs while they waited for their life's dream. Most states had waiting lists of at least two years and sometimes as long as five. Men who qualified were not automatically entitled to a block of land; rather, they had to wait until suitable land became available, and then they had to apply for a block in competition with others. On the other hand, newspapers also carried extensive stories warning of the 'pitfalls of soldier settlement'.[37] One of these pitfalls was land speculation. There was no doubt that some profiteers sought to exploit the demand for land, just as they had done after the First World War. It still took careful public servants to foil such schemes. In 1944 a Buderim landowner wrote to the Queensland Lands Department offering 1000 acres of prime 'virgin' land with 'dark chocolate soil' and a good modern home for soldier settlement. He wanted £3000 for the land, which he considered 'cheap according to ruling prices today and the quality of the soil'. The local Lands Department officer, however, reported that the

---

36 Rural Reconstruction Commission, Settlement and Employment of Returned Men on the Land, pp. 3–35.
37 See the Age, 18 July 1945; Courier Mail, 27 July 1945 and 15 March 1946; Sydney Morning Herald, 11 October 1945 and 24 August 1952.

land was, in fact, rough, broken, with poor yellow grey soil, no permanent water, and infested with lantana. He estimated its worth at £200 but considered it quite unsuitable.[38]

Despite the undoubted greater caution of the administrators of the Second World War soldier settlement scheme, accounts of the experience of settlement strike a chord with those of earlier settlers. In the 1950s Stan McRae took up a soldier settler block at Jerramungup, Western Australia, only to find that it was infested with rabbits. James Deegan was a settler in the same area. He found not only rabbits, but also the land flooded. Both complained of the poor housing provided by the government: two-bedroom asbestos houses with iron roofs. Worse was the price of stock. They and other settlers in the area were convinced that the government was charging an inflated price for sheep and that some of them were 'roughies'. Life there proved to be hard. It was a significant distance from any towns, the land was difficult to cultivate, and despite government assistance, after the living allowance ran out many relied on child endowment to survive. Deegan's wife came to wish 'that instead of dropping the atom bomb on Monte Bello ... they had dropped it on Jerramungup'. Fred and Ethel Grossman took up a block at Gairdner, Western Australia, only to find that it was infested with weeds and tiger snakes. James Nunn, a soldier settler on Kangaroo Island, found it difficult to clear his heavily wooded land, and he and his wife lived in a tent for four years before their house was built. In Victoria, Graham Budd and his family lived in a shearing shed with no water, and no power or sink for the first two years on the farm. He bitterly recalled that government officials had given the impression that 'one would be rich in no time'. This had not proved to be the case. Friends of the Bennetts, soldier settlers from Western Australia, wrote to say 'we have not made our fortune yet but are getting poorer each day'.

Although the plight of these settlers was similar, their allocation of blame differed. All agreed that the land they had settled was poor, government assistance inadequate, and prices for their produce low. James Nunn and Graham Budd thought the bureaucrats were most to blame. The commission, they believed, was after its 'pound of flesh', refusing to reduce rents or valuations when it was clear that the land could not produce enough to cover required repayments. Nunn resented the fact that 'conquering heroes' were 'being made subservient to the bureaucratic whims of people better paid than they were'. James Deegan, on the other hand, found that local inspectors were sympathetic to his situation, turning a blind eye to the fact that he kept pigs, enabling him to use the proceeds from this stock for his family rather than rent. Others blamed the resentment of locals for their troubles. James Oversby thought that many established farmers in the area resented the facilities given to soldier settlers. He felt these men dominated the local council, doing everything they could to prevent the growth of Jerramungup.

---

38 See Queensland Premiers Department Special Bundle, Soldier Settlement 1944–49.

Whatever the cause, settlers noted the failure of those around them: families left the land, indebted after years of labour; wives became sullen and withdrawn; and husbands, whose dream of manly independence was lost in debt, ceaseless labour, and domestic conflict, committed suicide. These experiences echoed the plight of the first generation of soldier settlers.[39]

Such accounts sit uneasily beside more recent studies, which suggest that soldier settlement after the Second World War successfully established men and their families on productive farms. We should be wary of generalising from oral history and autobiographical accounts in the light of these broader studies. Some are the bitter reflections of those who failed. Others are narratives often unconsciously structured around a trope of triumph against adversity, in which the obstacles and problems are magnified to highlight the achievement of survival. But, equally, they cannot be dismissed too lightly. Even Rosalind Smallwood's rosy picture of soldier settlement in 1950s Victoria has its share of settlers who struggled to survive. Moreover, Victoria had the most effective post-war settlement scheme and cannot be taken as representative of all states. But there are other factors that qualify this picture. Smallwood concludes her account in 1962. By this time most of the soldier settlers had been on the land only ten years, during a decade of high commodity prices and high tariff barriers. This helps explain a low failure rate. Others, however, were later hit hard by the 1967 drought and by falling wool prices, and later still by the 1973 oil crisis, which significantly increased costs of equipment and fuel. This was a familiar scenario. Seasons, price fluctuations, and market forces seriously affected the prospects of small farmers, be they soldier settlers or not. A 1972 study of a Victorian soldier settlement area found that half the farms were in serious debt and that many settlers were forced to take on outside work to keep their farms afloat. On Kangaroo Island only sixty-five of the original 174 settlers were still there by 1977. Yet despite these problems, a surprising number of those who survived, despite low incomes, felt that life on the land was worth the sacrifice. Joe and Jocelyn Price looked back on the tough times and considered them the 'best years of their life'. But then they had weathered all the ups and downs.[40]

All the evidence, however, suggests that the more carefully planned scheme for Second World War veterans was relatively successful. By the early 1960s about 12,000 ex-servicemen had been settled on the land. Success, however, varied from state to state. In Victoria only 4 per cent had failed, but in Tasmania a poorly administered and underfunded scheme had led to a failure rate of 28 per cent.

---

39 See J. Deegan, S. McRae, F. & E. Crossman, & J. Oversby, Oral History Transcripts, Battye Library; J. Nunn, *Soldier Settlers: War Service Land Settlement Kangaroo Island*, Investigator Press, Hawthorndene, 1980, pp. 27–97; Graham Budd Papers, *Autobiography*, vol. 1, La Trobe Library, MS 11560; A. G. Bennett Papers, La Trobe Library, MS 9559, MSB 54.
40 See Smallwood, *Hard to Go Bung*, pp. 222–35; H. S. Hawkins and A. S. Watson, *Shelford: A Preliminary Report of a Social and Economic Study of a Victorian Soldier Settlement Area*, University of Melbourne, School of Agriculture, 1972; M. McRae, *On the Block: Rocks, Rabbits and Reptiles*, Sunnyland Press, Mortlake, 1987.

In the other states, about one in ten had failed. More failed in the late 1960s and early 1970s, but overall most have considered this scheme a greater success than its predecessor. But it was not a profitable scheme for Australian governments. By the early 1960s total Commonwealth and state government expenses for settling men on the land after 1945 amounted to £106 million. In return, they had received repayments amounting to £26 million. More was returned in subsequent years, but there was no expectation or likelihood that receipts would ever match expenditure. Nor was there any outcry over government losses on this scheme. This is partly due to more sophisticated national accounting. Although actual monetary receipts would never match expenditure, Commonwealth and State governments held substantial equity in the land, amounting to a considerable financial asset. Moreover, profit and loss had to take account of the benefits of produce, trade, and taxes accruing from the agricultural sector. Successful soldier settlers were a benefit to the economy. The readiness to accept the direct costs of settling men on the land after 1945 stands in marked contrast to the response to the First World War soldier settlement scheme, where losses of £45 million over twenty-five years were seen as a 'serious failure'. Although these estimates took no account of the value of government equity in the land or the indirect benefits of agricultural production.[41]

An explanation for the difference in response may partly reside in the extent of individual failure. The Second World War scheme involved far fewer people – only one-quarter of the number in the first scheme – and failure rates of less than 20 per cent in most states were undoubtedly lower. How much lower, however, is in dispute. When Mr Justice Pike came to draw up the ledger of failure after the First World War, he concluded that only 29 per cent of soldier settlers had left their land. The rate varied from state to state. Tasmania was the worst, with 61 per cent failing, but only 17 per cent failed in Victoria. Saying 'only' is precisely to register a note of surprise. Given the outcry and widespread condemnation of soldier settlement after the First World War, such rates might seem low. Of course, some have disputed Pike's figures. Marilyn Lake estimates that by 1929 one-third had failed, and a decade later this had risen sharply to two-thirds and, in some districts, three-quarters. Others have claimed that Lake's figures are overly pessimistic. Perhaps the most judicious estimate is that of J.M. Powell, who argues that half the settlers had failed by 1939. While certainly a tragedy, it also means that half of the original settlers, 20,000 families, were still on the land twenty years after settling there.[42]

---

41 See Smallwood, *Hard to Go Bung*, p. 231; *Commonwealth Year Book*, 1960, p. 99; Rural Reconstruction Commission, *Settlement and Employment of Returned Men on the Land*, p. 6.
42 See 'Report of Mr Justice Pike on Losses Due to Soldier Settlement', p. 6; Lake, *Limits of Hope*, pp. 114 & 202; J. M. Powell, 'The Debt of Honour: Soldier Settlement in the Dominions 1915-1940', *Journal of Australian Studies*, no. 8, June 1981, pp. 66-7. For criticisms of Lake's figures, see C. Fahey, 'Review: *Limits of Hope*: *Australian Historical Studies*, vol. 23, no. 90, April 1988, pp. 140-1.

4 Soldier Settlement

A more useful point of comparison might be with the late-nineteenth-century selection schemes. Unfortunately, there is no overall estimate of the number of selectors who succeeded or failed, and moreover, the evidence is difficult to uncover. There are some partial estimates. The 1883 Morris and Rankin Report on New South Wales claimed that more than half, and possibly three-quarters, of the selectors had failed. Their figures, however, are vague and inconclusive. Our best guides are local and regional studies. Here there are differences. G.L. Buxton concludes that selection in the Riverina was remarkably successful, but Duncan Waterson's study of the agriculturally rich district of the Darling Downs estimates that two thirds of the original settlers failed. More sobering still is Bill Gammage's claim that eight out of every nine selections in Narrandera passed from their original occupants (although some of this was settlers selling at a profit). Those historians who have analysed the successes of selection have focused more on the increase in land under cultivation than on the number of original selectors who survived on their land. The weight of evidence on selection seems to indicate that it was a greater failure than soldier settlement after the First World War.[43]

If this is the case would a more accurate, although heretical, proposition be that soldier settlement was not the 'great failure' that its critics have sought to portray it as. There were many tragic failures – some through no fault of anyone, and a number through official ineptitude, poor planning, and occasional corruption – and the extent of human suffering for these families was significant. The fact that these problems afflicted men and their families who had already sacrificed so much is cause for even further regret. Planners and administrators of soldier settlement after 1945 were more careful, and the extent of failure was much reduced. But it was not eradicated. No government can entirely insulate farmers from the effects of drought, flood, poor seasons, the market forces of supply and demand, land speculation, or corruption. These are the lot of farming families, be they soldier settlers or civilian farmers. But the success rate for soldier settlers seems to have been higher than that for nineteenth-century selectors. The assistance provided by governments undoubtedly helped many soldier settlers to ride out some of the troughs of farming life that sent others under. In all, soldier settlement after 1918 and 1945 assisted as many as 30,000 families to settle, more or less permanently, on the land at a time when the thrust of change in the agricultural sector was towards large scale and heavily mechanised farming. This was a small but significant achievement, although certainly no comfort to those who found themselves placed on poor land with few resources.

---

43 See Report of Inquiry into the State of the Public Lands and the Operation of the Land Laws, 1883, p. 106; G. L. Buxton, *The Riverina 1861–91: An Australian Regional Study*, MUP, Melbourne, 1967, pp. 189–210; D. B. Waterson, *Squatter, Selector and Storekeeper: A History of the Darling Downs 1859–93*, SUP, Sydney, 1968, pp. 99–100; B. Gammage, *Narrandera Shire*, Narrandera Shire Council, Narrandera, 1986, pp. 81–106.

The success of soldier settlement says something important about repatriation. Much of our understanding of the history of soldier settlement has come from those settlers who failed and their defenders, who were determined to argue for a better deal for these men and their families. Our image of failure was fostered by these groups and by the planners of later schemes, who sought to clear the path to a fairer and more supportive policy. But the outrage that accompanied the First World War soldier settlement scheme tells us as much about the expectations of repatriation as it does about settlement itself. The planners of this first scheme were convinced that it would be sufficient to place the able-bodied on the land for the nation's debt of gratitude to be expunged. There was a continuing commitment to the injured and ill, but the able-bodied were men who had proved themselves in the most difficult circumstances and, given the right start, were thus able to look after themselves. To do anything else would have been to diminish their manhood.

Underpinning this was a belief that soldier settlement should not involve any long-term costs to the nation. It was this belief that made Mr Justice Pike's estimate of loss so alarming. From this assumption flowed a complex politics. On one side, any individual failure might be seen as the result of weakness, the product of 'misfits'. This was an uncomfortable and unsettling message, and one stoutly resisted by returned servicemen and their defenders. On their side, it was imperative to prove that soldier settlement problems were a failure of policy and administration. This view was given public and official endorsement. It framed the caution of later planners and administrators. After the Second World War, however, it was assumed that soldier settlement would be a continuing government commitment. This time it was seen as a normal expense of repatriation. What distinguished repatriation after 1945 was a belief that able-bodied men required more extensive and continuing assistance than had been the expectation in 1918. Repatriation, then, is in part a battle of perceptions and expectations, and it is this battle that has done much to shape historical understandings of soldier settlement.

5
Shell-Shock

Since 1915 we have witnessed an explosion of words describing the psychological effects of war. In popular parlance, *jelly shakes*, *shivers* and *bomb happy* mark out forms of war-induced mental breakdown with frankness and simplicity. Military and medical authorities were more laboured in their terminology, resorting to a panoply of inelegant and cryptic signifiers: war neurosis, commotional anxiety, disordered action of the heart, effort syndrome, combat fatigue, battle exhaustion, and post-traumatic stress disorder. Words are a way of capturing the world, confining and demarcating observable parts. But the proliferation of scientific terms gives us one indication of the variety and complexity of this field of enquiry, and the difficulty doctors faced in mapping the terrain. They, of course, had the harder task of moving beyond description to a language of cause and effect. One concept, however, has crossed the boundaries from the scientific to the popular: 'shell-shock'. C.S. Myers, research scientist at the Cambridge University Psychological Laboratory and consultant psychologist to the British Expeditionary Force, was one of the first to use this term. He was responding to widespread alarm at the number of soldiers stricken with symptoms of blindness, stammering, deafness, muteness, uncontrollable fits, and chronic shaking without any apparent organic cause. By December 1914 medical officers at the front were reporting that one tenth of all casualties seemed to be suffering from these conditions. Three years later the incidence had risen to two-fifths. At first a few officers noted that the worst cases seemed to occur among men thrown over or buried by exploding shells. Although apparently unhurt, these soldiers quickly developed alarming signs of injury and distress. Sir Frederick Mott, Wilfred Harris, and Myers, among others, proposed that minute lesions on the brain from the 'shock' of a near-by shell blast were the cause. By early 1915, however, Myers came to a different view. He believed that the shocks were psychological, not biological, and that the condition was curable through hypnosis and suggestion.[1]

The term *shell-shock* caught the public imagination. It rendered a vivid image of the cause of these painful and otherwise inexplicable conditions. By 1917, however, medical authorities were beginning to question the usefulness of this term. Further investigation revealed that many men suffering shell-shock had not been affected (psychologically or biologically) by an exploding shell; some were not on the front line or anywhere near gunshots, let alone shells, and yet they exhibited the classic symptoms of anxiety, neurasthenia, or hysteria. The problem obviously appeared, as Myers had proposed, to be psychological, but now in ways unrelated to shell explosions. The preferred term became war neurosis, although there were many specific conditions – such as conversion hysteria, commotional anxiety, neurasthenia, and disordered action of the heart – encompassed by this general classification. In 1922 the British War Office committee of inquiry into this condition concluded that *shell-shock* was a seriously misleading term, and recommended that it be officially abandoned, to be replaced by *war neurosis*. This did not dent its popular appeal. In Australia stories of the shell-shocked soldier were staple fare in *Smith's Weekly* throughout the interwar years. It remains a familiar term in popular language even today (in the 1990s the British cricket team was said to be 'shell-shocked').

But where popular opinion sustained the concept of shell-shock, which favoured the idea of a random and specific incident as the reason for the collapse of friends and relatives, doctors sought to indict some cause in their search for explanation. *War neurosis* was one term of attribution, suggesting that there was either something amiss with its sufferers or exceptional in the nature of modern warfare. Military and medical authorities pursued this line of enquiry, further refining their language in light of experience from subsequent conflicts. During the Second World War, 'battle exhaustion' became an important concept, especially in the USA. Later still, 'post-traumatic stress disorder' came to prominence in the analysis of persistent psychological problems in Vietnam veterans and those of later conflicts. The increasingly elaborate scientific language suggests greater precision; it might equally suggest bafflement. It is useful to step to one side of these concepts and debates – to disengage from psychological science and engage with history.[2]

The proliferation of words in the lexicon since 1915 for the psychological effects of war, however, opens up an important historical question. Shell-shock was thought to be something new and unique to modern warfare. Although some noted evidence of nervous conditions and hysteria among soldiers in the American Civil War, and Russian doctors used psychological treatments for a few soldiers

---

1 C. S. Myers, 'A Contribution to the Study of Shell Shock', *Lancet*, vol. 1, 1915, pp. 316–20; C. S. Myers, *Shell Shock in France, 1914–18*, CUP, Cambridge, 1940, pp. 12–25. For the alternative and earlier biological view, see W. Harris, *Nerve Injuries and Shock*, OUP, London, 1915.

2 See G. Elliot Smith & T. H. Pear, *Shell Shock and its Lessons*, Manchester University Press, Manchester, 1917; Thomas W. Salmon, *The Care of Mental Diseases and War Neuroses (Shell Shock) in the British Army*, National Committee for Mental Hygiene, New York, 1917; and John T. MacCurdy, *War Neuroses*, CUP, Cambridge, 1918. See also 'Report of the War Office Committee of Inquiry into Shell Shock', *British Parliamentary Papers*, vol. 1, 1922; 'The Soul Agony of the Shell-Shocked', *Smith's Weekly*, 8 May 1920; 'Shell-Shocked Morphia Fiend', *Smith's Weekly*, 17 March 1928.

5 Shell-Shock

in the 1904–5 Russo-Japanese War, its appearance in the First World War was on such an unprecedented scale that contemporary doctors and subsequent medical and military historians have concluded that there is something in the character of modern warfare that is inherently stressful; a type of stress unknown in previous conflicts. Shell-shock seemed to be something new. Scientists have argued that the intensity of modern warfare (the large numbers of combatants), the vastly increased destructive capacity of weapons (particularly shells, grenades, and automatic weapons), the protracted nature of the conflict (continuing for days at a time over a number of years), and the relative passivity of modern warfare (with soldiers being subjected to long periods of shelling and gunfire from unseen forces) created unique conditions for an increased incidence of stress and psychological breakdown. How these various factors operated is disputed, but the qualitative difference of modern warfare from the limited, occasional, and mostly face-to-face fighting of traditional battles is not questioned. Shell-shock, then, was apparently a consequence of modern warfare. Although military authorities were at first loath to accept that these conditions were psychological in origin, this has become the accepted conclusion.[3] But is shell-shock new? And if it is not, does this suggest that the neuroses of war are more complex (medically, socially, and culturally) than medical theory allows? In other words, while the extreme distress of soldiers, sailors, and airmen in war is all too real, do the terms *shell-shock* and *war neurosis* tell us as much about medicine and medical government of illness as they do about the effects of war? And what were the implications of an idea like shell-shock for the repatriation of returned servicemen and women?

We can illustrate this problem through some case studies. Bearing in mind the argument about shell-shock and modernity, how can we make sense of the case of a young man struck blind after a shell burst? He lay in bed with staring eyes, dilated pupils, declaring he was unable to distinguish light from darkness, but there was no sign of abnormality or injury to the eye, and the pupils reacted to light. Or explain another case of a soldier whose right arm was paralysed after intensive combat. Examination, however, found no injury to the arm, or to nearby muscles or nerves. Another case is that of a soldier who found it difficult to eat. He felt nauseous, threw up his food, and became seriously withdrawn and apathetic. These are very familiar symptoms in the medical literature on war neurosis but in actual fact they come from very different eras. The first two appear to be classic cases of hysteria, although contemporary psychiatrists would prefer the term *conversion reaction*; the latter might be seen as a depressive anxiety condition. Hysteria was more common in the First World War and much less frequent in the Second World

---

3   See J. Keegan, *The Face of Battle*, Jonathon Cape, London, 1976; M. Stone, 'Shell Shock and the Psychologists', in W. F. Bynum et al. (eds), *The Anatomy of Madness: Essays in the History of Psychiatry*, vol. 2, Tavistock, London, 1985, pp. 243–71; E. Showalter, *The Female Malady: Women, Madness and English Culture 1830–1980*, Virago, London, 1987, pp. 167–94; Belenky, 'Introduction', pp. 1–5.

War or Vietnam, so here we have one indicator of the different contexts from which these cases were taken. But a much clearer indication is the treatment for each of these conditions. In the first case the soldier was treated by a psychiatrist who used suggestion, and after a few days the patient was coaxed to full recovery of his sight. The third case was treated with a combination of psychotherapy and psychotropic drugs. Our initial impression seems confirmed: the first case is from the First World War and the third from the Vietnam War. What about the second case? The best clue, again, is not the symptom but the treatment. The soldier with the paralysed arm was thrown into an ice-cold river and left to drown or swim. He miraculously recovered the use of his arm and made it back to shore. This was a case from the Napoleonic Wars.[4]

The nineteenth-century case is not an anomaly; there were others like it in the literature. The point of these case studies has been to suggest that shell-shock may not be an entirely new phenomenon. Many of the conditions that came to be seen as psychological in origin in the First World War were familiar to military authorities, but before 1915 they were largely seen as forms of malingering. In fact, there is a considerable literature on 'feigned' illnesses among soldiers, stretching back to the seventeenth century. This was a far from crude field of enquiry. The analysis of feigned illness covered such problems as 'pretended' blindness, deafness, and paralysis of the limbs, melancholia, mania and hypochondria, epilepsy, sleeplessness, vertigo, fear, fever, delirium, and excitability of the heart – all symptoms and conditions deemed neurotic in the First World War. And there were various gradations of pretence. Gavin, writing in the early nineteenth century, identified four types: feigned (totally fictitious), exaggerated (where the condition was real but was said to exist in greater or different form), factitious (condition wholly produced by the patient), and lastly, aggravated (where the condition was increased by artificial means). There was also a sophisticated armoury of techniques for unmasking malingering. Those suspected of pretence were stimulated with electric currents, given strong smelling salts, thrown in rivers, given opium drafts and then tickled under the nose with feathers, given sudden frights, or just sent back to their units to fight. Others were more sympathetic. In the 1870s A.B.R. Myers argued that the high incidence of heart stress among soldiers was not feigned but a consequence of constricted military uniforms.[5]

---

4   The three cases are from A. W. Campbell, 'Remarks on some Neuroses and Psychoses of War', *MJA*, vol. 1, 1916, pp. 320–1; H. Gavin, *On the Feigned and Factitious Diseases of Soldiers and Seamen, on the Means Used to Stimulate or Produce Them and on the Best Modes of Discovering Imposters*, Edinburgh University Press, Edinburgh, 1838, pp. 97–100; B. Boman, 'The Vietnam Veteran Ten Years On', *Australian and New Zealand Journal of Psychiatry*, no. 16, 1982, pp. 114–16.

5   See Gavin, *On the Feigned and Factitious Diseases*, pp. 1–117; T. R. Beck, *Elements of Medical Jurisprudence*, 2nd edn, John Anderson, London, 1825, pp. 1–17; A. B. R. Myers, *On the Aetiology and Prevalence of Diseases of the Heart Among Soldiers*, John Churchill & Sons, London, 1870, pp. 6–39. All these works cite earlier authorities, such as George Cheyne, *The*

5 Shell-Shock

Other readings of the relationship between nerves, malingering and trauma, however, begin to appear in the late nineteenth century. The 'epidemic' of accident victims claiming compensation when they had no precise injury was popularly dismissed as 'railway spine'. But this term, in its very ambiguity, highlighted the difficulty of rendering the actuality of this condition: was it feigned or hysterical? Just before the outbreak of the First World War the literature on malingering was given greater credence by investigations into the injuries of workers. In 1913 Sir John Collie, who would soon become a prominent contributor to debates about war neurosis, published an extensive treatise on malingering and feigned sickness arising from workers' compensation legislation. Collie noted the large increase in such cases since the introduction of this legislation, and mapped out all the usual symptoms of malingering – hysterical paralysis, palpitations of the heart, loss of energy, disinterest and melancholia, and persistent aches and pains – none of which had an organic cause. Compensation, he concluded, was a significant inducement to 'deliberate fraud'. But he also embraced a new language of psychological motivation and 'unconscious exaggeration'. Here he admitted that there was a large grey area between the 'ingenious conscious deceiver' and those whose pains were psychic in origin – between the malingerer and the hysteric.

Collie provides a bridge to shell-shock. Despite his conclusion that deceit and exaggeration were at the heart of many of these claims for compensation, his text continually ruptures this belief. In his own desire for an exhaustive account, Collie undermines the argument for malingering, becoming so intent on exploring unconscious impulses, hysterical reactions, traumatic neurosis, and neurasthenic personalities that there seems remarkably little space left for 'pure deceit'. In emphasising hereditary and temperamental vulnerability to neurosis, he further underlined the mental origin of these complaints. And, in focusing on the large numbers of men suffering hysterical conditions arising from work accidents, he laid the ground for later theories of war neurosis. Even before the war some were coming to recognise that hysteria was not the exclusive preserve of women.[6]

Many of the psychological conditions of war that we have come to regard as modern in origin are, in fact, of considerable antiquity. What has changed is their incidence and more certainly the way they have been viewed. It did take some time for the malingering explanation to lose its hold on military authorities. During the First World War doctors resorted to electrical stimulation, confinement, punitive work duties, and ridicule in an effort to uncover 'malingerers'. Even in the Second World War, General George Patton, Commander of the United States Forces in Europe, was a noted sceptic of 'combat fatigue'.[7] Most medical and military

---

English Malady; or, A Treatise on Nervous Disorders of All Kinds, Strahan & Leake, London, 1733, and Dr Zacchias, *Questionum Medico-Legalium*, Frankfurt, 1688.
6 Sir J. Collie, *Malingering and Feigned Sickness*, Edward Arnold, London, 1913, pp. 1–97.
7 See A.J. Glass, 'Lessons Learned', in A.J. Glass & R.J. Bernucci, *Neuropsychiatry in World War II*, vol. 1, Office of the Surgeon General, Department of the Army, Washington, 1966, pp. 735–59.

authorities, however, embraced the psychological theory. But in the context of the literature on malingering, instead of just accepting the naturalness and obviousness of shell-shock, it might be more fruitful to ask how such an approach to these conditions was made obvious. How and why was the long-standing literature on malingering overthrown by a new discourse of neurosis? From an historical perspective the central issue is the making of shell-shock and the implications of this making for repatriation.

I

It was neither ignorance nor foolishness that prompted British military authorities to see men with no obvious physical problems complaining of stiff limbs, blindness, or deafness, or others unable to control fits of shaking or stuttering, as either cowards or malingerers. When the first cases began to stream into casualty stations towards the end of 1914, there was a long tradition of military observation and analysis to confirm their suspicions. Adding to this belief were the peculiar patterns of this 'malingering'. It seemed to occur almost universally in some units, while being hardly present in others, even though both were at similar points in the line and involved in fighting of similar intensity. These behaviours seemed to have the characteristics of epidemics, and this proved to be a continuing source of interest for those seeking to diagnose their nature. Of more immediate concern, however, was the number of such cases. As with any epidemic, although it infected some and bypassed others, the overall numbers affected rose dramatically. This had serious consequences for the fighting strength and morale of the forces. Alarmed authorities resorted to court martials, resulting in executions for deserting malingerers, in an effort to discipline the troops. And while the Australian government did not sanction execution for desertion, much to the consternation of the British War Office, Australian officers, like their British counterparts, forcibly returned many supposed malingerers to the line. The 1922 Shell Shock Inquiry concluded that some supposed cowards had probably been victims of war neurosis.[8]

The weight of numbers reputedly suffering these conditions, and moreover the number of officers from 'good backgrounds' afflicted, slowly eroded the cowardice and malingering argument. Before 1914 incidents of cowardice and malingering had been individualised. It was the fault of a single soldier, or a small group of soldiers or sailors, and exposure of the real nature of the behaviour and subsequent punishment was swift and direct. But the mass of malingerers in 1914 and 1915 rendered individualisation impossible. Moreover the excessive number of sufferers presented an uncomfortable picture of the character of the British and Empire

---

8 A. Babington, *For the Sake of Example: Capital Courts-Martial 1914–20*, Leo Cooper, London, 1983, pp. 189–207.

soldier. Was it really possible that so many volunteers, the cream of British Empire manhood, were cowards? It is not surprising, then, that, from the beginning, some authorities sought a medical explanation for this problem. The first line of explanation was that pursued by doctors such as Mott and Harris. They argued that these men did suffer from organic damage to the brain, but that this was 'microscopic' and not observable under typical conditions of medical examination. These were literally cases of shell-shock, where soldiers had suffered minute lesions to the brain from the direct shocks and vibrations of exploding shells, or the concussive consequences of being thrown or buried by these shells.

The concussive theory seemed plausible, but it was soon overwhelmed by facts that it could not explain. As the war on the western front progressed, an increasing number of cases of shell-shock occurred among troops who had been nowhere near direct shelling. Some were in the front line but had not yet been subjected to shelling; more disturbing still was the increasing numbers who had not even been in the line. The empirical spirit of medical officers demanded a different theory. If brain lesions and cowardice were ruled out as explanations, then shell-shock might be a psychological reaction to combat. This was the approach of an increasing number of psychiatrists and neurologists attached to the medical corps of all combatant forces. Some began to experiment with the new psychotherapeutic techniques that had found favour with a small number of doctors before the war. Hypnosis, suggestion, and persuasion techniques seemed to offer therapeutic benefits to soldiers with these conditions. A few even tried the new 'science' of psychoanalysis. Often these therapies worked with remarkable speed and efficacy. Soldiers brought in with paralysed limbs and hysterical blindness were rested, fed properly, and then gently counselled about the nature of their condition. Within a few days they had fully recovered and were able to return to the front. Many cases were not so easily cured, but the fact that psychological techniques demonstrably worked did much to cement their legitimacy among a previously sceptical medical profession. How they worked and why they worked was not always clear. This was the stuff of vigorous psychiatric and neurological debate. But the war provided the context for the continuation of a considerably longer struggle in psychological medicine between those who favoured physical explanations for mental conditions and those who believed that some of these problems, the neuroses, were psychological in origin. Shell-shock, then, provided a new arena for a theoretical debate of some duration, and the views about its nature, the explanations provided for its incidence, and the techniques used for its treatment arose out of these conditions of dispute.[9]

---

9 See Harris, *Nerve Injuries and Shock*, pp. 92–123; MacCurdy, *War Neuroses*, pp. 1–10; Myers, *Shell Shock in France*, pp. 12–28; Smith & Pear, *Shell Shock and its Lessons*, pp. 1–52; H.C. Miller (ed.), *Functional Nerve Disease: An Epitome of War Experience for the Practitioner*, Hodder & Stoughton, London, 1920.

The contours of this debate were well established by the early twentieth century. There appeared to be different types of mental phenomena (neuroses and psychoses), and three major factors were used to explain the causes of these disturbances: heredity and degeneration, physical illness, and psychological malfunctioning. The disputes within this field were numerous: between those who saw the neuroses and psychoses as fundamentally different and those who saw them as merely separate stages of the one condition, and between those whose focus was on hereditary predisposition and those who sought either psychological or physical forms of therapeutic intervention in the belief that these conditions were curable. In other words, there was a diverse ensemble of theories, practices, and techniques that constituted the field of mental disorder. This field of explanation was shaped by the pervasive debate about the relative effects of the mind and the body, heredity and environment. Those favouring physical and hereditary factors (the majority of psychiatrists before the war) sought to demonstrate that mental disorders were the result of physical processes, while those inclined to a psychological approach argued that the mind was capable of influencing the body. These points of dispute had important effects on the way shell-shock was perceived by the doctors. Military doctors had to confront an epidemic of male neuroses on a scale hitherto unimagined, and this raised new questions that required some reconsideration of the relations between mind, environment, body, and heredity.

It is not surprising that the first medical efforts to explain shell-shock focused on uncovering a physical cause. Medical officers, and consultant psychiatrists and neurologists, in attempting to overcome long-standing military beliefs that such behaviours were caused by malingering and cowardice, sought observable and concrete evidence to anchor their assertion that these were medical, not disciplinary, problems. The mounting numbers of cases at first aided their speculations and then undermined them. In the first few months of fighting the severity of shelling fostered the belief that these cases arose from the hidden effects of explosions. But the increasing incidence of men suffering from severe symptoms of stress, hysteria, and anxiety who had not been exposed to shelling forced medical officers to reconsider the problem. Despite the implausibility of the minute brain lesion theory, some doctors continued to argue that it was a valid diagnosis. Sir Frederick Mott, one of the first proponents of this theory, continued to believe in it even after the war. Some supporters of the psychological theory, however, saved a place for Mott's theory. In 1916, W. Ernest Jones, a prominent Melbourne psychiatrist, fully supported the idea that shell-shock was largely a psychological problem, but maintained that a small number of cases (particularly those with aphasia) suffered from 'commotional' shock. Some went to extraordinary lengths to support the commotional theory. A.G. Butler was one of these. In researching his medical history of Australia's involvement in the war, he followed up every possible lead to confirm the reality of the percussive effects of shells on the brain. He felt he had confirmed the reality of this condition after corresponding with Roy

Coupland Winn, a front-line medical officer in France and, after the war, Australia's first trained psychoanalyst – a fact that made him, in Butler's eyes, all the more reliable as a witness for the physical theory. Winn informed Butler that, while in France, he had been thrown into a foxhole by the force of an exploding shell. Upon recovering his senses, he noticed a rat running around the rim of the crater in an agitated and erratic fashion. Winn concluded that the rat had been shaken by the explosion and concurred with Butler that this seemed to suggest shells had direct concussive effects (it also confirmed the importance of rats in sound theorising). Here was proof for Butler that commotional shell-shock was real.[10]

Butler's obsessive interest in the reality of a physical cause for shell-shock betrays an anxiety about the implications of the psychological theory for his cherished Anzac legend. It suggested some weakness in the Anzacs, and for many years Butler maintained that the psychological, particularly the psychoanalytic, theory of shell-shock exaggerated the role of psychopathology in the genesis of war neurosis. Even so, Butler was too rigorous a scholar not to concede that the commotional cases were only a minority of shell-shock victims. Psychology did seem to offer a plausible explanation for the majority of cases. The fact was that many of these cases exhibited the classical symptoms of nervous disorder. As G. Elliot Smith and T.H. Pear concluded in 1917, there was nothing novel about war neuroses: they were exactly the same conditions that occurred in peace time. What was different was their prevalence. It was therefore a simple matter for doctors to categorise these conditions. They were familiar in the medical literature and consisted of two major classes of psychological illness: hysteria and anxiety.[11]

Despite the essential familiarity of these conditions, their incidence was remarkable. First, the number of reported cases far exceeded anything that had been experienced in peacetime, placing a great strain on medical personnel and resources. The longer the war went on, the higher the rate. By 1916 they were estimating that nearly half of all casualties were mental cases. One problem, however, was diagnosis. As many medical officers admitted, chronic overcrowding in field stations afforded few opportunities for extensive investigation of less serious complaints. Some were inclined to label almost any case not arising from wounds as shell-shock as a means of freeing beds for more serious cases. Shell-shock cases were thus quickly moved behind the lines, and often to hospitals in Britain, without any sustained medical examination. The loss of manpower, particularly as the war dragged on and recruiting became more difficult, was alarming. In 1916, British military authorities, concerned about the high incidence of this diagnosis, and fearful that many men were malingerers reporting these conditions in the hope of

---

10   See F. Mott, *War Neuroses and Shell Shock*, Hodder & Stoughton, London, 1919; W.E. Jones, 'Shell Shock', *MJA*, vol. 1, 1916, p. 191. See also R.C. Winn to A.G. Butler, 15 August 1932, and A.G. Butler, 'Notes re Shell Shock', in Butler Papers, box 67.
11   See A.G. Butler to Major J.V. Ashburner, 14 May 1941, Butler Papers, box 61; Smith & Pear, *Shell Shock and its Lessons*, p. x.

escaping the trenches, advised medical officers to refrain from entering a diagnosis of shell-shock in admission books. In 1917 they made this practice compulsory. Thereafter, they were required to enter 'NYD' (Not Yet Diagnosed), sometimes with a query ('shell-shock?'), and later 'NYDN' (Not Yet Diagnosed Neurosis). Australian authorities followed similar principles.

This classification corresponded with new systems of treatment. Instead of removing possible neurosis cases behind the lines and to hospitals in Britain, as formerly, the NYD cases were placed in special wards in Field Ambulance and Casualty Clearing Stations, where they could be attended by psychiatrists. It was found that, the sooner the soldier was treated, the greater the chances were of returning him to the front. The longer the soldier was away from the front, the less likely he was to recover sufficiently to return. The introduction of advanced psychiatric facilities, just behind the front line, meant that shell-shocked soldiers could be diagnosed, obtain much needed rest, and receive immediate psychotherapy to relieve them of any serious symptoms before they became too ingrained. Minor cases could be returned to the front and chronic cases removed to hospitals in Britain. A high proportion of soldiers treated in this way were able to return to combat within a few days.[12]

This system was a significant therapeutic advance, and one that addressed (but did not solve) the chronic manpower problems afflicting military forces. But it does complicate the statistics on the incidence of shell-shock. The new diagnostic categories meant that many who were formerly classified as shell-shock cases were now not entered in the books under this category. This probably explains the levelling off in the incidence of shell-shock from 1916. But, for historians, it also presents clear difficulties in measuring the extent of the problem. Did new classifications mean that many of the early cases were wrongly categorised, inflating the numbers, or that statistics after 1916 underestimated the incidence of shell-shock? Moreover, the increasing sophistication of diagnosis probably meant that cases of malingering, cowardice, or self-inflicted wounds, previously denied medical classification, were increasingly brought within the domain of psychiatrists. In the first years of the war the incidence of shell-shock was likely to have been under-reported.

These factors make any simple statement on the extent of shell-shock difficult. But the available evidence suggests that one-quarter to half of all casualties were psychological, and this is on the conservative end of the spectrum. This gives us an idea of the seriousness of the problem. It is more important, however, to focus on the ways in which the problem was understood. Even here, though, complex cultural factors shaped knowledge of these conditions. Australian medical authorities consistently reported fewer cases of shell-shock among the Anzacs compared with British figures. In 1916, at Pozieres, when the British figure was

---

12 See W.G. MacPherson, Surgeon General of British Armies in France, Memo, 13 February 1917, Butler Papers, box 68. See also Butler, *The Australian Army Medical Services*, vol. 3, pp. 121–8.

nearing 40 per cent, Australian doctors estimated that only one-quarter of ordinary soldiers, and even fewer officers, brought into Field Ambulance Stations were suffering shell-shock.[13]

Did this mean that Anzacs were less prone to shell-shock, or simply that Australian doctors were less willing to diagnose the problem? There are arguments for both these propositions. Later psychiatric research has suggested that the cohesion of a fighting unit plays a significant role in the genesis of war neurosis. The tighter the bonds of the unit, the higher the morale, and the less likely it was for war neurosis to be manifest. This is one explanation for the remarkable variations in the incidence of shell-shock, with some units suffering numerous cases and others in similar conditions having very few. The renowned 'mateship' of the Anzacs may have acted as a psychological bulwark against shell-shock, reducing its prevalence.[14] On the other side, if the repugnance towards psychological explanations of doctors like Butler is any indicator, then Australian medical authorities may have been more cautious in labelling men as shell-shock cases. Butler later argued that 'neurosis in the field' was of 'very minor importance', claiming that much so-called shell-shock was just fatigue. Major J.V. Ashburner, medical officer and psychiatrist, agreed.[15] Were these opinions, written many years after the war, rationalisations after the event or attitudes consistently held? If the latter, how many others were similarly sceptical, and how might this have affected the statistics? These are impossible questions to answer. What we do know is that, despite the lower incidence of shell-shock among the Anzacs, it was still, at one quarter of all casualties, a condition that alarmed medical authorities and weakened the fighting strength of the force.

The second peculiar feature of shell-shock was the large number of cases of hysteria – over one-third of all instances of war neurosis. Prior to the war, British doctors in particular had regarded this as a condition largely unknown among men, although in the decade before the war workers' compensation cases raised the spectre of a male variant. It was traditionally viewed as a woman's disease, as the etymology of hysteria (literally 'wandering womb') suggests. But the high incidence of male hysteria in war suggested that combat created mental stresses unknown in peacetime. British authorities noted other peculiarities. Hysteria seemed more common in the ordinary soldier, whereas anxiety was more usual among officers. Moreover, despite the alarming symptoms of hysteria, it was the easier condition to cure. The treatment of hysteria did the most to legitimate psychotherapy. Psychiatrists found that cases of hysteria were often easily overcome with rest, isolation, regular food, and the application of psychological therapy – persuasion,

---

13 Col. C.G. Manifold, 'Notes on Shell Shock Cases which Have Passed through Some Australian Field Ambulances', 1918, Butler Papers, box 61.
14 See Belenky 'Introduction', pp. 4–5; E. A. Strecker & K E. Appel, *Psychiatry and Modern Warfare*, Macmillan, New York, 1945, pp. 7–8; Myers, *Shell Shock in France*, pp. 40–1.
15 A.G. Butler to Major-General R.M. Downes, 3 May 1940, and Major J.V. Ashburner to A. G. Butler, 19 May 1941, Butler Papers, box 61.

suggestion, hypnosis, or less commonly, analysis. Those doctors who favoured the theories of Freud suggested that relapse was common after suggestion, and argued that sustained analysis was more effective in preventing recurrences. Most military psychiatrists, however, belittled the analytical approach as time-consuming and ineffective. But despite this opposition, Freudian theory provided the only real language to explain hysteria. Even among doctors who found the therapy of Freud preposterous (notably A.G. Butler), the arguments that hysteria represented an 'unconscious flight into illness' or a 'sublimation' arising from irresolvable conflicts between the order to fight and the desire to survive gained their particular impetus from the Viennese analyst.[16]

The language of the unconscious, however, did little to allay concern about the troubling character of shell-shock. While sublimation and repression were accepted as the psychological mechanisms impelling shell-shock, the reasons why some succumbed and others did not, and the reasons why some treatments were preferred to others, called on different cultural logics. Here doctors drew on a repertoire of ideas embedded in broader frameworks of gender, class, and race. Psychiatrists seeking to explain the different incidence of hysteria among soldiers and officers argued that soldiers had weaker personalities, making it more likely for them to take the 'flight into illness', while officers had a highly developed sense of duty and obligation. Officers had 'stronger characters', greater demands on them to lead, and as a consequence, they repressed their mental conflicts for longer. When they did collapse, their condition was more likely to be anxiety, and their repression more ingrained and difficult to cure. Here was a social Darwinist language of fitness, which rendered those from working-class backgrounds weaker and more vulnerable. But embedded in all this was an uncomfortable recognition of the feminised nature of hysteria. The idea of weaker nervous systems, even hysteria itself, paralleled ideas about the greater nervous vulnerability of women. In mounting these arguments, doctors edged ever closer to feminising soldiers. Resistance to this trend was no more apparent than in debates about treatment. Many doctors favoured persuasion and suggestion techniques because they were more manly. These relied on an assertion of the inherent reasonableness of the men, and demanded of them a conscious engagement of their will to be cured. Hypnosis was less popular, not just because of the vagaries of its operation, but also because it was an 'irrational' therapy – one that relied on an emotional release under induced unconsciousness with no corresponding demand that patients understand their

---

16 See F.C. Bartlett, *Psychology and the Soldier*, CUP, Cambridge, 1927, pp. 181–97; Miller, *Functional Nerve Disease*, pp. 3–111; Smith & Pear, *Shell Shock and its Lessons*, pp. 11–54; MacCurdy, *War Neuroses*, pp. 121–8. For evidence of Butler's antipathy to psychoanalysis and his resort to its language nonetheless, see Butler, *Australian Army Medical Services*, vol. 3, pp. 91–120. For Australian work on hysteria and war neurosis, see C. Godfrey, 'Some Cases of Stammering Treated by Psychotherapy', *MJA*, vol. 2, 1918, pp. 262–4; R.R. Stawell, 'The Recruit's Heart and Soldier's Heart', *MJA*, vol. 1, 1917, pp. 49–53; W.R. Regnell, 'The Psycho-Neuroses of War', *MJA*, vol. 1, 1919, pp. 455–60.

cure. Was treatment about the release of emotions or the mastery of them? The answer was not just a therapeutic one, but also an issue of masculinity. Ironically, the therapy that most relied on a conscious, rational understanding – psychoanalysis – was also the most suspicious. Perhaps its demand that the patient talk for long periods (in passive repose) blurred the boundaries of femininity and masculinity (for both patient and therapist) in ways that were too confronting for many doctors.[17]

The other surprising feature of the incidence of anxiety and hysteria was that shell-shock was more common among officers than soldiers. This certainly disturbed comfortable conclusions that shell-shock was a product of the enlistment of the 'unfit'. But it did resonate with nineteenth-century ideas that nervousness was most prevalent among those in sedentary and intellectual occupations. The over-exertion of the brain was thought to strain the nerves. Many officers came from these backgrounds. But military doctors also ascribed their problems to the greater demands of repression in the case of officers, and the greater difficulty they faced in reconciling external social demands (ideals of duty, honour, and glory) with their own unconscious desire to escape from harm. Codes of masculinity were integral to understanding the genesis of illness. Australian psychiatrists, however, found a different pattern. Among the Anzacs, officers had a lower incidence of shell-shock than ordinary soldiers. Again, it is impossible to discern whether this reflected patterns of diagnosis among Australian medical officers or something unique to the nature of the Anzac force. The fact that many Anzac officers were promoted from the ranks may have meant they were less likely to experience the psychological pressure of honour and duty, which was ingrained in the British officer class during their years in public schools and military academies. Anzac officers were volunteers, often from humble backgrounds, who by force of their personality and leadership were promoted to the higher rank, while British officers, at least in the early years of the war, were a distinct caste, inculcated with military ideals from an early age.[18]

The last peculiarity of shell-shock was its presence as neurosis. Although some soldiers were diagnosed with serious mental illnesses (psychoses), which in civilian life would have been sufficient to warrant certification, military psychiatrists found that the incidence of psychosis among soldiers was no different to that in civilian life. This in itself was puzzling, as medical examination or subsequent training should have weeded out those suffering severe mental disturbances. Psychiatrists went to some lengths to explain away this problem. Oliver Latham, a leading Australian psychiatrist and wartime medical officer, later concluded that the conditions of military life disguised symptoms of psychosis. He argued that there

---

17   See R. Leys, 'Traumatic Cures: Shell Shock, Janet, and the Question of Memory', *Critical Inquiry*, vol. 20, no. 4, Summer 1994, pp. 623–62.
18   See Smith & Pear, *Shell Shock and its Lessons*, pp. 11–54; MacCurdy, *War Neuroses*, pp. 121–8. On the Australian incidence, see Manifold, 'Notes on Shell Shock Cases'.

were many Anzacs 'doomed to insanity no matter what life they took up', but military life, the freedom from financial and family worries, and the healthy life of mateship, exercise, discipline, good clothes, and regular food 'kept many a potential psychotic free from mental ill-health for quite some time'. Once exposed to the conditions of combat, however, these incipient psychotics soon lapsed into serious breakdown. Latham's observations have a certain plausibility, but a more direct reason for the incidence of psychosis among Anzacs was that, in the anxiety over falling recruitments, some seriously disturbed volunteers were passed fit for service. Some were tragic cases, fortunately discovered before they were required to fight. In 1915 one young man, only released from Callan Park Mental Hospital three weeks earlier, was passed fit for service and sent to Egypt for training. Within a fortnight of his arrival he was found wandering over the sand-hills herding imaginary cows. He was returned home. How many others passed through the large holes in the examination net and found themselves at the front we will never know. But regardless of the cause, most military psychiatrists concluded that war did not exacerbate the genesis of psychosis, and while the foundations for this conclusion appear somewhat fragile, it was a fact that shaped medical perceptions of the nature of shell-shock.[19]

Shell-shock encompassed a range of neuroses, but not psychoses; it seemed to affect large numbers of soldiers; and officers seemed to suffer worse cases. While these were widely accepted features of shell-shock, their meaning was open to dispute. The key point of disagreement was over the origin of these nervous breakdowns: were they a product of the excessive stress of war, a stress sufficient to weaken even the soundest psychological constitution, or were there some inherent faults in these men that meant that some succumbed to shell-shock while others survived mentally unscathed?

On one side of this debate were those doctors who saw war as an exceptional context, something that created abnormal strains. A version of this approach was to deny that war said anything particular about the psychology or character of the soldier. Here the focus was on the role of fatigue and exhaustion in the genesis of shell-shock. Depleted constitutions made men vulnerable to the stress of combat, and over time, even the strongest succumbed, if only briefly, to nervous breakdown. British doctors such as MacCurdy and Bartlett placed fatigue high on their list of causal factors. And A.G. Butler, drawing on the testimony of soldiers such as Roy Coupland Winn, enthusiastically embraced the exhaustion argument, in part to confirm his belief that psychological theories were exaggerated. Winn, a believer in the psychological approach, confided to Butler that exhaustion had driven him to the edge of breakdown. Exhaustion probably played a significant role in many cases, but it is hard to avoid the feeling that its popularity as an explanation arose partly because it side-stepped the uncomfortable idea that some soldiers

---

19 O. Latham to A. G. Butler, 18 March 1935, Butler Papers, 3/9.16. For the case study, see Department of Veterans' Affairs, NSW, Case Files, M, CRS 138, sample no. 783.

suffered a psychological or physiological flaw. Shell-shock abraded against ideals of manliness, bravery, and courage, exposing the vulnerability of these cherished myths to the reality of combat. But exhaustion was an inadequate answer, something even Butler was forced to admit. There were too many instances of shell-shock in the first days of combat for fatigue and tiredness to be the only factors. While exhaustion may have explained the collapse of the strongest, it could not explain the genesis of all cases of shell-shock.[20]

Most doctors who saw war as the central cause of shell-shock, however, focused on the psychological effects of combat. War was seen to create conditions of extreme mental conflict, between imperatives to fight and desires to survive. Continued combat required an extraordinary effort of repression, and over time, mental defences weakened under this effort. Here was a diagnosis replete with Freudian language, but the advocates of this view, unlike Freud, sought to deny that there was anything constitutional in this breakdown. The most sophisticated proponent of this position was the noted British anthropologist and psychologist W.H.R. Rivers, superintendent of Craiglockhart Hospital for Nervous Diseases during the First World War. Rivers has gained a central place in the history of shell-shock. It was at Craiglockhart that he treated such notable patients as Siegfried Sassoon and Wilfred Owen, and their accounts of Rivers and his treatment reveal a complex and troubled therapeutic environment. Rivers himself seems to have been intensely involved in the therapy of some of his special patients, seeing Craiglockhart as his most important work. Sassoon, in particular, depicts Rivers as a beneficent, even saintly, father figure, providing a haven of sanity in an increasingly insane world. In this relationship we might see the operation of heightened forms of transference and counter-transference (to use the Freudian terms), and indeed this is partly the case, but it is not that simple. There are contradictions in Sassoon's account – or, more properly, elisions. Rivers, despite his sympathy and attachment to Sassoon, still attempted to render Sassoon's pacifism as an illness in an effort to alleviate his very real nightmares and anxieties. Moreover, Rivers remained caught within the contradictions of his roles as military doctor, psychological scientist, and confidant. He formed close attachments to particular patients, engaged vigorously in research into the causes of shell-shock, and earnestly sought to restore mental health, but with the consequence that cured soldiers went back to combat. And Sassoon had to struggle to reconcile Rivers' sympathy for his condition and the demand that he recant his political views. These dilemmas may have troubled Rivers, particularly when former patients, such as Owen, returned to the front only to be killed. Rivers died, still in his prime, just after the war.[21]

---

20 See MacCurdy, *War Neuroses*, pp. 49–50; Bartlett, *Psychology and the Soldier*, pp. 77–86; A.G. Butler to Major J.V. Ashburner, 14 May 1941, Butler Papers, box 61; Report of Major Roy Coupland Winn on the Battle of Messines, 1931, Butler Papers, box 43.

21 On Rivers and Craiglockhart, see Showalter, *The Female Malady*, pp. 167–94; R. Slobodin, *W.H.R. Rivers*, Columbia University Press, New York, 1978, pp. 44–85.

The importance of Rivers' theory of war neurosis was that it adopted all the central tenets of psychoanalysis except the one that most offended pragmatic British medical sensibilities. The adoption of psychoanalytic language was crucial because there seemed to be no plausible alternative. Freud provided the only coherent account of mental functioning. Many may have disputed elements of his theory and condemned analysis as a form of therapy, preferring, as they did, the easier and quicker results of hypnosis and suggestion, but why suggestion and hypnosis worked was inexplicable without some notion of unconscious conflict. Rivers went further than most in adopting Freudian concepts such as the unconscious, instinct, suppression, repression, mental conflict, and psychic censorship. Where he departed from Freud was in the function of sexual aetiology in neurosis. Rivers disputed Freud's assertion that 'disturbances in the sex instinct' were at the root of neurosis. This is how Rivers expressed it, and the crudity of this formulation tells us much about Rivers' desire to avoid Freud's unsavoury thesis. For Rivers, the war demonstrated the falsity of the sex explanation (and importantly after the war Freud revised his theory to include a new concept; the 'death instinct'). For Rivers the most crucial instinct challenged by war was not the sex instinct but the self-preservation instinct. In war, fear, anger, and terror confronted the instinct for self-preservation. While this conflict could be controlled by repression (arising out of a sense of duty and commitment to one's comrades), a failure in the equilibrium struck between instinct and control could cause the instinctive mechanisms of self-preservation to assert themselves, forcing an unconscious flight into aggression, immobility, or collapse. From this basic premise, Rivers carefully charted the different psychic mechanisms in the genesis of particular types of neurosis. Underpinning all this was a clear proposition that war was a unique context, and that, without combat, most of these men would have lead normal mental lives.[22]

The weakness in the psychological theory for other doctors, however, was that the reason for the sudden loss of equilibrium remained largely unexplained. All observers agreed that some soldiers succumbed to neurosis very quickly, some took much longer, while others never developed any significant symptoms (or none sufficient to warrant evacuation from the line). The vagueness of Rivers on this problem fostered, for others, a fundamental conviction – one of considerable longevity in psychiatric theory – that those who developed shell-shock suffered some predisposition to neurosis. Some of this predisposition was easy to detect. When American doctor Thomas Salmon inspected British facilities for the treatment of shell-shock, he was informed that almost one-fifth of all cases were mentally deficient. Australian psychiatrists and doctors, such as Oliver Latham and Professor R.J.A. Berry of the University of Melbourne, also believed that some Anzacs who developed mental diseases did so because of serious hereditary

---

22 See W.H.R Rivers, *Instinct and the Unconscious: A Contribution to a Biological Theory of the Psycho-Neuroses*, CUP, Cambridge, 1920.

deficiency. But serious deficiency only accounted for some of the problem. It was obvious that many men were more than capable of passing any physical or psychological examination but still suffered some inherent weakness of the nervous system. As one Australian doctor, Colonel A.M. Wilson, declared, 'the greatest predisposing factor is temperament'. There were some who were more 'naturally' nervous, and it was this type of soldier who succumbed to the stress of war. This was an approach supported by many psychiatrists and doctors.

When prominent Melbourne doctor J.W. Springthorpe discussed war neurosis, it was clear to him that there were distinct psychopathic and neurasthenic personality types. And while it would have been preferable if such types had been detected at enlistment, all admitted that these types were difficult to diagnose. What the war confirmed for psychiatrists and neurologists was their long-standing belief that the prevalence of a predisposition to mental disorder was much greater than the public or politicians had been prepared to accept. The excessive stress of war indicated just how widespread this vulnerability was, and underpinning this argument was an assumption that any stress, in wartime or peacetime, would induce breakdown in these men.[23]

Freudians were strange bedfellows for hereditary determinists, but bedfellows they were. Freud himself was rather circumspect about the function of psychoanalysis in understanding war neurosis. He suggested that the theory of sexuality was developed primarily to explain the transference neuroses and might not be suitable for analysing anxiety, paranoia, *dementia praecox*, or melancholia. Nonetheless, he proposed that there might be some narcissistic fixation in the development of traumatic neuroses, of which war neurosis was one type. Freud's followers, notably Sándor Ferenczi, Ernest Jones, and Karl Abraham, were more forthright. For them, the evidence that some soldiers developed neurosis and others did not made the sexual theory all the more pertinent. Jones argued that there were three factors in the genesis of shell-shock – hereditary predisposition, 'current difficulty', and unresolved infantile conflict – which together created 'wounded self-love'. Abraham and Ferenczi elaborated on the psychological mechanisms of self-love. For them, shell-shock was a response to trauma characterised by a retreat into ego-infantile narcissism, most commonly manifest in impotence and 'passive labile heterosexual impulses'. While all agreed that trauma was the precipitating factor, there was a clear implication that particular psychological types were more prone to the psychic reaction of shell-shock. In cruder hands, this idea of types could become even more central. For H.C. Miller, many shell-shock cases were

---

23 See Salmon, *The Care and Treatment of Mental Diseases and War Neuroses*, pp. 14–19; O. Latham to A.G. Butler, 18 March 1935, Butler Papers, 3/9.1; A. N. Wilson, 'Shell Shock and Allied Conditions' n.d., and J.W. Springthorpe, 'Suggestions as to the Better Treatment of our War Neuroses', 28 March 1918, Butler Papers, box 61. On Berry's views, see M. Cawte, 'Craniometry and Eugenics in Australia: R.J.A. Berry and the Quest for Social Efficiency', *Historical Studies*, vol. 2, no. 86, April 1986, pp. 45–6.

'mother's darling' boys, fixated on their parents and psychologically stunted at an earlier developmental stage.[24]

The idea of 'mother's boys' ran uncomfortably close to suggesting that homosexuality or repressed homosexual impulses lay at the heart of shell-shock. In this context, we can understand the desire that drove so many British psychiatrists to reject the sexual theories of Freud. Despite the work of pre-war sexologists such as Havelock Ellis and Krafft-Ebbing on the prevalence of homosexuality, and the trial of Oscar Wilde in publicising its existence, few were prepared to accept that such impulses, even if repressed, might affect over one-quarter of all army casualties. Nonetheless, the theory of types, as a means of explaining why some developed shell-shock and others did not, had its adherents. But regardless of the sophistication of the arguments, the stress on psychological types ran remarkably close to the idea of hereditary predisposition. Underpinning both was a suggestion that the 'unfit' (hereditarily or psychologically) had been allowed to enlist. And the extent of shell-shock further exacerbated long-standing racial fears. The much vaunted British race seemed to be in decline from the propagation of the unfit, although the war made the character and nature of fitness a far more complex problem than it had been in the nineteenth century. Australians perhaps took heart from the evidence that suggested that Anzacs had a lesser incidence of these problems, but many doctors after the war trumpeted the need to improve the stock lest the Australian race 'wither away'.[25]

II

What were the lessons of shell-shock? In civilian practice, the old divisions between physical and psychological theories began to blur. Shell-shock did not create a new understanding of mental illness – most psychiatrists drew on existing theories, and the therapeutic effects of psychotherapy were evident before the war – but it did shift the weight of professional opinion more towards sympathy for psychological approaches. In Australia it also encouraged the emergence of psychology as a distinct discipline. The first psychology courses in Australia were professed just after the war by H. Tasman Lovell at the University of Sydney. Psychology was no longer just a branch of philosophy concerned with the relations between mind and body, but a science of human behaviour, concerned with mental functioning, morale, the measurement of intelligence, the mapping of psychological types, and the means by which people could be better adjusted to their environment. One

---

24 See S. Ferenczi, K. Abraham, E. Simmel, & E. Jones, *Psychoanalysis and the War Neuroses*, International Psycho-Analytical Press, London, 1921 (Freud's views are in the introduction to this work); H.C. Miller, 'The Mother Complex', in Miller (ed.), *Functional Nerve Disease*, pp. 115–28.

25 J. Bostock & L.J. Nye, *Wither Away? A Study of Race Psychology and the Factors Leading to Australia's National Decline*, Angus & Robertson, Sydney, 1934.

of the pioneers of psychology in Australia, Elton Mayo, honed his theories in the treatment of shell-shocked soldiers in Queensland. After the war he sought to adapt his theories to the problems of industrial organisation, arguing that industrial unrest arose from unconscious maladjustment. There were, of course, still adherents of older views. W.A.T. Lind, pathologist with the Victorian Mental Hygiene Department, believed that the psychological approach was seriously flawed and that future research into the pathology of the neuroses would reveal their physical origin. Others remained implacable opponents of psychotherapy, particularly of psychoanalysis. The medical superintendent of Kew Mental Hospital, M.F.H. Gamble, condemned psychoanalysis as the outpouring of 'the morbid minded, one might say, paranoical sexual occultist of Vienna'. And throughout the inter-war years respected members of the psychiatric profession dismissed the theory as 'balderdash' and its practitioners as 'charlatans'. But, equally, there many advocates. Sydney Evan Jones and A.T. Edwards used free association, suggestion, and persuasion in the treatment of shell-shocked returned soldiers at the army psychiatric clinic at Broughton Hall in Sydney. A few others, with no formal training in psychoanalysis, notably R.A. Noble, used Freudian ideas, and analysis as well as suggestion, in their private practices. In the 1920s, examination papers at the University of Sydney for the Diploma of Psychological Medicine contained questions on psychotherapy, repression, and the theories of Freud, indicating that some teaching of these ideas was considered part of proper psychiatric training. Others went further. In 1922 Roy Coupland Winn went to England to undertake formal psychoanalytic training, returning later to establish a private practice in this field. Some, notably Paul Dane and J.K. Adey, were firm adherents of Freudian theory, while other prominent interwar psychiatrists were fellow travellers.[26]

The majority of the psychiatric profession, however, adopted a more eclectic approach. Serious mental illnesses were still the focus of extensive drug, surgical, and other physical treatments. Moreover, during the inter-war years there were many innovations in the treatment of psychoses: insulin coma therapies, and convulsion (cardiazol) and shock (electro-convulsive) treatments. The neuroses, however, were more usually treated with psychological techniques. While many concentrated their expertise in only one of these fields, others operated in both. Reg Ellery, a Melbourne psychiatrist, was one of the first to use cardiazol but was

---

26 See H. Bourke, 'Industrial Unrest as Social Pathology: The Australian Writings of Elton Mayo', *Historical Studies*, vol. 20, no. 79, October 1982, pp. 217–33. For more general discussion of the rise of psychology, see W.M. O'Neil, *A Century of Psychology in Australia*, SUP, Sydney, 1987, pp. 15–53. For the views of the opponents, see W.A.T. Lind, 'The Physical Basis of Insanity', *MJA*, vol. 1, 1922, pp. 466–8; M.F.H. Gamble, 'Prognosis in Mental Diseases', *Australasian Medical Congress Transactions*, 1920, p. 436; W.A. Osborne to Editor and J.M. McGeorge to Editor, *MJA*, vol. 2, 1936, pp. 385 & 383. For the views of the supporters, see R.A. Noble, 'Treatment of Functional Nerve Disease During and After the War', *Australasian Medical Congress Transactions*, 1920, pp. 429–32.

also a firm proponent of psychoanalysis. In Australia doctors such as John Bostock and R.A. Noble advocated a composite view of insanity. By this they meant that mental illness encompassed a range of conditions, and more importantly, many forms of disturbance were due to various combinations of social, psychological, or organic causes. In other words, some mental disorders were purely psychological in origin and others wholly organic, but most patients suffered from conditions that had psychological and physical factors. Mental illness, then, was a continuum, stretching from the psychological to the organic, and each illness was somewhere on that continuum. Patients had to be individualised, to sort out the particular combination of causes and to tailor the specific combination of physical and psychological treatments appropriate to each.[27]

One seemingly clear implication of shell-shock was that the extent of predisposition to neurosis in the community was far greater than had previously been thought. This was an obvious threat to public health. It was neither a new nor an unexpected view. Since the late nineteenth century, social Darwinists and eugenicists had long suspected that 'civilisation' was threatened by the 'unfit'. But 'fitness' here was seen in rather crude terms, measured by observable mental deficiency. The war suggested deficiency was both more extensive and more complex than previously thought. It was not just defects of intelligence, but also psychological complexes, maladjusted temperaments, and neurotic predispositions, that had to be confronted. Just as there were disputes over the nature of shell-shock, so there were differences as to the most important problems to be tackled after the war. For some, shell-shock made it evident that hereditary vulnerability to illness was widespread. This confirmed pre-war fears about the threat to the race posed by the propagation of inherited taints.

After the war eugenic societies were more numerous and better supported. They campaigned for the extensive use of intelligence and other mental tests in schools, juvenile courts, and prisons to uncover the 'unfit'. These people could then be prevented from passing on their 'degeneracy' to later generations. While most eugenicists supported measures for the compulsory segregation of the 'unfit', a few went further, advocating sterilisation. But others believed that much mental illness arose from psychological and social stress. They campaigned for preventative health measures to promote mental hygiene: sex education, child guidance, parenting advice, public campaigns promoting healthy lifestyles, relaxation and exercise, and the promotion of greater awareness of the problem of stress. These were measures of environmental reform. But as with the composite view of mental illness, the dividing line between nature and nurture was blurred. Prominent members of eugenic societies, such as doctor J.W. Springthorpe and educationalist K.S. Cunningham, were also members of the mental hygiene movement. There was

---

27 See R.A. Noble, 'Psychotherapy in Practice', *MJA*, vol. 2, 1923, pp. 564–6; J. Bostock, 'The "Composite" Point of View as to the Causation of Mental Disorder', *Australasian Medical Congress Transactions*, 1927, pp. 110–13.

broad acceptance of the view that heredity and environment both played a role in the production of 'social and mental deficiency', and while some were more affected by one rather than the other, public health demanded both approaches. Shell-shock crystallised long-standing disputes over the nature of mental illness, but it also promoted an awareness that no one theory could command the whole domain.[28]

There were also military lessons to be drawn from shell-shock. Belief in hereditary and psychological predisposition to war neurosis was widespread. It was imperative then, to ensure more rigorous examination of recruits. This was the central proposal of Thomas Salmon's report on shell-shock in the British Army in the First World War. The effect of 'careless recruiting', as he called it, was the most important lesson of this war. With the outbreak of the Second World War, the focus shifted again to the quality of the recruits. This was particularly the case in the USA, where enormous resources were devoted to psychological testing. In 1941 the Army Surgeon-General established a Psychological Branch, and by 1943 one-quarter of all psychologists in the USA (over 1000) were engaged in military psychology. They were employed in giving aptitude tests, refining classification procedures, investigating the problem of the 'abnormal' soldier, and trialling techniques for improving morale. Using a battery of sophisticated mental and psychological tests, American psychologists endeavoured to weed out those clearly unsuited to military life and to classify each recruit according to the service role for which he was best suited: combat or support, the specific service (army, navy, air force), and so on. The Americans were the most advanced in introducing these techniques, but all combatant nations implemented means for more rigorous scrutiny of recruits than had been the case in 1914, and many were hopeful that such measures would greatly reduce the incidence of shell-shock.[29]

Australian military authorities were slow to follow the American lead. Perhaps the lower incidence of shell-shock in the First World War fostered complacency. Perhaps it was reluctance to admit that a new generation of Anzacs might be unsuitable. Whatever the cause, Bill O'Neil, future professor of psychology at the University of Sydney and wartime tester, has charted the apathy of Australian military authorities. Although several psychologists working in the New South Wales Education Department and Sydney Technical College established the Volunteer Emergency Psychological Service to advise on the psychological needs of warfare, the armed forces were reluctant to make psychological testing a routine part of the recruitment process. It was not until 1941 that the army and the air force experimented with the use of psychological testing, but these were small and not very comprehensive investigations. Nonetheless, the fact that a number of recruits

---

28 See S. Garton, 'Sound Minds and Healthy Bodies: Re-considering Eugenics in Australia, 1914–1940', *Australian Historical Studies*, vol. 26, no. 103, October 1994, pp. 163–81.
29 Salmon, *The Care and Treatment of Mental Diseases and War Neuroses*, p. 19; C.W. Bray, *Psychology and Military Proficiency: A History of the Applied Psychology Panel of the National Defense Research Committee*, Princeton University Press, Princeton, NJ, 1948, pp. 1–12.

were failing tests alerted military authorities to the need for more systematic efforts. In 1943 the RAAF became the first service to establish a psychological section. Later that year the army established a similar unit, and psychological tests became standard procedure at the Australian Recruit Training Centre at Cowra. The focus of this work was to diagnose those unsuitable for combat and to assist in 'the allocation of recruits to specialised training programs'. Psychological testing led to the rejection of 12 per cent of those who came forward to enlist.[30]

Perhaps the caution of Australian military authorities also arose from their more sober assessment of the utility of psychological testing. As C.K. Parkinson, senior medical officer with the Repatriation Department, explained, 'many men of subnormal mental grade make useful soldiers'. If shell-shock had shown anything, it was that those with the highest intelligence were sometimes vulnerable to the most serious breakdowns. Probably more influential was the widely accepted view that the discovery of the psychologically unfit was difficult, even with testing. The mentally deficient, claimed Parkinson, were easily uncovered, but the 'psychopathic individual' was 'generally impossible to detect'. W.S. Dawson, Professor of Psychiatry at the University of Sydney, believed that the 'dull', the 'nitwit', and the 'martial misfit' were obvious, but for the 'psychopath', the psychiatric examiner had to rely on 'impressions'. He catalogued an extraordinary series of warning signs for the 'recognition of psychopathic types': untidiness, lack of cleanliness, lack of regard for discipline, shyness, bed-wetting, masturbation, homosexuality, irritability, depression, querulousness, alcoholism, homesickness, boisterousness, undue fatigability, chronic dyspeptics, indefatigable scribes and diarists, those picked on by fellow recruits, and those who attended sick parades with trivial complaints. Any of these were taken as signs of incipient psychopathology. To modern eyes, this list probably looks quaint and absurdly broad. Perhaps it was a measure of the unpredictability of psychological tests, and the fact that, in uncertain times, it was best to cover all possibilities. Perhaps they were aware of the fragility of their knowledge and feared for their reputations if they failed to lower the rate of neurosis in war. And in the early years of the war – its 'phoney' stage – psychiatrists had little idea about what the effects of war might be. Most assumed that psychological breakdowns brought on by combat would be similar to those in the First World War, but as the Second World War progressed, there were some surprises.[31]

In May 1941 Lieutenant-Colonel A.J.M. Sinclair and E.J. Cooper established a war neurosis clinic at Tobruk. Their work was the first substantial Australian investigation into mental disorders in the Second World War. Sinclair and Cooper

---

30 J.V. Ashburner, 'Psychology in the Australian Army', *MJA*, vol. 2, 1946, pp. 86–92. For a general survey, see O'Neil, *A Century of Psychology in Australia*, pp. 64–76.
31 See C.K. Parkinson, 'The Management of Neurotic Affections in Military Practice', *MJA*, vol. 1, 1940, pp. 94–7; W.S. Dawson, 'The Prevention of War Neuroses', *MJA*, vol. 2, 1941, pp. 375–8; C.C. Minty, 'War Neuroses', *MJA*, vol. 2, 1940, pp. 386–7.

confirmed two important facts in the treatment of psychiatric casualties. First, as in the First World War, the incidence of psychosis did not seem to be any greater than in civilian life. But although its incidence was constant, military psychiatrists were confident that the new convulsion and shock therapies would have a significant therapeutic benefit. Second, Sinclair and Cooper further confirmed the now well-established utility of early treatment. The sooner treatment was provided, the greater were the chances of returning the soldier to active duty. They reported that 60 per cent of patients treated at the clinic were returned to combat duty, and a further 23 per cent were fit for base duties. They also noticed other patterns that have a familiar ring. Almost one-quarter of the patients had a history of 'nervous breakdown', and half had a history of neurosis in the family. Half were also classified as 'inferior personality types'. Similar findings resulted from Sinclair's later work in New Guinea. This was evidence of the failure of recruitment examinations and for the need for more expert psychological testing, but it also reveals the strong desire to uncover predisposition as a major cause of neurosis. Given the breadth of criteria – from bed-wetting to diary-writing – it is not surprising that many investigations uncovered evidence of predisposition. The more interesting question concerns why predisposition was such a persistent explanation, especially in Australia. In contrast, this theory was relegated to the margins in American military psychiatry. Did the Anzac legend inhibit investigation of alternative theories of the inherent psychological trauma of war? Could a view of war as inevitably destructive sit comfortably with a glorification of a soldier ethos? The deeper cultural motivations of Australian psychiatrists remain elusive and largely the matter of conjecture. What we do know is that Sinclair and other military psychiatrists favoured predisposition and the utility of early treatment.[32]

Sinclair and Cooper, however, also uncovered peculiar trends in the incidence of war neurosis. Unlike in the First World War, they found very few patients with hysteria, and most of these were cases of 'fugue' rather than the formerly common problems of blindness, deafness, and stammering. The majority of patients, almost two-thirds, were diagnosed to be suffering from various anxiety states, and a further fifth had head injuries. This paralleled the findings of British, Canadian and American military psychiatrists. Hysteria afflicted only a small number of soldiers in the Second World War.[33] The reasons for this dramatic decline remain obscure.

---

32 E.L. Cooper and A.J.M. Sinclair, 'War Neurosis in Tobruk: A Report on 207 Patients from the Australian Imperial Force Units in Tobruk', *MJA*, vol. 2, 1942, pp. 73–7. See also A.J.M. Sinclair, 'Psychiatric Casualties in an Operational Zone in New Guinea', *MJA*, vol. 2, 1943, pp. 453–60; H.J.B. Stephens, 'Observations on Psychoses in Service Personnel in Forward Areas', *MJA*, vol. 1, 1946, pp. 145–7.

33 See also A.J.M. Sinclair, 'The Psychological Reactions of Soldiers: Lectures I and II', *MJA*, vol. 2, 1945, pp. 229–34 & 261–9. For discussions of international findings, see Strecker & Appel, *Psychiatry in Modern Warfare*, pp. 26–8; R.H. Ahrenfeldt, *Psychiatry in the British Army in the Second World War*, Routledge & Kegan Paul, London, 1958, pp. 181–248; T. Copp & B. McAndrew, *Battle Exhaustion: Soldiers and Psychiatrists in the Canadian Army 1939–1945*, McGill-Queens University Press, Montreal, 1990, pp. 49–95.

It paralleled a more general decline in the diagnosis of hysteria after 1918. By the 1930s hysteria was only a small part of civilian psychiatric practice – a far cry from the early days of Charcot, Janet, and Freud. Did this reflect a change in forms of medical classification or some more profound change in the modern psyche? The emergence of new diagnoses such as conversion reaction suggests that hysteria might have been submerged within new disease classifications. But this seems a less than satisfactory explanation. Military psychiatrists in the Second World War expected to find hysteria, and the fact that its incidence was low suggests a more fundamental change in the presentation of psychological conflict. Some have seen hysteria as the prime means for the expression of a feminine resistance to patriarchy. That still leaves the problem of male hysteria vague.

Is it possible that hysteria was more a disease of silence or, perhaps more appropriately, a bodily language when a verbal one was impossible? Freud dubbed his method the 'talking cure', in which the bringing of the psychic conflict at the heart of the symptom to consciousness abreacted its effects. In the 1920s and 1930s the impact of psychoanalysis on public culture was such that everyone was talking of complexes and repression. As the *Australian Woman's Mirror* proclaimed in 1936, psychoanalysis was 'a woman topic of the moment'. Modernity was marked by endless talking about symptoms, and in this culture, the silence of hysteria was difficult to sustain.[34]

Despite the presence of anxiety as the main neurosis of the Second World War, Australian psychiatrists took issue with the American research on the causes of this syndrome. American military psychiatrists had to confront anxiety neuroses on a large scale in the European and Pacific campaigns. They were vigilant in psychological testing of recruits but, nevertheless, found that some 'marginal' types managed to slip through the net. Sustained combat in Europe, despite improved testing, still resulted in a very high incidence of shell-shock. Moreover, it seemed that, the longer the soldier was at the front, the more likely it was that he would eventually succumb to some neurosis. This seemed to be the case even among the strongest personalities, although the rate of breakdown was crucially affected by the length of time in actual combat, the intensity of fighting, and morale in the unit. Two explanations were offered. First, the intensity of total war and the destructiveness of weapons were so much greater than in the past, even than in 1914–18, that anxiety was a normal reaction to such an environment. Second, sustained combat led to endemic exhaustion, weakening even the healthiest constitution. Strong personalities under extreme stress would thus eventually collapse. Perhaps American psychologists were reluctant to admit that so many had escaped their testing net. Whatever the cause, increasingly American psychiatrists

---

34   See 'What is Psychoanalysis?: A Woman Topic of the Moment', *Australian Woman's Mirror*, 19 May 1936. See also S. Gilman et al., *Hysteria Beyond Freud*, University of California Press, Berkeley, 1993; M. Micale, 'Hysteria and its Historiography: A Review of Past and Present Writings', *History of Science*, vol. 27, September 1989, pp. 223–62.

favoured exhaustion and fatigue as the causes of war neurosis in the 1940s: shell-shock was replaced by battle fatigue and combat exhaustion as clinical and popular terms.[35]

Australian psychiatrists were less enamoured of the exhaustion theory. Sinclair argued that, although over half of all patients in army neurosis clinics complained of exhaustion, less than one-tenth suffered from actual clinical exhaustion. Moreover, their experience of breakdown in Australian soldiers who had not experienced combat convinced them that breakdowns in social relationships, not exhaustion, triggered the collapse of many weaker types. Australian psychiatrists also found that the incidence of war neurosis was less than in the First World War, and certainly less in Australian forces than in American forces. Sinclair estimated that only 2 per cent of admissions to military hospitals in New Guinea were psychiatric casualties, and although he considered this an underestimation (with many psychiatric cases treated at the front line and others diagnosed with illnesses that were really psychiatric in origin), this figure still fell far short of the American figure of one-third of all casualties being psychiatric. The reasons for the difference may stem from the different combat role of Anzacs. Many Anzacs during the Second World War did not see the sustained combat experienced by American forces, being more involved in shorter but intense campaigns, particularly in the Pacific. Moreover, morale among the Australians seems to have been much higher. Once they were in New Guinea and the Pacific, Australians were fighting to defend home, boosting morale. The nature of their war and the morale of the forces – the Anzac spirit or, in Bean's words, mateship – may have more ably sustained the psychology of Australian soldiers. Equally, Australian military psychiatrists were less likely to see breakdown as an inevitable consequence of combat, checking their embrace of comfortable generalisations. The work of Australian doctors suggested that the Anzacs were not afflicted with psychiatric problems to the extent that other combatant forces were. This in itself was good for morale.[36]

The greater scepticism and eclecticism of Australian psychiatrists worked to the advantage of soldiers in later conflicts. After 1945 the increasing American interest in combat fatigue had disastrous military consequences. The belief that even the strongest succumbed to nervousness if subjected to sustained combat led to the 'tour of duty' policy in later conflicts, particularly Vietnam. Under this policy, men were enlisted for twelve-month tours, a length of time thought to be sufficiently short to prevent combat fatigue. But this meant that American soldiers enlisted as individuals, with a specific period of duty, not as members of units. They moved into and out of units according to their own individual

---

35 See Strecker & Appel, *Psychiatry in Modern Warfare*, pp. 3–19; Glass & Bernucci, *Neuropsychiatry in World War II*, pp. 735–59.
36 See Sinclair, 'Psychiatric Casualties in an Operational Zone in New Guinea', pp. 453–60; Dawson, 'The Prevention of War Neuroses', pp. 376–8; Editorial, 'The Nervous Disorders of Service Personnel: An Urgent Problem', *MJA*, vol. 1, 1944, pp. 515–6; Strecker & Appel, *Psychiatry in Modern Warfare*, pp. 3–21.

timetable. This broke down unit cohesion and weakened morale. Later studies have suggested that this lack of cohesion and morale made the combat soldier even more psychologically vulnerable to the stress of fighting, evident in high rates of drug addiction, alcoholism, and stress disorder. Australia's Vietnam forces, while still operating on a tour of duty principle, were more likely to enter and exit their tour as a unit rather than an individual soldier, making them more psychologically resilient. Moreover, some studies have suggested that the tour of duty system meant that many soldiers returned home before the full flowering of their psychological conflicts. They suffered delayed or what we have come to call post-traumatic stress reactions and, at home, were often distant from effective early psychiatric intervention, exacerbating their condition. The fatigue theory, despite its humane intentions, could have tragic consequences.[37]

III

In November 1950 prominent Australian novelist Miles Franklin wrote to Mollye Menken, the niece of her late friend and leading feminist Rose Scott: 'I have no more strength and I have to live in a disorganised litter, no strength for writing. I got your letter in March but have not earlier replied because I've been swamped. Had a sick nephew – war neurosis case – who kept me up night and day without sleep until he went to the repat hospital.'[38] Franklin's dilemma was that of many families. Shell-shock did not cease with the end of war. Many servicemen and women returned suffering psychological problems. Others developed problems sometime after their return. Australian governments accepted their responsibility to care for the mentally damaged soldier, providing psychiatric treatment in clinics and mental hospitals for the psychotic and neurotic returned serviceman and woman. They also provided pensions for those suffering from continuing mental problems, although the supposed genesis of the condition in combat made it difficult for servicewomen to obtain such pensions. In 1921 the Repatriation Commission confidently asserted that 'nervous diseases ... due to war service have ... ceased to be a prominent feature in hospitals and the streets'. Within a few years this assessment seemed somewhat optimistic. Repatriation authorities were alarmed by the increase in successful applications for pensions arising from neurosis. Between

---

37 See Belenky 'Introduction', pp. 4–5; H. Hendlin and A. Pollinger Haas, *Wounds of War: The Psychological Aftermath of Combat in Vietnam*, Basic Books, New York, 1984, pp. 3–12; G.H. Elder and E. Clipp, 'Combat Experience, Comradeship and Psychological Health', in J. P. Wilson, Z. Harel & B. Kahana (eds), *Adaptation to Extreme Stress: From the Holocaust to Vietnam*, Plenum, New York, 1988, pp. 131–56. On the greater Australian discipline and lower incidence of drug addiction, see B. O'Keefe & F.B. Smith, *Medicine at War: Medical Aspects of Australia's Involvement in Southeast Asian Conflicts 1950–1972*, Allen & Unwin, Sydney, 1994, pp. 201–24.

38 M. Franklin to M. Menken, 23 November 1950, Miles Franklin Papers, Mitchell Library MSS 363/20, p. 155.

1924 and 1940 the number receiving a pension for war neurosis rose 27 per cent, in comparison to a rise for all pensions of only 5 per cent. C.K. Parkinson, a medical officer with the Repatriation Department, argued that the existence of compensation for war neurosis was the underlying cause of this increase: it arose from 'the more or less subconscious desire for gain, sympathy and avoidance of civil responsibility'.[39] Some persisted in doubting that returned servicemen deserved a pension for war neurosis. They feared that the existence of a pension itself encouraged exaggerated and even fraudulent claims. Some believed that lax onus of proof and benefit of the doubt provisions undermined proper medical assessments of these disabilities. More than a few believed all of the above. How repatriation authorities responded to these problems depended on their understanding of the nature of shell-shock.

The immediate issue confronting military and repatriation authorities was treatment for shell-shocked returned servicemen. The first task – fundamental to psychiatric practice – was to sort those suffering from neuroses from those suffering from psychoses. But neurosis and psychosis also signified levels of curability. The latter were more likely to be seen as incurable, requiring certification and placement in a mental hospital. Although psychiatrists believed that there was nothing unique in the nature of returned-soldier mental illness and, moreover, that those suffering psychosis were more than likely to have developed the condition regardless of war experiences, returned-soldier groups insisted that returned men be treated in distinct institutions where possible, certainly in separate repatriation wards within mental hospitals, and that returned-soldier patients be further differentiated from civilian patients by different clothes. But the placement of returned men in mental hospitals, even when they were in separate accommodation, did not insulate them from the rapid decline in mental hospital facilities throughout Australia in the twentieth century. As psychiatrists concentrated their efforts on the treatment of the curable in clinics and private practices, mental hospitals struggled to retain staff, accommodation and recreation facilities aged, medical equipment became obsolete, and overworked staff increasingly resorted to restraint (strait jackets and muffs) to control patients. These conditions were the source of much complaint. From the 1920s, *Smith's Weekly*, and organisations such as the RSL and the Sailors, Soldiers and Airmen's Fathers Association, vigorously protested the inhumanity of these hospitals, the overcrowding, and the 'convict cut' clothes. Although psychiatrists claimed that repatriation patients received the most advanced convulsion, shock, and later, surgical treatment, the 1955 Stoller Inquiry into Australian mental hospitals was a damning indictment of facilities, and repatriation wards, although often better equipped than ordinary wards, did not escape this criticism.[40]

---

39 Parkinson, 'The Management of Neurotic Affections in Military Practice', p. 94. See Repatriation Commission, *Annual Report*, 1920–1, p. 15. The figures on pensions are from Butler, *The Australian Army Medical Services*, vol. 3, p. 965.

Returned soldiers with war neuroses, however, were treated in special clinics. During the First World War and immediate post-war years, to avoid the stigma of certification, the Australian Army established neurosis clinics, staffed by psychiatrists, to assist in the rehabilitation of shell-shock victims. At hospitals such as Lemnos in Perth, Millbrook Rise near Hobart, Bundoora in Melbourne, and Broughton Hall in Sydney, shell-shocked soldiers received psychotherapy, occupational therapy, rest, and medication to assist in their recovery. But there were also many private hospitals and sanatoriums, some run by the Red Cross and other charities, others established by donations from wealthy citizens. Recovery rates at these institutions, public and private, were high – as much as 90 per cent. So effective were they that the Repatriation Commission confidently predicted that they would soon be unnecessary. Broughton Hall ceased being a military hospital in 1922 and was handed over to the Mental Hospitals Department for use as an early treatment clinic for civilian patients. But the rise in the number of shell-shock and 'psychopathic' returned-soldier cases after the war prevented any wholesale closure of treatment facilities. Lemnos, Bundoora, and Millbrook Rise, as well as many private hospitals, continued to function as clinics for acute neurosis cases and, increasingly, as institutions for chronic psychopathic patients in the inter-war years and after the Second World War. And while these hospitals tried to differentiate the acute from the chronic, overcrowding and declining facilities eroded their therapeutic efforts.[41]

A.G. Butler was certain that nervous breakdown cases should only be temporary. The fact that men persisted with symptoms suggested to him that these were weaker vessels. Some psychiatrists were not so harsh. J.W. Springthorpe conceded that hysterics were easily and quickly cured but that 'psycho-neurasthenics' were much more persistent. For Springthorpe, a major problem was the lack of coordinated psychiatric treatment. Men were poorly diagnosed, many lying in ordinary hospitals before the mental origin of their complaint was recognised. Moreover, many were released from hospitals well before they were cured. Because the army and the Repatriation Commission were anxious to avoid certification and confinement in an ordinary mental hospital, shell-shock cases were rarely detained for treatment after demobilisation, no matter how necessary. For Springthorpe and other psychiatrists, war neurosis sufferers were returning to civilian life too quickly, and inevitably their weakened systems

---

40 See *Smith's Weekly*, 11 February 1922, 3 November 1945, 4 September 1948; Federal Executive Minute, 14 November 1919, RSL Papers, 963; Sailors, Soldiers and Airmen's Fathers Association, 'Report on War Neurosis', 8 August 1950; RSL, 'Report on Bundoora Hospital', 1952, RSL Papers, 1232 C; A. Stoller and K.W. Arscott, *Mental Health Facilities and Needs in Australia*, Government Printer, Canberra, 1955, pp. 81–3.
41 See Lemnos Hospital records, State Archives of Western Australia, WAS 242/3614; Military Mental Hospital Records, Victorian Public Record Office, VPRS 7527; Broughton Hall, No. 13 Military Mental Hospital, Case Papers, State Archives of NSW, 14/8956–8978; Minister of Repatriation to General Secretary, RSL, 2 February 1938, 'Mental Patients at Millbrook Rise', RSL Papers, 8950B; 'Millbrook Rise', Butler Papers, box 11.

succumbed to the pressures of life. The answer was to delay demobilisation until a cure had been effected. Psychiatrists during the Second World War, such as John McGeorge, were well aware of these problems and urged the government to make it compulsory for war neurosis victims to undergo twelve months of treatment before their release from the services. His suggestion was rejected. The government was on record as favouring discharge to civilian life as early as possible, so as 'not to foster the idea of inferiority' in these men.[42]

Efforts to ensure adequate treatment for shell-shock, however, did not address more fundamental suspicions about returned servicemen. Prevailing understandings of shell-shock ensured that psychiatrists and repatriation authorities were sceptical of the right of these men to a pension. Indeed, for them, the existence of the pension itself was at the heart of the problem. Butler attributed the rise in cases after the war to 'the possibility of inveighing a pension claim'. He was not alone in this suspicion. C.A. Courtney, Principal Medical Officer with the Repatriation Department, saw pensions as demoralising, 'begotten of the desire to find the onset of some form of ill-health as a means of ameliorating the effects of economic stringency'. Psychiatrists concurred. In 1942 John Bostock, Professor of Medical Psychology at the University of Queensland, declared that nervousness was a negligible complaint not worthy of a pension, and Andrew Dibden believed that a pension was 'a hindrance rather than an aid to the patient's recovery'. It fostered a desire to stay ill in the hope of obtaining compensation.[43]

The widespread belief among psychiatrists that many of the victims of this condition were hereditarily and neuropathically predisposed to nervous breakdown convinced them that such men were not entitled to compensation. This was clearly the belief with regard to more serious instances of breakdown. Of more concern was the vast number of soldiers who seemed to suffer some minor breakdown only to fully embrace the sick role when there seemed to be no real clinical reason for continuing nervous illness.

Some military medical officers, such as Colonel C.G. Manifold, argued that many front-line doctors had been too 'soft-hearted' towards exhausted soldiers. They diagnosed shell-shock far too readily, permitting men to 'wear the wounded stripe for life', and encouraging the 'weaker vessels in the regiment to seek relief and earn the distinction' of being wounded in action. If this was the case, then it undermined the case for pension compensation. Pension decisions revolved around the issue of war-caused disability. But if many cases of shell-shock arose

---

42 See A.G. Butler to General R. Downes, 12 December 1941, and J. W. Springthorpe, 'Suggestion as to the Better Treatment of Our War Neuroses', 23 March 1918, Butler Papers, box 61; 'Report by Dr J. McGeorge on Rehabilitation of War Neuroses', 1946, and Minister of Repatriation to General Secretary of RSL, 1 May 1943, RSL Papers, 1232 C.
43 A.G. Butler to General R. Downes, 3 May 1940, and Dr C.A. Courtney to A. G. Butler 13 October 1931, Butler Papers, box 61; J. Bostock, 'Nervousness: A Negligible and Not Pensionable Disability', *MJA*, vol. 1, 1942, pp. 133–5; W. A. Dibden, 'Psychiatric Casualties as a Repatriation Problem', *MJA*, vol. 1, 1945, p. 49.

from inherent deficiency, particularly those occurring in men who had not engaged in serious combat, then they should not be entitled to compensation. The problem was that overly sympathetic medical officers and hasty diagnoses had enabled some undeserving cases to obtain acknowledgment for illnesses that, in fact, arose from weaknesses that had nothing to do with war.[44]

Another issue was the belief that many of the nervous conditions of war were temporary, arising from exhaustion and justifiable fears. The rapid recovery rates, with more than half those treated at the front line being returned to their units within a few days, suggested that these were minor and transitory conditions. If this was the case, then there seemed to be no justification for increasing numbers of applications for war neurosis after the war. For Butler, Courtney, and others who believed in the transitory and environmental origin of shell-shock, the only reasons for the rising number of post-war psychiatric pension cases were either continuing stress in civilian life unrelated to war conditions, or the desire of some to remain ill in order to obtain compensation to which they were not entitled. Courtney, in particular, bitterly condemned the conspiracy of doctors and men to magnify their symptoms in order to obtain compensation. He accused some medical officers of being 'pension agents' and sarcastically noted the horror of applicants when informed that their nervous condition would cause them no organic disease or distress. He was 'more than ever astonished that medical guidance is so ignored in these pension questions'. Shell-shock, for Courtney, was another instance, perhaps the most glaring, in which medical facts were sacrificed to political expediency.[45]

Returned-services organisations and other self-styled champions of the returned man were, however, those most involved in insisting on the right of shell-shocked men to compensation. *Smith's Weekly* maintained a constant stream of articles on shell-shock and war neurosis, pointing to harsh pension decisions, which denied men with mental problems full compensation for their suffering. Some of the paper's claims were so exaggerated that returned-services organisations feared their effects on the campaign for full compensation. In 1950 the Sailors, Soldiers and Airmen's Fathers Association responded angrily to stories in *Smith's* that 95 per cent of pension claims had a war neurosis background.[46] The RSL, however, was well aware of the difficulties in granting pensions to shell-shocked soldiers. It monitored developments overseas for guidance on how best to secure the rights of their constituency. In this regard, Canada was the country most closely watched. After the First World War the Canadian government had ruled soldiers suffering from shell-shock ineligible for a pension. Instead, shell-shocked soldiers were given a one-off payment. In Canada the evidence for the inherent

---

44 C.G. Manifold 'Second Report on Shell Shock Cases which Have Passed through Some Australian Field Ambulances', 1918, Butler Papers, box 61.
45 C.A. Courtney to A.G. Butler, 13 October 1931, Butler Papers, box 42.
46 Sailors, Soldiers and Airmen's Fathers Association, 'Paper on War Neurosis', RSL Papers, 1232C. For typical stories, see *Smith's Weekly*, 28 June 1919, 14 November 1936, 2 October 1948.

predisposition to shell-shock took stronger hold than anywhere else. And the desire to ensure that pensions were not a drain on financial resources led to a conservative position on the relation between war and nervous breakdown. Throughout the 1920s and 1930s Canadian veterans' organisations attempted, with some success, to gain access to pensions for mentally damaged soldiers, and gradually pensions were granted for those suffering from chronic nervous conditions. In 1937, however, a proposed government conference of psychiatrists on shell-shock was opposed by the Canadian Legion, which feared that it would reveal that many cases 'were congenital and not war-caused'. The Legion agitated strongly, and the government eventually pigeon-holed the conference report for fear of the political consequences.[47]

The RSL in Australia recognised the need for vigilance concerning compensation for shell-shock. It clearly learnt much from the Canadian case, publicly rejecting predisposition and vigorously supporting theories of war causation. Both during and after the First World War and Second World War, it campaigned to obtain adequate treatment facilities and a right to a pension for these men. But behind the scenes it acknowledged that many suffered from either inherent deficiencies or personal and domestic worries. These were probably the cause of many nervous breakdowns, but to admit this was to undermine the case for compensation. Publicly the League proclaimed that any serviceman who was passed fit for service and who later developed nervous problems should be entitled to a pension, arguing that the field of neurosis was still vague and, hence, the benefit of the doubt should go to the soldiers. It also fiercely defended the principle that, once pensions were granted, they should not be taken away unless there was some fraud or infringement of the provisions. Here the RSL and other returned-services organisations were involved in a subtle cat and mouse game with psychiatric specialists, using expert evidence when it suited them, and ignoring it when it did not.[48]

According to Butler, less than 5 per cent of all war pensions were awarded specifically for war neurosis.[49] But psychological problems were noted on the files of many more pensioners than this. In our random sample, 28 per cent of First World War pensioners and 42 per cent of Second World War pensioners were said to be suffering from mental problems. Most of these men, however, had other conditions that were thought to be more significant in granting a pension. The higher figure for Second World War veterans is largely due to the very high proportion of prisoner-of-war pensioners believed to have psychological problems.

---

47 General Secretary, Canadian Legion, to General Secretary, RSL, 18 August 1937, RSL Papers, 8774B. See also Morton & Wright, *Winning the Second Battle*, pp. 133–5 &176–8.
48 See, for example, Congress Resolution, 'Mental Problems', 1935, RSL Papers, 8158–8159B; Western Australia Branch Report, 'Social Work and Psychiatry', 1944, General Secretary to Minister for Repatriation, 3 December 1945, and State Secretary, South Australian Branch, to General Secretary, 6 September 1949, RSL Papers, 1232C.
49 Butler, *The Australian Army Medical Services*, vol. 3, p. 965.

This is the flaw in Butler's calculations. Often pensions were cumulative, with incapacities for a variety of complaints added together for the final assessment. Only about half of those with psychological problems noted on their files received a pension specifically for war neurosis. Nonetheless, we can see that, in many cases, both returned men and local doctors, who provided them with the rationale to apply, considered psychological problems to be important.

The complex manoeuvrings around the problem of pensions for shell-shock are nowhere more apparent than in the assessment of specific cases. It is here that we can glimpse some of the dynamics in pensioning. Gordon S from rural Victoria served in Gallipoli and France, where he was wounded in action. He was awarded the Military Medal for bravery. In 1934 he applied for a pension for a gunshot wound to his right arm and for neurasthenia. Examining doctors found him 'anxious in expression, nervous, shaking and inclined to break down in tears'. He had exaggerated reflexes, and his heart action was slightly higher than average. The applicant claimed to have been taking nerve tonics. The problem for the consulting psychiatrist was how to explain the long lapse between the war and his application. This assessment became even more difficult when Gordon's former employer explained that he had been a 'steady worker, and abstainer', but that, due to lack of contracts, his employment had been terminated. The employer sought to help his former employee, maintaining that Gordon had been very nervous, often complaining of head and heart pains. Nonetheless, to what extent did unemployment affect his condition? The consulting psychiatrist clearly suspected that this was a major factor. But the military files suggested that Gordon had mild neurasthenia six months before his discharge. More troubling was the psychiatrist's conclusion that Gordon had an 'inborn predisposition to emotivity'. Here we have a familiar dilemma in the determination of shell-shock pensions. Was it predisposition, the effects of war, or the strain of post-war life that was the cause of the applicant's complaint? The obligation to give the benefit of the doubt weighed on the minds of the tribunal. It may have been due to war service – at least the mild neurasthenia noted in his file suggested so. But beyond these questions lay more complex imperatives. In this case, as with many others, the tribunal struggled to construct a coherent life story for the applicant. If some threads of connection to war could be written into the narrative, then it became possible to make a favourable decision. Gordon received a pension.[50]

The search for a thread connecting a soldier's problems to the war sometimes stretched the bounds of credibility. These decisions were not so much arbitrary, as many returned men liked to believe, as tendentious (often to the benefit of the applicant). But, for those rejected, the rationale must have seemed less than fair when viewed in the light of other cases. John B from Tasmania fought in Europe during the Second World War. In 1969 he applied for a pension for an anxiety

---

50   Gordon S, Department of Veterans' Affairs, Victoria, Case Files, AA, CRS B73, sample no. 127.

neurosis. The examining doctor found that he had been 'nervy' for years, but that the major cause of his condition was the 'unsatisfactory' state of his marriage: his wife suffered from phobias, and there were religious and social conflicts in the marriage. John became nervous and depressed. Graham W from South Australia served in the Middle East during the Second World War. On his return he discovered that his wife had deserted him for another man. He became depressed, drank, and by 1951, was seeking a pension for nervous anxiety. Although, in both cases, domestic stress was admitted to be the major factor in their condition, Graham's application was rejected and John's was accepted. Why? The distinguishing factor was that John had first become 'nervy' before his discharge, even though it took over twenty years for his condition to become serious, while Graham's condition developed after his discharge, even though it was only weeks after. John's narrative was more ambiguous, and in its ambiguity, there was room for doubt: his condition might have been due to war. Graham's case could not be invested with any such ambiguity.[51]

In some instances, however, pension tribunals granted pensions they later saw fit to revoke. Frederick B of Adelaide had served in France in the First World War but collapsed there and was diagnosed to be suffering from shell-shock and acute mania. Immediately on his discharge he lodged a successful application for a full pension due to shell-shock. At subsequent examinations, departmental doctors found him to be very unstable, suffering from tremors, profuse sweating, irritability, headaches, and general agitation. In 1932, however, a departmental officer noticed Frederick at the races, where he appeared quite normal. An investigation officer found that he was married (even though he claimed to be single), worked on his own soldier settler farm, and had a nice home. When confronted with these facts, Frederick denied them, and his brother argued vigorously that Frederick 'was off his head completely'. Departmental doctors assisting the investigation found that he had always been 'eccentric', even before the war, and prone to violent temper. The whole family seemed to be of 'a somewhat mental type', but the fact that the pensioner had kept down a good job, run his own farm, and maintained a family was the basis for cancellation of his pension.[52]

It is easy to see how the tribunal made a mistake in the case of Frederick. He had been diagnosed at the front and was therefore granted a pension. The fact that he was able to lead a normal life while feigning symptoms whenever he was required to front the Repatriation Commission tribunal only served to underline the undeserving nature of his case. How many more slipped through the net was a question of considerable concern to critics of the pension system. More troubling still were cases like Gordon S and John B, whose claim to a pension, on the medical evidence, was shaky at best. But benefit of the doubt worked in the favour of many

---

51   John B, Department of Veterans' Affairs, Tasmania, Case Files, sample no. 2; Graham W, Department of Veterans' Affairs, SA, Case Files, sample no. 197.
52   Frederick B, Department of Veterans' Affairs, SA, Case Files, AA, CRS CI37, sample no. 77.

applicants, despite the suspicion that, in some instances, the causes were not war related, or that men exaggerated their symptoms in order to gain a pension. This was not a concern confined to shell-shock cases, but the undoubted absence of precision in psychiatric science, its lack of a clear diagnostic test for mental illness, the vagueness of its categories, and the entrenched differences over the causes of neurosis unsettled those who sought to place pension determinations on a sound footing. While they conceded that there were many genuine sufferers, critics like Butler believed that:

> the way to make quite certain that there will be plenty of psychiatric casualties is to expect them, and to let it be known that they are expected ... I would not attempt to minimise the importance of the problem but I contend that ... 'bomb shock' in no way connotes 'peace with honour' and that though hysteria and neurasthenia are in some sense inevitable ... it must be regarded as a 'nervous breakdown' not as a battle casualty, and if not temporary only, is characteristic of an inferior type of man.[53]

It was a disquieting thought that Anzacs should be vulnerable to such complaints, but even more so that a few should be seeking to exploit shell-shock for their own advantage. This was an ungenerous assessment, although there were clearly instances that served to support it. Such suspicions, however, arose out of the way shell-shock was made by psychiatrists. It opened the way for scepticism, and in one sense, despite the advances of psychiatry, it had not entirely closed the door on the much longer tradition of fear that these conditions were forms of feigned illness and malingering.

---

53 A.G. Butler to General Rupert Downes, 12 December 1941, Butler Papers, box 61.

6
Home Fires

Captain Martin Donnelly was returning from four years at war. Sitting in the railway compartment, he was troubled by a 'certain bleakness ... that accompanies a stranger in a new world'. He had dreamt about his return to his wife Beth, and the brief happiness they had known before his departure. They had bought a small flat, and in the long wait for his return, Beth had refused to move back home to her family. She preferred to stay on in the flat. ' "I'll keep the home fires burning" she had said, "I'll find a way" '. She had found a way, and now Martin had received a note that Beth would not be at the station to meet him because the 'job was keeping her very busy right now'. Martin tried to convince himself that it did not matter, but it did. Her parting words had been 'only one thing can matter. The fact that you are coming back and that I'll be waiting'. 'Only now she wouldn't be waiting'. Beth had a job in an advertising agency. It was interesting and fun, and Martin did not have a job yet. But Beth was at the door when he returned:

> her warm fingers clasped his [and the] feeling of strangeness broke and he pulled her close to him. It was almost too wonderful ... and he kissed her often ... They looked into each others eyes a long time, and it was odd how much he had forgotten about her, or how much they had both changed. It gave him a feeling of insecurity ... He had gone away leaving a young, very young girl behind him. Now he returned and found a mature woman waiting ... 'I've been so afraid' said Beth. 'Afraid that you had changed. But you haven't. Oh, darling, how hard it is to see you again and not to cry'.

That night peace and contentment brought Martin the 'deepest, most quieting sleep he had had for a long time'. It did not last. Martin grew increasingly troubled by Beth's job. She was hardly ever at home, and his dream of married bliss soon faded. Worse, his own efforts to find a job were proving fruitless. Employers wanted men with experience, but his only experience was of war: 'My work is done he told himself Why should I be forced to start over again? I did my work. I did years of it'. But it was her job that gnawed at him. Finally he confronted Beth: 'this career business has got to stop. That's what's been the trouble with me ever since I got back'. She laughed, a hurt and angry laugh. Martin snapped and 'took his wife by the arm and slapped her across the face'.[1]

The story of Martin and Beth is fictional. And as typical romance fiction, one can reasonably expect travails in the course of love. It is one of many such stories that appeared in newspapers, journals, periodicals, radio programs, and films during and after the Second World War. In some respects, however, it is indistinguishable from popular romance fiction published at any time in the nineteenth or twentieth centuries. In other words, it is of its genre: two, fated to love each other, meet, undergo various tests of their love (initial misunderstandings, parental opposition, illness, misadventure, enforced separations, the attentions of others, perhaps even loveless marriages that they cannot leave, and so on) only to overcome all obstacles and realise their destiny. But there are also historical anchors for the story of Martin and Beth. War provided particular tropes for the romance narrative: men alienated from their lovers and families, feeling like strangers, unable to adjust to civilian life, struggling to find a niche in civilian society, and women who had grown up and changed since the departure of their men, and become independent and self-sufficient. All this and more provided a fund of material for writing specific stories. These narratives closely replicated the advice literature that sought to acquaint returned men and their families with the problems they would face and the adjustments that would be necessary to ensure successful repatriation. Indeed, the line between fiction and non-fiction was particularly blurred. Advice literature often resorted to exemplary tales to dramatise its message, and popular fiction drew upon the reservoirs of knowledge about the problems of returned servicemen and their families to frame its narratives. Both articulated for a broader reading, listening, and viewing public an understanding that the return of men to their families, and the resumption of normal family relations, would be far from smooth.

The passage from the 'barbarism' of war to the 'civilisation' of everyday life was expected to be difficult, and was indeed troubled for some. Repatriation was an organised effort to ease the material burdens of return – through medical and hospital benefits, pensions, employment preference, and training – but none of this could really address the individual negotiations each returning man had to make with his family. Equally, it could not ease the negotiations families had to undertake with returning men. There was a gap here, as experts recognised. And it was in this gap that advice literature, counselling services, family clinics, official exhortations, and fiction flourished. So much repatriation was really a private affair, and in the close confines of private life, it was women who were charged with the responsibility for ensuring the success of return. As William

---

1 W. Forrest, 'The Girl and the Malingerer', *Australian Women's Weekly*, 23 March 1946.

Fitzpatrick of the Victorian State War Council declared in 1917, 'women have more enthusiasm than men, and if we could engage their aid in this great work [repatriation] ... success would be assured ... women take in hand this labour of love'.[2] This was an extraordinary burden, which many willingly and successfully undertook. But advice literature and return fiction proliferated because, despite such labours, many marriages foundered and many families broke apart with the return of servicemen. War widows, on the other hand, had to struggle to bring up their families alone, and advice literature and welfare organisations here sought to address the problems of the family without a male head. And while these problem families may not be representative of all those who returned, the advice narratives shaped the expectations of all involved in repatriation.

I

The separation between home front and front line produced many feelings – nostalgia, longing, alienation – but it also fostered sex anxiety. We can see this in the earnest discussions of experts about the problems of readjustment after the Second World War. Most argued that First World War repatriation schemes had failed to address the personal problems of return, thus justifying expert intervention to prevent similar neglect of a new generation of diggers. There was certainly an element of self-promotion here, but it was experts who helped frame repatriation policies. There were many practical issues (such as pensions, training, and preference) of concern to advisers, legislators, returned-services advocates, and reformers. These were the focus of repatriation authorities after both wars. But discussion of the personal was more circumspect in 1918. In the 1940s such problems move to centre stage. One of the most important was the problem of sex adjustment: how were normal relations between the sexes to be resumed after the irregularities of war? The Australian Army Education Service was forthright in its warnings to returning men. It explained that 'fitting into the old routine won't be easy'. Army life had given them a 'freedom from responsibility', and moreover, 'the uniform' had given them 'an advantage in relations with the opposite sex'. The army was 'a holiday from the burdens of virtue'. The Education Service's rather simplistic solution to this dilemma was renunciation: 'you can fool around when you're in uniform but when you're in civvies you can't'. It went on to warn, however, that the 'resumption of home life may present problems'. For home life we should read marital sexual relations. How were men used to sexual liberty to readjust to monogamy and settled family life? Equally, how were women used to years of independence and self-reliance going to readjust to a social relationship of dependence? They predicted a return to stricter moral standards after the war, but for individual men and women, counselling and advice was necessary to restore

---

2 Fitzpatrick, *The Repatriation of the Soldier*, pp. 71–2.

harmonious relations. The Education Service was providing such advice for the returning man, hoping to acquaint him with the range of problems he might face. In doing so, it sought to render personal difficulties more general, defuse their destructive effects, and encourage men to seek help.[3]

Some experts offered advice to both men and women involved in readjustment. A.H. Martin, Director of the Institute of Industrial Psychology at the University of Sydney, was invited by the National Defence League to write a popular pamphlet for the families of returning servicemen. He argued that many families were complaining that returned men were 'utterly changed' – often 'irritable, fault-finding and impatient'. He sought to explain that returning men suffered 'from temporary warped personality'. Army life leads to 'regression to the primitive', and families needed to tread warily to ensure recovery. They had to avoid 'officiousness, condescension, nagging and correction'. If this advice was followed, he assured readers, few would need psychiatric care. Most would soon return to normal with 'home care and tact'. Such advice was directed as much to servicemen as it was to wives. It sought to acquaint women with the behaviours of returning men and the methods to deal with them, but it also made it clear to men that their behaviour was explicable, treatable, and temporary.[4]

Women also had their own journals of advice – notably the *Australian Woman's Mirror* and *Australian Women's Weekly*. Here women learnt that the 'return of warriors' meant the beginning of a new war: 'the battle of the sexes'. They were given direct advice on how to win this battle: it involved being tolerant of the husband's irritability and moods, accepting his sleeplessness and employment restlessness, being silent when he exploded for no good reason, and avoiding nagging or excessive sympathy. They were told that 'your soldier is not the same man who went away' and that it would take some time for him to readjust to married life. Some of the behaviour of their menfolk was actually 'delayed action shock'. But they were often reassured 'that any man can be ruled by a woman provided she doesn't let him know'. There was obviously little questioning here of the naturalness of traditional sex roles. Men were the breadwinners and women supervised the domestic sphere. The problem with returning soldiers seemed to be that many refused to assume their responsibilities as breadwinner, husband, and father. Women were advised on strategies for coaxing their men to return psychologically. Not all accepted such responsibilities. Jean Tait claimed that 'husbands expect too much'. But others rejected this view. One digger pleaded that a wife 'must allow [her] husband to feel that he is really needed'. Some might call this 'pandering', but the digger argued that returned men had suffered extreme blows to their 'self-esteem' when they found that women had been able to cope without them. Popular journals were not adverse to fostering a little debate to advertise their relevance, but for

---

3   Australian Army Education Service, *Human Problems After the War*, pp. 3–33.
4   Martin, *Welcome Home Serviceman!*, pp. 1–10.

the reading public, stories and letters framed readjustment as a difficult period for all concerned.[5]

There were more sober discussions of sex relations addressed to a specialist audience of doctors, social workers, psychologists, educationists, and repatriation officers. Reg Ellery, a prominent psychiatrist, wrote extensively on the problems of sex adjustment and war. His was a bleaker message. For Ellery, some servicemen were hereditarily unfit for war, and combat only exacerbated their problems after return. There were also many marginal neurotic types, whose exposure to war could cement mental and sexual maladjustment. First, there were men whose repressed aggressive instincts found an outlet in war. War gave new meaning to their manhood, but for Ellery, it 'made and marred them'. It raised them to new heights, only to cast them down when peace was declared. They returned 'harbouring righteous grudges' and living constantly in the past, resentful and incapable of adjusting to the present. Second, army life forced sexual adjustments on men that might 'persist in civil life'. It forced either 'an unnatural life of repression' or a search for 'substitute gratifications'. These latter gratifications included prostitution, masturbation, and more 'disturbingly', homosexuality and bisexuality. Finally, after years of separation and independence, 'women might be loath to surrender to husbands'. Any of these reactions (resentment, repression, substitution, independence) threatened post-war marital relations. In this literature the problems were more diverse, difficult, and sometimes more intractable, couched as they were within a language of drives, repression, and fixations. But despite the greater complexity of this expert discourse, its solution – counselling and professional assistance – was essentially the same as that of popular advice literature.[6]

The calm and objective tone of the popular and professional advice literature has a quaintly unreal quality. In its simple presentation of symptoms and solutions, it abstracts difficult human conflicts and emotions, seeking to make them commonplace and resolvable. Our access to the real processes of adjustment is more partial. Oral history is one source that suggests that readjustment was sometimes more tortured, scarring, and protracted than advice literature could admit. Joseph Kelly, a First World War veteran, found himself paralysed by depression for 'quite a long time'. Ray Tonkin, a Second World War veteran, was married only a short time before leaving for the front. After he returned he felt strange, driven by an overwhelming desire to hide under the bed. The few times he ventured onto the streets, he felt people were laughing at him. Some families and friends looked on, frustrated and unable to help returned men. Bob Percy, a veteran of Tobruk, seemed fine on his return. He bought a truck with his war gratuity and set up a cartage business, determined to be independent and provide for his family.

---

5 See J. Tait, 'Husbands Expect Too Much' and M.B., 'Dig has his Say', *Australian Woman's Mirror*, 4 September 1945 and 9 October 1945.
6 R.S. Ellery, *Psychiatric Aspects of Modern Warfare*, Reed & Harris, Melbourne, 1945, pp. 146–53.

But then he turned to drink, neglected the business, smashed the truck, and lived for many years in an old caravan.[7]

Reading oral histories and recollections, like advice literature, has an equally unreal quality. Often the narrative of the individual life seems to replicate the fictional accounts of readjustment. In their structure, and in the dominant motifs of strangeness, alienation, conflict, and slow recovery (or occasionally irreparable decline), both fact and fiction seem to work hand in hand. This is not to deny the reality of family conflict and marital tension. But neither should we walk boldly in the other direction, asserting that fiction accurately reflected reality. The relationship between the two is more complex. Reality gave fiction a repertoire of problems and possibilities with which to play, but fiction also gave its consumers plausible tropes and ways of understanding, explaining, and eventually retelling their own life story. We can see this operating in a rather directed way in the ABC Radio Listening Groups that discussed 'Problems in the Home' in 1947.

Experts advised listeners on marriage problems and techniques for 'getting it off your chest', but did so through fictional case studies of troubled marriages, often involving returned servicemen and their wives. Listening groups all around the country were guided in their analysis of the problems through study questions, but were also encouraged to discuss their collective interpretation of the problems, deciding who was in the right and what were the best means of resolving these problems. In this they brought lived experience to bear, but fictional experience also provided the context for their view of real marital problems.[8] The listening groups were particularly didactic. More commonly, stories, films, and radio programs played with conventional scenarios, reaffirming dominant motifs and structures, but also shifting, displacing, and inventing new twists in an effort to interest an audience. In these novelties we can glimpse interesting tensions and conflicts. Stories are a means of exploring deeper cultural meanings embedded in the process of readjustment after war. They move beyond the restrictions of advice literature to open out more complex, and often hidden, anxieties.

One of the most common genres for playing with the possibilities of returning soldiers was romance fiction. Here readers could be excited by the difficulties encountered on the path to true love and comforted by the final triumph of that love. Such stories were a staple of Australian women's magazines and periodicals, some of which commanded an enormous reading audience. Most were obviously generic, but their articulation of the course of return is illuminating. Moreover, the naivety of First World War stories provides the context for the explosion of

---

7 For Bob Percy's case, see Leonard Whittaker Papers, La Trobe Library, MS 12515. The oral histories are from South Australia State Library, Oral History Collection, OH 1/15 and 10/2.
8 L.B. Carter (ed.), Problems in the Home, ABC Listening Groups (4QR) Transcripts, 30 June 1947.

advice in the 1940s. Experience suggested that the comforting homilies of the 1920s had failed, and that return indeed was a problem. In 'Sweet Heart to Somebody', published in 1915, Miss Peppitt, an impoverished dressmaker, devotes her time to looking after her mother and spending her meagre savings on wool to knit socks for men at the front. One of her parcels is sent to Sergeant Skepp, a lonely, reclusive man, but there was 'no better soldier'. Skepp falls in love with the anonymous knitter, and after being wounded, he returns home to find her. After some extraordinary strokes of good fortune and coincidence, he finds Miss Peppitt, they instantly recognise each other's innate goodness, fall in love, and marry. The essential elements of many stories are here. Miss Peppitt is a 'true' woman – self-sacrificing, inherently good, and without a question mark against her character (in other words, constant labour has ensured that she has had no other man). Skepp is the classic 'still waters run deep', silent, but undoubtedly brave, man. Here manhood is signified not by physical capacity (Skepp is wounded and diminished in capacity) but by character (bravery, constancy). The didactic imperative of the story, however, is aimed at women. Purity, faithfulness, and war work will be rewarded with the love of a real man. More than this, real men are not represented by the classic hero figure, but by the silent, war-damaged man who has proven his worth through his injuries.[9]

The romance fiction of the 1940s could not realistically revolve around such obvious paragons of virtue as Miss Peppitt and Skepp. During the Second World War, romance fiction was affected by stories of women's entry into male occupations while men were away fighting (although the extent of this shift was exaggerated), and even more disturbingly, by the attraction of Australian women to 'yanks' (with the attendant suggestion that women might now be sexually experienced). These issues were added to the variety of hurdles confronting love, and many stories attempted to resolve them within the accepted confines of romance. In 'Welcome Back', Judy Barnett is the attractive daughter of a prominent local businessman, and her mother is the chair of the Veteran's Adjustment Committee. The committee decides to take on the case of Joseph Hartley, a former mill worker and veteran about to return to town. Joe is unsettled, shy, moody, unwilling to join in social activities, and reluctant to return to his old job – all the classic symptoms of 'returned soldier syndrome'. All the best efforts of the committee to reintegrate Joe just alienate him further. But Judy likes what she sees in Joe (ambition, drive, and commitment), and she pursues him and eventually breaches his defences. Joe gets a new and better (that is, white-collar) job, and they marry. There is a gentle parody here of 'do-gooders' like Mrs Barnett, and a clear message that love is more powerful than social work. Its modernity is signalled by Judy being the active pursuer (unlike Miss Peppitt who is entirely passive): the

---

9   J.S. Fletcher, 'Sweet Heart to Somebody', *Australian Home Journal*, 1 December 1915.

modern woman has to take matters into her own hands if returned men are to be reintegrated into romance.[10]

In 'Homecoming' Ted and John are both prisoners of war in love with the same woman, Margaret Berry. Only John is aware of the triangle, and he is troubled by guilt when he is chosen as one of five involved in an exchange of prisoners. He is returning to Margaret, and Ted has given him messages of his own love to give to her. But the problems of the triangle quickly dissipate when he arrives at Margaret's home (she is out at work) and is given a rather frosty reception from her mother. She informs John that Margaret has no interest in him and is engaged to 'a nice American officer'. John is crushed, but at that moment Margaret arrives home and embraces him enthusiastically (much to the consternation of her mother). All is quickly resolved – the yank had been foisted on Margaret by her mother, and she had no affection for Ted – and marriage follows. In 'Look Back in Love' we can see another familiar story-line. Debbie and Pete had been married briefly before his departure to war. Pete longs for his return and expects that things will be as before, with him as breadwinner and Debbie as housekeeper, but in his absence Debbie has found a good job. Pete is bitterly disappointed when Debbie hurries off to work instead of cooking him breakfast and picking up after him. Marital conflict ensues and divorce looks likely. They both come to their senses, however, realising their deep love. Pete declares that he is happy for her to work, and Debbie states her intention to resign to resume her domestic duties. Finally, they agree to a compromise: Debbie goes to work part-time. Here we have an idealised modern post-war marriage: one based on love and mutual sacrifice. Moreover, the hurdles of women's work, yanks, and unsettled returned men are seen as trivial or imaginary, easily overcome with persistence, compromise, and, of course, love.[11]

Romance fiction was primarily addressed to the woman reader, although some men undoubtedly read these stories. Men's magazines of the 1940s, however, also contained romance fiction addressed more directly to a male readership. And although the conventions of the genre were still apparent, there are interesting differences. There was a more frequent resort to first-person narratives than in the women's romances, which almost exclusively relied on the third person. Through these techniques, men were given a voice to articulate their feelings, while women's feelings, even in women's magazines, are at one remove from themselves, the object of some other subject. In men's magazines, the mix of first and third person helps render men as the protagonists and women as, often, mute and passive creatures (untroubled by employment or yanks) to be possessed by returning men. For

---

10 S. Oliver, 'Welcome Back', *Australian Women's Weekly*, 3 November 1945. For a discussion of the exaggerated extent of women's war employment, see K. Darian-Smith, *On the Home Front: Melbourne in Wartime 1939–45*, MUP, Melbourne, 1990, pp. 47–58.
11 See J. Leigh Cook, 'Homecoming', *Australian Woman's Mirror*, 7 August 1945; W.T. Budlong, 'Look Back in Love', *Australian Women's Weekly*, 22 September 1945.

example, in 'The Warriors Return', a nameless soldier and former prisoner of war, brutally tortured by the Japanese, returns to his wife Rene. They barely knew each other when they married and he fears her reaction because he has heard what women did while men were away fighting. His fears are groundless. She greets him passionately.[12]

Male romance fiction often played with return as a resolution of pre-war love entanglements. In 'The Return of Edward' the hero had left for war as a way of escaping the dilemma of a loveless marriage and a mistress he loved. He returns to find that he still hates his neurotic wife and longs for his mistress. Conveniently, his wife leaves him, and he is free to pursue his true love. In 'Digger Take a Wife' Jack Thurston returns home to the bush determined to resolve his love for Molly. Jack, Molly, and Ted had been an inseparable trio before the war, but it was Ted who had married Molly. Ted had been killed in the war, and Jack hopes to reveal his long-standing love for her. He finds her, the perfect bush wife (signifying a real Australian woman, with solid virtues, untainted by urban moral laxness and yanks), but Molly is sullen and distant, believing that he is returning to commiserate with her about Ted. In other words, she really loved Jack all along, but in their initial misunderstanding, neither can admit love. It begins to rain, and with a raging flood upon them, Molly's house is washed away. Clinging to a small raft, they both realise their mutual feelings. These are not complex or subtle stories, even in comparison with women's romance fiction. Moreover, they are curiously ahistorical. The war or the social dislocations of war occasioned by women's employment and sexual experience rarely figure here, or they are sometimes curiously and laboriously displaced by situating the story in the bush. Where women's fiction depicted the post-war world as one in which men and women had to accommodate themselves to new circumstances, men's fiction more often pictures war as a cleansing agent, a means of achieving repressed desires and returning to a pre-war world of true love. Women's fiction looks ahead to a new type of marriage brought on by the social transformation of war, while men's fiction fantasises a woman's unconditional submission to a man's love.[13]

The story of Jack, Molly, and Ted also points us towards a surprisingly frequent theme in return fiction: the soldier's desire for a mate's wife or girlfriend. Commonly these stories turn on two men at war, usually (but not always) close mates, who fall in love with the same woman. In each instance, however, the woman is already taken by one of the men, and the other mate refuses to reveal his desire. Fate conspires to ensure that the silent lover eventually replaces the original one. In 'Frail Bud' Bill Morris comes to realise that he does not love his own girlfriend but that of his mate Charlie Sinclair. Similarly, in 'Pin-Up Girl', Jack Tranter falls in love with the picture of a young woman found in the pocket of a dead soldier, Rex

---

12 S. Teece, 'The Warriors Return', *Cavalcade*, December 1946.
13 C.A. Adams and D. Blantyre-Gowland, 'The Return of Edward', *Man*, May 1944; C.R. Mentiplay, 'Digger Take a Wife', *Cavalcade*, January 1947.

Stanton. Of course, he determines to find the woman after the war and, like Bill Morris, after initial misunderstandings wins the heart of the woman he has come to love. Fate most commonly intervenes in the form of death (of the original lover), although in 'Frail Bud' it turns out that Charlie steps aside from the pursuit (by falling for someone else), leaving the field free for Bill. In each case the silent lover has never met the woman, but the letters or a photograph of the woman is what inspires him – as if these were emblems of the true woman (really the idealised male fantasy) – although, in each case, the reality eventually confirms the fantasy. There were occasional variations on this theme. In 'On Behalf of Harry' Gregory Day is sent by his seriously wounded and permanently disabled mate, Harry Martin, to break this news to Harry's fiancée. He is distressed when she shows no interest in marrying Harry, but his anger is tempered by his immediate feeling of love for 'Harry's girl'. His guilt overwhelms him, driving him to terrible accusations of betrayal. His dilemma is resolved when the woman reveals that she is not Harry's girl but her sister. Gregory is freed to pursue his true desire.[14]

It is difficult to decipher the issues at play in these stories of love for a mate's wife or girlfriend. For a female reader, they seem to suggest that a woman's true love may as yet be unknown to her (or that the man with whom she is currently involved is the wrong man) but that fate would ensure that her real love would return to take her hand. This is a common theme in romance fiction, and the war provided just another version of this scenario. For the male reader (and also perhaps the female reader), however, such stories prompted uncomfortable reflections on male sexual competitiveness. On one level, they suggested that war was a means of returning to a special love. But to do so often involved the death of another soldier. Desire and death were intimately linked here, with one being the means for the realisation of the other. Taken to an extreme, these stories hinted at (but, of course, never actually stated) a desire for the death of other soldiers as a means of self-fulfilment, revealing a sharp cleft in the idealised image of digger mateship. But other readings are possible. The frequent motif of these stories is that men assumed the role of a dead mate or fellow soldier: that of the lover of a particular woman. In these stories the bond between the two men, a bond blurred in death, becomes the dominant theme of the story. One man replaces another, almost becomes the other, and thus, in a curious way, this deathly bonding transcends the more mundane love of man and woman. In one sense, this motif presented the possibility that every returning lover brought back the desire of a digger who had died. In other ways, it hinted at a deeper homoerotic bond in the play of death and life that was mateship in war. There is no single answer here. For, even in this rather crude short-story romance fiction, there are ambiguities that open up a multiplicity of possibilities. Popular reflections on the meaning of love and war contained diverse potentialities, ones

---

14 'Frail Bud', *Australian Woman's Mirror*, 6 March 1945; Z. V. Webb, 'Pin-Up Girl', *Australian Woman's Mirror*, 23 October 1945; 'On Behalf of Harry', *Australian Woman's Mirror*, 27 June 1944. See L. Mann, *Flesh in Armour*, Allen & Unwin, Sydney, 1985 (1932).

that point to the cultural and psychological complexity of war for those at the front and those at home.

In most types of romance fiction the path to true love is essentially strewn with social and psychological obstacles. But some of this fiction seeks to deal with the physical problems that confronted returned men – specifically the possibilities for desire and love for those seriously wounded and disabled. For servicemen, the fear of being maimed and disabled was infused with concerns about a loss of manhood and their prospects for marriage – an idea that was more usually a euphemism for sexual performance. William Shaw Clayton, wounded at Gallipoli and in France, reported the frequent trench discussions on the 'all important [subject] of "the girl" ', in which the conversation turned on the chances of a fellow should he return 'seriously maimed ... one chap was much concerned as to how he would be treated by his fiancée if he should come home minus a leg or two'.[15] Such glimpses of the front line are rare. But if the proliferation of stories and films about the marriage prospects of disabled soldiers is any guide, then such fears were pervasive. In these stories and films, the focus was as often as not on the women who had to learn to desire these men as it was on the men who had to be reassured in their manhood.

Stories rendering a comforting picture of the return of disabled soldiers after the First World War were usually simple moral tales of romance and redemption. Here self-sacrificing and true women had no qualms or concerns about wounded and disabled men. Indeed, as with Skepp and Miss Peppitt, disablement was manly. This can also be seen in another First World War story, 'Sergeant Quinn VC', in which Quinn has lost an arm but is instantly recognisable as a hero because of his Victoria Cross. He asks the woman he loves and hopes to marry 'can you think of me [as a husband] – a disabled man?'. She, of course, sees the Cross and, instantly recognising him as a real man, puts 'her hand into his, like a child ... looks at him with shining eyes "with the Cross" she said'. The importance of such stories is that manhood itself comes to be signified by disablement and women are enjoined to submit ('like a child') to genuine desire.[16]

Similar motifs structured stories from the Second World War, although here the range of disabilities encompassed psychological, as well as physical, problems. In 'Snow is on the Grass Again' the male protagonist, Ben Underwood, a 'genuine war hero', is now in a repatriation hospital with a damaged back. Worse than this, however, he suffers from 'battle fatigue' and shows no interest in life. His fiancée breaks off their engagement (clearly an unworthy character), but Ben displays no feelings about this event. It is only when Pat, a war widow, dances with him at the hospital dance that he begins to recover. Pat is struggling (in this case to support a young child) and yet finds time to assist soldiers, a clear signifier of virtue. Love and marriage ensue, unencumbered by any qualms about disability.[17]

---

15   William Shaw Clayton Papers, La Trobe Library, MS 10434.
16   K. Tynan, 'Sergeant Quinn VC', *Australian Home Journal*, 1 December 1915.
17   D. Johnson, 'Snow is on the Grass Again', *Australian Women's Weekly*, 21 July 1945.

Some stories, however, explored more macabre elements of disability. In 'Please Don't Come Back' a female narrator talks of her marriage to Kim. It had begun happily enough, but after an accident, she had become blind and dependent. Slowly their marriage disintegrated, and after ten years they knew they hated each other. Kim eagerly goes to war to escape, and the narrator is left to fend for herself. With the help of friends, she gains a measure of independence and, more than anything else, prays that Kim does not return. He does, and she fully expects (and, in fact, hopes) that he will divorce her. But he says he no longer wishes to leave. Suddenly she realises something is wrong: he cannot leave; he has been wounded and is now blind. There are a number of peculiarities in this story. It is published in a men's magazine but has a woman author and, even more uniquely, a female narrator. Here the woman is the protagonist and the man rather passive and dependent. And driving this story is a narrative of equality in marriage, although now it is the equality of mutual disability that will keep this marriage together. Its moral resonates with that of similar women's fiction, but its publication in a men's magazine creates an obvious dissonance. What would the predominantly male readership make of this story? The underlying tone seems to be one more of threat than of romance – where a disabled soldier is forced into a relationship of equality with (perhaps even dependence on) someone whom he hated. It is a disturbing story, which might comfort some with the thought that wives will be prepared to stay with them despite their wounds, but which could equally serve to amplify anxiety about disability.[18]

In most of these stories disability is denied or rendered irrelevant. Only a few dared to confront the starker problems of negotiating marriage and disability, and most of these are from the 1940s, when discourses of sex and sex adjustment were more explicit than they had been twenty years earlier. The most famous of these texts is the Academy Award-winning film 'The Best Years of Our Lives', depicting the problems faced by three American veterans returning from the Second World War. One of these, Homer Parish, has lost both his hands (and is played by actual double amputee veteran Harold Russell). Homer (the very name highlights the everyman desire embedded in this character) undergoes a slow and painful adjustment to civil life, but a major stumbling block to his reintegration is the problem of desire – specifically, whether his girlfriend Wilma will overcome any repulsion she may feel for his disfigurement. Again it is women who bear the didactic brunt of this tale: it is they who have to learn to desire disfigurement. But the struggle of Homer here is also rendered more complex than in conventional romance. The film dwells on Homer's battle to regain his manhood (in a psychological sense) after the trauma of his accident. And it is only through the assertion of his manhood in a violent argument with another (male) customer in a drugstore that Homer regains the strength to resolve his sexual problems. He

---

18 B. Lee, 'Please Don't Come Back', *Cavalcade*, March 1946.

and Wilma go into his bedroom, where Homer reveals his stumps and the future that awaits her. Here the emasculation of Homer's hands is vividly represented, but is subtlety counterpointed by the rifles and bayonets on the wall of the bedroom. Homer, in his disfigurement, is a real man; Wilma desires him, which confirms his manhood; and their marriage promises full repatriation for Homer. Wilma here is more the agent of this reconciliation than a full character. Her desire is never problematised; it remains the model of marriage and motherhood. It only remains for Homer to overcome his own narcissistic inhibitions and fears for desire to be realised. In the film's focus on the traumas of Homer, Wilma's only role is to love unconditionally. Despite the novelty and complexity of this film, it resolves the problems of its characters within the conventions of romance fiction.[19]

There were a few stories that explored darker undercurrents in the reconciliation of desire and disfigurement. One that did, 'The Woman' by A.V. Neil, repays closer attention, not least because it links disfigurement with another staple of romance fiction: the desire for a mate's wife. Here two diggers, Frank Delaney and Steve Kellow, fighting in the jungles of New Guinea, had 'cobbered up, a sort of David and Jonathan business'. Frank Delaney was 'a little runt with an ugly mug', and Kellow was 'a good looking chap in a commonsense way'. They had been through many scrapes together, and Kellow had learnt to love and trust Delaney. One night Delaney pulled out a picture of his wife Louise, a 'ravishing' beauty with a 'laughing mouth' and 'deep, mysterious eyes'. The photo hit Kellow 'squarely beneath the belt'. The two, Frank and Louise, were incongruous – 'beauty and the beast'. Later Frank is killed in action, dying in Steve's arms with a strange smile on his face. Steve is determined to survive and to track down Louise. Later he is wounded and seriously disfigured. He writes to Louise, and despite his barely suppressed lust for his mate's widow, his shame at his 'knobbed flesh and hideous scars' prevents him from seeking a meeting. Louise, however, persuades Steve to visit, brushing aside his qualms about his disability as irrelevant. Steve is 'intoxicated' by this beauty who does not seem to mind his beastliness, just as she had not minded Frank's, and Louise makes it clear that she intends to seduce Steve.

Soon after, Louise and Steve marry. He reflects on Frank and fate: 'war in its vileness had snatched [Frank] from paradise and now Steven Kellow filled his place'. Soon after, Louise, wearing only 'a thin, silken robe', enters the lounge room where Steve is seated. He is overcome by her beauty, and at that moment the caged canary whistles 'a heart-breaking melody'. Steve exclaims 'my God Louise, you're as lovely as that bird's song'. A 'strange look' comes over Louise's face, and she walks over to the bird, takes it from the cage, strangles it, and throws it over the balcony. 'I hated that bird' she cried. 'He was beautiful. His body was beautiful. But there is only need

---

19   See D. Gerber, 'Heroes and Misfits: The Troubled Social Reintegration of Disabled Veterans in *The Best Years of Our Lives: American Quarterly*, vol. 46, no. 4, December 1994, pp. 545–74; S. Michel, 'Danger on the Homefront: Motherhood, Sexuality, and Disabled Veterans in American Post-war Films', in Cooke & Woollacott (eds), *Gendering War Talk*, pp. 260–79.

for one beautiful body here with us, my Steven'. At that moment her robe drops to the ground, but Steve is not looking at Louise; he is thinking of Frank and the strange smile on his face when he died: 'Kellow understood that smile now. Delaney was the lucky man. Delaney had escaped'.[20] Here a conventional romance scenario of the triumph of true love is overturned by a narrative of sexual threat and female domination. Disfigurement is just a fetish for the ultimate in female narcissism, and men become pawns in a sexual game that effectively renders them passive and emasculated. Although such malevolent themes were rare, the representation of Louise, and the anxiety it seeks to invoke in the male reader, provides us with a bridge to other, more pervasive, sources of sexual anxiety in the separation between front line and home front. In the distance that this separation created, there was ample space for a flourishing culture of suspicion. While digger culture paraded the joys of contact with women while serving overseas, men at the front still undoubtedly feared infidelity in their wives and fiancées. They were concerned that other men (shirkers in the First World War and yanks in the Second) were capitalising on their absence. In this space there was a deep reservoir of stories that articulated, shaped, and fanned these fears, drawing on a longer heritage of male anxiety about female desire.

II

As soldiers sank deeper into the mud of France, or gasped for breath in the humid jungles of New Guinea, their natural sense of isolation grew into a resentful feeling of abandonment. As wars ground on interminably, the metaphorical split between front line and home front widened. Men on the front came to feel that those at home (except for their families) had abandoned them. Politicians, profiteers, shirkers, and strikers were variously cast as the sources of the neglect, complacency, and exploitation that undermined the war effort and reduced the support vital for a speedy end to hostilities. In the First World War 'blowflyism' (following Cavill's 'Swat the Fly' cartoon) captured the demonology of the angry digger. But women were also the focus of considerable resentment. Here we can glimpse the intricate connections between war and masculinity. If battle was the assertion of manhood, then the symbolic fruit of that assertion was women. In numerous forms, soldiers were seen as having a rightful expectation of faithfulness from 'their women' and, more intriguingly, a reasonable expectation that they would be desired by all women. This dichotomous representation of women, as both faithful wife/mother and desiring lover/whore, drew on a long heritage of masculine images of women; war brought them into sharp focus. We can see the idealised image in the motto of the women's column in *The Soldier*, 'a mother's heart is always with her children, a wife is a key to the house'. Similarly, in 1946, *Reveille*, comforted the

---

20 A.V. Neil, 'The Woman', *Man*, February 1945.

returned man with an image of the discharged soldier in bed being brought bacon and eggs by a faithful wife. Alongside these images were more disquieting ones of female desire. In 1918 *The Bulletin* carried a humorous cartoon of fashionable flappers criticising a recent government repatriation decision: 'fancy the married men coming home first. Don't the military get things upside down!'. Men's magazines of the 1940s sanctioned more explicit depictions. In *Man* a scantily clad woman leans out of a window, anticipating the return of the 'ninth divvy'.[21]

The trouble with such representations was that they were male fantasies. And fantasies were likely to be disappointed, even more so in the context of the anxiety bred by separation. Counterpoised to images of welcoming wives and lovers were representations of female duplicity, betrayal, infidelity, and capriciousness. There is nothing unique in this. Popular journals such as *The Bulletin* had a long tradition of patronising chivalry and libertarian misogyny in their depictions of women. War, however, provided particular modes for their expression. During the First World War a pervasive theme of these images was that of women gaining pleasure from the presence of men at the front. It allowed them to satisfy diverse feminine needs. In one cartoon in *The Bulletin*, two military wives, decked out in all their finery, are discussing the effect of the war: 'Mrs Lieutenant Smith – "You were always complaining before the war about Dick's late hours, but now he's away all the time you seem as happy as a cricket." Mrs Captain Dick Brown – "Ah, yes. It's such a comfort knowing he was safe at the front when I last heard of him" '. In a similar vein, a cartoon pictured a young flapper talking to an old man: 'Old Thing – "It is gratifying to find all you young ladies still persisting with a cheerful heart in your efforts to drive the war on to a perfectly satisfactory conclusion." Young Thing – "Oh, I just love my bit! I've seven fiancés in Palestine and twelve in France, and if the war hadn't fizzled out till Easter I'd have made up the two dozen" '. In these depictions women joined the pantheon of forces who, for their own selfish ends, were eager for men to continue fighting and dying.[22]

The other dominant theme in this First World War literature was the betrayal of the digger by women consorting with shirkers and profiteers. Here war, instead of rewarding real men with the affection of women, allowed the shirker to exploit their absence. This might be seen as the fault of the shirker, but there were usually more sinister representations that suggested that this was woman's doing. In 1919 *The Soldier* published a particularly poignant drawing: 'The Girl Who Didn't Wait'. Here a distraught soldier is restrained and comforted by a mate as he sees his sweetheart on the arm of a rich, older man (linking both shirking, profiteering, and the betrayal of young men by older men). It might be contended that these are just images, but people lived through and expressed their fears in such depictions,

---

21 See *The Soldier*, 2 November 1917; *Reveille*, 1 March 1946; *The Bulletin*, 28 November 1918; Man, July 1945.
22 See 'Relieved from Anxiety', *The Bulletin*, 21 November 1918; 'Her Heart Was in her Work', *The Bulletin*, 23 January 1919.

which in turn arose out of currents of cultural anxiety. We can see the essentially blurred boundaries between representation and reality in frequent news reports of outraged diggers abusing civilian couples. In 1919 a returned soldier, Eric Bannister, was charged with assault after he saw John Price kiss a woman in George Street. He broke up the kiss shouting 'what right have you to kiss a girl when you haven't been to war' and punched Price in the face. Bannister was asserting his superior right of access to women and his belief that those who had not fought should be denied the normal privileges of manhood. Such rights and expectations were frequently offended by numerous reports of diggers returning home to find that their wives and sweethearts had taken up with men who had stayed at home. For newspapers, the more sensational the case, the better. In one account John Currans, a returned soldier from Dubbo, was reputedly 'cuckolded' by a half-caste Chinaman fruiterer. The racial dimension of this offence made it all the more dramatic. And the lesson was clear: women were faithless and in collusion with shirkers. There could be no greater betrayal in the eyes of many diggers.[23]

The currents of antagonism towards women in the 1940s were more explicit and sustained. The growth of a specific market for men's magazines provided an avenue for forthright commentary on the follies and deceit of women. Here, particularly in magazines such as *Man*, writers and cartoonists played freely with depictions of relations between men and women. During the war these magazines were dominated by stories and images of brave fighters. Men dominated visual representation: they held guns, fired canons, flew planes, and marched relentlessly forwards against the enemy, with weapons (those quintessential phallic symbols) thrust bravely forwards and upwards. But running as a counterpoint to these images were those of voracious, cunning, manipulative, and even murderous women. In one, a woman clad only in bra, pants, and stockings is speaking on the phone while holding a smoking revolver: 'No, Judge ... I'm not going on with my divorce' she says. We are left in little doubt as to who she has shot. Even after the war, when the images of the fighting man are replaced by pictures of attractive semi-clad women, these ideals of feminine desirability are countered by more threatening depictions. In one image a beautiful woman (drawn in typically exaggerated proportions) is again on the phone, with a much older man sitting on the sofa: 'Yeah, a S-U-C-K-E-R' she wryly spells to her friend at the other end of the line. In another variation on this theme, a woman and man passionately embrace on a lounge, with the woman declaring 'my husband has such a nasty mind. He suspects the truth'.[24]

Many of these images had no particular reference to the war and could plausibly be dated anywhere between the 1930s and the 1970s. But the very contrast between warriors and women in these images from the war and post-war years

---

23 See 'The Girl Who Didn't Wait', *The Soldier*, 27 June 1919; 'Peace and War', *Truth*, 17 November 1918; 'Currans' Cuckolded', *Truth*, 15 December 1918.
24 See *Man*, September 1943, May 1945, and January 1946.

sharpens the prevalent cultural suspicion of women. This is even more apparent in those images that have some direct connection to the war. Many of these have women manipulating or deceiving men in uniform, but more than this there is an overwhelming focus on women as the sexual aggressor. In one typical cartoon, an assertive woman grabs the arm of a frightened officer, dragging him back into a room, while declaring 'retreat another step Major and I'll scream'. This is a humorous reversal of the more usual case of the respectable woman screaming when assaulted by a man, but it is an all too frequent reversal, and in its very frequency, it almost becomes a norm. Other stories pointed to a darker vision of female sexual aggression. In 'The Living Myth' Deli suffers severe mood swings and seeks release through passion. She devours men, and when her husband restrains her, she attempts to kill him. By the late 1940s, men's journals are full of stories of women driving men to kill to satisfy the woman's needs, or women as sexual vampires preying on innocent male victims.[25]

These stories and images were published in a context of widespread reports about the faithlessness of wives. In tabloid newspapers such as *Truth* there were frequent lurid accounts of men returning from war to find their wives consorting with other men. In the Second World War, however, much of the focus of this reportage was not on the liaison between women and shirkers but with yanks. In popular literature after the war, such as Jon Cleary's *The Climate of Courage* (1954), Xavier Herbert's *Soldiers' Women* (1961), Lawson Glassop's *The Rats in New Guinea* (1963), and Dymphna Cusack and Florence James's *Come in Spinner* (1951), we are given a clear picture of the currents of anger and resentment towards women who had preferred Americans. One of the most bitter is Eric Lambert's, *The Veterans* (1954), a novel tracing the experiences of Bill Farr and his mates in the Ninth Battalion. Lambert amplifies the contrast between war front and home front by reversing the conventional chronology. The novel begins with return and ends with combat. He achieves this by focusing on a brief interlude in the war – after return from the Middle East and before embarkation for Borneo. Bill returns to find 'my sister was yank-mad ... my father ... making a fortune out of war contracts and ... that after three years away they were strangers to me and I was a stranger to them'. A key feature of the novel is the virulent disgust at the relationships between Australian women and Americans. It is a literary counterpart to Albert Tucker's powerful representations of Australian women fraternising with yanks as monstrous and disgusting figures. This impression is heightened in the second half of the novel, in which the men return to war only to die in the jungles of the Pacific islands. Implicit in this stark contrast between home and war is the sense that death in war was preferable, and more noble, than the demeaning alienation of life at home. Lambert, however, seems reluctant to develop the full implications of this condemnation of home. Bill survives and returns to a good and faithful woman and

---

25 See *Man*, June 1945; R. Thew, 'Crime Passionelle', *Cavalcade*, February 1949; 'Beauty as a Vampire', *Cavalcade*, April 1949.

a newborn son, although the future pleasures of suburbia seem strangely unreal in the context of the novel's earlier tensions. The more lasting impression is of a corrupt, selfish, and unconcerned home front.[26]

In women's journals, men's magazines, and newspapers there were daily stories of yanks attracting the attention of Australian women. And reports of liaisons with Black American soldiers amplified sex anxieties by adding the problem of race. Much of this reportage, both during and after the war, is framed by a moralistic demand that women maintain fidelity to Australian men. And like any moral crusade, it probably exaggerated the incidence of sin. Moreover, always in counterpoint to these stories of faithless women were depictions of respectable, hardworking, self-sacrificing, church-going girlfriends, wives, and mothers. But it is in the tensions between these two representational traditions that we can see anxiety. Equally the respectability of the many served to highlight the faithlessness of the few, and it is this latter group who were the focus of most commentary and who have lingered longer in popular memory. This critical reportage depicted women as superficial, impressionable, overly materialistic, and easily seduced by the smooth yanks who had more money to spend. Another undercurrent is an implicit critique of Australian masculinity: diggers were rough, crude, ill-mannered, unsophisticated, and more interested in mates than women, so it was little surprise that Australian women were 'yank-mad'. But the sustained production of images of women as sexual aggressors in men's magazines hints at darker dimensions to the liaison between Australian women and American soldiers. It suggested that it was women who were taking the initiative – who were after yanks – and that this was part of a deeper feminine conspiracy to entrap yanks for their money; and betray innocent and simple Australian soldiers. It was women who were at fault.[27]

There was an obvious and not very surprising double standard here. Servicemen were not expected to remain faithful to sweethearts while serving overseas; the high incidence of venereal disease in all wars, and the efforts of military authorities to contain its spread through the distribution of condoms and lectures on prevention, clearly mark a male military culture that tolerated, even celebrated, war as a time of sexual adventure. And within that culture women were the objects of the male sexual gaze, seen as ever-available, willing, and compliant. First World War digger journals defined a new Australian female type: 'The Tabbie' or 'Diggus Feminus', who 'Inhabits Australia' and 'is easily domesticated. Lives chiefly on chocolates, cakes and ice-cream. Very fond of theatres, movies,

---

26 E. Lambert, *The Veterans*, Frederick Muller, London, 1954. See also R. Campbell, *Heroes and Lovers: A Question of National Identity*, Allen & Unwin, Sydney, 1989.

27 See *Truth*, 22 and 29 June 1947; *The Bulletin*, 24 August 1946; 'The Passion Pit', *Australian Woman's Mirror*, 3 October 1944. See also Gerster, *Big-Noting*, pp. 172–202; D. Walker, 'The Writers' War', in J. Beaumont (ed.), *Australia's War 1939–45*, Allen & Unwin, Sydney, 1996, pp. 116–39. On concern about 'Negro' servicemen, see K. Saunders, *War on the Homefront: State Intervention in Queensland 1938–48*, UQP, St Lucia, 1993.

moonlight excursions and picnics. Variously called by the male of the species "The Tabbie", "The Bint", "The Clinger" and "The Skirt". Alternatively, women in these journals were seen as types: 'the bar girl', 'the bathing girl', 'the dancing girl', 'the flapper', 'the singing girl', 'the landlady's daughter', and for the purposes of contrast, 'the maiden aunt'. Similar images pervaded the men's magazines of the 1940s. Here women were 'comfort fund girls' ready to boost the morale of the digger. These types were male fantasies: two dimensional, abstract, occasionally inanimate (skirts), and available for male pleasure. But such images had their perils. While they spoke to the expression of male desire unshackled in war, they also under mined male confidence in the faithfulness of Australian women. If many women were available and willing participants in pleasure, then how could men be confident that wives, sisters, and girlfriends were not equally willing participants? Fantasy could be as productive of anxiety as it was of desire.[28]

But there were generational problems, just as there were gender ones, inherent in such anxieties. The war and post-war emphasis on sexual pleasure, drinking and dancing, and new styles of dress, music, and entertainment were responses to a 'moribund' culture that was seen to have sacrificed youth for its own ends. Youth culture, particularly in the 1920s, celebrated a modernist aesthetic of movement, action, directness and rejection of ornamentation. We can see this in painting and architecture, but also in popular dress – in the straight, figure-concealing lines and short-cropped hair of the 1920s flapper. The flapper became a site of considerable cultural anxiety, fostered by her function as a symbol of the modern age, being youthful, energetic, and a seeker of pleasure.[29] This embrace of difference was of concern to parents, politicians, church leaders, and social reformers, who feared that it threatened the essential social institutions of marriage and the family. In this climate of moral fear, social reformers finally succeeded in implementing legislation that they had advocated for many years, such as compulsory notification of venereal diseases, early closing of hotels, confinement of the hereditarily unfit, censorship of foreign literature, and later, restrictions on American films and music. The fact that this legislation was not very successful points to the persistent assertion of a popular right to pleasure and relaxation, but these reform efforts signified the concern that many felt about the breakdown of traditions brought on by the upsets of war.[30]

---

28 See 'The Tabbie', *Aussie*, no. 10, January 1919; 'The Aussie Girl', *Aussie*, no. 3, March 1918; 'Homeville Comforts Fund', *Cavalcade*, September 1945.
29 See M. Eksteins, *The Rites of Spring: The Great War and the Birth of the Modern Age*, Anchor Books, New York, 1990. See also B. Cameron, 'The Flappers and the Feminists: A Study of Women's Emancipation in the 1920s', in M. Bevege, M. Janes, & C. Shute (eds), *Worth Her Salt: Women at Work in Australia*, Hale & Iremonger, Sydney, 1982, pp. 257–69.
30 See M. McKernan, *The Australian People and the Great War*, Nelson, Melbourne, 1180, pp. 1–93; Reiger, *The Disenchantment of the Home*, pp. 178–209; R. White 'Americanisation and Popular Culture in Australia', *Teaching History*, vol. 12, no. 2, 1978, pp. 3–21.

Reformers and moralists in the 1940s feared a repeat of the social uncertainties of the 1920s. The earnest prognosis of the Australian Army Education Service, that post-war Australia would see a return to stricter moral standards, may have been more hope than belief. Many others predicted unsettled times. Some believed, in the light of the 1920s experience, that any uncertainty would be temporary. 'Morals went out the window when war came in' declared Arthur Rainsford, just as they had done during the previous war, but this was temporary, and 'nothing terrible happened after all'. Sometimes this 'wartime frenzy' was the subject of comic caricature. As one writer declared, 'peace happiness is that period of goofiness which is the inevitable reaction to long years of war'. But others had a darker prognosis of post-war pestilence, plague, racketeering, organised crime, sexual promiscuity, broken marriages, and atomic destruction.[31]

Not least of these problems was the threat to relations between the sexes. War had seen women move into men's occupations and women made vulnerable to the charms of yanks. Would libertarian sexuality continue in the post-war world? Was it possible to restore normal relations between the sexes? What were the prospects for stable family life? These were the questions that dominated public discourse on sex and marriage in the 1940s. The experience of post-war disturbance in sex relations in the 1920s served as a warning to many. But the cultural climate of the 1940s was vastly different to that of the 1920s and demanded different solutions. The crude efforts at repression from moralists in the 1920s would not work in the 1940s. Even in mainstream women's journals, such as the *Australian Woman's Mirror*, the efforts of moralists were easily parodied and rendered comic with epithets such as 'matronly'. The place of sex within culture had been irrevocably transformed by the growing popularity of sexology and psychoanalysis in the 1930s – a popularity not unrelated to the problem of shell-shock. By the 1940s sex could not be denied; it had to be regulated, channelled into marriage, and even promoted as a good in itself.

A new group of helping professions – psychologists, psychotherapists, marriage guidance counsellors, and advice columnists – were on hand to assist in this process. There were frequent articles on how women could overcome 'frigidity', 'sex as the new religion', and the need for sympathy, understanding, and sexual compatibility in marriage.[32] Much of this ideological work had begun well before the cessation of hostilities. The problem of women entering men's jobs, and thereby being unsexed, was tackled by maintaining and reinforcing traditional gender

---

31 See A. Rainsford, 'As it Was Is Now', *Cavalcade*, April 1946; 'Freak Wagers', *Cavalcade*, November 1945; T. Egan, 'Peace the Killer', *Cavalcade*, December 1945; R.G. McClymont, 'Post-War Problems', *Reveille*, 3 January 1945; 'Refugee Flat Racketeers', *Smith's Weekly*, 3 November 1945; Carl Lyon, 'Servicemen Beware of These', *Australian Woman's Mirror*, 12 February 1946.
32 See for example 'Passion Pit', *Australian Woman's Mirror*, 3 October 1944; M. Birge, 'Frigidity is a Personal Problem', *Cavalcade*, April 1946; D. Scott, 'Your Chance of Staying Married', *Man*, December 1944; 'When Your Man comes Back', *Australian Woman's Mirror*, 24 April 1945.

distinctions, most obviously in pay, but more subtly in the frequent stories and advertisements that encouraged women in the forces and factory work to maintain their femininity, beauty, and desirability for the eventual return of men by using particular soaps, make-up, perfumes and other items essential to sexual attractiveness. Marilyn Lake has given us important insights into how 'Rosie the Riveter' was persuaded to return to the home in order to make way for the repatriated man. During the war men's jobs were feminised – the women who worked in them were continually constructed as still feminine – and thus the return to traditional women's work became merely another feminine task, one that many women, tired of doing two jobs (public and private), were eager to embrace.[33]

Thus sex, instead of being a threat to marital stability, became its chief bulwark. But it was sex defined within narrow terms. The new psychological experts may have seen repression as unhealthy, but sexuality in their eyes was best expressed within terms of monogamous, heterosexual marriages, achieving its full flowering in mutual sexual satisfaction, equal and complementary roles (breadwinner and housewife), and the raising of a family. These demands to fit back into conventional roles were all the greater with returned men. As many warned, in the 1920s and again in the 1940s, returned soldiers were bound to be 'fatalists, difficult to place in their former spheres of life, a trifle rusty in the head, and generally dissatisfied with their former surroundings'.[34] What was needed was a healthy dose of independence on the part of these men. But equally crucial was family life. In the 1920s it was hoped that settlement on the farm, or sound training in a trade, was the best means of ensuring that men assumed their breadwinning role. By the 1940s, experts were less confident that work alone would suffice. It also required the 'sympathetic understanding, unwavering tolerance and infinite patience' of Australian women.[35] In this recipe for marital harmony it is possible to see what we have come to know as 'the 1950s' (suburbia, nuclear families, material prosperity, social stability) – as the imagined solution to post-war sex anxiety and marital disruption.

III

In 1920 Frederick D went to the address of his estranged wife and three children, shot the locks off the door, entered, and in a struggle, shot her in the head. His wife had left the family home to escape his drunkenness and violence. With three children to support, she had taken out a maintenance order the day before she was killed. In his defence, Frederick claimed that he bore no malice against his wife, had not intended to kill her, and had broken down the door because he believed he

---

33 Marilyn Lake, 'Female Desires: the Meaning of World War II', *Australian Historical Studies*, vol. 24, no. 95, October 1990, pp. 267–84.
34 'An American Speaks', *Repatriation*, vol. 1, no. 12, March 1920, p. 16.
35 Martin, Welcome Home Serviceman, p. 1.

would not be admitted, that his wife's fatal injuries had resulted from her attempts to take the gun from him, that his wife had deceived him because his children were not really his, that she had undergone abortions without his permission, and that, as a returned soldier suffering from the effects of gas and shell-shock, he was prone to headaches, dizziness, and amnesia. Frederick was acquitted. This was an extreme case of returned-soldier violence. Newspapers, however, reported frequently on returned men committing a range of crimes against the person – rapes, many in broad daylight, carnal knowledge, sexual assaults, and murders. Similar lurid reports littered the tabloid papers in the 1940s. There was much public sympathy for these men, as the result of Frederick D's trial suggests, but the tide of returned-soldier crime began to alarm those charged with the maintenance of justice. Magistrates began to grow 'tired of appeals for leniency from returned soldiers', admonishing them to take responsibility for their actions and declaring that next time the punishment might be made to fit the crime.[36]

Rates of crime, particularly that related to sexual assault and family violence, were taken by many returned-soldier groups, politicians, and reformers as clear signs of the social disruption caused by returned men and by repatriation policies that had failed to integrate them into civilian life. *Smith's Weekly*, in particular, made much of the failures of the repatriation system and of bureaucratic persecution, focusing on the plight of many former soldiers who were forced to commit crimes through poverty, or driven to crime because of the effects of gas and shock. After the Second World War, commentators warned that 'after battles crime takes a new lease of life'.[37] Another popular indicator of returned-soldier disruption was divorce. Social commentators advised on such matters as 'Your Chance of Staying Married' when 'more marriages than ever are becoming unstuck'. Crimes and divorce are hardly the preserve of returned men, but rising rates of both after war suggest disruption on return, and were certainly read as such by many social commentators.[38]

Patterns of arrest – for crimes against the person, such as violence, murder, and rape – do indicate a sharp increase, (20 per cent) in the two years immediately after both the First and the Second World Wars. And in each case, the rate plateaus for at least five years thereafter. These figures give a clear indication of a short, sharp intensification of personal conflict with the return of servicemen. In part, this arose from the presence of more men in the community. Crimes against the person fell dramatically during the war years, and in many respects, the post-war surges were merely a return to pre-war norms. Similarly, divorces jump sharply in

---

36 The case of Frederick D is analysed in J. Allen, *Sex and Secrets: Crimes Involving Australian Women since 1880*, OUP, Melbourne, 1990, p. 134. See also *Truth*, 15 December 1918, 29 June 1920, 9 January 1921, and 20 April 1947. The comments of the magistrate are from *Truth*, 13 June 1920.
37 See Gordon H. McGregor, 'Wolves of War', *Man*, January 1946; *Smith's Weekly* 21 February 1920, 29 April 1922, and 6 May 1922.
38 D. Scott, 'Your Chance of Staying Married', *Man*, December 1944.

the immediate post-war years. From 1918 to 1921 the number of divorces more than doubles, and from 1944 to 1947, divorces increase by 55 per cent. As with crime, these years represent a peak, with the number and rate of divorces remaining fairly steady, even declining, in subsequent years. These divorces may just represent the return of men, allowing marriages that had been over for some time to be formally dissolved. So many marriages broke up after the war that many feared the 'destruction of the Australian family'. Within a few years these alarming predictions were calmed by the levelling in the divorce rate. But there were some peculiarities in post-war divorce, most notably the number of men petitioning for divorce in the mid-1940s. This suggested that some hasty wartime romances did not stand the test of return, and that servicemen who returned to find their wives living with other men acted quickly to sever the relationships. Post-war crime and divorce rates were seen as evidence of the failure of servicemen to adjust to civilian life, but the statistics are not that clear. To glimpse the pressures of return, we need to move beyond the rough impressions of statistics to a closer examination of particular crimes and marriages.[39]

Much of the post-war increase in crimes against the person was directed against women. Moreover, these crimes took on new and more violent forms. This is particularly evident in cases of femicide. Before the First World War most instances of husbands murdering wives involved a routine domestic beating that went too far. Women were murdered in their homes after violent, usually drunken, attacks by their husbands – the last in a series of beatings that escalated in intensity over the years. After the war, however, more were murdered by husbands in public places, usually with guns, and most commonly after the wife had left the marriage and was claiming maintenance for the children. Many of the men charged were returned soldiers, often using weapons they had brought back from the war. Their anger and bitterness at their wife's desertion may have been fed by the literature of female duplicity and betrayal that permeated Australian popular culture. It was a literature that almost seemed to justify their actions. When combined with pleas that, owing to the stress of war, they were not responsible for their actions, we see the context in which many were acquitted or convicted of lesser charges, such as manslaughter. The case of Frederick D was hardly unique.[40]

Similar considerations acted in favour of returned soldiers charged with rape, carnal knowledge, or sexual assault. There was nothing new in defence counsel attempting to besmirch the character and morals of the accuser, but after both World Wars, returned-soldier defendants had the excuse of shell-shock or battle fatigue to fall back on if other arguments failed. Juries were often sympathetic.

---

39 Crime and divorce statistics are from S.K. Mukherjee et al., *Source Book of Australian Criminal and Social Statistics 1900–1980*, Australian Institute of Criminology, Canberra, 1981, pp. 8 & 21. For contemporary comments, see C.E. Martin, *Divorce and the Family*, Australian Institute of Political Science, Canberra, 1951, pp. 1–16; W.D. Borrie, 'The Family', in G. Caiger (ed.), *The Australian Way of Life*, Books for Libraries Press, Freeport, NY, 1953, pp. 23–44.
40 Allen, *Sex and Secrets*, pp. 130–56 & 218–31.

When one returned soldier knocked down a married woman in a park in broad daylight and attempted to rape her, he showed little interest in the fact that there were witnesses. He was later arrested but found not guilty when previously certain witnesses suddenly found their memories more hazy than they had previously thought. When such defences failed, as they did in rare instances, there was instant outrage on the part of the defenders of the wronged returned men. In 1921 a returned soldier was convicted of rape and sentenced to death. Over the next five days there was a sustained public protest arguing that the girl must have consented and that the crime was seduction, not rape. The sentence was commuted to imprisonment. Only when the person raped or assaulted was a young boy were convicted returned soldiers denied a spirited public defence. Overall, conviction rates for sex offences were lower after 1915 than they had been in the 1880s.[41]

Crime gives us a particular insight into domestic and sexual tensions generated by war, but the bulk of strained returned-serviceman marriages rarely figured in these records. Most couples existed peaceably enough, some even prospered, but others created their own private hell. It is the latter that concerned reformers and returned-soldier groups. Repatriation case files are one of our few means of exploring the everyday tensions that poisoned the lives of some returned-serviceman families. These were families enduring the added strain of disability and illness. We cannot hope to explore all the dimensions of conflict in case files framed by competing narratives but through these veils the nightmarish life of many 'repat' families is evident. Nor can we be certain about the exact role of the war in the genesis of these problems. Unhappiness and conflict are hardly the preserve of returned-serviceman families. But because these lives are captured in the Repatriation Department welfare net, they are presented to us as war problems. More significantly, it was the generation of knowledge about these families that convinced contemporaries that there was, indeed, something especially troubled about the family life of these men.

In 1925 the wife of one returned man wrote to the Minister of Defence seeking assistance. The local repatriation doctor had said her husband's nerves were bad. She was inclined to blame the after-effects of a serious gunshot wound to the head, as he was always complaining about headaches. He had failed to turn up for his last pension review, and the pension had been cancelled. She was seeking its resumption, as her husband was unable to work. In documenting her case (supported by statements from local doctors), she detailed a history of violence and misery. Her husband was continually depressed, complaining of headaches and declaring that he wished he had been killed in France. He could not stand the noise of the children and had attempted to strangle them a number of times. Once he picked up their three-week-old baby, threw it under the bed, and bundled all the bed clothes on top of it to stop it crying. A few weeks later he almost strangled

---

41 Allen, *Sex and Secrets*, p. 152. See also *Truth,* 15 December 1918, 9–16 January 1921, and 1 June 1947.

their eldest girl. She had suffered for eight years before writing. The pension was reinstituted. A year later the husband began to wander away from home, and the wife followed, living in the bush, going from camp site to camp site in an effort to persuade him to return home. In 1929 he left for good. In a case from Western Australia local doctors sought to have a returned soldier committed to a military mental hospital after numerous assaults on his wife and sons. He suffered serious dizzy spells and depression, and was frequently irritable and morose. He refused to have any food in the house and slept out in the garden like a tramp. Two of his three sons were boarded out in foster homes because of his violent dislike of them. Despite this violence, his wife wanted him to stay home, as some days he was normal and on other days he was changed – he changed very quickly. In 1929 he was admitted to a mental hospital and committed suicide four years later.[42]

Similar problems plagued the families of Second World War veterans. In 1969 a Red Cross social worker was asked by the Repatriation Department to report on the circumstances of Eric P and his family in suburban Adelaide. Mrs P had complained to the department that her husband was improvident with his pension. The social worker found them living in a large, pleasant-looking brick house in a good suburb. Inside, however, she found Eric drunk. On further investigation, she discovered that Eric was frequently drunk, particularly after pension day, and, on these occasions, he was often aggressive, hostile, and physically violent towards his wife and children. He had been like this for twenty-three years. He claimed he did not have enough money and had taken to charging items in his wife's name. But the social worker also concluded that Mrs P contributed to the problem. She continually 'nagged' her husband, calling him a 'no-hoper'. He refused to accept treatment for alcoholism, blaming his condition on war nerves. The social worker recommended that his pension be placed in trust, to save the family from bankruptcy, and arranged for Eric to see a psychiatrist.[43]

These few cases hardly do justice to the range and complexity of problems that afflicted many returned-serviceman families. Reading between the lines, however, we can discern some of the many factors contributing to this unhappiness. Alcoholism, financial worries, mental instability, marital incompatibility, and illness, however, are hardly problems unique to families receiving repatriation benefits. Would these domestic problems have erupted regardless of war? It is an unanswerable question. War, however, gave families, social workers, and doctors a means of writing a coherent narrative about each case. Many experts acknowledged peculiar pressures on returned-serviceman families. And the linking of war with family instability sanctioned palliative measures. This concern and the forms of intervention advocated by family reformers, returned-services organisations, and repatriation authorities echoed a

---

42 Department of Veterans' Affairs, NSW, Case Files, AA, CRS C138, sample no. 758; Department of Veterans' Affairs, WA, Case Files, AA, CRS K60, sample no. 56.
43 Department of Veterans' Affairs, SA, Case Files, sample no. 167.

broader discourse on the modern family. No longer was family life and, more particularly, child rearing the preserve of parents. By the 1920s it was already the object of professional scrutiny, debate, and social policy – with social-security payments for struggling families, baby health clinics, child-guidance centres, marriage-guidance counselling, and a panoply of family and child-rearing experts advising on the physical and psychological needs of the child. The returned-serviceman family was one subset of this larger field of social endeavour. If a new order was to be achieved, declared the Director of Youth Welfare in New South Wales in 1946, 'the care and education of a new generation must be regarded as a social responsibility'. And within this domain of practical knowledge and social intervention, repatriation authorities, and returned services' and dependents' organisations isolated two problem families: those of war damaged soldiers and those of men who died as a consequence of war service.[44]

IV

At first glance, the problems of families coping with a recently returned serviceman are vastly different from those of the family where the father and breadwinner failed to return from war. But there was a common thread: the importance of fathers. Underpinning concern about returned-servicemen families was a fear that the war-damaged soldier family, or the family robbed of its paternal anchor, might seriously impair children. And it is in the increasing discourse on the 'soldier father' and 'fatherless family' that we can see one of the most fundamental changes in repatriation. After the First World War, authorities were primarily concerned with the material dimensions of reintegration. Men needed employment, training, land, and pensions to ensure their successful return. Widows and children needed pensions to compensate them for the loss of their breadwinner. But in the 1920s and 1930s the focus began to shift to the psychological consequences of failing returned-serviceman families. By the Second World War it was accepted that material assistance was still vital, but experts were more active in publicising the difficult private tasks of 'the soldier and his child' and of 'fitting the soldier father into the family again'. And when the RSL addressed the problem of widows and children of servicemen, it did so under the banner of 'our dependants!'. What linked these statements was a concern with proper fathering. Returned men had to be eased back into fathering, and in the absence of fathers, others had to assume this role. Running alongside a vast literature on mothering was this smaller, but equally

---

44 See H.L. Harris, *Doing Our Best for Our Children*, Angus & Robertson, Sydney, 1946, p. viii. See also Reiger, *The Disenchantment of the Home*, pp. 32–127; M. Gilding, *The Making and the Breaking of the Australian Family*, Allen & Unwin, Sydney, 1991.

important, literature on fathering, largely generated by the observation of war families.⁴⁵

A husband and father should be a sober and industrious breadwinner. This simple assumption took on the force of natural law for many who saw fit to comment on repatriation. For those families robbed of their breadwinner, the state needed to assume the role of breadwinner to ensure that these families were not disadvantaged by their sacrifice for the nation. As a special correspondent for the *Sydney Morning Herald* declared in 1917:

> Few realise the vastness of the problem of how best to do the fair thing by the soldier's dependants. To them perhaps no definite promise was made, but the moral duty that rests upon the community is no less strong on that account. Nor does the claim for special consideration rest on ethical grounds only. It may be based upon the more selfish foundation of self-interest. As a community, we cannot afford to allow a large section of our people to be materially prejudiced through the part their breadwinner took in the war.

Pensions, training, employment preference, and land were all means of assisting men to resume their breadwinner role. These policies, according to this correspondent, were essential, but the task went well beyond just taking 'proper care of the breadwinner ... [so] that the dependants may be left to look after themselves'. Such policies took no account of the problems of the dependent children of men who had not returned or of men who, because of war injuries, could never resume full employment. These children, especially young sons, might be forced to leave school at an early age to earn the money required to compensate for the partial or complete loss of their father breadwinner. Their future would be blighted thereafter.⁴⁶

The tenor of this argument echoed many others. It was an attack on the inadequacies of government provision for injured soldiers, widows, and their children, and a plea for more generous assistance. But it also went beyond the typical concerns of such pleas, explicitly in its condemnation of the 'look after the breadwinner and the dependants will look after themselves' attitude of repatriation authorities. It clearly saw the long-term costs of poor provision for soldiers, widows, and dependants in the stunted future of the next generation. The force of such views was felt in 1921 with the introduction of the Soldiers' Children Education Scheme, which aimed to keep the children of war widows and the permanently incapacitated war-damaged soldier in appropriate education. This government scheme was supplemented by private efforts. Legacy, the RSL, and Remembrance Clubs raised

---

45   See Anon., 'The Soldier and his Child', *Australian Woman's Mirror*, 29 May 1945; H. Tasman Lovell, 'Fitting The Soldier Father into the Family Again', *Sydney Morning Herald*, 28 June 1945; and 'Our Dependants!: The Women and Children', *Reveille*, 3 January 1950.
46   'Repatriation: The Case for Dependants', *Sydney Morning Herald*, 21 July 1917.

funds for the education of soldiers' children, and prominent philanthropists, such as the Baillieus in Melbourne and Samuel McCaughey in Sydney, donated substantial sums for the endowment of scholarships and bursaries, administered by the Soldiers' Children Education Board. By 1948 nearly 33,000 children had been assisted under these schemes. But there were occasional tensions between the aspirations of the children and what the Board was prepared to fund. In 1950 Elise Paterson was eager to undertake medicine at the University of Melbourne, but her school and the Board considered that she had little chance of success and only supported her to become a dietitian.[47]

Fathering and substitute fathering entailed more than just the satisfaction of the material needs of dependants. It also involved paternal guidance and instruction. This was particularly evident in the efforts of organisations such as Legacy. Established in 1923, Legacy aimed to assist the families of soldiers who had died as a result of war injuries. War widows and children were already assisted by women's groups such as the War Widows' Association, the Widowed Mothers' Association, and from the 1940s, the War Widows' Guild. These groups worked hard to assist war widows and their children, providing emergency sustenance relief, assisting with school fees, running vocational guidance classes to facilitate employment for widows, and most importantly, acting as a voice to defend their pension rights. Legacy, however, sought to act as a father might: raising funds to assist war widows with rent, school fees, and clothing, but also organising working bees to repair homes, providing holidays for widows and children, monitoring the education and vocational prospects of children, and running recreation clubs and gymnasiums to ensure that children were able to participate in sporting and other outdoor activities. Through the latter, they sought to instil the values of patriotism, obedience, service, and respect for the Anzac spirit. Legacy saw its role as giving 'the utmost advantage to the children whose fathers left them behind for us to look after'. And to this end, it attached an individual adviser to each war-widow family. The adviser acted as paternal monitor of the family's progress, ensuring that the family received the assistance it needed, and serving as confidant and counsellor for the mother, and male role model for the children. The adviser's vision was a manly one: standing in for fathers as guardians of the material and moral needs of children, and ensuring that children had healthy bodies, sound minds, and correct outlooks.[48]

The fear of degeneracy was very real for doctors, social reformers, academics, and politicians after the First World War. The 'science' of eugenics had its advocates before 1914, but after the war the belief that Australia's racial stock had been

---

47 'Case of Elise Paterson', RSL Papers, 510X. See also Lloyd & Rees, *The Last Shilling*, pp. 238–9.
48 See E.O. Milne, 'Can Psychology Be Applied to the Relief of the Digger and Digger Junior', *Reveille*, 1 September 1928. See also Lyons, *Legacy: The First Fifty Years*; M. Smith, 'War Widows: The Forgotten Victims of War', *Journal of the Australian War Memorial*, no. 5, October 1984, pp. 9–14.

depleted with the death of the fittest in battle, and a concern that the next generation might suffer from acquired deficiencies as a consequence of absent fathers or a father's war injuries, promoted greater interest in eugenic policies. Eugenics had always been accompanied by a certain amount of debate regarding the relative influence of heredity and environment, and although some were committed to an absolute belief in one rather than the other, most accepted that both played a role. Eugenics was concerned with the means of ensuring the propagation of the fit and preventing the reproduction of the unfit. After the war numerous organisations emerged, such as the Public Health Society, the Racial Hygiene Association, the Mental Hygiene Movement and the Eugenics Society of Victoria, concerned with promoting measures to permanently confine the unfit and introducing reforms to improve the health of those vulnerable to degeneracy from illness or familial, educational, or social maladjustment. In this context there were understandable fears that the children of war-damaged soldiers and war widows might be adversely affected by their environment. In 1923 Dr Katie Ardill-Brice – doctor, Red Cross nurse during the war, and consultant to the Racial Hygiene Association – persuaded the RSL to establish a health clinic for women and children in Sydney. Here the wives, widows, and children of servicemen received free medical tests, advice, and treatment. It supplied extra milk and nourishment to children suffering malnutrition, monitored cases of tuberculosis, advised new mothers on feeding, tested the health of babies and school-age children, and used the services of a volunteer optometrist. This clinic operated for over thirty years and saw nearly 3000 patients in that time.[49]

In 1932 the Victorian State President of the RSL, believing that 'the children of returned soldiers suffered from disabilities possibly to a greater extent than other children in the community', established a Children's Health Bureau in Melbourne. The medical officer at the Bureau was Alfred Plumley Derham, a returned soldier, doctor, and member of both the Victorian Eugenics Society and the Mental Hygiene Movement. Derham saw the Bureau's role as one of providing preventive medical advice and health education. It sought to provide medical supervision rather than just treatment for illnesses, and from the beginning, subjected children to intelligence, as well as medical, tests to ensure that they were given the most appropriate care. It averaged 2000 attendances a year in the 1930s, a significant number, which Derham attributed to the anxiety of parents, eager to reassure themselves that their children 'had not inherited war disabilities, nervous and physical, from which their soldier fathers suffered'. Derham's investigations, however, were less than reassuring on this question. In 1935 he reported:

> a very strong impression ... that very many children present a problem in behaviour ... In most cases these difficulties are traceable not to inherited faults

---

49   See 'RSL Women's Clinic', *Reveille*, 1 March 1929; 'Our Dependants! The Women and Children', *Reveille*, 3 January 1950.

but [chiefly to] the state of tension existing in the household, usually owing to the lack of complete harmony and co-operation between the parents. This disharmony is in many cases attributed by the wife to a nervous irritability or instability of the husband traceable to war service ... The belief that these difficulties are due solely to war service and therefore inevitable tends to prevent the sufferers from seeking medical advice ... I fully realise the terrible effects of the Great War on the physical, nervous and mental condition of soldiers ... it would be almost impossible to exaggerate the tragic effects of war on the health, happiness and prosperity of the whole community. There is no doubt that those who served and their immediate relations bore the brunt of the strain and will carry the effects to their graves ... [but the war is often] an excuse for his or her natural irritability, selfishness and lack of self-control.

Derham's analysis of the problems of returned-soldier families is strangely contradictory. He concedes that maladjustment seems more prevalent in soldier families but suggests that this might be due more to natural causes than to war. Derham's difficulty highlights the impossibility of attribution for family problems. Many were hardly unique to returned soldiers. There is every likelihood that such problems had as much to do with opportunity, education, and poverty as they had to do with war service. But to explicitly confront this question would rupture the rationale of returned-services organisations. If these were social rather than war problems, there was no place for war-service welfare. Instead, those with investments in repatriation clung tenaciously to their belief in the vulnerability of the returned man's family.

Children's health clinics were also situated at the crossroads between treatment and government. While they provided a vital medical service to many returned soldier and war-widow families, they also sought to regulate the conduct of those families. There were preferred ways of being a parent: certain assumed responsibilities, duties, obligations, and modes of behaviour. Parents in troubled families could not be left to their own devices; they had to be advised and educated. The efforts of agencies such as the Children's Health Bureau to fulfil this educative and governmental role sometimes met with hostility and resistance. This is strikingly evident in the case of Joe Knuckey. In 1933 Joe, then sixteen years old, was brought to the Bureau by his mother because of his severe stammering. The investigating doctor concluded that tensions in the home and, more particularly, the attitude of the mother, and possibly the father, towards Joe – they were consciously or unconsciously blaming him for the affliction – exacerbated the stammering. Joe seemed to be 'living in fear' of his mother. The doctor advised a change in their relationship to each other. Mrs Knuckey was less than happy with this diagnosis. She wrote to the Bureau stating that 'we have always tried to give all our children the best education possible ... [we] have always been careful to prevent them from mixing in bad company ... and Joe has always been treated the same as our other children'. This being the case, she was at a loss to see how the 'home environment' was at fault. She rejected the advice, declaring 'I feel that I cannot do any more, as it will not be possible to make any alterations in our mode of living'. In her view, the doctor seemed to be suggesting that 'unless the emotional atmosphere of the home is changed he will have to be removed to another environment, which is quite out of the question'. Derham attempted to ameliorate the situation, apologising for a 'certain misunderstanding', but reiterated that the boy did have a 'serious speech impediment', which required some 'alteration in your general attitude to the boy'.[50]

Increasing familiarity with cases like that of Joe Knuckey convinced many charged with assisting returned-soldier and war-widow families that the need for psychological assistance was as great as the need for material assistance. If the next generation were to be fit and productive citizens, then the psychological poisons of family life required address. This awareness framed the proliferation of psychological advice literature during and after the Second World War. Experts were confident that provision of the material and health needs of returned-soldier families was well in hand. It was the more difficult problem of parental and family attitudes and relationships that required serious scrutiny. Yet the problem of parental resistance suggested that experts had to tread lightly. Advice literature in popular journals and magazines, family problem programs on radio, and concerted efforts to advertise the existence of treatment clinics for family problems were the most common vehicles for government policy on this issue. And it was through these initiatives that the question of parenting was discussed. Mothers were advised to be regular in giving babies food, to show imagination in their diet, to hold their tongue because children were observant, and to avoid nagging at all costs. Mothers needed to avoid parental anxiety and cater for the psychological, as well as the physical, needs of children, which included sex education. Mothers also had to be aware of the upsetting effect that a returning father might have on children. Some children had been without paternal guidance for many years, and may have become spoilt. On the one hand, mothers had to provide space for children to get to know their fathers. Fathers, on the other hand, were advised that they had to win the confidence of their children again. They had to devote time to the task, and become involved in their welfare without spoiling them, and both mothers and fathers had to learn to hide their own tensions and conflicts. Although the return of men from the war was an unnatural event, parents had to work to make it seem natural, to avoid unsettling children.[51]

---

50 See 'Report on Children's Health Bureau 23 May 1935', Children's Health Bureau, *Annual Reports*, 1933–51; A.P. Derham, 'Address at Meeting of Legacy Club', 17 October 1936, Correspondence re Knuckey Case, in A.P. Derham Papers, 5/1–5/3/5, Melbourne University Archives.

51 See, for example, Z. Benjamin, *Education for Parenthood*, Australian Council for Education Research, Melbourne, 1944, pp. 3–48; Mother MD, 'How Fare Wartime Mothers', *Australian Woman's Mirror*, 13 June 1944; Australian Army Education Service, *Mans Place in Nature*,

These were unrealistic expectations. Return could hardly be anything but unsettling, and as the experience of experts after the First World War indicated, some returned-soldier families never recovered their equilibrium. But there was a buoyancy and optimism in the post-war literature of the 1940s. Psychology seemed to have a new prestige, and experts were anxious to ensure that science, especially the sciences of psychology and education, were brought to bear on the pressing problem of family stability. Frequent references to the 'new order' bolstered the claims of psychological professionals. Their program was an explicit rejection of 'traditional family know how'. As child expert Zoe Benjamin proclaimed, 'today there is a great creative force which is expressing itself in a desire for the building of a better world ... [and] the happiness and unhappiness of the new world ... must result from the character of the men and women who are that world'. The key was education and the 'complete sweeping away of traditional attitudes' in the rearing of children. If families were to conduct themselves properly, the resistance of parents such as the Knuckeys would have to be overcome. But as the experts and repatriation authorities of the 1950s and 1960s came to recognise, problems and maladjustments among returned-soldier and war-widow families were more intractable than these confident predictions recognised.[52]

Nonetheless, the sense that 1945 heralded a new world bolstered the spirits of reformers and post-war reconstructionists. This world not only promised material well-being, full employment, and a social-security safety net but also a new world of relations between the sexes and between parents and children. This was a time of utopian imaginings, some of it found in fictional narratives like that of Martin and Beth that opened this chapter. True to the conventions of most romance fiction, it is not surprising that Martin and Beth overcome their travails and find enhanced love. But it is the form of that love that is interesting. Both are shocked by Martin's violent action in slapping his wife, but instead of divorcing, they resolve to heal their marriage. Martin decides to accept Beth's job; Beth comes to accept Martin's need for a wife. She offers to become a full-time housewife, but Martin is unhappy with this solution. They also agree to compromise. She will work part-time. Here is an image of marriage that embodies compromise and equality. It was a novel fantasy, but one that was soon subsumed into a more conventional image of domesticity and suburbia. The cold war, the atomic bomb, immigration, and men's demand that women accept the natural differences in sex roles dominated the cultural landscape of many Australians after the war. This was an unsettling context, in which images of external threat were counteracted by ideals of social harmony and the 'Australian way of life'. The excitement of the new order was supplanted by the familiarity and security of an older vision of social order: patriotism, loyalty, conformity, material prosperity, and domesticity. And underpinning all this was a post-war demand

---

Department of the Army, Melbourne, 1945; Lovell, 'Fitting the Soldier Father into the Family Again'; Anon., The Soldier and his Child'.
52   Benjamin, *Education far Parenthood*, p. 3.

of returned men that women make way for their return. They did not want a world of compromise and accommodation to women's needs. They demanded a reward for their sacrifice, and that reward was seen to be women relinquishing their employment, serving men's domestic needs, and bolstering the manhood of men by recognising their status as breadwinners. The hunger for a new order and for a breaking with tradition that seems so evident in much of the literature addressed to women in the early 1940s had to wait for a later generation and a new cultural context.

7
Prisoners of War

In late 1945 Australians witnessed the return of prisoners of war from Japanese camps in South-East Asia. They had been amply warned about the 'appalling enemy atrocities', torture, starvation, and conditions 'worse than pigsties' that these men had suffered. Women had also suffered. Imprisoned Australian nurses were proudly proclaimed as survivors of 'Japanese atrocity camps'. 'Grim official pictures' of the emaciated inmates of Changi helped inscribe the image of these horrors into the imaginations of all Australians. And this image has remained vivid. In the 1980s, when Vivienne Lowe recalled the welcomes for returning soldiers, she remembered the 'great cheering ... except when the prisoners of war came home. We just all stood there and cried because they couldn't walk and were driven along in trucks ... that's not what they really wanted, so we had to try not to show it'. Vivienne's memory poses us a problem. It seems to contradict contemporary reports, which trumpeted the 'joyous welcome' for prisoners of war, the 'wonderful week of reunions' for ex-prisoners, and the numerous images of returning prisoners giving a 'rousing cheer' on landing and being greeted enthusiastically by friends and relatives. Undoubtedly, in the weeks since their liberation many of these men and women had put on sufficient weight to give, at least in the published pictures, a semblance of health. In the reports of welcomes there seemed very little to distinguish the prisoners of war from other returning veterans – the same cheering crowds, the same laughing faces, the same passionate embraces, and the same proud families now restored to completeness. But in the memories of Australians like Vivienne, and in the minds of many former prisoners, they were different. While prisoners of war in Europe and the Middle East in the First and Second World Wars had suffered considerable privations, the experiences of prisoners of the Japanese were of an unimaginable type and scale: not the terrifying annihilation of combat, but the insidious bodily decay wrought by torture, starvation, and disease. These men and women marked out a new and nightmarish dimension of Australian war experience.[1]

Was imprisonment just another facet of war service, or something different? Or to put it in other terms, were former prisoners returning veterans like any others, or a special class of veteran? In the complex interplay of visual images, reportage, stories, memories, and public policy, we can see a tension: between the desire to regularise the experience of prisoners, to blur the distinction between them and other veterans, and the need to mark out their special claims to recognition. This is nowhere more obvious than with regard to repatriation. Governments since 1945 have generally sought to accommodate the rehabilitation and medical problems of former prisoners within the existing systems of benefits and entitlements available for all veterans. But ex-prisoners – and organisations, such as the Ex-Prisoners of War Association or the Ex-Prisoners of War and Relatives' Association, which have represented them – continue to press for special benefits to compensate for their greater health and welfare problems. This conflict between the normal and the exceptional inevitably shapes efforts to write of the experience of former prisoners of war.[2]

I

For many years the story of prisoners of war, particularly those in Japanese camps, barely rated a mention in general histories of Australia, even in military histories. Lionel Wigmore, in the Official History series, devotes one-fifth of his volume on the 'Japanese thrust' to prisoners, but this hundred or so pages is dwarfed by those devoted to other military events in the twenty-two volumes. Yet, of the 22,000 Australian prisoners of war held by the Japanese, one-third died in captivity, representing one-quarter of all Australian combat deaths in the war, and almost half of all those killed fighting Japan. In comparison, of the 8000 Australians in German prisoner-of-war camps, only 265 died. The dimensions of this tragedy and its human significance are belied by its relative neglect by historians. In recent military histories prisoners are accorded a passing mention, peripheral as they are to the main story of military campaigns. Equally general histories of twentieth-century Australia relegate prisoners of war to the margins of national history – a far cry from the thousands of pages devoted to Gallipoli. Nor is the prisoner-of-war story the focus of special celebration or commemoration. Tobruk or Kokoda spring more immediately to mind here. For historian Hank Nelson, this effacement of the prisoners of war from Australian history is regrettable. While the 'horror, stoicism and gallantry of Gallipoli have become part of a common tradition ... the ex-prisoners are granted just the horror'.[3]

---

1   The mortality rates in Japanese prisoner-of-war camps were unconscionably high, but the rates in camps in Eastern Europe during WWII were double those in South-East Asia. See H. Nelson, *Prisoners of War: Australians Under Nippon*, ABC Books, Sydney, 1985, p. 216.
2   See *Sydney Morning Herald*, 1 September 1945, 18 September 1945, 12 October 1945, and 23 October 1945; *Courier Mail*, 15 September 1945 and 27 September 1945; *Australian Women's Weekly*, 29 September 1945. The recollections of Vivienne Lowe are quoted in Darian-Smith, *On the Home Front*, p. 230.

Much of Nelson's work, and that of others like Joan Beaumont, aims to redress this neglect. Instead of focusing on the 'unique and unprecedented nature of their treatment', Nelson seeks to restore their experience to the mainstream of Australian history. This is no easy task. Their absence from military and national history is hardly surprising. It is precisely the peculiarity and ambiguity of their imprisonment that pushes prisoners to the margins. Where the story of war is one of action, bravery, stoicism, victory, or defeat, imprisonment is a story of passivity, victimisation, confinement, and grim survival. This problem is all the more acute for prisoners of the Japanese. Prisoners of war in Europe have been able to proclaim their history of resistance and daring escape. In popular books and films, such as *The Wooden Horse* and *The Great Escape*, British, American and Commonwealth prisoners have been rendered heroic men of action, in a lineage stretching back to the siege of Troy. This trope reached a pinnacle of comic absurdity in the popular American television series of the 1960s, 'Hogan's Heroes', in which the prisoners are made into the effective commanders of the camp and the German guards become their passive dupes. It is impossible to conceive of a comic account of a Japanese prisoner-of-war camp. There the scale of human suffering was too great. And although there have been efforts to write the prisoners of Japan into the 'heroic escape' narrative, the links to a larger prisoner-of-war tradition are rather strained. As most have admitted, escape from camps in Asia and the Pacific were infrequent and futile. Prisoners of war in these camps do, in important ways, stand in contrast to the male warrior ideal that infuses the myth of war. More disturbingly, enforced passivity conjures up a feminised condition, an association all the more potent because women were also prisoners of the Japanese, suffering many of the same privations and hardships as men.[4]

The prisoner-of-war experience may not be easily assimilated into the Anzac legend as military history, but it has had remarkable appeal as autobiography, memoir, and diary. Since 1945, personal accounts of prisoner-of-war experiences have enjoyed considerable popularity. This is even more curious given their grim horror and repetitiveness. And while this literature may have failed to transform traditional narratives of war or nation, it has rendered the experience of internment explicable. Robin Gerster suspects that these accounts appeal to a deep xenophobia in Australian culture. While racial themes pervade these accounts, this does not appear to be the whole story. More crucial is the normalisation of captivity. There is a continuing heroic theme in Australian war literature. The best-selling Australian

---

3   Nelson, *Prisoners of War*, p. 4. See also H. Nelson, 'Measuring the Railway: From Individual Lives to National History', in H. Nelson & G. McCormack (eds), *The Burma-Thailand Railway*, Allen & Unwin, Sydney, 1993, pp. 10–26.

4   The gendered character of the prisoner-of-war experience is discussed insightfully in J. Beaumont, *Gull Force: Survival and Leadership in Captivity 1941–45*, Allen & Unwin, Sydney, 1988, p. 2. For one effort to incorporate prisoners of Japan into the noble escape tradition, see C. Burgess, *Freedom or Death: Australia's Greatest Escape Stories from Two World Wars*, Allen & Unwin, Sydney, 1994.

war novels of Lambert, Cleary, Glassop, and others may have effected a cynicism about the home front, and adopted some of the ironic undertones of British and American literature, but their core themes remained the mateship, vigour, and anti-authoritarian fighting spirit of the ordinary Anzac. Similar themes pervade the prisoner-of-war accounts. In these, brave men and women battle an 'evil foe' and, by dint of tenacity, bravery, and mateship, triumph over the inhumanity of their captors. In effect, the prisoner-of-war narrative has become as emblematic of the Anzac legend as Gallipoli, Kokoda, or Tobruk.[5]

In part, our understanding of the prisoner-of-war experience is a product of this literary effort to turn individual horror and suffering into something more meaningful. For if the prisoner experience is to enter history, passivity and victimisation have to be transformed into activity and agency. And this is precisely what the extensive prisoner-of-war literature has done: it has turned the victims of 'atrocity camps' in the first newspaper reports into actors in a larger human drama. But although much of this drama is framed by the Anzac legend, it never entirely fits. It is precisely the largeness of this drama that complicates imprisonment as a national story. If Australian history is about the distinctive features and characteristics of its people and culture, then the universal qualities of human perseverance embodied in the prisoner-of-war experience resist easy incorporation into a narrow national history. We can see uncomfortable tensions here: between the desire to mark out a specific Australian experience and the need to place it in a broader human story. The prisoner experience has indeed entered history, but in problematical ways for national history.

Despite this, what is most surprising is the speed with which the prisoner-of-war experience was transformed into history. Journalist and inmate of Japanese prisoner-of-war camps Rohan Rivett published his account of the experience, *Behind Bamboo*, in 1946. Rivett, a mere twelve months after release, begins the process of placing the camps in the distant past: 'when our minds go back to these years which stretch like a deep abyss across the plateau of our lives, we will tend to think of the brighter side'. This is a double manoeuvre, which pushes the experience into the past and highlights the 'brighter side', but at the cost of rendering the experience, for modern readers at least, almost farcical. This account is a 'boys own' adventure story – escapes, near misses, mishaps, surprising coincidences, betrayal, capture, and minor victories over Japanese guards – an effect amplified by the frequent echoes of the English public school. Here the inmates are 'the old dysenterians', and it is this indefatigable attitude that serves to demarcate the prisoners from the 'limited and obsessed' minds of their captors. The extraordinary deprivations of the prisoners are likewise oddly displaced by making them a part of a 'down and out' story. Each bowl of rice is savoured as better than a meal at the best restaurant in Paris. These diverse effects serve to

---

5   See Gerster, *Big-Noting*, pp. 225–39; Walker, 'The Writers' War', pp. 116–39.

heighten a sense that the prisoners triumphed over their circumstances because of qualities of comradeship, coolness under pressure, resourcefulness, and humour. But, for Rivett, the prisoner-of-war experience also confirmed that our closest ties, in temperament and attitude, were to the British and that, with the cessation of hostilities, Australia's future lay in the Commonwealth. Here the prisoner-of-war experience becomes another chapter in a larger imperial story of the inherent superiority of the British race.[6]

Race is also a central theme in Russell Braddon's best-selling account of his prisoner-of-war experience. *The Naked Island*, first published in 1952 and in its fourteenth printing by 1977, is a more vivid and arresting narrative than Rivett's. Here a spare dramatic realism heightens the horror of confinement and the tragedy of brave men succumbing to torture, ill-treatment, and starvation. But for Braddon, like Rivett, the survival of the prisoners is a 'tribute to the Britisher's capacity for living fearlessly and gently'. While this tone of British racial superiority strikes a discordant note with modern Australian nationalist sentiment, it undoubtedly found a receptive audience among Australians who had lived through the war and understood the 'depravity and barbarity' of Japanese atrocities. Braddon crystallised the fears of many Australians of the 1950s with his apocalyptic prophecy of a brutal warrior class hell-bent on a 'one hundred years war of Asia against the white man'. Many prisoners saw their experience in racial terms – as civilisation against barbarism, West against East – and any historical account of these events that does justice to the ways in which the prisoners lived and understood them has to take on the burden of these sentiments. But it is this trope of racial conflict that problematises the incorporation of the prisoner experience into history in contemporary multicultural Australia in the 'Asian century'. It is not surprising, then, that many historians have sought other ways of writing this story.[7]

The experience of Australian nurses likewise received early treatment. In 1954 two popular accounts of prisoner-of-war nurses were published: Betty Jeffrey's *White Coolies* (reprinted nine times by 1957) and Jessie Simons's *While History Passed* (reprinted three times in 1954). Both have much in common with Rivett's account – notably, the vaguely unreal tone of a 'girls own adventure' and the undercurrent of racial commentary. Here the Japanese are 'like monkeys', and the nurses are brave, resourceful, and plucky. The savagery of the Japanese, notably in their slaughter of the nurses on Banka Island, is contrasted with the caring and civilised demeanour of the captives, a contrast rendered ironic by Jeffrey's reference to them as 'coolies'. The only excuse that Simons can find for the Japanese atrocities is that 'their inheritance is largely pagan'. But there are uncomfortable elements in this situation that required careful negotiation. The narrative has to resolve the difficulties implicit in the idea of captive women, although the faintly erotic subtext

---

6   R. Rivett, *Behind Bamboo: An Inside Story of the Japanese Prison Camps*, Angus & Robertson, Sydney, 1946. The opening quotation is from p. 311.
7   See R. Braddon, *The Naked Island*, T. Werner Laurie, London, 1952.

of threat may have added to the popularity of these books. This is highlighted in the foreword to Jeffrey's account. Here the Matron-in-Chief of the Royal Australian Army Nursing Corps, Colonel Sage, obscures the gender of the captives. These women are seen to exhibit the same qualities as the men: they fought 'just as surely as ... the soldier with rifle and tank', exhibited courage and bravery, 'grand humour', resourcefulness, and 'an ability to overcome the greatest problems'. Colonel Sage, however, takes a step back from this disquieting association, asserting that their action arose not from a lust for battle, but from a 'natural instinct to tend the sick', but even with this caveat, there is an uncomfortable blurring of gender boundaries. Similarly, Simons finds that the lasting value of the experience was comradeship, in a way that directly paralleled the mateship of the Anzac ethos. Jeffrey's account, in particular, is an effort to resolve this ambiguity by reinstituting clear gender roles through a subtext of sex and desire. Here the nurses retain their virtue (any hint of molestation or rape is firmly denied – something more recent scholarship has contested – suggesting more complex undercurrents of disavowal) but do not lose their desire. The nurses find the 'slit eyes and bandy legs of their captors repellent' and long 'to see a sun-tanned digger'. On their release they are 'excited to see real men again' and are overjoyed at being able to put on lipstick and be called girls. In the end, *White Coolies* is a story of the maintenance of womanhood under adverse circumstances, distancing these nurses from the masculine narrative of courage and bravery.[8]

In the hands of writers in the 1960s and 1970s, however, the prisoner of war experience could become the means to explore the roots of Australian xenophobia and boorishness. In John Romeril's play 'The Floating World' (1975), Les and Irene Harding are the quintessential Australian suburban bigots – crude, drunken, sexist, swearing, anti-Asian caricatures. Only slowly does it become apparent that Les' bigotry hides a deeper anguish, masking his horrific experiences on the Burma-Thailand railway and the palpable post-traumatic stress that afflicts his marriage. There is a marked ambivalence in Romeril's depiction of this suburban couple. While tapping into the deeper personal undercurrents of this behaviour, the attitudes and actions of Les and Irene are so repugnant as to overwhelm any sympathy an assumed educated middle class audience might feel for them. In some of these later generation literary accounts, often written twenty to thirty years after the end of the war, the prisoner of war symbolises an older, intolerant Australia. New generations needed to move beyond the past. This critical commentary, however, became complicated by the growth of oral testimony of the prisoner experience which opened out a more complex picture for future generations.

Through the 1960s former prisoners produced a small but steady stream of accounts of the prisoner-of-war experience. One of the most popular was Ray Parkin's three-volume account of the sinking of the *HMAS Perth*, his capture,

---

8   B. Jeffrey, *White Coolies*, Angus & Robertson, Sydney, 1954; J.E. Simons, *While History Passed*, William Heinemann, Melbourne, 1954.

enforced labour on the Burma-Thailand railway, and eventual transfer to a labour camp in Japan. Its interest and popularity arose partly from its literary qualities. Where Rivett, Jeffrey, and even Braddon offered first-person description and recollection, Parkin transformed his narrative into something resembling fiction, using third-person commentary, dialogue, characterisation, and imaginative recreation of places and events to heighten the drama of the account. In this fictionalising, it succeeds far more than earlier accounts in recreating the gritty reality of capture and imprisonment. But there are other imperatives that cut across this realism. Parkin steps back to place the narrative within some larger picture, and in struggling to make believable the unimaginable, he understandably falls back on classical allusions. These increasingly come to characterise much prisoner-of-war literature, conveying the sense that the experience was a test of character that served to strengthen and transform the individual.

For Parkin, this was like 'crossing the Styx and passing through a world of illuminating enchantment ... here was a test'. Having seen the darkest underworld, the hero is able to survive all subsequent tests of courage, bravery, and resourcefulness. Running alongside this narrative of individual triumph is a collective story of men banding together to defeat a seemingly invincible foe. Parkin resorts to one of the most common allusions in this literature: Shakespeare's St Crispin's day monologue in *Henry V*. The Australians are a happy band of brothers 'in this state together' and are able to gain an almost spiritual 'tolerance ... of intolerance'. In the reference to Henry V, Parkin is able to place the prisoner-of-war experience in a larger human drama, in the mainstream of British courage and fortitude. But, in doing so, he, like Rivett and Braddon before him, undermines the sense that there is anything distinctively Australian in this experience.[9]

The second volume in Parkin's trilogy anticipates the popularity of diary accounts of the prisoner experience. *Into the Smother* is written partly in diary form, but the entries are heavily edited and placed within a broader narrative context utilising Parkin's more usual fiction technique. In the 1980s, however, the diary form became a publishing phenomenon, achieving enormous sales and publicity for former prisoners such as Stan Arneil and Edward 'Weary' Dunlop. This may suggest both a greater willingness on the part of ex-prisoners to talk about their experiences and a public desire for authenticity. They struck a chord with a new wave of enthusiasm for oral histories of the lives of ordinary men and women, in which the individual and the mundane came to stand for the extraordinary, the unique, and the lived experience of history. This social history genre was nowhere more evident than in the prisoner-of-war diaries. Here the spare, cryptic entries of daily suffering – 'cholera cases are now eighteen with ten suspects. My ulcer is giving me hell and I have had very little sleep' – give concrete form to the tragedy

---

9   R. Parkin, *Out of the Smoke*, Hogarth Press, London, 1960; R. Parkin, *Into the Smother: A Journal of the Burma-Siam Railway*, Hogarth Press, London, 1963; R. Parkin, *The Sword and the Blossom*, Hogarth Press, London, 1968.

of ill-treatment, illness, and starvation, and heighten the extraordinary triumph of those who survived. But why this sudden spate of prisoner-of-war diaries? Were these men, nearing the ends of their lives, seeking to carve a small place in history, fearful that it would forget them and their fallen comrades? Were they unhappy with the way their lives had thus far been represented? Were they hoping to exorcise the ghosts of the past? Did they feel able, at last, to free themselves from the horror of their experience sufficiently to talk about it again?

Dunlop believed that his diaries should remain unpublished for forty years for 'fear that they might add further to the suffering of the bereaved, and add to controversy and hatred'. But Dunlop also distrusted his original harsh judgements of captors and circumstances. Then in the evening of his life, he was able to put things in perspective. And it is this problem of perspective that is interesting. For Dunlop, 'in the annals of human suffering, Australians had written something very special of their own' as prisoners of war. Yet, almost in the same breath, he robs their efforts of a distinctively Australian character, for what was 'most uplifting of all is the timeless, enduring, special brotherhood ... whose devotion and pride smacks of the St Crispin's Day of *Henry V*'. Similarly, Sue Ebury, Dunlop's biographer, strives for classical references to give meaning to the life. Dunlop is a brave Ulysses returning home or a latter-day Christian on his Pilgrim's Progress.[10] Just as with Parkin, Rivett, and Braddon, men of Dunlop's generation were comfortable with the classics that had been an elementary part of their education. But they did more than comfort. Enduring symbols of sacrifice in war provided the only language for the ennoblement of internment. The alternative was a nihilistic modernism that focused on horror and the essential meaninglessness of war – hardly a comforting means of remembrance.

This use of literary and classical allusion highlights the existence of two fields of meaning for the camp experience: as a chapter in the Australian national story and as something more universal. In one sense, much of the writing by former prisoners of war is a conscious effort to merge their experience into a larger Anzac history. But just like the Anzac legend itself, mateship derives added meaning from its connection to a larger history of brotherhood, evident in the frequent references to *Henry V*, *The Iliad*, and other classic war narratives. Perhaps the profound emotional resonance of Anzac itself arises because it embodies a message that is at once distinctively Australian and yet something more timeless. But this only complicates the incorporation of the prisoner experience into nationalist history and literature. Since the earliest account of Rivett, comradeship has been a dominant motif in the prisoner narrative. For ex-prisoner Kenneth Harrison, writing in 1966, this was a 'story of their sturdiness of spirit, their humour and integrity – and their mateship'. This sentiment is echoed by Rowley Richards in his account of 'a group of Australians ... supporting each other in their fight to retain

---

10 E.E. Dunlop, *The War Diaries of Weary Dunlop: Java and the Burma-Thailand Railway*, Nelson, Melbourne, 1986, pp. xv-xvii; Ebury, *Weary*, pp. 395 & 526.

pride, courage and humanity'. For Stan Arneil and Tom Uren, the abiding lesson of the camps was the importance of the cooperative or collective principle. The prisoner narrative may have been tied to other messages and meanings, such as Empire loyalty and racial antipathy, but mateship is the link.

This is equally apparent in the efforts to move beyond memory to history. In 1959, as a young parliamentarian, Tom Uren spoke of how the comradeship of the Australian prisoners meant that the rate of survival of Australians was far higher than in British camps, where strict military hierarchy was maintained and 'the law of the jungle prevailed'. This was a message taken up in historical accounts of the camps. Russell Braddon made it a central theme in his histories as well as his novels about prisoners of war. It is a message that reaches its apotheosis in Patsy Adam-Smith's study *Prisoners of War* (1992). Adam-Smith contrasted atrocities perpetrated on the prisoners with their 'strength, manliness and humanity ... of spirit'. In her account, the horrors of imprisonment almost become an experience to aspire to, for it was 'a further edge of mateship that all soldiers experience, and if we ridicule this it is only because we envy them this rare oneness with each other'. The problem with Adam-Smith's account, however, is that it is as much myth as history, barely distinguishable from the accounts and recollections of survivors. This is hardly surprising, given is reliance on oral testimony. It remains a powerful and moving evocation of the feelings of returned soldiers and provides an invaluable insight into how memory shapes, and is in turn shaped, by history. But Adam-Smith uncritically accepts memory as fact, and while this is a strength in recollections, it is a weakness in history.[11]

Prisoner brotherhood has also found a significant place in literature. One evocative fictional realisation of the prisoner-of-war experience is David Malouf's *The Great World* (1990), in which he charts the lives of two men of different temperament, disposition, and background: Digger Keen and Vic Curran. They meet as prisoners of war and form an indissoluble bond of mateship, saving each other's lives and surviving against the odds. After the war they go in very different directions, Digger retaining a quintessential working-class Australianness and Vic embracing the new post-war ideal of social mobility and entrepreneurial endeavour. Digger and Vic become a means by which Malouf can write a sweeping narrative of the fate of the national ethos in a period of rapid Americanisation and social prosperity, processes that threaten an Australian identity founded on Anzac and perpetuated in Changi. Malouf resolves this conflict in favour of Australian mateship. Ultimately this relationship is more important and enduring than wealth

---

11 See K. Harrison, *Road to Hiroshima*, Rigby, Adelaide, 1983 (first published 1966 as *The Brave Japanese*), p. 280; R. Richards and M. McEwan, *The Survival Factor*, Kangaroo Press, Sydney, 1989, p. 205; S. Arneil, *One Man's War*, Sun, Melbourne, 1982, p. 4; T. Uren, *Straight Left*, Random House, Sydney, 1994, pp. 36–7; H. Clarke, C. Burgess, & R. Braddon, *Prisoners of War*, Time-Life Books, Sydney, 1988; P. Adam-Smith, *Prisoners of War: From Gallipoli to Korea*, Viking, Melbourne, 1992, p. 580.

and progress, as symbolised by Vic literally, in his dying breath, crawling back towards the spiritual bond of mateship with Digger.[12]

The prisoner of war experience and its capacity to reveal deeper currents in Australian culture is evident in the increasing literary interest in stories of war imprisonment. Australian writers in recent decades have moved beyond the savage satire of writers like John Romeril in the 1970s to open up more sympathetic and complex insights into the experience. Malouf's wonderful novel is a case in point. So too is Richard Flanagan's award winning *The Narrow Road to the Deep North* (2013). Here Flanagan deploys many of the conventional tropes of not just prisoner-of-war accounts but returned soldier accounts more generally – the mateship of war, the horrors that bound men together, the betrayal of women, lust for another's wife (although here not of a mate at the frontline) and more importantly the post-war ennui that engulfed them; the fruitless search for meaning in a world they increasingly find dull, domesticated, alien and suffocating in its social conventions. The main character Dorrigo Evans, a prominent post-war doctor and advocate for prisoner veterans has a loveless marriage, a fruitless outlet in loveless affairs, and a passion for the veteran cause to keep the flame of mateship alive. But Flanagan's deeply moving novel also opens out new perspectives on the prisoner experience, reflecting in many ways the extraordinary developments in the oral accounts of war imprisonment. While his depiction of the horrors of the camp and the cruelty of the guards is searing in its realism, Flanagan explores aspects of the Japanese experience, almost sympathetic portraits of some of the captors and the post-war confrontation with their past, while also exploring undercurrents of class selfishness in characters such as Rooster McNeice. Not all Australians were virtuous victims of imprisonment. Flanagan seems, in part, to be reflecting the more complex ex-prisoner accounts that, years after release, allowed them to seek an accommodation not only with their experience but the reality of coming to terms with Asia.

These autobiographical, historical, and literary evocations of mateship, however, have been the focus of careful revision. Historians such as Beaumont, Daws, Nelson, and Henning suggest that the writings of Adam-Smith, Braddon, and others might work well as myth and recollection, and even better as literature, but fail to understand the complexity of the prison-camp system and the dynamics of survival. Indeed, such revisions raise doubts about whether there was anything distinctive about the Australian experience of internment. Rather, it seems to parallel those of many other nationalities imprisoned during the war. Gavin Daws' study of American prisoners of war demonstrates that mateship was hardly unique to the Australians. For Daws, tribalism and 'little brotherhoods' marked the experience of all prisoner groups, and while there may have been differences in degree, they were an ever-present dynamic of camp life. Moreover, as other

---

12   D. Malouf, *The Great World*, Chatto & Windus, London, 1990.

historians have argued, survival had as much to do with the variables of time and place as it did with mateship. Some camps were more harshly administered; others were more poorly supplied and located in areas near inadequate water supplies, exacerbating already serious problems of disease. There were other factors. In Ambon, for instance, bad morale, in-fighting, and poor leadership meant that two-thirds of all Australian prisoners died – more than double the rate on the Burma-Thailand railway. In other words, mateship provided little defence against particular conditions. Moreover, under extreme stress, the bonds of mateship collapsed. Sharp differences in the mortality rates for officers and men also suggest that the burden was not born equally. Officers were not required to work, and this was a vital factor in reducing their incidence of fatal illness and injury.

Beaumont has gone further than most in exploring the material and cultural underpinnings of the mateship ethos. She has argued that the style of leadership was a major factor in rates of survival. In camps where officers successfully blurred the distinctions of rank, morale was higher and qualities of resourcefulness, ingenuity, and humour were thereby fostered. Officers on Ambon failed this test, and the weakened bonds of brotherhood were counted in lost lives. In the last analysis, however, this revisionist work has reaffirmed the importance of mateship to the survival of Australian prisoners of war. Under the right conditions and with appropriate leadership, Australian forces banded together more effectively, as evidenced by their higher survival rates. What we now have is a more complex understanding of the dynamics underpinning the mateship ethos and an awareness that there was no single prisoner-of-war experience.[13]

The prisoner-of-war story – in autobiography, literature, and history – has most commonly been one of collective bonding. But in some accounts, it also represents another type of story: that of personal growth. In these accounts, Rivett's hope that, with time, men would look on 'the brighter side' came to fruition. In private letters, memoirs, and reminiscences, many former prisoners, like other servicemen, recalled their front-line experiences as the pinnacle of their lives, the time when they lived most fully and meaningfully, when their deepest friendships were formed. With the healing powers of time and the powerful nostalgia that shapes recollections, prisoners of war also came to see their time in the camps as fundamental to their future. By 1987 John Lane could see a shape to his life. His was a story of pre-war innocence, a test of fire in the prison camps, and a final emergence into mature adulthood. For Stan Arneil, 'the greatest privilege of my life [was] to have been part of that group'. Similarly, Tom Uren found in the camp experience the fire in which the legacy of his mother's instinctive hatred of social exploitation was tempered into a life-long belief in the principles of

---

13 See G. Daws, *Prisoners of the Japanese*, William Morrow, New York, 1994, pp. 17–28; Nelson, *Prisoners of War*, McCormack & Nelson, *The Burma-Thailand Railway*; Beaumont, *Gull Force*, P. Henning, *Doomed Battalion: Mateship and Leadership in War and Captivity*, Allen & Unwin, Sydney, 1995.

socialism. Weary Dunlop came to see the prisoner-of-war experience as a 'gift'. It had bequeathed to him something 'so rich as the gratitude and love of such men and women'. These accounts are, in fact, a type of *Bildungsroman* – a narrative of growth to self-discovery. This is a popular genre in Western literature, and these recollections share its form. It is this generic power that invests these accounts with a universal message for readers – one that makes them as much literary as historical.[14]

These are inspiring stories of human triumph, but they are deceptive guides to the meaning of war internment. The majority of prisoners of war have not felt able or inclined to record their experiences or understanding of captivity, and its effect on their life remains elusive but no less important. One way of working around this absence is to ask what it was that enabled a few men and women to tell their story. Many of the published accounts, particularly those published since the 1960s, are marked by an extraordinary tolerance of their former captors. For Weary Dunlop, Tom Uren, and lesser known writers, such as Rowley Richards and Kenneth Harrison, the Japanese were undoubtedly cruel and sadistic, but there were also individual Japanese who were 'considerate and comradely'. All came to believe that people should not be seen as races but as individuals, each with the capacity for humanity and, in Dunlop's words, 'an equality in the face of suffering and death'. Perhaps the most remarkable rapprochement with the Japanese, particularly given that it was written in 1966, is Kenneth Harrison's expression of admiration for 'the brave Japanese'. Not only does Harrison focus on a few kind and gentle Japanese guards, but he also comes to see the ordinary Japanese soldier as marked by an admirable spirit and commitment to their national ideal.[15]

This transcendent capacity for tolerance is one of the most remarkable characteristics of many returned prisoners. And in this spirit of accommodation and tolerance, these men and women were able to find a voice to speak of their experiences. But was this a common reaction? Some of the earliest anecdotal and written evidence suggests that hatred and contempt for captors were (understandably) the more common responses. Bitterness, however, is not the most productive state for recollection and reminiscence. Equally, the realities of the book market militate against the publication of stories of defeat, anger, and lifelong resentment. It takes a rare ability to turn unmitigated horror and tragedy into something poignant and meaningful. Don Wall's studies of the Sandakan death march are a case in point. Even this atrocity is counterpointed by a greater story of almost spiritual brotherhood, in which brothers and friends die within days of each other, as if fate governed all and mateship was sustained in the moment of death.[16] The traces we have of the prisoner-of-war experience, then, are shaped

---

14 See J. Lane, *Summer Will Come Again: The Story of the Australian Prisoners of War Fight for Survival in Japan*, Fremantle Arts Centre Press, Fremantle, 1987; Arneil, *One Man's War*, p. 5; Uren, *Straight Left*, pp. 32–8; Dunlop, *War Diaries*, p. xvii.
15 See 'Foreword', in Harrison, *Road to Hiroshima*.

by a narrative of mateship triumphing over inhumanity even in death. Exemplary and inspiring as they are, they cannot be taken as the norm. They provide us with a way of making sense of the Japanese prison camps and a way of writing the prisoner-of-war experience into history, but they cannot illuminate the bleaker struggle of men and women who returned from these camps suffering serious physical and psychological scars.

II

In 1946, a special Repatriation Committee was established to report on the problems of former prisoners of war. The committee included prominent doctors and former prisoners, such as Weary Dunlop and Lieutenant Colonel A.E. Coates, as well as medical experts, such as psychiatrist Alan Stoller. It concluded that many ex-prisoners of war, particularly those in Japanese camps, suffered 'from an indefinite malaise or "feeling out of sorts", together with an undue tendency to fatigue ... associated in some cases with symptoms of emotional or other psychological disturbance ... caused by the after effects of severe hardships and continued and recurring physical illnesses'. Even before the cessation of hostilities, the Director-General of Manpower had come to similar conclusions. He believed that returning prisoners 'may be labouring under certain handicaps resulting from the development of mental attitudes aroused by a long period of imprisonment'. When the evidence was scrutinised, it suggested that these problems were not suffered to the same extent by prisoners of war in European prison camps. Did this mean that former prisoners of war in Japanese camps required separate investigation, treatment, and consideration? The committee's response was inevitably contradictory.[17]

By early 1946 it was obvious that former prisoners of war were having particular difficulties re-establishing themselves in civilian life. The repatriation committee investigating the issue agreed that special problems for these ex-servicemen and women existed, but concluded that 'they should not be handled as a class apart from other discharged servicemen and women ... [but] encouraged to feel that some ... of their difficulties were confronting ... other members of the forces'. Moreover, 'no stress should be laid on the psychological factor' as it was 'common throughout the forces'. A draft medical report prepared for the committee was even more emphatic. It blamed the 'preconceived idea that [the prisoner of war] must inevitably be the subject of psychological damage ... such problems as

---

16 See D. Wall, *Sandakan Under Nippon: The Last March*, self-published, Sydney, 19S8; A. Moffitt, *Project Kingfisher*, Angus & Robertson, Sydney, 1988.
17 Report of the Repatriation Committee on Repatriated Prisoners of War, 4 July 1946, A. E. Coates Papers, AWM PR 89/186. See also 'Statement of Director General of Manpower', 5 December 1944, RSL Papers, 544C.

remain are physical rather than psychological'. This report cited evidence from a leading Sydney psychiatrist that the incidence of neurosis among prisoners of war was minimal and what cases did occur were mild. In 1947 one psychiatrist argued that camp life was even conducive to mental health.[18] Two things appear striking here. The first is the desire to deny that former prisoners faced any unique psychological problems. The second is the conflict between the idea that the prisoners had peculiar problems and the belief that their problems were the same as other returned-service personnel. The question was whether these differences were ones of degree or kind. But the answer lay not merely in a difference of interpretation or emphasis, for it bore very directly on the provision of repatriation benefits for returned prisoners. Should they receive special treatment and benefits?

The answer of the repatriation committee was to keep the prisoners of war within the established benefits system. This decision was qualified by the belief that the health of prisoners of war required continued monitoring, and indeed this committee operated for a number of years, scrutinising any evidence for the existence of special problems for returned prisoners. Similarly, the Director-General of Manpower believed that the policies of employment preference and vocational training were adequate to the needs of returned prisoners, but he also argued that these men and women required 'special toleration and sympathetic consideration'. As a consequence, former prisoners would 'be dealt with by the most experienced employment officers'.[19] These were well-intentioned but ineffective gestures. A better indication of actual practice is the fate of the government records. Somewhere in the bowels of the repatriation bureaucracy, a simple decision was made not to separate the files of prisoners of war from those of other returned service personnel. These records, which could have provided the evidence of the problems arising from imprisonment, were kept in general archives, merged into the mass of departmental files, thereby complicating any process of specifying the distinctive problems of former prisoners as a class. Instead, like other returned service personnel, they had to fight for benefits on an individual, case-by-case, basis. Former prisoners, and the organisations that represented them, had to rely on their collective experiences and their own expert witnesses to press their claims for special recognition.

One of the difficulties they faced was that there was no clear scientific consensus on the effects of confinement. Towards the end of the war there was much speculation about rehabilitation after internment. An influential article on the 'prisoner of war mentality', published in the *British Medical Journal* in 1944, argued that the 'depression and irritability of camp attitudes would persist after

---

18 Draft Report by Drs Fisher, Bye, Furner, Harvey, & Hunt, A.E. Coates Papers. See also O. Ponyton, 'Some Observations on the Psychological and Psychiatric Problems Encountered in a Singapore Prison Camp', *MJA*, vol. 2, 1947, pp. 509–11.
19 Report of the Repatriation Committee on Repatriated Prisoners of War, 4 July 1946, A.E. Coates Papers. See also 'Statement of Director General of Manpower', 5 December 1944.

discharge'. This was dubbed the 'barbed-wire attitude' (later a syndrome). It involved four phases. First, prisoners suffered acute mental stress on capture, which degenerated into severe depression when the enormity of confinement hit home. Second, prisoners entered a period of convalescence as they began to form new associations and routines in the camps. But there was continuing frustration at the perceived lack of action by home governments to save them. Third, there was a long period of boredom and demoralisation, exacerbated by sexual deprivation and fear of becoming forgotten men. Finally, there was the exaltation of freedom, characterised by false hopes about post-war prosperity and pleasure, which were soon dashed. In the first months of return, the behaviour of ex-prisoners was characterised by bouts of restlessness, irritability, disrespect for authority, irresponsibility, fear of enclosed spaces, fear of crowds, cynicism, and quick and violent tempers.[20]

In the 1940s and 1950s Australian doctors rejected the idea of the 'barbed-wire syndrome'. The disturbed and restless behaviours were real enough – no one could ignore them – but the cause, in their view, was physical rather than psychological. Their conclusions may have been influenced by the widespread belief that Australian prisoners had sustained their morale far more effectively than British prisoners and had, therefore, insulated themselves against this syndrome. Equally, they were aware of a central flaw in the 'barbed-wire' theory. As the special repatriation committee on prisoners of war argued, there was no 'internment psychology', as the symptoms of restlessness, violence, cynicism, and disrespect were common to many veterans. Instead, Australian experts giving evidence to repatriation authorities continued to focus on the physical basis for these behaviours. They concluded that the long-term effects of starvation and the continuing irritation of infection and infestation were undermining the rehabilitation of former prisoners. In 1950 a report to the repatriation committee on prisoners argued that there was 'an almost universal complaint of some gastrointestinal upset and of various nervous symptoms', but nerve problems were 'due to prolonged nutritional deficiencies'. In the same year, Alfred Plumley Derham, – prominent Melbourne doctor, member of the Repatriation Assessment Appeal Tribunal, and former prisoner of war – confided to Weary Dunlop his belief 'that the cause of much ill-health and anxiety states in ex-prisoners of war was due to unsuspected amoebiasis'.[21]

Does it matter whether the symptoms of restlessness, anxiety, and upset were psychological or physical? It clearly mattered to those on committees inquiring into these problems. Psychological explanations conjured up the spectre of inherent

---

20 P.H. Newman, 'The Prisoner of War Mentality: Its Effect after Repatriation', *British Medical Journal*, 1 January 1944, pp. 1–8.
21 See Report of the Repatriation Committee on Repatriated Prisoners of War, 4 July 1946, A.E. Coates Papers. See also Report on the Residual Effects of Nutritional Disease Afflicting Prisoners of War, 1950, in Derham Papers, 7/1/1. For Derham's views on amoebiasis, see A.P. Derham to E.E. Dunlop, 14 August 1950, Derham Papers, 7/1/2.

weakness and mental fragility. And although repatriation authorities were willing to recognise combat stress and post-war psychiatric problems as war-caused, anxiety was shaky ground on which to build a campaign for general recognition of disabilities arising from service, particularly when many prisoners had not been in actual combat. It was this ambiguity, as much as entrenched medical theory, that underpinned the desire to found prisoner-of-war problems in the physical effects of captivity. A psychological basis for a repatriation pension application was always vulnerable to rejection on the grounds that it was not war-caused nor unique to prisoners. An argument that physical and mental disabilities arose from the actual conditions of prisoner-of-war camps was a more secure foundation for successful pension claims.

The intensity of argument for a physical basis for disabilities also owed something to the growing perception among former prisoners of war that governments were losing sympathy for their plight. This seemed obvious in the refusal of the Chifley government to grant compensation to former prisoners and their families for losses and deprivations incurred during imprisonment. The Ex-Prisoners of War Association first raised this issue in 1946, claiming that former prisoners deserved payments of three shillings for each day in captivity to compensate them for the fact that they did not receive full armed-services rations while being held captive and had missed out on proficiency pay allocations because they could not pass appropriate tests. This 'subsistence pay' claim was rejected by the government on the grounds that it was impossible to calculate the extent of disadvantage and any compensation would need to be tied to reparations from Japan. The Liberal Party made a 'three shillings a day' promise to ex-prisoners in the 1949 election, but when the Menzies government assumed office, it also tied compensation to reparations, a view supported by the Owen Committee, charged with investigating the basis of the 'subsistence pay' claim. Moreover, the Owen Committee and the government rejected the argument that these payments should be made as a right of service and paid to all former prisoners. In 1950 the government established a trust fund from Japanese reparations to benefit former prisoners suffering economic or physical hardship. This was the source of continuing frustration to returned-services organisations, particularly as Britain, Canada and the USA had already developed compensation schemes for all ex-prisoners of war. The Owen Committee rejected the idea of per diem compensation, claiming that 'cruelties and privations ... cannot practicably be related to ... a daily ... allowance'. Instead, compensation would be merged into the repatriation system, a move opposed by returned-services organisations on the grounds that it made compensation a benefit for injury rather than a right of service.[22]

The repatriation system was geared to the assessment of injury and illness, and the payment of compensation for any disabilities arising from war service. Attempts by prisoner-of-war groups to press for recognition of their disabilities

---

22 The various moves in this struggle are evident in the file 'POWs and Compensation', RSL Papers, 2387C, and also successive issues of the journal of the Ex-Prisoners of War Association, *Barbed Wire and Bamboo*, 1950–52.

as a group or to claim compensation as a class could not be accommodated into a system of case-based assessment and individualised payment. The struggle for prisoners of war, as for other servicemen and women, was to expand the range of disabilities and illnesses accepted as war-caused. And here prisoner-of-war representatives joined with other returned-services groups in pressing for more generous application of benefit of the doubt and onus of proof principles. Weary Dunlop, for instance, devoted considerable time and effort to giving evidence in support of pension claims by former prisoners. He also gave evidence as a witness in the landmark Law case (1981), which widened benefit of doubt provisions for all returned-service pension applicants. Nonetheless, there were tensions between returned-service groups and prisoner-of-war associations. In the 1970s Dunlop was instrumental in the campaign for the recognition of cancer as a war-caused disability for former prisoners. But the RSL rejected this special claim, arguing that all veterans should be recognised as having equal access to such a benefit.[23]

III

By 1948 the first evidence began to appear suggesting that prisoners of war were experiencing greater levels of disability than other veterans. The repatriation committee on prisoners of war responded to this anecdotal evidence by investigating the disabilities of a small sample of ex-servicemen. It found that physical and psychological disabilities were more evident in ex-prisoners than other veterans. Repatriation Department doctors reported that many former prisoners of war were suffering chronic diarrhoea, and an increasing number were found to have 'functional nervous disorders'. In 1950, in response to this evidence, the Repatriation Department conducted a health survey of 12,000 former prisoners of war. This survey confirmed the earlier findings.[24] Overseas research added to the weight of evidence suggesting that former prisoners carried a considerable physical and psychological burden. In 1954 Bernard Cohen and Maurice Cooper, in one of the first systematic follow-up studies of American prisoners of war, found that veterans held captive in Japanese prison camps had a marked excess of mortality and a higher rate of hospitalisation than either prisoners of war in Europe or ordinary veterans. Almost 90 per cent of Japanese prisoners of war suffered vague complaints such as head, back, and stomach aches, lethargy, general debility, sore feet, and sleeplessness – double the rate for other prisoners of war. More alarming was the high proportion of 'accidental deaths' (usually involving alcohol and car accidents) and suicide. Similar British and American studies since the 1960s have confirmed these initial findings. Prisoners

---

23 Ebury, *Weary*, pp. 614–17.
24 See Minutes of Repatriation Committee, 12 November 1948 and 15 December 1948, in Derham Papers, 7/1/1.

of the Japanese died earlier than other veterans, particularly in the first ten years after release, and usually from trauma (accidents and suicide). There was a higher incidence of problems such as tuberculosis and cirrhosis of the liver, but mortality from chronic and degenerative diseases did not appear to be in excess of comparable male cohorts: There was also a high rate of psychiatric problems among former prisoners of war. Gilbert Beebe, in a study of American former prisoners, concluded that the most significant long-term effect of incarceration was psychological, 'characterized by a variable loss of ego strength'.[25]

Australian research from the 1960s was more equivocal. G. Freed and P.B. Stringer found few significant differences in mortality between former prisoners of war and the general male population of the same age. There were exceptions, paralleling those in the overseas literature. Ex-prisoners had higher mortality rates from tuberculosis and cirrhosis of the liver, and younger prisoners of war had excessive mortality from suicides and accidents.[26] Although these studies varied in their assessment of the impact of imprisonment, by the 1970s there was a considerable body of Australian and international scientific research that argued that former prisoners of the Japanese did suffer disproportionately as a group. To the consternation of prisoner-of-war groups, this evidence did not seem to be having an impact on repatriation decisions. They declared that pension claims by prisoners of war were being rejected. And the Repatriation Department seemed reluctant to undertake sustained research into their plight. After the pioneering 1950 health survey, little systematic analysis of ex-prisoner problems had been undertaken by Australian governments. In 1983 the Ex-Prisoners of War Association undertook its own morbidity study to convince the government of its case. It concluded that former prisoners of war did suffer an excess of gastro-intestinal, heart, skin, respiratory, and nervous problems. The report argued that these men and women were 'the survivors of a disaster of huge proportions'. And in a clear rebuttal of Repatriation Tribunal arguments, the report urged that it was 'important to recognise that not all the disabilities, so reluctantly revealed by the men, are due to age, but to a great extent are the end product of ... the stresses, both mental and physical, endured as prisoners'.[27]

---

25 See B.M. Cohen & M. Z. Cooper, *A Follow-Up Study of WWII POWs*, USA Government Printing Office, Washington, 1954; G. Beebe, 'Follow-Up Studies of World War II and Korean War Prisoners', *American Journal of Epidemiology*, vol. 101, no. 5, 1975, pp. 400–22. See also M. Dean Nefzger, 'Follow-Up Studies of World War II and Korean Prisoners', *American Journal of Epidemiology*, vol. 91, no. 2, 1970, pp. 123–38; R.J. Keehn, 'Follow-Up Studies of World War II and Korean Conflict Prisoners', *American Journal of Epidemiology*, vol. 111, no. 2, 1980, pp. 194–211; J.L. Patrick & P.J.D. Heaf, *Long-Term Effects of War-Related Deprivation on Health*, British Council of World Veterans Association, London, 1982.

26 G. Freed and P.B. Stringer, 'Comparative Mortality Experience 1943–1963 among Former Australian Prisoners of War of the Japanese', *Medical Research Bulletin*, vol. 2, 1968, pp. 4–28.

27 I.L. Duncan et al., *Morbidity in Ex-prisoners of War*, Prisoners of War Association, Sydney, 1985.

Like many returned-services groups, prisoner-of-war organisations expressed continued dissatisfaction with repatriation decisions. They sought an acceptance of the justice of their claims, but the pension and appeals tribunals were only prepared to act on an individual basis, determining each claim on its merits. Men who had lived through 'hell' had to face the inquisitorial processes of the pension system – a system designed to test the validity of claims and uncover malingering. These adversarial tests angered and frustrated former prisoners and their families, who believed that, having survived imprisonment, they had nothing left to prove. Nonetheless, the available evidence suggests that the claims of former prisoners met with some justice before repatriation tribunals. In the pension case files, we can see not only an accumulation of evidence for the greater physical, social, and psychological burden of former prisoners, but also a preparedness to be generous in the assessment of their claims. In our random sample of pension cases, on every criterion of disability – be it economic (such as job restlessness or time off due to ill health), social (such as marriage breakdown and divorce), or medical (such as continuing health and psychological problems) – former prisoners were recorded as having a higher incidence than other veterans of the Second World War. A greater proportion of former prisoners of war received a pension than other veterans. Moreover, they were more likely to have their claim assessed at a higher rate and, over time, have their pension rate increase more quickly. Twenty years after their initial pension claim, 53 per cent of Second World War pensioners were receiving a higher assessment rate, whereas 68 per cent of prisoners of war were assessed at a higher level. Of course, this reflects the reality of the greater disabilities and ill-health of former prisoners as much as generosity. But this is just the point. Many prisoners suffered more than other veterans, and this suffering was reflected in the granting of pensions.[28]

Even a casual glance at individual cases reveals a distressing incidence of individual and domestic tragedy on return. Two cases hardly do justice to the variety of problems these men confronted, but they are suggestive. In 1959 Rod H sought a pension for rheumatism, but this was rejected by the tribunal. He did have serious problems, but in the view of the attendant medical officers, these were a consequence of neurasthenia. Rod suffered general tiredness, lack of energy, sleeplessness, depression, and poor appetite. Although his former employer considered him to be a good worker, Rod felt unable to go to work. By 1975 Departmental medical officers described him as 'tense, anxious, depressed, apprehensive, intolerant of the slightest noise'. His wife said he fell to pieces easily. He had not worked since the 1950s. In 1948 Horace W, a former banker, was

---

28 See random sample of Department of Veterans' Affairs, Case Files. There are 769 cases in the WWII sample, ninety-six of whom are former prisoners of war. My evidence for the frustration and anger of former prisoners and their families is anecdotal, but nonetheless revealing, arising in the course of conversations with the children of former prisoners (who wish to remain anonymous).

granted a pension for nerve problems. Before the war he had been active in sport and a good student. But he 'fell apart' in a prisoner-of-war camp. Now he was described as 'sluggish, moody, depressed, and anxious', suffering from headaches and anorexia. He had lost all sexual desire. By 1950 his desire had returned but had been accompanied by chronic premature ejaculation. According to his wife, his performance was 'unsatisfactory'. He was found to have severe repressed aggression and an expressed desire 'to do violence to his wife'.[29]

It is impossible to say whether these are typical prisoner-of-war cases. Such a thing does not really exist. Both Rod and Horace exhibit a number of problems common to many prisoner-of-war pensioners: depression, anxiety, lassitude, and loss of appetite. It is tempting to see the last as perhaps some unconscious desire for their former prisoner-of-war state – a ghostly echo of the common veteran nostalgia for their war years. Then again, these symptoms and problems were also found in many veterans who had not been prisoners of war. It is difficult to define a distinct prisoner-of-war syndrome. What the case files reveal is that, on the whole, former prisoners of war suffered typical returned serviceman problems and that, as a class, they had a higher incidence of problem than other classes of veteran. Of course, we face a 'chicken and an egg' problem here. Did the official desire to respond favourably to former prisoner war claims produce evidence of their greater economic, social, physical, and psychological vulnerability, or did this greater vulnerability push the tribunals into accepting the justice of their claims? Medical research suggests the latter. If this is true, then we can conclude that, statistically at least, former prisoners of war received a measure of comparative justice, which recognised their greater physical and psychological problems. What concerned former prisoners, however, was that this was not recognised as a general fact but had to be fought case by case. It remained a benefit, not a right.

By the 1980s, medical research into prisoners of war focused overwhelmingly on the psychological consequences of service. Although the physical effects were still evident in the high rate of gastrointestinal disorders and liver cancer, long-term studies showed only a marginal excess of mortality among former prisoners of war. What was significant was a high rate of mortality in the first fourteen years after release, particularly among younger former prisoners, and an alarming incidence of depression among those who survived into the 1980s. Both suggested that psychological problems were the most enduring consequences of imprisonment. Psychiatrists speculated that depression might be the long-term effect of post-traumatic stress disorder. Research on prisoners of war contributed to a larger psychiatric interest in 'traumatic stress' and 'survivor guilt' – an interest arising out of related studies into the psychological consequences of events such as the Vietnam War and the Holocaust. Some of this research, however, indicated that

---

29 See Department of Veterans Affairs, Tasmania, Case Files, M, CRS P693, prisoner of war sample no. 6; Department of Veterans Affairs, NSW, Case Files, prisoner of war sample no. 11.

prisoners who returned to take up active public careers, particularly those committed to a political cause, had the highest levels of psychological health.[30]

It is hard not to feel some ambivalence about this corpus of scientific research. It certainly describes a problem (even if it may not explain it well) and provides firm evidence for the long-term effects of prisoner-of-war service. And slowly governments have come to accept this weight of evidence in their provision of benefits. In 1974, former prisoners of war were granted free medical care for all disabilities, whether war-caused or not. Five years later widows of former prisoners were also granted free medical facilities. In 1992, widows were automatically granted war widow status, therefore relieving them of the onerous task of proving that their husbands had died as a consequence of their imprisonment. But even scientific evidence is captive to the forces of political expediency. In the mid-1980s, benefits, such as free nursing-home care, were scrapped in an effort to find savings to balance budgets. Prisoner-of-war activists, however, continued to push for greater recognition of their entitlement and for increased benefits. In 1994 Tom Uren argued that all former prisoner-of-war TPI pensioners should receive twice the normal pension and qualify for free nursing-home accommodation, in recognition of their 'special suffering'. The Minister for Veterans' Affairs, however, rejected this argument, claiming that 'it would be unfair to other veterans to give special favours to ex-POWs'. In the realms of public policy, governments balance diverse constituencies and imperatives: social justice versus economic responsibility; all veterans against special cases; the public and specific publics. And former prisoners were continually caught in a larger dilemma – one that goes to the heart of their place in Australian culture. To what extent were they a special case, different from other veterans? Their typicality allowed them a place in the Anzac legend; their specialness undermined their incorporation in that legend, while at the same time advancing their claim for benefits.[31]

On the other hand, the arid psychologising of much of this scientific literature inevitably trivialises both the problems confronting former prisoners of war and their triumph over extreme adversity. To analyse the extraordinary post-war contributions to Australian society of men like Weary Dunlop and Tom Uren as adaptations to psychological stress is to diminish the exemplary character of their lives. And while the exhausting public career of Dunlop, which exacted a considerable price from his family, may be ripe for psychological analysis, it reduces a complex life to a mere reaction to trauma. If anything characterises his life and

---

30 The medical literature on these problems is voluminous. Some examples include O. Dent, et al., 'Post-war Mortality among Australian World War II Prisoners of the Japanese', *MJA*, vol. 1, 1989, pp. 378–82; C. Tennant, K. Goulston, & O. Dent, 'Australian Prisoners of War of the Japanese: Post-War Psychiatric Hospitalisation and Psychological Morbidity', *Australian and New Zealand Journal of Psychiatry*, vol. 20, 1986, pp. 334–40. See also Wilson, Harel, & Kahana (eds), *Human Adaptation to Extreme Stress*.
31 See the *Australian* 19 July 1995, p. 8 Vietnam See *Sydney Morning Herald*, 10 July 1981; *Australian*, 11–12 July 1981.

the lives of many other former prisoners it is their capacity for the transcendence of suffering. While many suffered the effects of imprisonment long afterwards, some also forged a great accommodation with their past, and in doing so, offered a model of tolerance for future Australians. And it is this that makes the prisoner-of-war story both part of Australian history and yet not part of this story. Prisoners of war have come to be seen as inheritors of Anzac, representing the virtues of mateship, brotherhood, sacrifice, courage, and resourcefulness. Even more, they offer a means, however small, to incorporate women into the legend. Yet so many of their problems and reactions were common to veterans from many countries and many wars. And, in the end, their survival represents a chapter in a more universal saga of human triumph over adversity. They are both special and yet typical – unique yet universal – and in their ambiguity they can stand for many things. And, while this can undermine the campaign for adequate benefits, it can allow former prisoners to symbolise significant values in Australian culture.

8
Korea and Vietnam

From late 1941, the focus of Australia's military effort in World War II shifted from Europe and the Middle East to our immediate region – Asia, Melanesia and the Pacific. In early 1942 Singapore fell and a month later the Japanese invaded New Guinea. This focus proved to be more than a response to the immediate strategic needs of the Allied military effort to defeat Japan. For the next thirty years, as Cold War concerns about increasing communist influences in the region escalated, Australia's strategic and military efforts were largely concentrated in East and South East Asia. While there were flashpoints, Australia had an almost continuous military and military adviser presence in the region from 1945. There was an Australian contingent as part of the Allied occupation forces in Japan from 1945 to 1950. And as early as 1948 Australia was asked to contribute to a British Commonwealth force to manage the 'Malayan emergency'; a commitment that lasted throughout the next decade. During the 1950s the Australian Government supported US and British efforts to combat communist incursions in Vietnam, Laos, Thailand and in 1965 Australia committed troops to Borneo to assist in controlling the escalating confrontation between Malaya and Indonesia. Indonesia, Australia's nearest neighbour, was a locus of concern given the wild fluctuations in the political rhetoric and allegiances of President Sukarno. Sukarno's interest in West New Guinea were watched closely.[1] Australia suffered small numbers of military casualties in many of these confrontations but there were also two major military engagements in this period that involved significant numbers of Australian troops and created new challenges for the re-integration of Australian servicemen and women into civilian society – Korea and Vietnam.

---

1   For an overview of these conflicts see Peter Edwards with Gregory Pemberton, *Crises and Commitments: The Politics and Diplomacy of Australia's Involvement in Southeast Asian Conflicts 1948–65*, Allen & Unwin, Sydney, 1992.

I

For many of the veterans of the Korean War it was 'the forgotten war'.[2] On the 25 June 1950, when Soviet-backed North Korean forces broke through the 38th parallel (the agreed boundary between communist controlled northern Korea and Western controlled southern Korea), Allied forces were caught off guard and had to scramble quickly to arrest the surge of communist forces deep into the southern half of the peninsula. The fledgling United Nations was charged with co-ordinating the response to this invasion, and while contingents from over twenty countries formed the United Nations force the United States bore the brunt of the military engagement. US troops were immediately mobilised from Japan and Europe, with General Douglas MacArthur placed in charge of the United Nations force. Australian military authorities and the government, however, were woefully unprepared. The only available Australian forces for deployment were in Japan. It took almost 3 months for an Australian army brigade to arrive in Korea and the 3 RAR (Royal Australian Regiment) did not commence operations until October. Closer to hand were air force and naval resources. Within a few days of the invasion Royal Australian Navy ships were committed to action, destroyers and frigates undertook regular patrols and engaged shore batteries in combat. Later the aircraft carrier, HMAS Sydney and its Fleet Air Arm squadrons attacked supply lines and supported ground troops. Naval and air support became a vital part of this conflict. Australia committed 77 Air Squadron to the war and it remained in action throughout. Once army units were on the ground Australian forces saw some of the most intense fighting in crucial engagements such as the battles of Kapyong and Maryang San.[3]

The Korean War was a major conflict. Estimates for many forces are rough, with as many as 147,000 South Korean, 520,000 North Korean and 900,000 Chinese battle casualties. The United States had over 50,000 killed in action or died of wounds or disease, 100,000 wounded and over 8,000 missing in action. Australia's manpower contribution was comparatively small but still significant. From June 1950 to July 1953, Australia committed 17,000 sailors, soldiers and airmen to serve in Korea, with more in medical, nursing and support units. In all 339 Australians were killed there, 1216 wounded and 29 became prisoners of war.[4] By any measure this was a significant military commitment, which came at some considerable cost. Indeed, the casualty rate for Australian forces in Korea was higher than that for the later war in Vietnam. But Korea was also a different war for the Anzacs. In terms of strategy the more effective integration of air, sea and ground forces in combined

---

2   See Ron Thiele, *Korea: The Forgotten War 1950–53*, Parker Pattinson, Douglas Park, 2003.
3   Jeffrey Grey, *A Military History of Australia*, CUP, Melbourne, 1990, pp. 196–209, and Ben Evans, *Out in the Cold: Australia's Involvement in the Korean War 1950–53*, DVA, Canberra, 2000.
4   Grey, *A Military History of Australia*, p.207.

assaults on North Korean forces represented a significant development. For service personnel on the ground, however, there were more pressing concerns. The rough mountainous terrain and extremes of temperatures – very hot in summer and freezing in winter represented major health and logistical challenges. Especially in winter, for armed forces more experienced in jungle and desert warfare, the frozen terrain, and the ever-present risk of frostbite, represented forbidding conditions for which they had little training or preparation.

This might explain why one of the short official histories of Australia's involvement in the Korean War is titled '*Out in the Cold*'.[5] But there are other meanings embedded in this phrase. Unlike earlier Anzac forces Australian regiments and squadrons were part of a larger United Nations force. Under the United Nations banner, however, Australian forces were only one part of a larger British Commonwealth Contingent. And while ostensibly this Commonwealth Contingent was part of the larger United Nations effort, in reality American commanders, primarily General MacArthur (until his controversial sacking by President Truman in April 1951), were responsible for all the major military decisions. A distinctive Anzac presence was obscured by these larger considerations. But there were other dimensions to this sense of being on the outer. The key battles of the Korean War were largely fought in the first year. From late 1951, however, the war entered a stalemate situation with opposing forces dug-in on opposite sides of the 38th parallel. For service personnel, this was in one sense a return to the trench warfare of 1916 and 1917. Unlike the First World War, however, servicemen were largely confined to defending their area and rarely ventured out of their entrenched positions. The war was now at a stand-off. The cold, the boredom and the lack of action sapped the morale of fighting forces. More importantly, many of them felt that Australians at home had lost interest in this conflict. There was little to engage news services as they moved onto other stories after the excitement of the battles of 1951. Australian servicemen and women were mired in a nether world of inaction, frostbite and boredom.

These problems were exacerbated by the distance from Australia. Although Korea was relatively close to Australia, at least by air, the logistics of leave to Australia were complex and costly. Australian service personnel instead took rest and recreation leave in Japan rather than Australia, and were thus separated from their families for long periods. Nonetheless, Australian military authorities learnt some valuable lessons that paid dividends in later conflicts, most importantly Vietnam. The concern about the incidence of 'battle fatigue' or 'combat exhaustion' during the Second World War demanded a new type of response. Australian military authorities adopted the new policy of a 'tour of duty' for service personnel. This generally meant that men were offered five days leave in Japan after four months and three weeks after eight months in Korea, with a significant rotation

---

5   Evans, *Out in the Cold*.

back to Japan after 12 months, to ensure that service personnel were never at the frontline for extended periods to better ensure their mental fitness. In the first months of this policy each serviceman clocked up their weeks on an individual basis, which meant that in the middle of a battle men had their leave fall due. This created logistical problems and Australian military authorities, unlike their American counterparts who sustained the individual rotation concept for the next twenty years, began to rotate units rather than individual servicemen.[6] This enhanced the psychological resilience of Australian units under very trying conditions.

The cessation of hostilities in Korea were deeply ambiguous. There was no victory to declare, not even a peace treaty, instead merely a negotiated truce that reaffirmed the old boundary of the 38th parallel. The parallel was marked by a demilitarised zone and armed forces at the ready on each side of this zone. The Americans kept a significant force at the ready on the South Korean side. There was thus no Anzac triumph to proclaim for those who waited at home. Nonetheless, the welcome home parades were well attended and the veterans of the Korean War, many of them also veterans of the Second World War, received the same entitlements to repatriation benefits as earlier Anzacs had received – pensions, training, war service homes, soldier settlement, medical and convalescent benefits for the ill and wounded. But some Korean veterans reported a climate of contempt for their efforts. Although generally the RSL leadership welcomed them, some Korean veterans who applied for membership at local RSL branches were turned away: 'Korea isn't a war' was a phrase that some claimed was thrown in their faces in pubs and clubs.[7] And it wasn't until April 2000 that a memorial specifically for the Korean War was unveiled in Canberra. Korea faded from the news and public memory very quickly. It was to be a later Asian conflict that ignited Australian conflict at home and brought Vietnam veterans into the heartland of domestic politics. Vietnam left a legacy for Australian politics and culture, which Korea did not. Yet Australia's involvement in Korea was significant. It seemed to its veterans to have been ignored by politicians and public alike, while Vietnam was burned into the memories of those who fought and those that home who opposed the war. It was the Vietnam war that redefined the idea of 'troubled returns'.

II

Colin Simpson died in 1981. Simpson, married to Lorraine and the father of two boys, lived in an unfashionable but comfortable outer-western suburb of Sydney and enjoyed the usual pleasures of Australian suburban life. In 1975, not yet thirty

---

6   See Norman Bartlett (ed.), *With the Australians in Korea*, AWM, Canberra, 1960, pp. 141-2.
7   Cameron Forbes, *The Korean War: Australia in the Giants' Playground*, Macmillan, Sydney, 2010, p. 472.

years old, doctors found he had cancer (lymphoma), and although it went into remission, it reappeared three years later. As he and Lorraine struggled to come to terms with the illness, friends and neighbours who had served in Vietnam also seemed to be troubled by health problems: cancers, anxiety, rashes, sleeplessness, moodiness, fatigue, and worst of all, an uncommonly high incidence of birth defects in their newborn children. Was their neighbourhood of young families cursed, a 'street of tragedy', as the newspapers trumpeted? A year or two later, Simpson began to read about a new organisation of returned soldiers, the Vietnam Veterans' Association (VVA), which claimed that many returned men were suffering serious health problems from the effects of herbicides used during the war. Simpson was convinced that he had been sprayed, remembering the planes that distributed a fine mist across the countryside, the leafless trees, and the dead foliage around the camps. He contacted the VVA and was added to their grim 'cancer register'. But Simpson was a particularly credible case for the claim that chemicals were the cause of many health problems among veterans. His memory of the sprays and the lifeless environment seemed to place him in a direct relationship to dioxin herbicides (popularly known as 'Agent Orange'), despite government claims that Australian veterans had not been exposed. The Association decided to run a test case to prove that these sprays were responsible for a range of health problems in veterans and that the sufferers of these problems deserved pensions as victims of war-caused disabilities. 'Operation Simpson', as it came to be known, was under way.[8]

In 1980 Simpson's application for a pension to compensate him for lymphoma arising from exposure to Agent Orange was rejected by the Department of Veterans' Affairs. The department claimed that there was no evidence linking such herbicides to health problems. In February Simpson appealed this decision to the Repatriation Commission. It was rejected in August 1981. He had died in July. In September, the VVA sponsored an appeal to the Repatriation Review Tribunal, this time seeking a widow's pension for Lorraine on account of Simpson's death from war-caused illness. In a landmark decision, the tribunal awarded Lorraine the pension, finding 'that it is a real possibility that the applicant's cancer resulted from herbicide exposure arising during service in Vietnam'. Although the Department of Veterans' Affairs issued a statement declaring that the Simpson case would not be taken by the department as a precedent, a few cases succeeded. Carol Dunn received a widow's pension in 1984 for the death of her husband nine years earlier from testicular cancer. The tribunal again accepted that herbicide exposure was a contributing factor to Dunn's death. In the same year, attempts by the Repatriation Commission to overturn these precedents were rejected by the Federal Court. Successful Agent Orange cases were rare, but pension claims were far from hopeless. On the contrary, many veterans claiming health problems from exposure

---

8   See *Sydney Morning Herald*, 10 July 1981; *Australian*, 11–12 July 1981.

to Agent Orange were actually given pensions by the Repatriation Commission, although these were explicitly granted for reasons other than herbicide exposure.[9]

Given the success of these pension claims, why was the VVA so determined to push for official recognition of herbicide exposure as the cause of so many post-war problems among veterans of the Vietnam War? Few were denied a pension, even if the Department of Veterans' Affairs disputed the cause. Yet the Association continued to agitate for a full judicial inquiry into the effects of Agent Orange on veterans and their children. It was a position that drove a wedge between the Association and other returned services groups, especially the RSL. William Keys, then Secretary of the League, explained that he was against such an inquiry because it would 'put a weapon in the hands of those who want to tighten up the benefit of the doubt clauses'. This would be disastrous, as these clauses were 'the most generous in the world and are the means by which we are now achieving substantial benefits for our people'. Others concurred. Bruce Ruxton, President of the Victorian Branch of the RSL, in a typically robust statement, wrote to the Association President Phill Thompson: 'try being nice for a change and endeavour to off-load the chip on your shoulder ... we won't discriminate in the RSL ... you want Vietnam veterans as some sort of special category thus creating discrimination'.[10] Ruxton had a point: some Vietnam veterans saw their experience as essentially different to that of other veterans. It was this sense of difference that fuelled the Association. As Thompson declared in 1982, 'the Vietnam veteran is the victim of a new style of warfare and new problems', and although they 'served this country with great honour and distinction ... neglect and lack of understanding... was their lot on their return'.[11] The actions of the VVA seemed to be less about gaining pensions for veterans (this was a concern, but it was already happening, even if for the 'wrong reasons'), than about contesting their status as returned soldiers. They were laying a claim to a distinctive experience, just as prisoners of war were doing, and using this to press for special consideration. But where prisoners of war were seeking increased benefits and entitlements, Vietnam veteran groups also seemed to be asking for recognition of their war as essentially different to any previous Australian military engagement. Theirs was a statement of belief as well as a plea for benefits, and as such, it was as much a contest of meaning as fact. It is this contest that highlights a central problem for the historian of the Vietnam War. In what ways was the experience of Vietnam veterans different to that

---

9   For details of the Simpson Case, see Vietnam Veterans' Association of Australia Circular, October 1982. On later developments, see Repatriation Review Tribunal, Statement of Decision, 17– 19 September 1984; *Evans v. Repatriation Commission*, Federal Court Decision, 5 September 1984, in Vietnam Veterans' Association (VVA) Papers, AWM, PR 87/163, series 7, box 73.
10 William Keys to Phill Thompson, 4 August 1982, and Bruce Ruxton to Phill Thompson, 7 March 1985, VVA Papers, box 74.
11 President's Address to Open the Queensland Vietnam Veterans Counselling Service Centre, 21 July 1982, VVA Papers, box 81.

of veterans from other conflicts? And how has this debate over difference affected the repatriation of the Vietnam veteran?

III

What happens when history becomes memory – not history as what actually happened (no matter how elusive that might be), but history as what people wrote, told, and believed happened? Here memory does not merely add to, become, or correct history, but can cut across it. The consequences of such a jumble of memory and history are evident in our understandings of the Vietnam War. In 1987 and 1988 Australians warmly embraced Vietnam veterans in 'welcome home marches', and many veterans wept at this expression of thanks for their sacrifice. 'Huge crowds' engaged in 'great emotional outpourings' – 'cheers and tears' – to give veterans the welcome that had been 'denied' them on their return. These marches 'purged the anger, frustration, bitterness, confusion and rejection which has possessed these men'. Interspersed with the reports of the welcome were the memories of veterans that gave shape to the embrace. Phil Holmes from Brisbane spoke for many when he remembered the coldness of their original reception: 'they didn't want to know us when we came back. You got abused if anyone found out you had been there'. Peter Kilby's memories were even more disturbing: 'I got pig's blood thrown at me the last time we marched in Sydney'. Almost all recalled coming back with a sense of failure, the war having not been won, only to be greeted by angry anti-war protests. And many of the oral histories and recollections of veterans published since the 1970s have affirmed this story of rejection.[12] What, then, are we to make of different images of return? There is much visual and written reportage that returning soldiers from Vietnam received warm welcomes. Even as late as 1971, well after the significant moratorium marches against the war, newspapers reported large crowds and 'barrages of ticker tape' for returning veterans. Contrary to numerous accounts and memories of veterans being smuggled in late at night to avoid protesters (although such subterfuges did happen), military authorities ensured that returning units paraded through capital cities to 'blizzards of paper' and rousing cheers. And while these may have lacked the joy of victory parades, they were frequently represented as enthusiastic welcomes from large crowds of grateful Australians. Occasional references to protesters stressed that they were small in number, their chants drowned by cheers for the men, and their efforts usually discouraged by police confiscation of their placards.[13]

---

12 See *Sydney Morning Herald*, 4 October 1987; the *Australian*, 5 October 1987. Some of the relevant oral testimonies and recollections include Rintoul, *Ashes of Vietnam*, Edwards, *Vietnam: The War Within*, K. Maddock (ed.), *Memories of Vietnam*, Random House, Sydney, 1991. See also P. Hamilton, 'The Knife Edge: Debates about Memory and History', in K. Darian-Smith & P. Hamilton (eds), *Memory and History in Twentieth Century Australia*, OUP, Melbourne, 1994, pp. 9–32.

This is not to deny the reality of protests. There were many, some of them very large. And they drew on a broad cross-section of support, including radicals, liberal and church pacifists, and mothers opposed to conscription. Some of these protests did disrupt returns. There was even one case of a marching soldier being splashed with red liquid, although it seems more likely to have been dye than 'pig's blood'. But a perusal of the newspapers suggests that these protests rarely coincided with welcome home parades. Moreover, the red dye incident seems to have been an isolated one (and does not appear to have involved Kilby). And while there were cases of soldiers being denounced and abused on their return, and some radical groups urging victory for the North Vietnamese, these seem not to have come from the mainstream protest movement. Many protesters at the time (and since) have maintained that their opposition was to the war, not the soldiers. In the heat of the moment, such subtle distinctions were probably lost on veterans, but by any calculation, the supporters and welcomers far outnumbered the protesters.[14]

This alternative reality of welcome has not become part of the history or memory of Vietnam veterans. But rather than just proclaiming the falsity of these memories, we need to see them in their context, more as projections of the tumultuous social and cultural changes that have come to be associated with the 1960s. Throughout the West, changing dress, hairstyles, and music, and emerging sexual liberation, gay liberation, women's liberation, new left, student protest, anti-colonial, and antiwar movements received extraordinary media coverage. And despite the fact that some of these movements were far from new, they were represented as signifiers of global cultural upheaval. In this context, the anti-Vietnam protests could be read – much like the May 1968 riots in Paris, student sit-ins in Berkeley, Stonewall in New York, or the Cultural Revolution in China – as symptoms of an upheaval in established values. From the perspective of the 1990s these radical dreams or nightmares (depending on your perspective) seem sadly exaggerated. But such a view is informed by the smug cynicism of hindsight. At the time, even in Australia, where some of these challenges lacked the strength and broad appeal of similar groups in Europe and the USA, social values were undergoing profound change.

Protesters were undoubtedly a minority, and the anti-war movement was consistently opposed by the majority of Australians, but their visibility in media and popular culture was all too evident. And protest had effects. Involvement in the war was supported by Australians until 1968; thereafter, most came to favour withdrawal. And more importantly for soldiers, many of the values associated with love and peace involved new and alien codes of masculinity. Long hair, sensitivity, and a partiality for

---

13 See, for example, *Sydney Morning Herald*, 11 March 1971 and 10 November 1971.
14 See A. Curthoys, '"Vietnam": Public Memory of an Anti-War Movement', in Darian-Smith & Hamilton, *Memory and History in Twentieth Century Australia*, pp. 113–34; A. Curthoys, 'The Anti-War Movements', in J. Grey & J. Doyle (eds), *Vietnam: War, Myth and Memory*, Allen & Unwin, Sydney, 1992, pp. 81–107.

drugs seemed to overturn the traditional masculine warrior ethos of bravery, courage, strength, and fortitude. One of the virtues of soldiering had always been the status of true manhood that it conferred. Now young men and women seemed to desire something other than the warrior ideal. Such differences in values, behaviours, and even appearance signified a growing rupture between Vietnam veterans and their society. While the veterans had numerous supporters, many of these were older Australians. Their peers, however, seemed to be heading in a different direction.[15]

The protests and movements for social change that framed the departure and return of Vietnam veterans were obviously disturbing. In the memories of many veterans, the protest movement looms large as a betrayal of soldiers by those at home. They claimed they had been 'stabbed in the back' – left to defend the country alone while others sought to undermine the war effort.[16] But the protest movements also acted to amplify more traditional tensions between front line and the home front. Such alienations fostered a sense among soldiers that they were isolated: victims of government and public neglect, inadequately supplied, and forgotten by those they left behind. This traditional antagonism to the home front is evident in the novels written by Australian Vietnam veterans. In such works as William Nagle's *The Odd Angry Shot* (1975), Rhys Pollard's *The Cream Machine* (1972), and David Alexander's *When the Buffalo Fight* (1980), the soldiers are 'frustrated pawns', 'shit-shovelers', 'dust pounders' fighting for no seeming purpose or objective, just trying 'to stay alive' in a nightmare world of jungle warfare. In this mire, mateship is the only life raft. In counterpoint to the camaraderie of the band (or the 'cream' in Pollard's ironic turn of phrase), is the betrayal by those at home. Some of this focused on the protesters. In *The Cream Machine* this is graphically represented by the discovery of a Monash University protest badge on the body of a dead Viet Cong soldier. In *When the Buffalo Fight* the protesters even invade the home of one of the officers, harassing Major Ryder's wife with anti-war slogans. And throughout these novels there is a constant stream of abusive references to protesters. They are 'bleeding hearts', 'tear jerking, psalm singing, eloquent intellectuals a million miles from the action'. In *The Odd Angry Shot* one soldier denounces the 'Peace, Love and Brotherhood' brigade, wishing he 'could have emptied every round of ammunition in the country into them'. The significance of this antagonism is all the more evident in its absence in novels written by men who did not serve overseas, such as John Carroll's *Token Soldiers* (1983), or in its curious erasure in Tom Jeffrey's 1979 film of *The Odd Angry Shot*. For the men at the front, the bilious effects of protest were very real.

---

15 P. Cochrane, 'At War At Home: Australian Attitudes During the Vietnam Years', in G. Pemberton (ed.), *Vietnam Remembered*, Weldon Publishing, Sydney, 1990, pp. 165–85. For the shifting opinion-poll evidence, see M. Goot & R. Tiffen, 'Public Opinion and the Politics of the Polls', in P. King (ed.), *Australia's Vietnam: Australia in the Second Indo-China War*, Allen & Unwin, Sydney, 1983, pp. 129–64. Other useful discussions of the changing cultural context that confronted returning soldiers include D. Horne, *The Lucky Country Revisited*, Dene, Melbourne, 1987; R. Gerster and J. Bassett, *Seizures of Youth: 'The Sixties' and Australia*, Hyland House, Melbourne, 1991.

16 For accusations of betrayal, see *Sydney Morning Herald*, 14 December 1971.

But there are other fears and anxieties about home evident in this literature. Common adversaries are the 'sticky-fingered politicians' and 'mongrel bastard' public servants who sent men to this 'hell-hole'. The government does not care about their fate and is only using them for its own game of political advantage. Even veterans of previous wars are 'turd burglars spinning yarns in RSL clubs', insensitive to the needs of the men in Vietnam. Added to this frustration is the evident antagonism towards military authority. Officers are represented as obsessive enforcers of petty rules, but are also revealed to be inadequate to the demands of leadership when the real fighting begins. It is almost as if the enemy are the government and the military. The Vietnamese are almost entirely absent as characters in these novels, except in *When the Buffalo Fight*, where a few are personalised as tragic victims of war and some even granted a grudging respect as fellow sufferers, a counterpoint that only heightens the sense of betrayal. Underpinning some of this antipathy to authority is the theme of class. In most of these novels the ordinary soldiers are seen as poor working-class victims sacrificed to political expediency while 'silver-spooned' types evade enlistment. Even more pervasive is the fear that their wives and girlfriends are cheating on them. Almost every soldier in these novels is plagued by such anxieties, and more than a few of them face the reality of sexual betrayal. Most of the loyal band of brothers receive 'dear john' letters 'giving them the arse' (while they, of course, resort to bargirls). Running through all these narratives is a barely suppressed anger towards women at home; they are heartless, manipulative, lying, and deceiving. This, in turn, forces the men back onto themselves. It is mateship that gets them through, and it is not surprising that these novels end with some ambivalence about return. What awaits them are their betrayers, and what they are losing are their mates.[17]

If we see these sentiments in a longer perspective, however, what is striking is not the special alienation of the Vietnam veteran but the entirely conventional nature of their antagonisms and frustrations. While the rapidity of the transition from home to war and back again may have exacerbated the violence of this rupture, in many respects the emotions portrayed in such accounts, and many subsequent oral testimonies, parallel those of veterans of the First and Second World Wars. The First AIF focused on 'shirkers' and 'strikers', and the Second looked to 'yanks' and 'profiteers', as sources of betrayal. Soldiers in both world wars had a sense, like Korean veterans, that they were being forgotten, pawns in larger political games. Worse still was the pervasive sense of female betrayal – the 'girl who wouldn't wait' in 1918, and the girls in the 1940s who were 'yank-mad'. For Vietnam veterans we have a familiar demonology of profiteers, strikers, 'bloody

---

17   W. Nagle, *The Odd Angry Shot*, Angus & Robertson, Sydney, 1975; R. Pollard, *The Cream Machine*, Angus & Robertson, Sydney, 1972; D. Alexander, *When the Buffalo Fight*, Hutchinson, Melbourne, 1980. See also J. Carroll, *Token Soldiers*, Wildgrass Books, Melbourne, 1983; Gerster, *Big-Noting*, pp. 237–58; P. Pierce, 'Australian and American Literature of the Vietnam War', in P. Pierce, J. Grey, & J. Doyle (eds), *Vietnam Days: Australia and the Impact of Vietnam*, Penguin, Melbourne, 1991, pp. 237–74.

politicians', and unfaithful women. And given the political conflicts arising from the conscription referendums of 1916 and 1917, the anger towards the anti-conscription movement of the 1960s and 1970s looks no less traditional. Perhaps these are the similarities of genre, with novelists drawing on a well-established corpus of figures and feelings to propel their narratives and strengthen the central theme of mateship. But the pervasive sense of alienation experienced at the front that is remembered in oral testimony suggests that such similarities were more than genre. Soldiers who went to Vietnam were, of course, already bearers of an Anzac ethos, an integral part of which was a rupture between home and war, and in the military they were inculcated into the culture of soldiering that found its own definition in opposition to home. The presentation of experience was inevitably shaped by the demands of literary form (be it novel, autobiography, or remembrance). And styles of storytelling influenced the way soldiers understood and recounted their own experience. They expected alienation and betrayal, were told they would be its victims, and experienced its effects.

In other ways too, the experience of return for Vietnam veterans paralleled that of veterans from other wars. While the silent majority in all wars returned to lead ordinary lives back in the community, a significant number found it hard to settle into old routines and habits. Terry Burstall, a veteran of the battle of Long Tan, left the army in 1968 but found that he could not adjust. He went to Papua New Guinea and led the life of a virtual recluse for three years before returning to Brisbane. There he needed 'adrenalin highs' to keep any interest in life and worked as a bouncer at a nightclub in the Valley, where he was badly injured several times. It was a familiar story. Some found it impossible to return to civilian life and returned to soldiering as mercenaries. Mark Rose just pursued odd jobs in North Queensland, Papua New Guinea, and the Philippines. As with veterans of other wars, some had volunteered for service because they had been unsettled at home. Their return was to old alienations. But others suffered new problems, and now had the war to explain their dissatisfactions. They complained of illness, lassitude, nightmares, and lack of interest in life. The files of the Department of Veterans' Affairs reveal a depressing number of such stories. John L is typical. He led an itinerant life on return, mostly farm labouring, prawn-trawling in the north, and butchering. He lived in tents, moving from town to town, and suffered insomnia, nightmares, headaches, and violent outbursts of temper. He expressed 'bitterness and anger towards the government', describing them as 'traitors and hypocrites', and had difficulty initiating or maintaining relationships with the opposite sex. In almost every respect, such stories are remarkably similar to those of troubled war pensioners from earlier conflicts.[18]

---

18 T. Burstall, *The Soldier's Story: The Battle of Xa Long Tan Vietnam, 18 August 1966*, UQP, St Lucia, 1986. The oral histories are from Rintoul, *Ashes of Vietnam*, pp. 211–13, and the case of John L is from Department of Veterans' Affairs, Queensland, Case Files, sample no. 128. Some

There is much to be gained from focusing on the commonalities of the returned serviceman and servicewoman experience. But bemoaning the blinkers of Vietnam veterans who have failed to see the universality of their experience is also limiting. Even respected and well-researched histories of the Vietnam War have tended to focus on the rejection rather than the welcome of returning soldiers. As John Murphy argues, the 'saddest irony was that veterans were denied the simple dignity and solace of the returning soldier'.[19] And there is a kernel of truth here. The Vietnam War was a more morally ambiguous conflict than Australia's earlier international engagements, a sense exacerbated by the extent of national and international opposition. Moreover, the confusion over whether it was an Australian victory but American defeat (or even whether it was a 'war') clouded perceptions of the virtue and heroism of veterans. Even a defeat, as Gallipoli had shown, could be turned into national myth, but something that was as murky and confused as Vietnam defied easy incorporation. Nor were the names of Vietnam veterans usually added to the numerous community war memorials that proliferated in Australia. This was partly because many communities suffered no losses in a conflict that involved only 50,000 Australians, fewer than those killed in the Great War.

The symbolism of Anzac during the 1970s and 1980s was focused on remembering the dead from the First and Second World Wars, rather than the smaller engagements of Korea, Malaya, Borneo, and Vietnam. Some Vietnam veterans complained that they were being written out of Anzac history – the poor cousins, even the black sheep, of the legend. And the absence of separate memorialisation of their contribution to the legend (until the dedication of the Vietnam War Memorial in Canberra in 1992) served as a stark symbol of their outsider status. Even efforts by Vietnam veterans' groups to establish special memorial days (notably for the Battle of Long Tan) were criticised for being political and dismissed by army representatives as 'single unit actions' and hence inappropriate for celebration. Ironically, as this neglect has come to be redressed in recent years, it is the anti-conscription protesters of the 1960s and 1970s who are complaining about being written out of history. Some have even sought incorporation by adopting the rhetoric of Anzac: the protests are described as battles and the protesters 'gallant men' who 'fought' with 'real heroism'. In one instance, they are even accorded an 'honour roll'.[20]

---

important revisionist work has begun to note these similarities. See, for example, J. Ross, 'Australia's Legacy: The Vietnam Veterans', in Pemberton, *Vietnam Remembered*, pp. 187–213.

19 J. Murphy, *Harvest of Fear: A History of Australia's Vietnam War*, Allen & Unwin, Sydney, 1993, p. 278.

20 The most extraordinary example of this incorporation, is B. Scates, *Draftmen Go Free: A History of the Anti-Conscription Movement in Australia*, self-published, Richmond, 1989. For comments on Long Tan Day, see Colonel E Pfitzner, Department of Defence, to Phill Thompson, President of the VVA, 16 January 1984, in VVA Papers, box 77.

What distinguishes the Vietnam story from the stories of returned men from the First and the Second World Wars is the extent to which the angry and resentful soldier has come to stand for the real experience of Vietnam. Such men were always a minority, but where the 'disturbed and maladjusted' veteran from earlier wars was part of a dark, unstated, and intensely private history for particular families, overshadowed by the rich public imagery of the Anzac legend, the alienated Vietnam veteran has become an iconic figure in history, memory, and popular culture. In the complex circularity of life and reportage, stories and images of alienated veterans focused media attention on instances of veteran violence, in turn producing and amplifying such images. Newspaper reports of crimes – particularly violence, murder, and rape – noted whenever possible the status of offenders as Vietnam veterans. Even more mundane events, such as shoplifting or fits of rage in public places, found an explanation in the veteran experience.

In a common cry, the *Australian* declared that 'suicide and murderous reactions' marked many veterans, particularly those exposed to Agent Orange. Such reportage almost amounted to mass hysteria in the early 1980s, when some horrendous crimes were blamed on supposed veterans. In 1983 one Melbourne paper reported on a Vietnam veteran who shot dead his estranged wife and her flatmate, and then killed himself. It later turned out that he had not served overseas. Such reports are hardly peculiar to Vietnam veterans. There are many accounts of men from earlier wars committing crimes, but these are submerged into a larger iconography of the digger. The Vietnam veteran was for a time excluded from the Anzac legend, and the greater presence of the media in popular culture only served to further entrench a stereotype of the alienated Vietnam veteran in the public mind. This flowed over into literary production. In many novels and plays, the returned man of the First World War or the Second World War often found completion in the bosom of a welcoming family, no matter how embittered he had been at the front. Typically, Bill Farr, in Eric Lambert's *The Veterans*, finds solace in the thought of his return to Betty and his newborn son. But the few novels about return written by former Vietnam veterans present a starker picture. Merv Ryan's *Vietnam Conscript* (1992), for instance, plays with the conventional figure of the returned man in love with his mate's wife, but here the mate has survived, and the means of achieving this love becomes a bloody trail of murder and suicide.[21]

This image of the disturbed Vietnam veteran has been challenged by historians such as Jeffrey Grey and Ian McNeill. They argue that the incidence of disturbed behaviour, or what has come to be known as post-traumatic stress disorder, is far lower in Australia than in the USA. They rightly point out that the majority of Australian veterans returned to lead productive and stable lives, indistinguishable in their quota of misery and happiness from that of the ordinary citizen. Confusion

---

21 M. Ryan, Vietnam Conscript, Access Press, Perth, 1992. For reports of alienated veterans, see the *Australian*, 19 April 1982, *Sydney Morning Herald*, 18 November 1980, *Herald* (Melbourne), 30 September 1980; *Sun* (Melbourne), 6 January 1983.

in the popular mind between the American and the Australian experience of combat in Vietnam is seen as the origin of the myth of the disturbed Australian Vietnam veteran. In one sense, this is an important distinction. The Australian experience was different. Australian units were fewer and were engaged in a specific exercise of containment and eradication of the North Vietnamese forces from one province. Their military objectives were clear and, unlike the United States forces, they were successful in achieving their admittedly limited aims.

From a military point of view, the Australian involvement in the war was a success. Moreover, the discipline and morale of Australian troops was generally better than that of United States forces. The incidence of drug addiction and disease was lower (although alcoholism was high), and desertion, serious disobedience, and 'fragging' (the killing of officers by soldiers) was virtually unknown in Australian regiments. Australian forces, however, were not entirely free of problems. Peter Bourne, an American psychiatrist attached to Australian forces in 1966, noted that Australian soldiers seemed to suffer from isolationism. Confined to a backwater in the overall conflict, they resented their marginal status and adopted a 'distanced' attitude to others (friend and foe) in Vietnam. This cemented the bonds within the units (something that made Australians more psychologically resilient in battle) but fanned their resentment towards authority, both in Vietnam and at home. The consequences of this isolation have yet to be fully explored. Whatever the effects, these revisionist historians are right to distinguish Australian from American military experience. But on another level, this misses the point. The cultural context of return for Australians was shaped as much by American influences as Australian. It is impossible to entirely disentangle the Australian popular memory of Vietnam from the American when so many American stories and films gained ready acceptance and popularity in Australia. Australians, veterans and non-veterans, consumed the wider American story of Vietnam disenchantment, and it is this that frames many of the memories of rejection.[22]

Vietnam has functioned as a metaphor for loss in American culture. It bridges the 'Camelot' of the Kennedy administration and the disgrace of Watergate. It seems to span a time of innocence, when the USA embodied integrity, social cohesion, and international peace, to a time of economic decline, proliferating poverty, race and sex conflict, urban decay, endemic crime and political upheaval. Of course, such powerful dichotomies are chimerical. The 1950s and early 1960s were hardly free of social conflict, and the seeds of contemporary social and economic decline were sown well before Vietnam. Contemporary disenchantment, however, has fanned a romanticised memory of the American past. But the Vietnam War did operate as a powerful agent for social disillusion, and a sense

---

22 J. Grey, 'Memory and Public Myth', in Grey & Doyle, *Vietnam: War, Myth and Memory*, pp. 137–53; I. McNeill, 'The Australian Army and the Vietnam War', in Pierce, Grey, & Doyle, *Vietnam Days*, pp. 11–61. See also P. Bourne, *Men, Stress and Vietnam*, Little Brown, Boston, 1970, pp. 167–86.

of decline and disintegration. It was then the longest American war and the first in which the USA was on the losing side – itself a dramatic signifier of decline. Within this frame of reference, the focus has shifted onto the moral, social and political decay of the USA. Films, because of their very popularity, are one means of investigating the ways in which this idea of decline played itself out in popular culture.

Was loss a function of the inherent madness of war and the Russian roulette of life, as in Francis Ford Coppola's *Apocalypse Now*, Michael Herr's *Dispatches* or Michael Cimino's *The Deer Hunter*? Was it the consequence of a military machine whose function was to produce crazed psychopaths, as in Stanley Kubrick's *Full Metal Jacket*? Or was it some powerful Manichean split in the American soul, as in Oliver Stone's *Platoon*? The question is unanswerable. But peopling these and other narratives is an extraordinary panoply of disturbed veterans, shattered and forever transformed by war: Nick in *The Deer Hunter*, drug addicted and obsessed with a game of life and death; murderous avenging angel Travis Bickle in Martin Scorsese's *Taxi Driver*, depressed and suicidal Robert in Hal Ashby's *Coming Home*, or rambling and maniacal Kurtz in *Apocalypse Now*. Even when the veteran is not mad, he is inevitably rendered a stranger to American society: John Rambo in *First Blood* is violently expelled from society and exacts his revenge, but even Michael in *The Deer Hunter* finds it difficult to return to old ways and friendships. Running counter to such characterisations, however, is a theme of war experience as one of personal growth. For Luke in *Coming Home* or John Kovacs in Oliver Stone's *Born on the Fourth of July*, the war and its direct physical consequences (paralysis) foster alienation and despair. But each overcomes his spiritual malaise to find a new and authoritative voice in American culture (as an anti-war activist). Even Michael in *The Deer Hunter* undergoes a life-affirming transformation, leaving behind a narrow and painful masculine ethos for a newer, nurturing maturity. But dominating these representations is a vision of war as psychically and emotionally scaring, and the veteran as violent, depressed, or suicidal. The alienated veteran came to signify the deeper moral decline of American society.

The cultural dilemmas and narratives in which these struggles are fought out are not necessarily Australia's problems. The Vietnam War affected far more people, and touched more significant cultural nerves, in the USA than ever it did in Australia. Nonetheless, these popular films and books helped cement an image of the damaged and alienated veteran in the Australian public mind as much as in the USA. They fostered an image of the veteran as social antagonist, something that frequent newspaper reports of ill, criminal, murderous, and suicidal veterans seemed to confirm as fact. Some Australian veterans resented such representations. John Embelton reacted angrily to television programs on embittered and ill Vietnam veterans, claiming that he 'returned fit and well' and that such stories fostered unnecessary 'shame'. In his view, there was no evidence of problems in his family or in the families of his returned comrades. But other veterans embraced the evidence of problem and alienation in order to assert that governments had not done enough to assist the war-damaged veteran. Like their counterparts from earlier wars, they believed that the home front had little sympathy for their plight and were determined to demand their rights. They had to turn to the repatriation system for justice. But here they faced a dilemma. Many were afflicted with a hatred of the system that had betrayed them, and yet this system was all there was to provide the welfare they needed. It was a conflict that others had faced before them, and one that fostered suspicion and resentment.[23]

IV

In the 1970s, representatives of the RSL were anxious to ensure the integration of Vietnam veterans into the League. 'Our boys return home ... so now let's bring them into the RSL' declared Frank Buxton of the New South Wales Branch. Buxton and others saw that the future of the League inevitably lay with this new generation of diggers. As the returned men of the First and the Second World Wars 'pass on more quickly ... membership must continue to dwindle' unless they are replaced by 'the young veterans of today'. And in 1972 the League placed Vietnam veterans at the head of the Anzac Day march in Sydney in recognition of the leadership role they would assume in the future.[24] Vietnam veterans did join the League – 15,000, or nearly one-third of the returned forces, in the decade after the war. This rate paralleled that for returned men from earlier conflicts and suggests that, for many Vietnam veterans, the League was a congenial institution. Some, however, complained of their treatment by established members. Like their brethren who returned from the Second World War or the Korean War, Vietnam veterans found a League dominated by men of an earlier generation anxious to maintain their position. In the raucous atmosphere of male bravado in League's clubs, older men undoubtedly ribbed their younger colleagues about how, in their day, war was much tougher. When Second World War veterans returned, they were chided about how real war was trench warfare. When Vietnam veterans returned, they were told that the jungle campaigns of New Guinea and Borneo were much tougher than those of South-East Asia, and a year's tour of duty was said to be a 'piece of cake' in comparison the long haul of the Second World War. Vietnam veterans resented their nickname – 'the odd angry shotters' – which belittled their fighting effort. In the friendly bombast of male 'big-noting', the nuances of the Vietnam conflict – the greater fire-power of weapons, the complexity of guerrilla war in which civilian and soldier were often indistinguishable, and the

---

23 J. Embleton to VVA, 30 November 1983, VVA Papers, box 90.
24 F. Buxton, 'Our Boys Return Home ... So Now Let's Bring Them into the RSL, *Reveille*, 1 January 1972. On the Anzac Day march, see *Reveille*, 1 May 1972.

lack of relief in the shorter tour of duty – were unlikely to carry much weight with older veterans.[25]

For returning men, the day-to-day life of the League may have been marked by generational rivalry, but the officials of the League acted to press the claims of Vietnam veterans for full repatriation entitlements. Throughout the late 1960s and early 1970s the League campaigned for greater benefits for these veterans. Under the Repatriation Act, servicemen and women who had served in Vietnam were entitled to education and employment retraining programs and allowances, war-service homes, re-establishment loans, and pensions. The League argued that these benefits were insufficient. It pushed for soldier-settlement schemes. It also sought increased benefits to match those available to ex-service personnel from earlier wars. In 1970 the President of the League, Sir Arthur Lee, complained that, unlike veterans of the Second World War, who were entitled to two or more years training, men and women who served in Vietnam received only one year of funded training. Equally, the League sought to obtain full benefits for injured and ill national servicemen who had not served overseas. These were small gestures, as long years of campaigning by the League had ensured generous benefits for servicemen and women. But it seems clear that the League were just as vigilant in campaigning for Vietnam veterans as they had been for those who returned from earlier wars. It was vital to the League's future to demonstrate their relevance to a new generation.[26]

It is a testament to the League's commitment to the welfare of servicemen and women that it supported increased benefits for Vietnam veterans at a time of unparalleled criticism of repatriation. The late 1960s and early 1970s was the height of the 'Be in it Mate' controversy. A number of critics were claiming that many veterans were receiving benefits for complaints that had no relation to war service, and that the repatriation system was 'feather bedding'. As journalist Peter Samuel argued in 1972, it was 'a vast national welfare system administered for ex-servicemen, by ex-servicemen in the interests of ex-servicemen at tax-payers' expense ... and never objectively appraised'. Attempts by the RSL to increase the number of illnesses deemed to be war-caused were condemned as a 'disgrace' and a 'comic opera'. The Federal government sought to allay public concern by establishing a number of inquiries into repatriation: a 1970 Senate committee and, a year later, the even more extensive Toose Commission. The RSL responded angrily to such developments, at times verging on the intemperate, declaring that the chair of the Senate committee would be 'pulling a rickshaw' if it had not been for the veterans of the Second World War. The leadership of the League were all too aware of the need to defend the system. William Keys, Secretary of the RSL, wrote to the President in 1972, urging that the League 'not sit quietly by while repat is

---

25 There are a number of letters about the 'rocky' relationship between the RSL and Vietnam veterans, mainly from aggrieved Vietnam veterans, in VVA Papers, box 91.
26 See *Sydney Morning Herald*, 24 April 1970 and 20 December 1971.

attacked unmercifully'. A year later he condemned the Senate report as 'superficial ... designed far more to assist the taxpayer than the incapacitated ex-serviceman and his dependants'.[27]

This was not a favourable context for pushing for more assistance for veterans. Nonetheless, the League pressed forward. But the hostile climate may have had an effect on the tenor and extent of the League's agitation. Usually the League was asking to bring benefits for Vietnam veterans into line with those available for other ex-service persons. By inclination, the League sought to see veterans as a single group with common problems and needs. It was not likely to be sympathetic to arguments that veterans of a particular conflict had different problems. This inclination and the climate of criticism stunted awareness of particular issues. In 1972, the *Canberra Times* reported that Mr Justice Toose had asked the RSL to investigate claims that Vietnam servicemen had been exposed to toxic defoliants. It was an issue that the League preferred to subsume into an older campaign for the recognition of diseases arising from exposure to gas in the First World War. Even these more traditional issues were the subject of widespread public criticism. The League was unlikely to raise an entirely new problem at this time. The defoliants problem disappeared, only to return a decade later. Ironically it became the cause of a major rupture in the veteran community, convincing some Vietnam veterans that the RSL was sacrificing their interests to those of older members.[28]

Did Vietnam veterans suffer a disproportionate share of war-caused problems arising from the nature of their service? At the simplest level, there is a lack of detailed studies of social and health problems among veterans. More significantly, few studies have broached a comparison between Vietnam veterans and those from earlier wars, and any attempt to do so rests on a shaky foundation; different age and marriage cohorts, different historical contexts, different forms and levels of medical treatment are among the factors that obstruct accurate statistical comparison. When we consider Vietnam veterans alone, difficulties remain. Some of the few studies that have attempted to assess the impact of service in Vietnam have come to contradictory conclusions. Studies of mortality among Vietnam veterans have generally concluded that there is 'no evidence of excessive death among veterans' in comparison with men of a similar age. If anything, the mortality rate among veterans seems to be lower than that for their civilian counterparts, although it is conceded that veterans passed rigorous medical examinations before service and were therefore already a particularly healthy population. This very concession points to the difficulties of any direct comparison. But, in general, such studies have found that low educational achievement, blue-collar occupations, a less stable employment

---

27   William Keys to W. Newington, 23 June 1973, and Keys to Sir Arthur Lee, 16 March 1972, in RSL Papers, 1988 series, box 33. For some of the criticism, see, P. Samuel, 'Repat – Can it Survive?', *The Bulletin*, 7 October 1972; *Sunday Mail* 26 February 1972.
28   *Canberra Times*, 25 February 1972.

record before service, and in-service disciplinary actions were more significant indicators of post-war mortality than service itself.[29]

On the other hand, studies of psychological problems suggest high rates of anxiety, tension, hostility, nightmares, guilt, alienation, hypochondria, depression, and alcoholism amongst Vietnam veterans. The accumulating evidence of such problems has fostered the image of the Vietnam veteran as being uniquely prone to post-traumatic stress disorder. But as we have seen, such problems were far from rare among veterans from earlier wars. The terminology may be different – *shell-shock*, *combat exhaustion*, or *post-traumatic stress* – but a substantial minority of veterans from all twentieth century wars seemed to have suffered from anxiety, nightmares, depression, or other associated problems after return. What distinguished the Vietnam veteran was the low incidence of psychological problems reported in combat. Some psychiatrists have argued that this arose from the reluctance of army doctors to diagnose psychological problems in Vietnam, preferring to file them as disciplinary. Thus, the incidence was under-reported. But this seems to be little different to the response in earlier wars. There has always been a reluctance to diagnose psychological problems for fear of fostering malingering. Other psychiatrists have argued that the limited tour of duty for Vietnam veterans meant that many of the stress problems associated with combat occurred after discharge, rather than during service. The implication in such studies is that veterans from earlier wars, who usually served for more than a year, sometimes as many as four years, were more likely to develop symptoms at the front. If this is the case, there may be little difference indeed between the veterans of all modern wars in their response to combat. At the very least, 10 per cent – and more likely somewhere between one fifth and one-quarter – of veterans from the First World War, the Second World War, and Vietnam seem to have returned suffering from various symptoms of stress, anxiety, and depression. One of the darker and, as yet, unwritten stories of war is that of the long-term psychological damage of a substantial proportion of those who return, and of the families who have to live with angry, depressed, and resentful men.[30]

Another way of attempting to explore the consequences of service in Vietnam is to examine war-pension files. Even here the evidence is ambiguous when we

---

29 See Australian Veterans' Health Studies, *The Mortality Report*, vols I & II, AGPS, Canberra, 1984; M. A. Adena et al., 'Mortality among Vietnam Veterans Compared with Non-Veterans and the Australian Population', *MJA*, vol. 143, December 9–23, 1985, pp. 541–4.

30 The literature on this topic is enormous. See, for example, J. A. M. Cugley & R. D. Savage, 'Cognitive Impairment and Personality Adjustment in Vietnam Veterans', *Australian Psychologist*, vol. 19, no. 2, July 1984, pp. 205–16; C. Tennant, J. H. Streimer, & H. Temperly, 'Memories of Vietnam: Post-Traumatic Stress Disorders in Australian Veterans', *Australian and New Zealand Journal of Psychiatry*, vol. 24, 1990, pp. 29–36; B. Bowman, 'The Vietnam Veteran Ten Years On', pp. 107–27. For evidence of the reluctance of Vietnam veterans to seek assistance, see I. K. Waterhouse, *Evaluation of the Vietnam Veterans Counselling Service*, Department of Veterans' Affairs, Sydney, 1985.

consider such indicators as marital problems, employment instability, symptoms of psychological disorder, alcoholism, or changes in the rate of assessed disability. But we can gain some comparison with war pensioners from earlier conflicts. Vietnam pensioners, for instance, have higher rates of marital difficulties, particularly rates of divorce, than other war pensioners. But this, in part, reflects easier access to divorce. Vietnam pensioners are also more likely to experience time off work due to ill health. But, on the other hand, they exhibit greater employment stability than other veteran pensioners. And the fact that over 70 per cent of Vietnam war pensioners were in the same occupation ten years after discharge does much to dispel the image of the disturbed and restless veteran. The number of war pensioners granted a pension for psychological problems was undoubtedly high: nearly 40 per cent. This is almost double the rate for pensioners from the Second World War and three times that of pensioners from the First World War, but no higher than that for prisoners of war from the Second World War. Moreover, nearly 40 per cent of Vietnam veterans have no mention of any psychological problems (pensionable or otherwise) on their files. Alcohol abuse was notably higher among Vietnam war pensioners, but rates of increase in pension assessments, a measure of increasing ill health, were greatest among prisoners of war. In other words, repatriation pension boards certainly noted evidence of significant social and health problems in Vietnam pensioners, but overall, prisoners of war seem to have been the group most affected by war service. While Vietnam veterans had a high representation for some indicators, they were poorly represented for others. And it is always possible that such differences reflect as much the assumptions of the assessors, particularly in their willingness to diagnose stress in Vietnam veterans, as the actual incidence of a problem.[31]

There may be other ways of looking at this evidence. What it does suggest is that Vietnam veterans were integrated into the repatriation system. They sought pensions and were given them. Indeed, by the early 1980s, 6800 Vietnam veterans, 5170 wives and widows, and 8758 children were receiving war pension assistance. This meant that about 14 per cent of Vietnam veterans were receiving pensions ten years after the war, a rate only marginally less than that for veterans of the Second World War at a similar period. Both rates were certainly less than the 22 per cent of First World War veterans receiving pensions in the late 1920s, but then morbidity rates in that war had been much higher. Furthermore, the rate of rejection of pension applications seems to have varied little for veterans since 1929 (when appeal mechanisms were first instituted). Usually two-fifths of initial applications were rejected, regardless of war, and equally, successful appeals against rejections have indicated a remarkable consistency since 1945 (about four-fifths). In short, Vietnam veterans seem to have suffered no more or less discrimination

---

31 These conclusions are based on a correlation of different indicators from our random sample of Department of Veterans' Affairs case files.

(or favouritism, depending on one's perspective) in the repatriation system than veterans from other wars.[32]

In 1982 the Secretary of the Department of Veterans' Affairs, Derek Volker, attempted to persuade Vietnam veterans that they were receiving adequate treatment in repatriation matters. For Volker, the evidence suggested that the system was generous to Vietnam veterans and their families, and 'rightly so'. Overall, the evidence suggests that Volker was fair in his assessment. But some Vietnam veterans were not so easily convinced. A vocal minority were angry at what they perceived to be government prejudice. The feeling persisted that they had been betrayed by politicians. Distrust of government was evident in the refusal of some Vietnam veterans to seek any assistance from the Department of Veterans' Affairs. Others, who had experience of the department, complained that they were not receiving fair treatment. Independent inquiries seemed to support some of these claims. A 1983 Victorian Ombudsmen Report into pension claims concluded that many applications were inadequately investigated, medical officers seemed to lack a familiarity with relevant medical literature, and too often, unexplained symptoms were ascribed to hereditary problems. This investigation itself was far from being a model of rigour (it was based on only nine case files), but it added fuel to the resentment of some veterans. Moreover, it echoed the complaints of many war pension applicants since the introduction of the repatriation system. But some Vietnam veterans believed they were being uniquely discriminated against and unfairly treated by the department.[33]

V

The veteran community has never had a single voice. While the RSL has traditionally been the largest and most influential returned-services organisation, there were always others, some disaffected with the political stance of the League and others seeking to provide a focus for smaller constituencies (prisoners of war, limbless soldiers, blinded soldiers, tuberculosis sufferers, widows, Korean veterans, and others). It is not surprising, then, that Vietnam veterans sought to give voice to their own concerns. What is surprising, although not unprecedented (as the Returned Soldiers' Labour League of the 1920s or the Queensland Digger's Club of the 1930s indicate), is their estrangement from the League. The antagonism was mutual. As Phill Thompson argued, 'the RSL is an example of leaders of the ex-service community who have been diverted from the proper path ... better

---

32 These statistics are calculated from figures in Repatriation Department and Department of Veterans' Affairs, Annual Reports, 1929–1985.
33 D. Volker, Address to VVA conference, 25 May 1982, VVA Papers, box 89; Victorian Ombudsman, Report on Complaint by Vietnam Veterans' Association on Defective Administration of Claims, 1983, VVA Papers, box 85.

known for their role as watchdogs for ... community moral principles ... and a particular set of political beliefs'. Bruce Ruxton of the RSL, on the other hand, found the VVA leadership 'most irrational, illogical and irratic [sic] ... just a tool of the ALP'. Neither group, however, commanded the allegiance of the majority of Vietnam veterans. Where the League had about one- third of Vietnam veterans as members, the VVA had, at most, 8000 members (more likely 5000), little more than one-tenth. Most veterans returned to lead lives uninvolved in veteran politics. But it is clear that the majority of its membership were more bitter about their treatment by the Department of Veterans' Affairs than they were about the RSL. The latter may have failed to represent their interests, but the former provided pensions that were either insufficient or granted on the wrong basis.[34]

The VVA seems to have emerged in late 1979, when a small group of veterans began to meet in Melbourne to discuss their mutual experiences and problems. In their view, they had returned to a 'community indifferent or hostile' to their plight, 'an unresponsive RSL', and a 'flawed repatriation system'. In part, the inspiration for this group was the emergence of a Vietnam veterans' movement in the USA, which was actively lobbying for a better deal for veterans. But a perusal of the Association papers also suggests that many of its members had grievances directly related to their experience in Australia. They contain numerous letters from veterans complaining about their treatment by the Department of Veterans' Affairs; it was frequently criticised as 'slack', 'hostile', 'demeaning', and 'dismissive'. They complained bitterly that department officers accused them of being 'malingerers', and the Association lost few opportunities to condemn the 'lack of sympathy and rudeness of Departmental officers'.[35] Nor was it hard to publicise evidence of what might be charitably described as inefficiency and insensitivity. The Victorian Ombudsman's report on the handling of cases, despite its flaws, was a useful weapon in the campaign to highlight the failures of repatriation. Lack of investigation helped foster an image that repatriation had become routine, perfunctory, and more importantly for the Association, unable to recognise or come to grips with new problems. Further investigations revealed that at least one medical officer in the department was prepared to declare that the majority of Vietnam veteran war-neurosis pension claims were 'malingered for purposes of money, prestige or avoidance of life's problems'. Equally disturbing was the inappropriate humour in departmental publications. The VVA was particularly offended by an item in *Repat Chat*, the newsletter of the department's social clubs.

---

34 Phill Thompson to President of the Launceston RSL Sub-Branch, 22 September 1983, VVA Papers, box 91; Bruce Ruxton to Dr Michael Barr, 6 August 1982, box 85.
35 For an account of the formation of the Association and a useful insight into the anger underpinning its formation, see 'Let's Finally Bring the Vietnam Veterans Home', *Debrief*, March, 1983, pp. 10–15. For other evidence of the Association's criticism of the Department, see VVA Press Release, 20 February 1983, box 81, and for a typical veteran letter complaining about his treatment, see N. Matthew to Senator Gietzelt, Minister for Veterans' Affairs, 5 November 1983, VVA Papers, box 91.

It trumpeted a 'newsflash – another side effect of exposure to Agent Orange ... evidence of itchy feet is found in 100% of the Central Office Library Staff'.[36]

Some of this may be isolated prejudice or misplaced humour. But in the climate of hostility surrounding relations between the department and veterans, it crystallised an image of a bureaucracy insensitive, even antagonistic, to the needs of ex-servicemen and women. Such an image proved hard to shake, and the attempts of departmental officers to reassure veterans fell on stony ground. In 1983, for example, Derek Volker, Secretary of the department, was at pains to assure veterans that the department had a very good record in granting claims for pensions to veterans of Vietnam: one-third of all claims for pensions on the basis of exposure to chemicals had been accepted by the Repatriation Board; almost half of the rejections appealed were accepted by the Appeals Board; and all of those who went even further and appealed to the Repatriation Review Tribunal were granted. The VVA response to Volker's earnest defence gives us an important insight into the Association's antagonism to the repatriation system. On one level, the criticisms of the insensitivity, rudeness, and antagonism of repatriation officers were hardly new. Such allegations had been around for many years, and veterans of earlier wars were as active in their condemnation of the department as those from Vietnam. All veterans resented the veiled hints that they were 'bludgers', and the atmosphere of interrogation and trial that structured their dealings with the department. Finally, the whole process of rejecting claims and then granting many of them on appeal seems to have affected veterans of all wars.

Embedded in this structure were charity mentalities, seeking to place hurdles in the way of claimants so that only the 'deserving' received benefits. This was the source of much complaint, and the RSL was ever vigilant in opposing these procedures to ensure that men got their pensions as a right rather than an act of benevolence. But if the RSL was there to press home these criticisms, why did an association of Vietnam veterans feel the need to replicate these efforts? Here we can begin to glimpse the motivations of the VVA. It was not the case that Vietnam veterans were being denied pensions. On the contrary, as Volker made clear, many, even those claiming exposure to chemicals, received them. Although some claims were initially rejected by the Board, if veterans were prepared to pursue all the avenues of appeal their chances of success were great. It was not the denial of pensions that angered the Association but the belief that they were being granted for the wrong reasons. The department was granting pensions for many reasons, but not explicitly for herbicide exposure. The Association, unlike the League, did not just want more generous pension provisions or greater rates of success in claims; it also wanted an admission, a statement of fact, that Vietnam veterans had

---

36 *Repat Chat*, June 1980. See also Victorian Ombudsman, Report on Complaint by Vietnam Veterans' Association on Defective Administration of Claims, 1983. For the views of Dr Rose, see Senate Standing Committee on Science and the Environment, *Pesticides and the Health of Australian Vietnam Veterans*, AGPS, Canberra, 1982, p. 126.

suffered as a consequence of contact with herbicides during service. This became the key plank of the Association's platform.[37]

What brought Vietnam veterans in the Association together was a shared history of problems. In late 1979, when the first gatherings of veterans met to discuss their grievances, they found that most of them had experienced or had veteran friends who suffered from a diverse range of complaints, such as anger, anxiety, depression, sleeplessness, moodiness, uncontrollable fits of rage, bouts of impotence, and difficulties adjusting to work or family life. A large number also seemed to have contracted cancer, particularly lymphomas – something that men in their thirties found difficult to comprehend. Finally, veterans complained that a large number of their children seemed to be suffering birth defects, while their brothers, sisters, and friends who had not served in Vietnam had normal children. It was not so much the existence of these complaints that brought these men together, but a shared conviction that there was a particular reason for these problems. They blamed exposure to toxic herbicides during service, especially 2,4,5-T and 2,4-D (Agent Orange). Their conviction arose from recent reports in the USA about the effects of herbicides on American veterans. From 1964 until 1970, in Operation Ranch Hand, Agent Orange and other herbicides had been used in large quantities by United States forces in an attempt to destroy the ground cover that shielded enemy forces. By the late 1960s there was a body of scientific evidence suggesting that exposure to herbicides containing dioxin (such as Agent Orange) caused birth defects in mice. Other evidence increased public and scientific concern. In the 1960s and 1970s, studies of workers in herbicide factories and of families in rural districts exposed to herbicide spraying suggested a link to cancer and birth defects.

Despite this evidence, a connection between herbicides and the health problems of veterans was not made until 1978. Sometime in 1977 Maude de Victor, a benefits counsellor with the Veterans' Affairs Department in Chicago, met a veteran who claimed his cancer was caused by Agent Orange. She was intrigued, and began to ask other ill veterans about their contact with herbicides. She found most recalled coming in contact with Agent Orange. In 1978 she published the statistics on this link but was largely ignored by the department. A few months later a local television station ran a story on her assertion. Soon after, Paul Reutershan, a veteran with terminal cancer, contacted Edward Gorman, a personal injury lawyer in Long Island, New York, seeking representation to pursue compensation from chemical companies for his illness. He died later that year, but Gorman continued the case on the behalf of Reutershan's family, who later formed the Agent Orange Victims International Organisation. The efforts of veterans themselves to gain acknowledgement of the role of herbicides in their problems met with a frosty reception, both from established veterans' organisations and the Veterans'

---

37 *Australian*, 26–27 February 1983.

administration. These veterans formed the Vietnam Veterans Association of America and began to seek compensation in the courts. So began the long history of legal battles over Agent Orange.[38]

The experience of American veterans struck a chord. Australian veterans convinced that their problems arose from exposure to herbicides established the Vietnam Veterans' Association of Australia in 1980. Colin Simpson was an early participant, and he became the case the Association hoped would establish a precedent for various illnesses arising from Agent Orange exposure being war-caused. Federal Labor Party politician, Clyde Holding, attended some of these early meetings. Holding had opposed conscription for the war but now found himself convinced of 'the intrinsic merit of the veterans' case'. He urged the ALP to adopt the Agent Orange case, declaring the VVA 'the single most dynamic political grouping within the RSL'. Outside Parliament, other voices in support of the Vietnam veteran case began to be heard. In 1980 a controversial book by journalists John Dux and P.J. Young surveyed the available scientific literature on herbicides and illness and concluded that 'the weight of evidence ... runs heavily against Agent Orange'. In another popular account, social scientist Jock McCulloch argued that a conspiracy of political and commercial interests was acting to suppress information about the effects of dioxins. The new Association proved remarkably adept at monitoring and disseminating the scientific research that proved a link between herbicides and ill health. Increasing media focus on their claims fuelled scientific interest in herbicides. Scientists keen to make their mark set about testing the supposed links; some finding a connection, others not.[39]

An appreciation of the escalating media interest in the veteran cause is vital for any understanding of the Agent Orange controversy. Leading members of the Association, such as Holt McMinn and Phill Thompson, proved to be skilled users of news media, releasing astute press statements, appearing in various news forums to argue their case, encouraging others to argue for them, and stirring controversy by criticising governments, bureaucrats, and the RSL. This was grist to the media mill. Throughout the 1980s the Association was able to feed the media, which in turn played a significant role in shaping popular perceptions. Headlines such as 'Orange Reaps Bitter Harvest for Vets', 'Poisons Linked to Deformed Babies', 'The Survivor who Became a Victim', 'War Vets Betrayed by Government', and 'Battling the Black Legacy of Vietnam' were obviously more dramatic and appealing than the sporadic attempts to report the other side of the story, which were diminished

---

38 See P. H. Schuck, *Agent Orange on Trial: Mass Toxic Disasters in the Courts*, Belknap Press, Cambridge, Mass., 1986.
39 For example 'Swedish Study links 2,4,5-T with Cancer', *Canberra Times*, 8 April 1981. See also J. Dux and P. J. Young, *Agent Orange: The Bitter Harvest*, Hodder & Stoughton, Sydney, 1980, p. 271; J. McCulloch, *The Politics of Agent Orange: The Australian Experience*, Heinemann, Melbourne, 1984. For Holding's views, see Clyde Holding to Bill Hayden, 20 March 1980, VVA Papers, box 78.

in appeal by such headers as '2,4,5-T One of the Safest' or 'Defoliants Protected Troops'. The media does not just produce or reflect; it also consumes, and organisations prepared to provide a steady diet of appealing material can command a disproportionate share of media coverage. The VVA understood this and assiduously cultivated its media contacts, writing to congratulate sympathetic journalists, such as Fia Cumming, on their 'good investigations'. As a consequence, the plight of the Vietnam veterans captured popular sympathies. Coverage of the veterans' cause attracted the attention of film-makers and musicians. Bill Bennett directed a feature movie, *A Street to Die*, which closely paralleled the facts of the Colin Simpson case. Similarly, the rock group Redgum wrote a song about Vietnam, 'I was Only Nineteen', which became a national success in 1983 (although it may not have been so popular had it retained its original title and chorus line 'a walk in the light green').[40]

Agent Orange marked an important shift in the media response to repatriation. In the early 1970s the Repatriation Commission was widely criticised for encouraging welfare dependence and fraud. A decade later the media focus was still on corruption, but now it was a government conspiracy to hide the truth of Agent Orange and unjustly deprive innocent victims of the compensation that was their due. Here was an archetypal media story: the battlers done over by 'big brother', the duplicity of a modern government that sacrificed the health of soldiers despite knowing the dangers, and underpinning all this, the whiff of secrecy and cover-up that pervaded media reports. But perhaps it was not just the elements of the conventional good story that framed this tragedy. Media sympathy for veterans reflected a broader shift in popular perception. In American and Australian novels, plays, stories, and films of the late 1970s and early 1980s, the Vietnam War was increasingly seen as folly: not only unnecessary, but also pointless, wasteful, and mad. Soldiers and veterans of the war were represented as pawns in the hands of unsympathetic governments, trained to be psychopaths and scarred by the horrors of their experience. Here was a powerful vehicle for expressing profound popular cynicism about political institutions. And veterans claiming ill health due to herbicides could become the quintessential victims.

The vocal Vietnam veterans campaign and its command of public sympathies embarrassed the Department of Veterans' Affairs and the Fraser government. Their denial of any link between Agent Orange and the poor health of veterans fostered an image of an uncaring government with something to hide. The Association seemed to be winning the media debate, and in an effort to placate public opinion, the government sponsored various inquiries into the links between herbicide exposure and veteran health – mortality studies, birth defect surveys, and Senate inquiries – all of which provided little substantiation of the Association's

---

40 *Australian*, 26 December 1979, 5 February 1981, 19 April 1982; *Sun Herald*, 10 May 1981; *Canberra Times*, 25 May 1985; *Sun Pictorial*, 14 November 1979; Adelaide *Advertiser*, 31 March 1981. See also Malcolm Barr to Fia Cumming, n.d., VVA Papers, box 85.

assertions.[41] The Association forcefully countered with its own studies and expert opinion, which purported to demonstrate a positive link. Finally, in 1983 the new Hawke Labor government, fulfilling an election promise, but against the advice of the RSL, instituted a Royal Commission of Inquiry into the effects of Agent Orange on veterans. The Evatt Royal Commission provided a forum for different interest groups to fight out their case: Vietnam veterans (whose legal costs were funded by the government) pressing for a recognition of their plight; the RSL anxiously protecting the benefit of the doubt clauses to ensure continued liberal treatment of all pension applicants; the scientists proclaiming their professional expertise; the Department of Veterans' Affairs keen to ensure that precedents were not established that would cripple the entire repatriation system; the government concerned to avoid political fallout; and the chemical companies determined to avoid costly compensation claims.

The story of the Evatt Royal Commission has been well told elsewhere. Its consequences for veterans, however, were far from satisfying. On the one hand, images of a small band of veterans, led by the resolute Phill Thompson (who was forced to deliver the veterans' closing arguments after legal counsel refused to act when funding ran out), battling the corporate giants of Monsanto and other chemical companies invested the battle with a 'David and Goliath' dimension that captured public sympathies. On the other hand, the RSL was partly right: the push for a judicial commission was a tactical mistake on the part of the VVA because it meant that the medical evidence had to be subjected to a rigorous standard of proof. In effect, the veterans had to prove a direct correlation between exposure to herbicides and subsequent ill health and birth defects. This was much more than was required by repatriation tribunals, which operated on the basis of allowing veterans 'reasonable doubt'. And while sentiment may have disposed many to favour the veteran case, the limited scientific evidence at that time for a direct causal relationship did not withstand serious scrutiny. The increasingly desperate efforts of the veterans to defend their case in the face of the searching cross-examination of chemical company lawyers makes for painful reading. It is possible that the perceived unjustness of the treatment of the veterans at the commission contributed to the wave of public support for the 'Welcome Home' marches a few years later. In his 1985 report, Mr Justice Evatt declared 'Agent Orange is not guilty'.[42]

---

41 Some of these inquiries included R. MacLennan et al., *Case-Control Study of Congenital Anomalies and Vietnam Service*, AGPS, Canberra, 1983; Australian Veterans' Health Studies, *Pilot Study Report*, 4 vols, AGPS, Canberra, 1983; Senate Standing Committee on Science and the Environment, *Pesticides and the Health of Australian Vietnam Veterans: First Report*, AGPS, Canberra, 1982; Australian Veterans' Health Studies, *The Mortality Report*. Some of the critical research supporting the case of the veterans includes P. Hall & B. Selinger, 'Australian Infant Mortality from Congenital Abnormalities of the Central Nervous System: A Significant Increase in Time', *Chemistry in Australia*, vol. 47, no. 10, 1980, pp. 420–2.
42 See Royal Commission on the Use and Effects of Chemical Agents on Australian Personnel in Vietnam, Report, 9 vols, AGPS, Canberra, 1985. The quote from Evatt is from vol. 8, ch. 15, p.

This was not the end of the story. The VVA bitterly condemned the commission report, claiming that it contained 'serious errors of fact, misstatements, omissions and lacked an appreciation of biological principles as well as common sense'. Moreover, large sections of it seemed to quote and paraphrase the submissions of the chemical companies. To veterans, this was evidence of bias, and they vowed to continue their campaign. And they did so, although tragically Phill Thompson, the stalwart of the veteran campaign, stricken with cancer, committed suicide a year after the report was handed down. In 1986 the Minister for Veterans' Affairs, Senator Arthur Gietzelt, assured the Association that the government 'rejected the language in which much of the report was couched' and promised to investigate their claims of bias. But he also rejected arguments that the commission report would prejudice claims for pensions. He urged Association members to examine the practices of the department, where they would see liberal tribunals sympathetic to their plight.[43]

The subsequent history of pension decisions supports Gietzelt's optimism. Many Vietnam veterans have had their legitimate claims for a pension accepted by repatriation tribunals. Moreover, in recent years a number of particular illnesses, notably some cancers, have been accepted by these tribunals as possibly caused by Agent Orange and hence service related. This might appear to be a rebuttal of the Royal Commission's findings, and news reports have been anxious to report these decisions as 'a bitter victory' over the commission, but in fact, they reflect the different standard of proof applicable in repatriation determinations: they now only require a 'reasonable hypothesis', while the Royal Commission had to determine whether a positive causal relation existed.[44] Moreover, the findings of the Commission did not stifle research into herbicides and birth defects. There have been a number of major international studies since that have confirmed a strong correlation between herbicides and birth defects.[45] And in 1991, the US Congress authorised the Department of Veterans' Affairs to presume a number of medical conditions as due to Agent Orange exposure.[46] While this was too late for veterans like Colin Simpson and Phill Thompson it has provided a measure of comfort for many of those who devoted their energies to the Agent Orange campaign.

While the cut and thrust of the commission proceedings and their consequences are fascinating, a more fundamental and intriguing question looms. Why was it

---

38. See also E B. Smith's chapters in O'Keefe & Smith, *Medicine at War*, pp. 283–363; Lloyd & Rees, *The Last Shilling*, pp. 355–79.
43 Address by Senator Gietzelt to Seventh Annual Congress of the VVA, 3 May 1986, VVA Papers, box 89. For Association criticisms of the Royal Commission report, see VVA Press Release, 26 November 1985, box 87; *Canberra Times*, 25 November 1985.
44 See, for example, *Sydney Morning Herald*, 8 October 1994.
45 For example, Anh D. Ngo, Richard Taylor, Christine L. Roberts, Tuan V. Nguyen, "Association between Agent Orange and birth defects: systematic review and meta-analysis". *International Journal of Epidemiology*, vol. 35 no. 5, 2006, pp. 1220–30.
46 'Agent Orange – Office of Public Health and Environmental Hazards', Department of Veterans' Affairs, 1991.

necessary to blame Agent Orange when access to pensions was, by any criterion, liberal? Even if the department's tribunals rejected Agent Orange as the cause, many of those seeking pensions for chemical exposure were granted them on other grounds. Why belabour the point if it had little material effect? This obviously puzzled the RSL, exacerbating tensions between the two organisations. But it did matter to the VVA.

The Association doggedly pursued their campaign hoping to establish two principles in the repatriation system. The first was that children of servicemen could be casualties of war. The veterans' argument that their children suffered birth defects as a consequence of exposure to herbicides was an extension of existing repatriation concepts of compensation for war-caused disability. Wives and children had long benefited from war pensions, but these were forms of compensation for the loss of a breadwinner. The Vietnam veterans were seeking to have the actual physical and mental disabilities of their children recognised as war caused. But the issue of defects was too ambiguous to allow them simply to be included among pensionable disabilities. If the veterans' claim had been accepted, there would have been no reason to draw the line at their children. Grandchildren and great grandchildren could have had legitimate claims, and this would have implied that the descendants of veterans were entitled to compensation in their own right, not as an addition to a veteran's pension, perhaps long after the original pensioner had died. This was a nightmarish prospect for governments, bureaucrats, and taxpayers anxious to reign in the burgeoning costs of repatriation. If the numerous birth defect studies had established a positive link between herbicide exposure and hereditary disability, there might have been no legal necessity to compensate them (as pensions were specifically for servicemen and women, or the families of deceased personnel), but there might have been a moral obligation to do so. Such possibilities were side-stepped by the Royal Commission's conclusion that there was no relation between exposure and an increased incidence of birth defects.

The second, and more recondite, challenge of the Association concerned veterans themselves. Many Vietnam veterans returned suffering from myriad symptoms of anxiety and depression. This was not unusual. For returned servicemen of the First World War these were often ascribed to shell-shock or war neurosis, while for those returning from the Second World War, such symptoms were classified as combat exhaustion or battle fatigue. Similar symptoms in Vietnam veterans were usually diagnosed as post-traumatic stress disorder. A whole corpus of medical discourse, beginning with the early theories of C.S. Myers on war hysteria, served to position these behaviours as psychological reactions to modern warfare. There were differences of opinion over the precise psychological mechanisms involved, the characteristic conditions of particular wars, the different timings of breakdown, and the best forms of treatment. But what was common to all these discussions, at least since 1915, was the belief that these behaviours and symptoms were psychological reactions to combat.

Repatriation authorities had accepted psychological disabilities as pensionable. Veterans often claimed that they felt belittled by the attitude of departmental medical officers when seeking pensions for shell-shock or war neurosis. The implication of malingering permeated these proceedings. But officially, psychiatrists, senior officers of the department, and politicians were firm in their conviction that such conditions were war-caused and rightly pensionable. Vietnam veterans had similar complaints about the attitudes of medical officers, but they were no less entitled to pensions, and repatriation authorities continued to assert their entitlement. Indeed, there was much official sympathy for the plight of Vietnam veterans and their families ravaged by the effects of traumatic shock. The fact that Vietnam veterans suffered similar problems to earlier returned men and women only further justified their claims. This was the view of the RSL. In 1983 William Keys wrote to Mr Justice Evatt arguing 'that many of the sorts of problems ... among Vietnam veterans are typical problems which have occurred with other groups of ex-service personnel ... war is a stressful and personally damaging activity'. Derek Volker of the department agreed. For Volker there was a 'decided prevalence' of neuropsychiatric conditions among 'the veterans of all wars', and these were reactions 'to the stress of battle'. Keys and Volker were not disputing the reality of anxiety and depression. On the contrary, they were affirming it, giving it a history, and thus incorporating it into the domain of repatriation. Similarly, when challenged about Agent Orange, Senator Tony Messner, Minister for Veterans' Affairs in 1981, had no difficulty in acknowledging that veterans were suffering from serious and undoubtedly pensionable problems, but they were problems arising from war trauma.[47]

For the VVA it was not pensions that were at issue but the whole domain of psychological explanation that governed repatriation decisions. Time and again they disputed the psychology of stress, trauma, and neurosis. They set themselves in opposition to this long history of psychological debate. Instead they favoured a discourse of physical disorder. For these veterans, many of the symptoms of so-called post-traumatic stress were more appropriately attributed to the effects of herbicide exposure. For the Association, many veteran problems were the consequence of 'toxic brain dysfunction', the symptoms of which were 'similar to those of Vietnam post-traumatic stress reaction'. Although not entirely opposed to psychological approaches – indeed it supported the establishment of special counselling services for Vietnam veterans to ease their readjustment to civilian life – the Association believed the majority of veterans were not receiving the correct diagnosis. In their view, this dysfunction arose from chemicals, and the refusal of the department to recognise this meant that many veterans were receiving the 'wrong treatment'. Officials of the Association stressed the need to 'challenge the orthodox psychiatric assumption of the Department of Veterans' Affairs'. And when departmental officers sought to refute such assertions by reaffirming the war

---

47   William Keys to Justice Evatt, 25 November 1983, VVA Papers, box 88; Address by Derek Volker to VVA Conference, 29 May 1982, box 89; *Sydney Morning Herald*, 9 July 1981.

stress argument, the Association rejected such rebuttals as further evidence of the government's refusal to accept the chemical theory.[48]

The idea of 'toxic brain dysfunction' came from obscure European sources and did not command the support of most experts in the field. But this is not about the rights or wrongs of such research but why the Association embraced the chemical explanation despite the weight of contrary opinion? The rebuttal of the psychological argument, in part, seems to represent a refusal to accept its causal mechanisms. At the heart of most psychological theories of war, whether in Freudian or behaviourist guise, was an assumption that there was some inherent weakness in the individual that made him or her more vulnerable to stress. The VVA was refusing this implication, arguing instead that the cause of veterans' problems lay outside themselves, in chemicals and their toxic effects. More than any other veteran group, the Association refused to drink the acidic draught of the psychological theory, no matter how useful it had been for obtaining benefits. Principle mattered more than outcome.

Many Vietnam veterans believed their war had been different. Although they had fought bravely, they had confronted not only a style of warfare unknown to other veterans, but also an insidious new weapon (herbicides), which through no fault of their own, wreaked havoc on their post-war lives. We may doubt the uniqueness of this war and its effects on returned men and women, but we cannot doubt the corrosive effects of the image of Vietnam. Vietnam veterans were mourning their exclusion from the legend. The scars of supposed community neglect and the painful aura of defeat that tainted their efforts were profound. In rejecting psychological explanations, the veterans were proclaiming not only their innocence, but also their claim to be victims of war. They were not the psychopathic failures of popular myth but men who had fought bravely and bore the marks of their sacrifice. By disavowing stress reactions, they were asserting their right to be accepted as true members of the Anzac family. As Phill Thompson argued, 'they never lost a battle and discharged their duty as well and as honourably as their fathers, and their fathers before them'.[49]

Australians have accepted this right. In the 'Welcome Home' marches, and in the dedication of a special memorial to the Vietnam forces in Canberra, there was a long overdue effort to incorporate these men and women into the Anzac legend. In dedicating the new memorial in October 1992, Brigadier Colin Kahn, himself a veteran of Vietnam, salved some of the bitter wounds of this conflict:

---

48 See 'Let's Finally Bring the Vietnam Veteran Home'; National Welfare Adviser of the VVA to Phill Thompson, 25 March 1981, and Press Release on Claims of Dr Griffith Spragg, 13 October 1982, VVA Papers, box 78.
49 Phill Thompson, Speech Opening the Queensland Vietnam Veterans' Counselling Centre, 21 July 1982, VVA Papers, box 81.

> This is the dawning of a highly significant and memorable day in Australia's military history, and in particular in the history of the war in Vietnam ... In veterans, it will today evoke sadness, pride and humility; in the future it will remind society of Australians' sacrifice in war which personally touched so few, but evoked such strong feelings in so many. It will help the nation to understand the value of the Vietnam veteran's service ... It will help, above all, to ensure that those who died, rest higher, than any achievement that we who remain behind, may have attained ... Now, 20 years after the war, at this the most hallowed of all shrines throughout the country for our war dead, we put further to rest the remaining phantoms from which some of our colleagues and next of kin still suffer.[50]

Many individual veterans still bear the physical and psychological scars of service. Nor has the VVA entirely abandoned its sense of grievance at the refusal of governments to acknowledge their claims. But the oceans of discontent are calmer. The symbols of connection have, in some sense, been forged, uniting Australian veterans of all wars.

---

50 Brigadier Colin Kahn, 'Reflections: Dedication of the Australian Vietnam Veterans' National Memorial, Canberra', *Journal of the Australian War Memorial*, no. 22, April 1993, pp. 42–3.

Epilogue

Canberra is the right place for a memorial. It has that sense of seasons, redolent of life, death, and renewal, that lies at the heart of war and its remembrance. Memorials are not only a means of acknowledging the sacrifice of those who served, but also our way of making the war dead live again in the hearts of those who survive. One of the joys of researching this book has been the opportunity to work at the Australian War Memorial in Canberra. In my lunch breaks I often used to wander down the hill to Anzac Avenue. Autumn was a favourite time: clear skies, brilliant sunshine, just a hint of approaching winter, a mild chill on the breeze, the burnished reds and yellows of the leaves enticing the melancholy of remembrance. Like most daily visitors to the Avenue (in the 1990s), my attention was drawn to the Vietnam War Memorial. This was a war of recent memory. But I am also drawn to this memorial because it is different. Anzac Avenue is full of statuary to war, most of it conventional – soldiers, groups of soldiers, men on horseback – symbolising the transcendent nobility of those who sacrificed themselves for the national good. There are a few more abstract pieces, but even in their abstractness they have the two-dimensional erectness of more traditional symbols.

In shape, size, and orientation, it is hard not to escape the conclusion that these forms are there to affirm a certain type of manly endeavour: not just to mourn loss, but also to commemorate the glory of sacrifice. The War Memorial precinct as a whole is riddled with these contrasting imperatives: the melancholy remembering spaces – the Court of Honour, the Pool of Reflection, the Hall of Memory, the Stone of Remembrance, the eternal flame, and the Tomb of the Unknown Soldier – and the vigorous signifiers of glory, many of the museum exhibits, the four freedoms, and the numerous statues in the Avenue. The last link us to classical ideals of citizenship and polity. Here are our warriors, those who have created and perpetuated our civilisation, just as the warriors of other civilisations have done (although sadly we are yet to fully recognise the sacrifice of Australian Aboriginal and Torres Strait Island peoples in the defence of this, their land). One can see similar stone symbols in most parts of the world, and each is a challenge to future generations to carry the standard. But in the age of mass death in war, when democracy demands that all citizens (nowadays even women) be prepared to risk death in the defence of national ideals, the quantum of grief accompanying this sacrifice is potentially overwhelming. Memorials are a means, perhaps inevitably inadequate ones, of both grieving and celebrating these acts of sacrifice. What attracts me to the Vietnam Memorial is that it is an attempt to reconcile the commemorative with the contemplative, but in a way that harbours remembrance more than glory. There is something dissonant about this memorial – it echoes the Hall of Memory up the hill rather than the statuary in the Avenue.

Everyone must approach a memorial such as this with their own particular views and emotional baggage. But in shape and form the Vietnam Memorial seems to combine the thrusting potency of Greek stelae with the encircling of Celtic henges. The small brass plaque to one side presents the intention of the sculptor: 'such forms have always symbolised commemoration and contemplation and remain amongst the most durable and potent of our creation'. Inside the circle, words and an image act as reminders of 'the actual and hidden reality of war', while the purpose of the blank wall is 'to receive thoughts and emotions'. Above is a ring containing the names of all those who died. The explanatory plaque also suggests that the water surrounding the circle is a moat bridged by a ramp, conjuring an image of a castle keep, safe and protective. This allusion echoes war, but my sense is that it is much more a 'feminised' space of protection. In totality the memorial is overwhelmingly maternal, with the amniotic fluid of life flowing outwards, and with the names of the war dead returned to the neck of the womb. This may not be everyone's impression, but I sense that it is there for many. And what more appropriate symbol could there be for the Anzac sons and daughters of the Vietnam War: enveloped in a maternal embrace and at last returned to the nation. It provides welcome succour, not bombast, return rather than rejection.

On one of my walks down to the Vietnam Memorial I saw the usual small crowd, negotiating their way around and through the memorial, snapping pictures, reading inscriptions, pausing, looking, remembering. But nearby I was taken by some shadowy forms that seemed to be edging rather uncomfortably around the sides of the memorial, a little hesitant to enter. Finally, they did, glanced nervously around, and quickly departed. They were two soldiers. A little later, as I was returning to the Research Centre, I noticed these young men again, now gazing in awe at the striking pose of the three soldiers, cast in bronze, further up the hill. This is a far more conventional representation: erect and vigorous soldiers, gigantic in their nobility, triumphant in their monumentalism. These young men lingered on each piece of equipment, touching the bronze in nervous excitement, lost in the reverie of their own imaginings of combat. The unsettling maternal embrace of the Vietnam Memorial had been left behind for something more paternal, manly, and familiar. They were free of the memory of loss and lost in the imagining of glory.

I found this a disquieting scene. Perhaps memorials are as much about forgetting as remembering. Then again, maybe it is that memorials have to wrestle with different meanings embedded in the complex history of war, return, and remembrance. Memorials exist in an uneasy tension between the need to ease bereavement and the desire to inspire future generations. It is not something easily resolved. We celebrate the virtues of mateship, fortitude, stoicism, self-sacrifice, and initiative – the defining virtues of our Anzac tradition – but they are values that exclude others of equal worth. What of the virtues of tolerance, amelioration, and harmony? What of recognition for women's traditional contribution to nation-building through birth and nurturing, or of Aboriginal respect for the land? And lurking beneath the worthy Anzac tradition is a darker story of premature death, grief, the shattered lives of many who survived, and the emotional wounds inflicted on those to whom they returned. Why has nation come to be entwined with death? Can we have one without the other? Is one worth the other? Perhaps the challenge is to create a new polity without forgetting the old: to broaden our national values without losing the old and to find meaning in being Australian without suffering the futility of war and all its consequences. Or is willing sacrifice and the embrace of death for the collective the only way we can assure ourselves that where we live has any worth?

Select Bibliography

The range of archival, oral, manuscript, and printed sources that I used in this study in 1996 will be obvious in the footnotes. In addition, Australia has been singularly blessed with an excellent series of official histories of Australian involvement in war, originating with the magnificent work of C. E. W. Bean and continuing with admirable histories of the Second World War, the Korean War, and the South-East Asian conflicts. Those interested in specific aspects of repatriation could find no better starting point than the volumes on medical aspects of the First World War by A. G. Butler. The following is just a small selection of other relevant secondary readings that I found particularly useful. It is by no means comprehensive.

Adam-Smith, P., *Prisoners of War: From Gallipoli to Korea*, Viking, Melbourne, 1992.
—— *The Anzacs*, Penguin, Melbourne, 1991.
Andrews, E. M., *The Anzac Illusion: Anglo-Australian Relations during World War I*, CUP, Melbourne, 1993.
Barter, M., *Far Above Battle: The Experience and Memory of Australian Soldiers in War 1939–1945*, Allen & Unwin, Sydney, 1994.
Bassett, J., *Guns and Brooches: Australian Army Nursing from the Boer War to the Gulf War*, OUP, Melbourne, 1992.
Beaumont, J. (ed.), *Gull Force: Survival and Leadership in Captivity 1941–45*, Allen & Unwin, Sydney, 1988.
—— *Australia's War 1914–18*, Allen & Unwin, Sydney, 1995.
—— (ed.), *Australia's War 1939–45*, Allen & Unwin, Sydney, 1996.
Campbell, R., *Heroes and Lovers: A Question of National Identity*, Allen & Unwin, Sydney, 1989.
Cannadine, D., 'War and Death, Grief and Mourning in Modern Britain', in J. Whaley (ed.), *Mirrors of Mortality: Studies in the Social History of Death*, Europa Publications, London, 1981.
Cochrane, P., *Simpson and the Donkey: The Making of a Legend*, MUP, Melbourne, 1992.
Cooke, M. & Woollacott, A. (eds), *Gendering War Talk*, Princeton University Press, Princeton, NJ, 1993.
Cooper, H. M., Munich, A. A., & Squier, S. M. (eds), *Arms and the Woman: War, Gender and Literary Representation*, University of North Carolina Press, Chapel Hill, 1989.

Copp, T. & McAndrew, B., *Battle Exhaustion: Soldiers and Psychiatrists in the Canadian Army 1939-1945*, McGill-Queens University Press, Montreal, 1990.
Damousi, J. & Lake, M. (eds), *Gender and War: Australians at War in the Twentieth Century*, CUP, Melbourne, 1995.
Darian-Smith, K., *On the Home Front: Melbourne in Wartime 1939-45*, MUP, Melbourne, 1990.
Darian-Smith, K. & Hamilton, P. (eds), *Memory and History in Twentieth Century Australia*, OUP, Melbourne, 1994.
Daws, G., *Prisoners of the Japanese*, William Morrow, New York, 1994.
Ebury, S., *Weary: The Life of Sir Edward Dunlop*, Viking, Melbourne, 1994.
Eksteins, M., *The Rites of Spring: The Great War and the Birth of the Modern Age*, Anchor Books, New York, 1990.
Ellis, J., *The Sharp End of War: The Fighting Man in World War Two*, David and Charles, London, 1980.
Evans, R., *Loyalty and Disloyalty: Social Conflict on the Queensland Homefront 1914-18*, Allen & Unwin, Sydney, 1987.
Fry, K., 'Soldier Settlement and the Agrarian Myth after the First World War', *Labour History*, no. 48, May 1985, pp. 29-43.
Fussell, P., *The Great War and Modern Memory*, OUP, Oxford, 1975.
—— *Wartime: Understanding and Behavior in the Second World War*, OUP, Oxford, 1989.
Gammage, B., *The Broken Years: Australian Soldiers in the Great War*, Penguin, Melbourne, 1975.
Gerster, R., *Big-Noting: The Heroic Theme in Australian War Writing*, MUP, Melbourne, 1992.
Gregory, A., *The Silence of Memory: Armistice Day 1919-1946*, Berg, Oxford, 1994.
Grey, J., *A Military History of Australia*, CUP, Melbourne, 1990.
Grey, J. & Doyle, J. (eds), *Vietnam: War, Myth and Memory*, Allen & Unwin, Sydney, 1992.
Henning, P., *Doomed Battalion: Mateship and Leadership in War and Captivity*, Allen & Unwin, Sydney, 1995.
Higonnet, M., Jenson, J., Michel, S., & Weitz, M. (eds), *Behind the Lines: Gender and Two World Wars*, Yale University Press, New Haven, 1987.
Huggonson, D., 'Aboriginal Diggers of the 9th Brigade First AIF', *Journal of the Royal Australian Historical Society*, vol. 79, 1993, pts 3-4, pp. 214-23.
Hynes, S., *A War Imagined: The First World War and English Culture*, Collier Books, New York, 1990.
Inglis, K. S., 'The Anzac Tradition', *Meanjin*, no. 1, March 1965, pp. 25-44.
—— *C.E.W. Bean: Australian Historian*, UQP, St Lucia, 1970.
—— 'A Sacred Place: The Making of the Australian War Memorial', *War and Society*, vol. 3, no. 2, September 1985, pp. 99-126.
—— 'Entombing Unknown Soldiers', *Journal of the Australian War Memorial*, no. 23, October 1993, pp. 4-12.
Jackomos, A. & Powell, D., *Forgotten Heroes: Aborigines at War from the Somme to Vietnam*, Victoria Press, Melbourne, 1993.
Jeffords, S., *The Remasculinization of America: Gender and the Vietnam War*, Indiana University Press, Bloomington, 1989.
Keegan, J., *The Face of Battle*, Jonathon Cape, London, 1976.
—— *A History of Warfare*, Pimlico, London, 1993.
Koven, S., 'Remembering and Dismemberment: Crippled Children, Wounded Soldiers, and the Great War in Britain', *American Historical Review*, vol. 99, no. 4, October 1994, pp. 1167-202.
Kristianson, G. L., *The Politics of Patriotism: The Pressure Group Activities of the Returned Servicemen's League*, ANU Press, Canberra, 1966.
Laqueur, T., 'Memory and Naming in the Great War', in J. Gillis (ed.), *Commemorations: The Politics of National Identity*, Princeton University Press, Princeton, NJ, 1994.
Lake, M., *Limits of Hope: Soldier Settlement in Victoria 1915-38*, OUP, Melbourne, 1987.

Select Bibliography

—— 'Mission Impossible: How Men Gave Birth to the Australian Nation – Nationalism, Gender and Other Seminal Acts', *Gender and History*, vol. 4, no. 3, 1992, pp. 305–22.

Leed, E. J., *No Man's Land: Combat and Identity in World War I*, CUP, Cambridge, 1979.

Leys, R., 'Traumatic Cures: Shell Shock, Janet, and the Question of Memory', *Critical Inquiry*, vol. 20, no. 4, Summer 1994, pp. 623–62.

Lindstrom, R. G., Stress and Identity: Australian Soldiers During the First World War, MA thesis, University of Melbourne, 1985.

Lloyd, C. & Rees, J., *The Last Shilling: A History of Repatriation in Australia*, MUP, Melbourne, 1994.

Lyons, M., *Legacy: The First Fifty Years*, Lothian, Melbourne, 1978.

McHugh, S., *Minefields and Miniskirts: Australian Women and the Vietnam War*, Doubleday, Sydney, 1993.

McKernan, M., *The Australian People and the Great War*, Nelson, Melbourne, 1980.

—— *All In! Australia During the Second World War*, Nelson, Melbourne, 1983.

—— *Here is their Spirit: A History of the Australian War Memorial 1917–1990*, UQP, St Lucia, 1991.

McKernan, M. & Browne, M. (eds), *Australia: Two Centuries of War and Peace*, AWM and Allen & Unwin, Canberra, 1988.

Maddock, K. (ed.), *Memories of Vietnam*, Random House, Sydney, 1991.

Moffitt, A., *Project Kingfisher*, Angus & Robertson, Sydney, 1989.

Morton, D. & Wright, G., *Winning the Second Battle: Canadian Veterans and the Return to Civil Life 1915–30*, University of Toronto Press, Toronto, 1987.

Mosse, G. L., *Fallen Soldiers: Reshaping the Memory of the World Wars*, OUP, New York, 1990.

Nelson, H., *Prisoners of War: Australians Under Nippon*, ABC Books, Sydney, 1985.

Nelson, H. and McCormack, G. (eds), *The Burma-Thailand Railway*, Allen & Unwin, Sydney, 1993.

O'Keefe, B., 'Butler's Medical Histories', *Journal of the Australian War Memorial*, no. 12, April 1988, pp. 25–34.

Pemberton, G. (ed.), *Vietnam Remembered*, Weldon Publishing, Sydney, 1990.

Pierce, P., Grey, J. & Doyle, J. (eds), *Vietnam Days: Australia and the Impact of Vietnam*, Penguin, Melbourne, 1991.

Powell, J. M., 'The Debt of Honour: Soldier Settlement in the Dominions 1915–1940', *Journal of Australian Studies*, no. 8, June 1981, pp. 64–87.

Pryor, L. J., The Origins of Australia's Repatriation Policy, MA thesis, University of Melbourne, 1932.

Robson, L. L., *The First AIF: A Study of its Recruitment 1914–1918*, MUP, Melbourne, 1982.

Roe, J. (ed.), *Social Policy in Australia: Some Perspectives 1901–1975*, Cassell, Sydney, 1976.

—— 'Chivalry and Social Policy in the Antipodes', *Historical Studies*, vol. 22, no. 88, April 1987, pp. 395–410.

Roe, M., 'Comment on the Digger Tradition', *Meanjin*, no. 3, 1965, pp. 357–8.

—— 'C.E.W. Bean: Progressive and Nationalist', *Veritas*, vol. 3, no. 1, 1980, pp. 1–9.

—— *Nine Australian Progressives: Vitalism in Bourgeois Social Thought 1890–1960*, UQP, St Lucia, 1984.

Ross, J., *The Myth of the Digger: The Australian Soldier in Two World Wars*, Hale & Iremonger, Sydney, 1985.

Sekuless, P. & Rees, J., *Lest We Forget: The History of the Returned Services League 1916–1986*, Rigby, Sydney, 1986.

Serle, G., 'The Digger Tradition and Australian Nationalism', *Meanjin*, vol. 24, no. 2, June 1965, pp. 149–58.

Skocpol, T., *Protecting Soldiers and Mothers: The Political Origins of Social Policy in the United States*, Harvard University Press, Cambridge, MA, 1988.

Smallwood, R., *Hard to Go Bung: World War II Soldier Settlement in Victoria 1945–1962*, Hyland House, Melbourne, 1992.

Smart, J. & Wood, T. (eds), *An Anzac Muster: War and Society in Australia and New Zealand 1914–18 and 1939–45*, Monash Publications in History, no. 14, Monash University, Melbourne, 1992.

Thomson, A., *Anzac Memories: Living with the Legend*, OUP, Melbourne, 1994.
Throssell, R., *My Father's Son*, Mandarin, Melbourne, 1990.
Wall, D., *Sandakan Under Nippon: The Last March*, self-published, Sydney, 1988.
Wall, R. & Winter, J. (eds), *The Upheaval of War: Family, Work and Welfare in Europe 1914-1918*, CUP, Cambridge, 1988.
Whalen, R., *Bitter Wounds: German Victims of the Great War 1914-39*, Cornell University Press, Ithaca, 1984.
Wheeler, L., 'War, Women and Welfare', in R. Kennedy (ed.), *Australian Welfare: Historical Sociology*, Macmillan, Melbourne, 1989, pp. 172-96.
White, R., 'Motives for Joining Up: Self-Sacrifice, Self-Interest and Social Class 1914-18', *Journal of the Australian War Memorial*, no. 9, 1986, pp. 3-16.
—— 'The Soldier as Tourist: The Australian Experience of the Great War', *War and Society*, vol. 5, no. 1, May 1987, pp. 63-77.
Wilcox, C. (ed.), *The Great War: Gain and Losses – Anzac and Empire*, AWM & ANU, Canberra, 1995.
Williams, J. F., *The Quarantined Culture: Australian Reaction to Modernism 1913-1939*, CUP, Melbourne, 1995.
Winter, J., *Sites of Memory, Sites of Mourning: The Great War in European Cultural History*, CUP, Cambridge, 1995.

Index

Aboriginal peoples *see* Indigenous Australians
Abraham, Karl 161
Adam-Smith, Patsy 221, 222
Adelaide 4
Adey, J. K. 163
Africa 5–6, 68
Agent Orange 239–240, 247, 257, 258–264
Agent Orange Victims International Organisation 258
AIF 3–5, 9, 12, 27, 105
AIF Education Service 3, 105, 181, 198
Alamein 70
alcoholism *see* drinking
Alexander, David 243
Alice Springs 55
All for Australia League 62
ALP *see* Australian Labor Party
American Legion 53
American Veterans' Association 53
anti-war protest 8, 16, 241
anxiety 146, 152, 155–157, 167, 168, 176, 207, 227, 244, 253, 258, 263
Anzac Day 9, 40, 51, 67, 69, 71, 250
Anzac legend 10, 23, 33, 43–50, 69, 71, 102, 153, 215, 247
Ardill-Brice, Katie 207
Armistice Day 52, 67
Armistice 3, 60, 67
Arneil, Stan 219, 221, 223
artificial limbs 81, 85, 119
As You Were 17
Ashburner, Major J. V. 155
Ashby, Hal 249
Ashford, William 119

Ashmead-Bartlett, Ellis 39, 42
Asia 5, 6, 213, 215, 217, 218
Assessment Appeals Tribunal 84
Atkinson, Meredith 2
Aussie 3, 32
Australian 247
Australian Imperial Forces
Australian Labor Party 8, 13, 54, 59, 65, 78, 86, 92, 256, 259, 261
Australian Legion of Ex-Servicemen and Women 52
Australian War Memorial 9, 21, 43, 69, 267–269
Australian Woman's Mirror 168, 182, 198
Australian Women's Weekly 182

Baillieu, W. L. 76, 80, 206
Ballarat 36
barbed-wire syndrome 227
Barbusse, Henri 39
Bartlett, F. C. 158
Barwick, Sir Garfield 115
Bathurst 45
Bayonet 97
Bean, C. E. W. 9, 10, 23, 32, 37, 40, 45–50, 71
Beaumont, Joan 215, 222
Bedford, Randolf 49, 57
Beebe, Gilbert 230
benefit of doubt 115, 229; *see also* pensions
Benjamin, Zoe 210
Bennett, Bill 260
Berry, R. J. A. 160
birth defects 239, 258, 261–263; *see also* Agent Orange
Bone, Muirhead 39

Bonython, John Langdon 76
Borneo 50, 235, 246, 250
Bostock, John 164, 173
Bourne, Peter 248
Bowles, Leslie 38
Boyd, Martin 19
Braddon, Russell 217, 219–221, 222
Brady, E. J. 121, 123, 124
Brennan, Christopher 42
Bridgetown 73
Brisbane 5, 6, 61, 241, 245
Britain 2, 9, 13, 24, 33, 39, 41, 47, 57, 75, 78, 79, 100, 103, 112, 122, 153, 217, 228, 235
British Legion 53
British Medical Journal 226
Brookes, Norman 80
Broughton Hall Psychiatric Clinic 163, 172
Bruce, Stanley Melbourne 107
Bulletin 23, 41, 193
Bundoora Hospital 172
Burchill, Elizabeth 21, 22
burials 33–35
Burma-Thailand Railway 30, 218, 223
burnt-out soldier 96
bushman 4, 41
Butler, A. G. 14, 26, 31, 48, 103, 112, 118, 152–156, 158, 172–174, 175, 178
Buxton, Frank 250
Buxton, G. L. 143

Cairns, Jim 8
Callan Park Mental Hospital 29, 158
Calwell, Arthur 8
Campbell, Norman 11
Canada 2, 67, 68, 75, 96, 99–103, 100, 174, 228
Canadian Legion 53
Canberra 70, 238, 265
Canberra Times 252
cancer 96, 114, 116, 229, 232, 239, 258, 262
cancer register 239
Carroll, John 243
casualties 24, 24, 32, 68, 78, 145, 153–155, 167, 169, 235, 236, 263; *see also* mortality, wounds
casualty stations 10, 150, 154
Catholics 13, 57
Cavill, Harold 59, 192
Chaney, Fred 89
Change Over 18
Changi 213, 221
charity 11, 80–84, 90, 93, 103–104, 118, 126, 132, 257

Chauvel, Charles 19
Chifley, Ben 82, 86, 228
children 22, 79, 85, 93–94, 99, 101, 133, 202–210, 239, 254, 258, 263
Children's Education Scheme 205
Children's Health Bureaus 207, 208
Chisholm, Ann 80
Cimino, Michael 249
cinema *see* films
citizenship 41, 55, 63, 87
civilisation 77, 121, 134, 164, 180
Clayton, William Shaw 189
Cleary, Jon 195, 216
Coates, A. E. 225
Cold War 235
Cole, G. D. H. 2
Collett, H. B. 64
Collie, Sir John 149
combat 6–8, 21–24, 27–29, 31, 46–48, 78, 105, 147, 169, 195, 214, 236
combat fatigue 7, 145, 149, 155, 158, 168, 228, 237, 253, 263; *see also* shell-shock
commemoration 33–39, 42, 52, 67, 69, 72, 214; *see also* war memorials
Commonwealth Rehabilitation Training Scheme 82, 99
communism 235
Concord Repatriation Hospital 117
conscription 10, 12, 35, 57, 59, 59, 65, 245, 246
convicts 49
Coombs, H. C. 82
Cooper, E. J. 166
Coppola, Francis Ford 249
Cossington-Smith, Grace 45
Country Women's Association 73
Courier Mail 8
Courtney, C. A. 116–117, 173–174
Craiglockhart Hospital 159
crime 49, 200–202, 247
Crowley, Grace 45
Culverhouse, F. V. 10
Cumming, Fia 260
Cunningham, K. S. 164
Curtin, John 86
Cusack, Dymphna 195

Dane, Paul 163
Dark, Eleanor 45
Darwin 6, 68
Davison, Frank Dalby 42
Daws, Gavin 222

Index

Dawson, W. S. 166
Defence, Department of 10, 83, 112, 202
Dellit, Bruce 37
demobilisation 2–3, 7, 61, 75, 112, 172
democracy 35, 41, 60–61, 268
Dennis, C. J. 42
dependence 23, 87, 104–106, 108–109; *see also* charity, masculinity
Depression, Great 25, 37, 64, 94, 96
Derham, A. P. 207–209, 227
digger 3, 19, 23, 32, 48, 51, 62, 69, 77, 181–182, 192
Diggers' Association 54, 255
disabilities 27, 28, 95, 107, 189–190, 202, 228–231; *see also* rehabilitation, repatriation
divorce 28, 200–201, 254
dole bludgers 11
domestic violence 199, 201–203, 247
Doyle, Sir Arthur Conan 70
drinking 3, 55, 72, 248, 253, 254
Duckboard 63, 97
Dunlop, Sir Edward 'Weary' 30, 219–220, 224–225, 227–229, 233
Dunn, Carol 239
Dux, John 259
Dyson, Will 43

Ebury, Sue 220
Edwards. A. T. 163
Eldershaw, M. Barnard 45
Ellery, Reg 163, 183
Elliot, Brigadier-General Pompey 105
Ellis, Havelock 162
Elmore, Charles 70
Empire 5, 13, 40, 40, 57–58, 80, 82, 91, 122, 131, 150
employment preference 14, 36, 65, 82, 90–92, 180
enlistment 111–112
Entitlement Appeals Tribunal 84; *see also* Repatriation Commission
Esson, Loius 44
eugenics 164, 206
Europe 3, 5, 39, 42, 44–45, 62, 68, 168, 213, 215, 242; *see also* France, Germany, Italy
Evatt, H. V. 113
Evatt Royal Commission 261
Ex-Prisoners of War and Relatives' Association 214
Ex-Prisoners of War Association 214, 228

families 12, 29, 32, 71, 130, 134–135, 143, 180, 192, 199–210, 213, 231, 249, 253, 255; *see also* children, fathers, home, marriage
fascism 47
fathers 204–210
femininity 21, 25, 134, 157, 268
feminism 42, 48, 57, 242
Ferenczi, Sándor 161
Ferguson, Helen Munro *see* Munro Ferguson, Helen
Ferguson, Patricia 22
films 109, 184, 190, 215, 249, 260
Financial Review 88
First World War 2, 6, 10, 12–15, 24, 26–29, 31–32, 33, 45, 51, 53, 78, 87, 99, 105, 119, 137, 139, 144, 147–149, 167, 175, 189
Fisher, W. A. 62
Fitchett, W. H. 40
Fitzpatrick, William 90, 180
flappers 193
Four Corners 66
France 2, 10, 30, 31, 33, 35, 39, 41, 47, 69, 77, 78, 103, 116, 153, 176, 189, 192, 193, 202
Franklin, Miles 170
Fremantle 4, 17
Freud, Sigmund 51, 156, 160–162, 168

Gallipoli 1, 10, 25, 31, 33, 39–42, 45, 47–50, 57, 58, 62–63, 68, 69, 70, 76, 214, 216, 246; *see also* Anzac legend
Galsworthy, John 39
Galton, Francis 2
Galway, H. L. 42
Gamble, M. F. H. 163
gambling 3, 72
Gammage, Bill 39, 143
gas 10, 111, 114, 252
Gay, Robert 9
gender *see* femininity, masculinity
Germany 5, 34, 39, 41–42, 47, 53, 67, 68, 78, 214
Gerster, Robin 215
GI Bill of Rights 99
Gietzelt, Arthur 262
Gilmore, Mary 42
Glassop, Lawson 195, 216
Grand Army of the Republic 53
Grant, Doug 55
Graves, Robert 39, 42
Grayndler, Edward 76
Great Britain *see* Britain
Great Depression *see* Depression, Great

Great War *see* First World War
Greer, Germaine 29
Grey, Jeffrey 247
Groom, Littleton 81

Harris, Wilfred 145, 151
Harrison, Kenneth 220, 224
Hemingway, Ernest 42
Henning, Peter 222
Herbert, Xavier 195
Herr, Michael 249
Hines, Colin 138
historians 33, 50, 62, 77, 78, 86, 98, 120, 147, 154
Hobart 5, 172
Hoff, Raynor 37
Holding, Clyde 259
Holloway, E. J. 122
Holman, William 81, 91
home 3–4, 20, 181, 184; *see also* families, marriage
homosexuality 51, 162, 166, 183; *see also* sexuality
Hordern, Samuel 76
Horne, Donald 29, 89
hospitals 65, 73, 80, 85, 88, 98, 171
hostels 81, 85
housing, war-service 65, 85, 99, 238, 251
Howse, Sir Neville 112
Hoyle, Alan 6, 17
Hughes, William Morris 12, 59, 75, 81, 84, 90, 104, 112
humour 31, 108
Hyde Park War Memorial 37
Hynes, Samuel 39, 43
hypnosis 145, 156
hysteria 146–149, 152, 153, 155–157, 167, 247, 263; *see also* shell-shock

Idriess, Ion 42
illness 27, 28, 78, 89, 92, 95, 100, 111, 147, 156, 174, 202, 225, 254, 261
immigration 64–65
Imperial War Graves Commission 33, 35–36; *see also* commemoration
India 2, 67, 68
Indigenous Australians 9, 22, 55, 77, 267
Industrial Workers of the World (IWW) 59
influenza 14, 15
Inglis, Ken 55
Ireland 3, 13, 35, 41, 48, 61
Italy 67

James, Florence 195
Japan 5, 7, 67, 213, 215, 217, 219–230, 235
Jebb, Richard 46
Jeffrey, Betty 217–218
Jeffrey, Tom 243
Johnston, George 98
Jones, Ernest 161
Jones, Sydney Evan 163
Jones, W. Ernest 152
Joseph, E. J. H. 17, 130, 133

Kahn, Colin 265
Kangaroo Island 140, 141
Kapyong 236
Kew Mental Hospital 163
Keys, William 240, 251, 264
Khaki and Green 32
King and Empire Alliance 62
Kipling, Rudyard 36, 39, 46
Knibbs, George 78
Knox, Adrian 80
Kokoda 7, 48, 68, 70, 214, 216
Korea 32, 69, 82, 85, 235–255
Korean veterans 238
Krafft-Ebbing, Richard 162
Kubrick, Stanley 249

Labor Party *see* Australian Labor Party
Lake, Marilyn 41, 134, 142, 199
Lambert, Eric 195, 216, 247
Lane, John 223
Laqueur, Thomas 34
larrikin 3, 42, 72; *see also* Anzac legend
Latham, Oliver 157
Lawrence, D.H. 62
Lawson, Henry 41
Lawson, Louisa 42
leadership 223
Leary-Smith, F. J. 3
Lee, Sir Arthur 251
Leed, Eric 23
Legacy 37, 52, 72, 205–206
Lemnos Hospital 172
Licensed Victuallers Association 4
Limbless Soldiers' Association 52
Lind, W. A. T. 163
Lindsay, Jack 44
Lindsay, Norman 44
Lithgow Small Arms Factory 55
Long Tan, Battle of 245, 246
Longstaff, Will 43

Index

Lovell, H. Tasman 162
loyalty 13, 61–64
Lutyens, Edward 35

MacArthur, Douglas 236
MacCurdy, J. T. 158
Maistre, Roy de 45
Malaya *see* Malaysia
Malayan and Far Eastern Association 52
Malaysia 6, 52, 69, 82, 85, 235, 246
malingering 88, 148–150, 152, 154, 178, 231, 264; *see also* charity, shell-shock
Malouf, David 221
Man 193
manhood 1, 23, 29, 35, 48, 51, 109, 110, 185, 189, 190, 192, 194; *see also* masculinity
Manifold, Colonel C. G. 173
Manning, Frederic 43
Manpower, Director-General of 225
manpower 14, 153
marriage 22, 45, 101, 106, 109, 182, 184, 197–202, 231, 254; *see also* families
Martin, A. H. 182
Maryang San 236
masculinity 22, 30, 48, 72, 104, 107–107, 109, 134, 157, 191, 218, 242, 249, 250, 267; *see also* manhood
Masefield, John 42
mateship 17, 21, 23–24, 30, 47, 50–51, 72, 155, 169, 188, 220–224, 244, 269; *see also* Anzac legend
Mayo, Elton 122, 163
McCaughey, Samuel 206
McCrae, Hugh 42
McCulloch, Jock 259
McGeorge, John 173
McMinn, Holt 259
McNeill, Ian 247
Medical Journal of Australia 117
Melbourne 4–5, 8, 36, 69, 91, 116, 128, 152, 161, 172
Melbourne Legacy Club *see* Legacy
memorials, war 34–39, 53, 69, 246; *see also* Australian War Memorial, Vietnam War Memorial, commemoration
memory 10, 16–74, 184, 221, 241, 248, 267
Menin Gate 35
Mental Hygiene Movement 207
Menzies, Sir Robert Gordon 13, 89, 228
Messner, Tony 264
Michel, Sonya 109

Middle East 2, 25, 33, 50, 69, 177, 193, 195, 213
Millbrook Rise Hospital 172
Millen, Edward 59, 77, 81, 84, 103
Miller, H. C. 161
modernism 39, 42–44, 220
Monash, Sir John 75
Monash University 243
Monsanto 261
Moore, H. J. 77
Moran, Herbert 51
moratorium marches 8, 66; *see also* anti-war protest
mortality 26, 32, 229, 252; *see also* casualties
Mosse, George 53
Mott, Sir Frederick 145, 151, 152
mourning 33, 63, 71; *see also* commemoration
movies *see* films
Mt Remarkable Training Farm 128
Munro Ferguson, Helen 80
Murphy, John 246
Myers, A. B. R. 148
Myers, C. S. 145, 263

Nagle, William 243
Nash, Paul 39, 44
National Defence League 182
nationalism 13, 40, 48, 56–60, 64, 67; *see also* patriotism
Nelson, Hank 214, 222
nervous breakdown 29, 145, 153, 158, 167, 172, 173; *see also* shell-shock
neurasthenia 146, 149
New Guard 62
New Guinea 5, 50, 68, 167, 169, 192, 235, 245, 250
New Zealand 2, 48, 67, 96, 100, 103
Newcastle 64
Noble, Ralph 163
Northern Territory 22; *see also* Alice Springs
nurses 2, 21, 52, 67, 87, 102, 213

O'Brien, J. P. 6, 54
occupational therapy 100, 106
Old Guard 62
O'Neil, William 165
onus of proof 100–115; *see also* benefit of doubt, pensions
Operation Ranch Hand 258; *see also* Agent Orange
Order of the Cincinnati 53
O'Reilly, Dowell 42

Owen Committee 228
Owen, Wilfred 39, 159
Oz 66

Palestine *see* Middle East
Palmer, Nettie 44
Palmer, Vance 19, 42, 44
Papua New Guinea *see* New Guinea
parades 4, 7, 16, 238; *see also* welcome
Parer, Damien 48
Parkin, Ray 218
Parkinson, C. K. 166, 171
Parkside Mental Hospital 116
patriotic funds 12
patriotism 39–50, 55, 57–58, 63–64, 80, 210; *see also* nationalism
Patton, General George 149
Pear, T. H. 153
Pearce, George 80
pensions 78–117, 231, 239, 240, 254, 262; *see also* repatriation: benefits
  old age and invalid 55, 84, 94, 96, 104
  service 85, 96
  totally and permanently incapacitated (TPI) 100, 110, 117, 233
  war 11, 27, 65, 75, 78, 79, 83–87, 99, 101–104, 116, 119, 173, 175, 205, 231, 254, 263
Perth 5, 36
Pike Report 119, 128, 131, 137, 142, 144
pioneers 4, 48, 133
Pollard, Rhys 243
poor law 11
post-traumatic stress disorder 253, 263; *see also* shell-shock, war neurosis
post-war reconstruction 15, 65, 82, 99, 210
Powell, J. M. 142
Pozieres 70
Preston, Margaret 45
Prichard, Katharine Susannah 19, 25, 45
prisoners of war 2, 5–7, 26, 112, 175, 186, 213–233, 236, 240, 254, 254
profiteers 12, 59, 192–193, 244
psychiatry 95, 106, 116, 147, 151–152, 154–158, 160–163, 166–176, 178, 183, 203, 225, 228, 230, 232, 248, 253, 264; *see also* hysteria, nervous breakdown, shell-shock, war neurosis
psychoanalysis 151, 157, 160–164, 168, 198
psychology 18, 24, 25, 28, 51, 87, 106, 110, 124, 145–150, 151–153, 154–162, 162–170, 173, 175, 182, 189, 198, 204, 209, 225, 227, 229–231, 232–233, 253, 263, 264
psychoses 152, 157, 163, 171
psychotherapy 148, 151, 154, 155, 162, 172

Queensland 6, 54, 63, 88, 93, 120, 122, 127, 129, 131, 139, 163, 245; *see also* Brisbane

race 40, 46–47, 49, 55, 58, 162, 196, 217, 224
Racial Hygiene Association 14, 207
Ramsay, Jack 71
rape *see* sexual assault
Red Cross 15, 33, 80, 172, 207
Red Flag Riot 60, 62
Redgum 260
rehabilitation 75, 80, 81, 99, 105, 106, 108, 110, 172, 214, 226; *see also* repatriation
religion 38, 53
Remarque, Erich Maria 39, 42–43
Remnants from Randwick 108
Repat Chat 256
repatriation 144, 147, 170, 183, 189, 202, 204, 210, 225–228, 230–232, 250, 254, 256
  benefits 10, 59, 61, 73, 78, 85–89, 103, 115, 226, 238, 251
  boards 83
  committees 83, 225
  criticisms of 88, 256–266
  funds 75, 80, 83
  legislation 75, 76, 81, 83, 90, 102, 113, 251
  Repatriation Commission 75, 83–84, 95, 97, 111–113, 116, 170–172, 239, 260
  Repatriation Department 11, 83, 88–89, 92, 95, 97, 109–110, 117, 203, 229
  Repatriation 11
  Repatriation Review Tribunal 239, 257; *see also* Assessment Appeals Tribunal
repression 51, 106, 156, 159, 162, 168, 183, 187, 198
republicanism 57, 61, 66
Returned and Services League (RSL) 52–56, 59, 62–69, 72–74, 83, 90, 93–96, 103, 112–115, 131, 137–139, 171, 174, 204, 207, 229, 238, 240, 244, 250–252, 255–257, 259–264; *see also* returned-services organisations
Returned Army Nurses Association 52
Returned Nurses' Association 67
Returned Sailors and Soldiers' Imperial League of Australia (RSSILA) 52
Returned Sailors, Soldiers and Citizens' Loyalty League 52

Index

Returned Soldiers and Nurses' Association 52
Returned Soldiers and Patriots' National League 52
Returned Soldiers' Association 40, 52, 56, 58, 83; *see also* Returned and Services League (RSL)
Returned Soldiers' Labour League 52
returned-services organisations 14, 21, 26, 31, 36, 40, 43, 52–57, 59, 63, 72, 90, 97, 104, 114, 128, 174, 255; *see also* Returned and Services League (RSL)
Reveille 63, 97
Richards, Rowley 220, 224
riots 60
Rivers, W. H. R. 159
Rivett, Rohan 216
Roe, Michael 58
Rolph, Trooper 98
romance fiction 180, 184–191, 210
Rottnest Island 4
Royal Australian Air Force (RAAF) 29, 139, 166
Rural Reconstruction Commission 128, 138; *see also* soldier settlement
Russia 61, 62, 67
Ruxton, Bruce 240, 256
Ryan, Merv 247

sacrifice 32–39, 41, 55, 71, 220, 234
Sailors and Soldiers Fathers' Association (Sailors, Soldiers and Airmen's Fathers Association) 52, 171, 174
Salmon, Thomas 160, 165
Salt 18, 108
Samuel, Peter 251
Sandakan 224
Sane Democracy League 62
Sassoon, Siegfried 39, 42, 159
Schaffer, Kay 134
Scorsese, Martin 249
Scott, Rose 42
Second World War 5–7, 10, 15–17, 24, 26–29, 32, 38, 48, 51, 52, 54, 65, 68, 82, 85, 91, 99, 105, 120, 137, 140, 144, 146, 166, 168, 175, 180, 231, 250
selectors 143; *see also* soldier settlement
Services' Welfare Fund 52
servicewomen 1, 6, 19, 21, 25, 26, 33, 75, 87, 100, 102, 170, 268
sex antagonism 185–201, 244–245
sex relations 179–204; *see also* families, marriage
sexual assault 200–202, 247
sexuality 45, 51, 108, 181, 189–193, 196–199, 232; *see also* homosexuality
Seymour, Alan 66
shell-shock 95, 201, 232, 253, 263, 264; *see also* hysteria, nervous breakdown, post-traumatic stress disorder, war neurosis
shirkers 13, 58, 91, 192, 244
Shrine of Remembrance, Melbourne 37, 69
Simons, Jessie 217
Simpson, Colin 238, 259
Simpson, John 48
Sinclair, A. J. M. 166–169
Singapore 235
Smith, G. Elliot 153
Smith, Sir James Joynton 90
Smith's Weekly 90–91, 95, 97, 146, 171, 174, 200
social Darwinism 23, 23, 41, 49, 156, 164
socialism 59, 105, 224
soldier settlement 64, 76
  boards 127, 131, 136
  commissions 128, 129, 132, 136
  conferences 121, 123
  inspectors 135, 140
Soldier Settler League 131
Soldiering On 32
Soldiers' Home League 52
Soldiers' Welfare Fund 73
South Australia 14, 122, 127, 128; *see also* Adelaide
Soviet Union 236
spiritualism 71
Springthorpe, J. W. 161, 164, 172
St John's Ambulance 80
State War Councils 83, 181
Stawell, Sir Richard 114
Stoller, Alan 171, 225
Stone, Oliver 249
strikes 12, 58, 65, 92, 192, 244; *see also* trade unions
suicide 28, 229, 247, 249
Sukarno 235
Sydney 5, 36, 68
Sydney Morning Herald 40, 88, 97, 205

Tasmania 16, 127, 128, 136, 141; *see also* Hobart
Taylor, George Augustine 28, 57, 58
Taylor, Griffith 122
The Soldier 28, 56–60, 90, 124, 192
Theodore, E.G. 121
Thirkell, Angela 3
Thompson, Phill 240, 255, 259, 261, 262, 265

Thomson, Alistair 71
Throssell, Hugo 25
Tiveychoc, Alan 16, 51, 72
Tobruk 7, 166, 214, 216
Tolstoy, Leo 47
Toose Commission 115, 251
Totally and Permanently Incapacitated Association 52
tour of duty 7, 18, 24, 169, 237, 250, 253
Townsville 60
Toynbee, Arnold 2
trade unions 12, 54, 59, 63, 88, 92, 105; *see also* strikes
training courses 75, 238, 251
Truman, Harry S. 237
Tubercular Sailors, Soldiers and Airmen's Association 52
tuberculosis 14, 81, 96, 111, 114, 207, 230
Tucker, Albert 195
Tudor, Frank 77
Turner, Alexander 17
Turner, Frederick Jackson 46
Turnor, Christopher 123

unemployment 14
United Kingdom *see* Britain
United Nations 236
University of Melbourne 206
University of Sydney 49, 162, 163, 182
Uren, Tom 221, 223, 233
USA 2, 8, 15, 33, 41, 67–68, 79, 99, 101, 103, 146, 149, 165, 167–169, 228, 236, 242, 247, 248, 249, 256
USSR *see* Soviet Union

Vaughan, Crawford 122
venereal disease 14, 96, 196
veterans 6, 11, 52, 53, 183, 213; *see also* Korean veterans, Vietnam veterans, servicewomen
Veterans' Affairs, Department of 84, 95, 233, 239, 240, 245, 255, 256, 260–264; *see also* Repatriation Commission, Repatriation Department
Victoria 63, 127, 140, 141; *see also* Melbourne
Vietnam 235
Vietnam Veterans' Association 52, 53, 239–240, 256–266
Vietnam Veterans Association of America 259
Vietnam veterans 7–10, 15, 18, 26, 69, 138, 244, 250, 252, 265
Vietnam War Memorial 246, 265, 267–268

Vietnamese 243, 244, 248
Villers-Bretonneux 35
Vision 44
vitalism 44
vocational training 81, 85, 99, 204, 226
Volker, Derek 255, 257, 264

Wakelin, Roland 45
Wall, Don 224
Waller, Napier 38
war 16, 19–21, 31, 43, 47, 51, 147, 180; *see also* First World War, Second World War
  American Civil 24, 34, 53, 78, 146
  Boer 34, 68, 76
  Korean 236, 246, 250
  Napoleonic 148
  Russo-Japanese 147
  Vietnam 7, 8, 18, 22, 24, 27, 50, 66, 69, 82, 85, 148, 169, 232
war gratuity 81, 85, 183
war memorials *see* memorials, war
war neurosis 145–150, 153–155, 170–173; *see also* post-traumatic stress disorder, shell-shock
War Widows' Association 206
War Widows' Guild 206
Waterhouse, Earle 29
Waterson, Duncan 143
Watson, John 119, 123
welcome 4–6, 15, 213, 241, 261, 265; *see also* parades
welfare state 83, 86–87, 104
Western Australia 13, 25, 64, 73, 116, 125, 127, 134, 140, 203; *see also* Perth
Whalen, Lesley 89
'White Australia' policy 44, 55
White, Major-General C. B. B. 105
Whiting, John 117
Whiz-Bang 63
Widowed Mothers' Association 206
widows, war 87, 95, 99, 102, 114, 181, 205–207; *see also* War Widows' Guild
Wigmore, Lionel 214
Wilde, Oscar 162
Willis, Hastings 110
Wilmot, Frank 44
Wilson, Colonel A. M. 161
Winn, Roy Coupland 153, 158, 163
Women's Auxiliary Australian Air Force 102
Wood, George Arnold 49
Woodward, Oliver 4

Index

World Veterans Federation 99
World War I *see* First World War
World War II *see* Second World War
wounds 31, 111; *see also* casualties

yanks 185, 192, 195, 198, 244; *see also* USA
YMCA 80
Young, P. J. 259

www.ingramcontent.com/pod-product-compliance
Lightning Source LLC
Chambersburg PA
CBHW080439170426
43195CB00017B/2820